TOURING
NEVADA

TOURING NEVADA

A HISTORIC and SCENIC GUIDE

MARY ELLEN and AL GLASS

UNIVERSITY OF NEVADA PRESS
RENO, NEVADA
1983

PHOTO CREDITS: The photographs in this book are all by Al Glass with the exception of those on the following pages. Stephen Trimble, Santa Fe, New Mexico: cover, 115, 137, 193. Tom Brownold, Flagstaff, Arizona: ii, 47. John Running, Flagstaff, Arizona: 1, 89, 159. Special Collections Department, Getchell Library, University of Nevada-Reno: 30, 45, 116 (top), 143, 160. Edna Patterson Collection, Northeastern Nevada Museum, Elko: 59. Nevada Historical Society, Reno: 105, 199 (top). Helen J. Stewart Collection, Dickinson Library, University of Nevada, Las Vegas: 166. Las Vegas News Bureau: 170. Natalie Glass: photo of the authors, back cover.

University of Nevada Press, Reno, Nevada 89557
© Mary Ellen Glass 1983. All rights reserved
Printed in the United States of America
Designed by Dave Comstock

Library of Congress Cataloging in Publication Data

Glass, Mary Ellen.
  Touring Nevada.

  Includes index.
    1. Nevada—Description and travel—1981–   —
Tours.
I. Glass, Al, 1926–   . II. Title.
F839.3.G53 1983   917.93′0433   83–1047
ISBN 0–87417–074–5

Second Printing 1986

CONTENTS

ESSAYS

MAPS

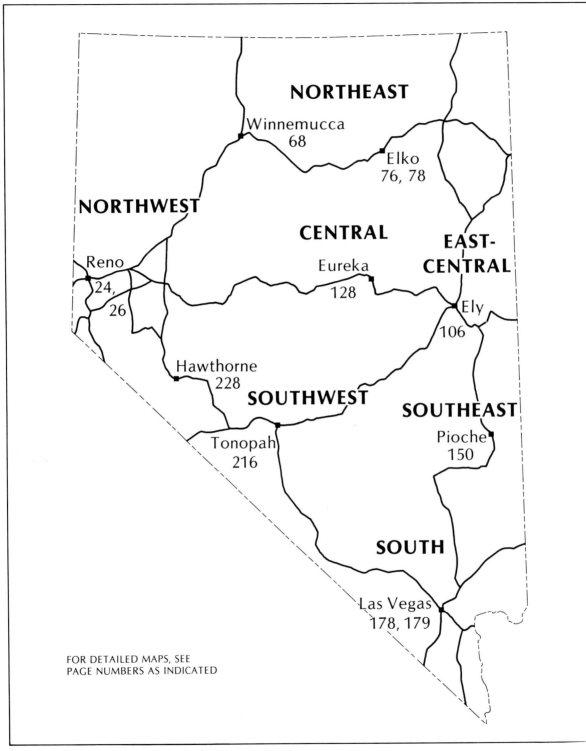

NORTHEAST

Winnemucca
68

Elko
76, 78

NORTHWEST

CENTRAL

**EAST-
CENTRAL**

Reno
24,
26

Eureka
128

Ely
106

Hawthorne
228

SOUTHWEST

SOUTHEAST

Pioche
150

Tonopah
216

SOUTH

Las Vegas
178, 179

FOR DETAILED MAPS, SEE
PAGE NUMBERS AS INDICATED

The seven geographic regions described in *Touring Nevada*

INTRODUCING: NEVADA!

WELCOME. You have an opportunity to visit some of the most interesting, historic, and scenic spots in the West. We hope this book will guide your steps.

Nevada lies in the Great Basin of the western United States. With 110,000 square miles, it is the seventh-largest state in the Union. The population is under one million, with an average density of about nine people per square mile. The largest population centers are around Las Vegas, where more than half our people live; Reno, since 1960 the second city in size; and the Carson-Tahoe area. The other urban centers are mainly those of the county seats.

The principal business in Nevada is tourism. There are, historically and currently, other industries and facets to the economy, but tourism comes before any of those. For the most part, it has been that way from the beginning.

The first settlements arose in response to the needs of the great westward movement of the nineteenth century; they provided food, lodging, and fodder for cross-country travelers. Almost inevitably, miners came along in the wake of wagon trains to explore and then exploit the natural resources of the Great Basin, and mining camps succeeded the embryonic commercial centers. Statehood came with the influx of the first mining discoveries.

Mining, however, has inexorable cycles, and by the late nineteenth century, borrasca (decline) had followed bonanza. Despite strenuous efforts at road building and track laying, and attempts to create a new economy, more than a third of the population departed at the end of the first boom. Some politicians and others began to question whether Nevada should have become a state at all. The mining camps which became ghost towns numbered in the hundreds.

A second bonanza-borrasca-ghost town cycle began in 1900. This time, the population did not decline so dramatically at the end of the period because people began to realize that something more than mere utilization of natural resources would be required to maintain the economy. The best solution to the problem proved to be a return to tourism, enhanced especially after 1931 by legalized casino gambling.

The promotion of tourism has taken many forms. Stage stops on primitive wagon roads have evolved into the world's most expansive hotels and casinos. World championship prizefights—Corbett and Fitzsimmons at Carson in 1897, Gans and Nelson at Goldfield in 1906, Jeffries and Johnson at Reno in 1910—drew people from all over the nation. The needs of early-day ranchers for some type of entertainment became Nevada's famous rodeos and fairs.

Mining has continued to be important. The state saw a third great mining boom in the mid-1950s—until that time, its largest. In the late 1970s and early 1980s, yet another mineral bonanza began, this time on a scientific and sophisticated scale that seemed to promise some years of activity. Another significant economic advantage derives from the "freeport" law that allows goods in transit to be warehoused in Nevada without assessment for property and inventory taxes. Some manufacturing takes place at various places around the state, especially in southern Nevada. The agriculture of the state is primarily in the north, consisting mainly of businesses connected with livestock.

The enterprises obscured by the tourist industry are important, of course, but they are less colorful and less likely than gambling or outdoor sports to attract people to come here to visit. A major portion of the Silver State's economy exists because people like you came here as travelers; we have written this book in part for you. We have also written the volume for people who have recently decided to settle here. Most of all, we wrote for anyone who wants to know more about this exciting, colorful, beautiful state of Nevada.

Offered an opportunity to create a new kind of tour guide, we didn't hesitate. As natives of Nevada, we have always traveled widely over the area, enjoying the out-of-doors and thinking that some day we would write a book so that others might also appreciate the features we liked. So this book is a personal look at Nevada through native eyes. We hope you will find it useful.

Acknowledgments

This book never could have happened without the assistance of the people who supported our efforts. This is to thank them all sincerely.

We especially enjoyed meeting the rangers and attendants at the Nevada state parks. In every case, they made us proud of their devotion to the system, their knowledge of the areas, and their helpful and friendly attitudes.

We were similarly impressed by the librarians and museum curators and attendants whom we met in our travels. The counties of this state are fortunate indeed to have knowledgeable, involved professionals and volunteers to care for the needs of travelers and researchers. Courthouse officials also helped us with our special requirements, and we thank them warmly.

Every greeter in a chamber of commerce where we stopped offered excellent advice and often gave us material to study. These people are genuine assets to every community where they exist, and we appreciate them greatly.

We owe special thanks for additional favors and attention to several people who went extra miles, provided needed research material, or gave added hospitality to us while we visited their homes or offices. These include: Ruth Tipton, Golconda; Edna Patterson, Elko; Richard Lane, Northeastern Nevada Museum, Elko; the staff of the Ruby Lake National Wildlife Refuge, especially Stephen Bouffard, who conducted our tour of the marshes; John Lancos, Red Rock Canyon Recreation Area; Peggy Trego, Unionville; Danny Robb, Tonopah; Duane Kern, Elko; Fred, Dorothy, and Pete Barnes, Getchell Mine; Sunny Martin, Ely; Hamilton and Patricia Vreeland, Reno; Jack Munson, Nevada Northern Railroad, East Ely; Max Blackham, Kennecott Copper Corporation, McGill; Norma Joyce Scott, Hawthorne; Della Phillips, Tus-

carora; Kathy Richardson, Belmont; Dorotha Itza, Lovelock; and numerous other nice people whose names we did not record, but who helped us with unique information about their communities.

We could not have completed our work without the staffs of Nevada's major research centers. At the University of Nevada Reno Library, we are particularly grateful to the people of the departments of Special Collections (with extra thanks for additional work to Karen Gash, Ellen Guerricagoitia, and Tim Gorelangton), Government Publications (especially Steve Zink, Juri Stratford, and Naoma Hainey), and Reference (notably LaMar Smith and Richard Grefrath). At the University of Nevada Las Vegas Library, we especially appreciated Annadean Kepper. The Nevada Historical Society in Reno, principally Phil Earl and Eric Moody, helped us immeasurably, and so did Guy Louis Rocha, director of the Nevada State Archives. We extend our warm thanks to all of them.

We owe a debt of gratitude for a gift of time to Harold G. Morehouse, director, and Ruth H. Donovan, assistant director, University of Nevada Reno Libraries.

We are sincerely grateful to Evelyn Wagner and the other members of the staff of the University of Nevada Reno Oral History Program for their cheerful endurance of our comings and goings; without Mrs. Wagner, there would have been no goings.

Finally, we give a continuing "thank you" to Robert Laxalt, director, Nicholas Cady, editor, the Editorial Advisory Board, and the staff of the University of Nevada Press. Their professional and good-humored approach to the completion of this book has made it all seem worthwhile. We also sincerely commend Amy Mazza's maps.

Although everyone tried to help us, we must assume responsibility for ignoring good advice and for committing the errors that surely appear here. We hope the mistakes are few, and that we have not embarrassed our friends in making them.

Mary Ellen and Al Glass
Reno, 1982

USING *TOURING NEVADA*

This book divides the Silver State into seven major areas. The divisions are not purely arbitrary; the sections contain elements of common history. The various areas share social and economic features within themselves, which range from exploration to mining to modern tourism. A brief chapter on the area's history precedes each group of tours, and there are from two to six tours in every section.

Each tour is designed as a one-day trip, although travelers are urged to take more time. The tours suggest ways of seeing attractive or important scenic, historic, scientific, and geologic areas. The authors have taken every trip, in the one-day time span laid out, but we have also pointed out campgrounds and commercial centers that might be useful when extending a tour to more than a single day.

Touring Nevada's primary purpose is to show the first-time visitor or the long-time resident some accessible and interesting places. This is not a "ghost town" guide (there are plenty of those), but what we hope is a different way of looking at the state in its modern dress. There are only a few "dirt road" byways included here, and no need for a four-wheel-drive on any trip. The reader is urged, however, to heed warnings about roads, weather conditions, and local regulations.

A few words of caution for uninitiated travelers to Nevada: although touring in this state should not be considered dangerous, a prudent driver should make sure that the vehicle is in top shape and that no trip begins without a few extra supplies. The roads across some of the deserts of the Great Basin are very long, and water is scarce. So be certain that the gasoline tank is full, the spare tire is in good condition, and the water jug is ready. A first-aid kit is always a good thing to have along, and so is an extra blanket; you do not expect to use them, but it is well to have them available. And please, take along a bag for disposal of your garbage. Litter is an ugly thing to leave on a beautiful landscape.

Remember to take your camera! There will be many fine opportunities for photography along the way.

Where to Find Maps

The Nevada State Highway Department annually publishes an official map of the state. This map is distributed free at museums, libraries, and similar public places in Nevada. That map, used together with the maps in this guide, will help with planning trips around the state. If you are a member of an auto club, the maps distributed free to members can be very helpful. The state Department of Transportation also publishes the Nevada Map Atlas, much more detailed than the official map, and available from the state highway office in Carson City. There are perhaps a dozen other sources (some of which are mentioned in this text) for various other kinds of maps. The Forest Service, the Bureau of Land Management, the Geological Survey, and other government agencies will also provide maps free or at low cost to people calling at their offices.

Route Numbers and Mileages

Various and changing government regulations keep highway route numbers in transition (and map-makers employed). If the route numbers on your map disagree with those we have noted, put the blame where it belongs; the highway numbers used in this book reflect the latest numbering scheme and were posted by the roadside the last time we passed the spot.

We have calculated the mileages as carefully as an accurate odometer would allow. If your car's mileage differs in some places, it will not be a great difference—a tenth of a mile or so.

A Note on Sources

We have used a wide variety of research materials in composing this book—standard histories, local histories, reports, promotional materials, guidebooks, and ephemera. Useful items included oral histories from the Oral History Program at the University of Nevada Reno. All of the short quotations, unless otherwise attributed, are from the oral histories. The authors (or speakers) of the oral histories are quoted simply as they narrated the events, without attempt to modify the words to make the style more literary. Other short quotations have standard identifications of the sources.

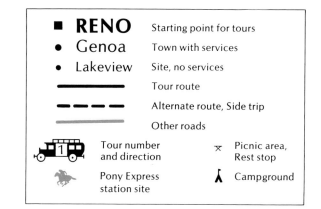

NORTHWESTERN NEVADA

NORTHWESTERN NEVADA

orthwestern Nevada is the womb of the state's history. The earliest settlers, the initial travelers and wagon trains, the premier permanent settlement, the original mining booms, the first push for statehood, and the first science, agriculture, and industry all came to northwestern Nevada. The land at the northwestern edge of the Great Basin, like that of much of the rest of the West, belonged originally to Spain. After the revolution of 1821, Mexico supposedly owned the territory but made no effort to occupy it. The Treaty of Guadalupe Hidalgo in 1848 gave title to the section to the United States of America; by that time, what would be Nevada was becoming well known.

Explorers and Early Travelers

The first white man to come into the northwestern Great Basin was probably Jedediah Strong Smith, a fur trapper. Smith trekked from west to east across the area in 1827, crossing the Sierra Nevada south of present-day Gardnerville. Two years later, in 1829, Peter Skene Ogden, another trapper, led his men into the sink of the Humboldt River south of where Lovelock arose, seeking fur animals. In 1833 and 1834, Joseph Walker, for whom a mountain pass, a river, and a lake would be named, came into northwestern Nevada from east to west, along the Humboldt River. Walker led his party through present-day Pershing, Churchill, and Lyon counties, then south through what would be Carson Valley, and into California. These were not mapping explorations, or intended to be trips of discovery, but rather voyages for profit in furs. Still, the trails blazed along the Humboldt River and over the Sierra Nevada endured, providing routes for those who would come on other errands.

In 1843, the first great westward migration was under way; the Oregon Trail to the north became the site of rather heavy traffic. Under the circumstances, the United States government needed accurate infor-

mation about the area and thus appointed John C. Frémont, a lieutenant of the Topographical Engineers, to survey the region. The Oregon survey completed, Frémont's party turned south toward what he would call the Great Basin. They came into what is now the northwest corner of Nevada, heading southerly. On January !0, 1844, the group came to Pyramid Lake and named it for a rock formation near the shore. From Pyramid, Frémont's party went up the Truckee River about to the site of present-day Wadsworth, crossed over to the Carson River and went downstream to the Carson Sink, then turned west again to traverse the snow-clogged Sierra Nevada into California in mid-January. In that month-long ordeal, Frémont and his cartographer Charles Preuss first saw Lake Tahoe. The return journey in 1844 took the group over the Old Spanish Trail (see Southern Nevada tours). On a second trip, this time east to west in 1845, the Frémont party again crossed the Sierra, over what became Donner Pass.

Frémont's importance is not just in his trailblazing or mapmaking. He is responsible for many place names he designated along his routes: the Humboldt River, called after a famous German naturalist; the Carson and Walker rivers, passes, valleys, and lakes named to honor guides with the party; the Great Basin, denoting the first realization of the system of interior drainage in the region. He was less successful in naming the Salmon Trout River (the Truckee) and Lake Bonpland (Tahoe).

Even while mapping was incomplete, the westward movement across the Great Basin had begun. In 1841, the Bidwell party brought wagons along the Humboldt, south across the Humboldt Sink, and over the Sierra south of present-day Gardnerville. The Donner party, having suffered numberless disasters and misfortunes (see Northeastern Nevada tours), floundered through the Truckee Meadows and into the Sierra in 1846; nearly half the group died there. In that same year, the Applegate cutoff to Oregon from the California Trail was established, later to become the Lassen Road across northwestern Nevada.

With the discovery of gold in California and acquisition of the territory by the United States, what had been sporadic trespasses on foreign soil swelled to a continuous stream of traffic. The Humboldt River emigrant trail, with the stream providing sustenance to the travelers, was the most popular of these routes. People and wagons entered Nevada's northeastern corner and traveled down the Humboldt to the Humboldt Sink. The crossing of the Forty Mile Desert came next, a stretch without fuel, water, or other supplies, and the scene of a great deal of dreadful suffering. Then there was Ragtown, on the bank of the Carson River, where wagon-train travelers could refresh themselves, rinse dust-covered clothing, and prepare for the crossing of the Sierra just ahead. Some chose to follow the Truckee River route, others the Carson River route, and mostly, the pioneers safely reached California. Much literature dwells on the hardships of the trail and the likelihood of catastrophe, but the fact remains that most of the people who started for California actually did arrive there. Even the Donner party, by most reckoning the outstandingly disaster-prone group of the lot, lost less than half its members. The Oregon- or California-bound travelers used the Great Basin at that time merely as a pathway; it was some time before the trappers, mappers, trail-blazers, and emigrant trains actually left genuine settlers in their wake.

Genoa

In 1850, the U.S. Congress decreed that the land acquired by the Treaty of Guadalupe Hidalgo would be divided into the state of California and the Territories of Utah and New Mexico. Most of the Great Basin, with its western boundary at the California state line, thus became part of Utah Territory. The Mormon leader, Brigham Young, was appointed territorial governor. Although still largely unsettled, the western section had experienced a growth in traffic, especially after the discovery of gold in California.

Small commercial establishments sprang up to serve this growing traffic. One of these, in Carson Valley at the very edge of Utah Territory, was set up in 1850. The trading post, a collection of temporary structures, became a permanent settlement with the construction of a log cabin store in the summer of 1851. As an outpost of the Utah theocracy, the center took the name Mormon Station. The population of the surrounding valleys—Eagle Valley, Jacks Valley, Washoe Valley—began to grow in response to the success of this first commercial venture and the continuing traffic to California.

By 1855, the place had a considerable colony of Mormon settlers. Mormon Station was the population and commercial center for what became Carson County. Then came a dispute between the Mormons and the U.S. government, and many of the Latter Day Saints departed in 1857, abandoning their houses and farms, or selling at low prices, but expecting the remaining ''gentile'' settlers to pay for anything they acquired. The Mormons never returned in force to Carson Valley, but their legacy was a dispute over the ownership of and payment for their deserted properties. With the residents still declining in 1862 to pay, a Mormon elder, Orson Hyde, delivered a curse that was designed to frighten money out of the ''gentiles.'' That also was unsuccessful, and Mormon dominance in western Nevada declined and then died out. The former Mormon Station became the town of Genoa. Within only two more years after the departure of the Mormons, the gold and silver discoveries on the Comstock Lode changed the character and then the government of western Utah Territory.

Genoa society and economy contained several interesting features in those early years. Nevada's long-lasting *Territorial Enterprise* was first published there. Other newspapers included the *Genoa Record* (later merged with the *Gardnerville Courier*) and the *Douglas County Banner*. Genoa was on the Pony Express route of 1860–1861 and was a stage stop for the trans-Sierra wagon roads. The first commercial skiing in the Sierra probably took place out of Genoa, with a local resident and Norwegian immigrant who called himself ''Snowshoe Thompson'' carrying the mail over the mountain passes in winter. The far-western section of

". . . You shall be visited of the Lord of Hosts with thunder and with earthquakes and floods, with pestilence and with famine until your names are not known among men, for you have rejected the authority of God, trampled upon his laws and his ordinances, and given yourselves up to serve the god of this world; to rioting in debauchery, in abominations, drunkenness and corruption. You have chuckled and gloried in taking the property of the Mormons, and withholding from them the benefits thereof. You have despised rule and authority, and put God and man at defiance. . . .

"I care not what our mill and land claims are, or were considered worth—whether five hundred thousand dollars, or five cents—twenty thousand dollars is our demand; and you can pay it to us, as I have said, and find mercy, if you will thenceforth do right, or despise the demand and perish.

". . . Without hypocrisy, deceit or falsehood, I remain as heretofore, a servant of God."

— Orson Hyde.
January 27, 1862

"In the valley here, there was three big Freds. There was Fred Dressler, Fred Dangberg, and Fred Frevert. They was big fellows. Fred Dangberg would hire somebody. They'd come around at night; he'd take them out and show them the moon. He said, 'That's the Dutchman's sun.' They worked all night. They were all Dutchmen, the original ones that settled here. . . .

"The Dangbergs generally would send so much money to one of their friends or maybe their relatives to come out on. Then they'd work. . . . Once in while they got one out here and he worked for them for a little while, and as soon as he found bigger wages he quit and paid them off. . . . Old Fred Dangberg used to be able to drive from his place into Carson City on his own land all the way through at one time."

— Harry Hawkins, son of
Carson Valley pioneers

Utah became a part of Nevada Territory in 1861, and Genoa became the seat of Douglas County when the state of Nevada was organized in 1864.

Despite its status as county seat and first town, Nevada's birthplace did not become a metropolis. In time, roads were built to bypass the site in favor of other towns in the valley. By 1880 only a few hundred people lived there, with five hotels (actually boarding houses) to serve the existing tourist traffic. Fires and floods and avalanches off the flanks of the Sierra erased much of the original community.

Still, if Genoa was not a metropolis, at least it acted as the valley's commercial and governmental center for many years. Then the other little towns began to spring up. Gardnerville was established about 1887, arising from the needs of ranchers in the southerly end of Carson Valley. There, hotels, stores, homes, and other buildings marked the rural agricultural community. A number of active German immigrant families in the valley gave the section a rather Teutonic atmosphere. Although the Germans never constituted a majority there, their industry and energy made Carson Valley widely known as Nevada's "Pennsylvania Dutch" area. After the turn of the century, Gardnerville gained another aspect of fame. Basques who had immigrated to the United States to tend sheep all over the northern part of Nevada established some of their traditional-style boarding hotels there. In time, these became important centers for native celebrations and, inevitably, for the serving of ethnic food. In the late twentieth century, the Basque restaurants of Gardnerville are among the best in the state.

Minden was a town of even later origin. The Dangberg family owned the site from the 1850s. In 1906, with the prospect of having the Virginia and Truckee railroad run to Carson Valley from Carson City, H. F. Dangberg, patriarch of the family, offered the railroad a right-of-way in return for a terminus of the tracks. With that bargain, Minden came into being on the Dangberg ranch, named to honor Dangberg's birthplace in Germany. The energy that created the town in the beginning soon resulted in added status for Minden, and a further decline for Genoa. In 1916,

Genoa lost the county seat to the newer town. Yet, Genoa would not become a ghost town.

Revered by Nevadans as the state's natal site, Genoa has retained a fair amount of commerce and a great deal of charm. The courthouse built in 1865 later became a school, and finally, a museum. The valley's first Masonic Hall remains intact, and so do several structures from the early days, many of them lovingly maintained by descendants of pioneer settlers there. The Nevada State Park System took over protection of some of the townsite, establishing Fort Genoa State Park. In the 1980s, Genoa residents still feel their importance as occupants of Nevada's first permanent settlement and have proved that by keeping the town and its environs attractive.

The Comstock Lode

The discovery of the Comstock Lode marked the beginning of Nevada's rise as a state. The Gold Canyon area had been prospected since about 1850, with some minor discoveries of gold there. By 1859, the time of the discovery of the great silver lode, the Gold Canyon placers had yielded less than two thirds of a million dollars, all in gold, for perhaps as many as 180 miners. Still, the prospectors continued to hope that something might be uncovered. Then in January 1859, men whose names became a vital part of Nevada lore made the discovery that changed the history of the American West. James "Old Virginny" Finney and three associates made a good gold strike; soon, monuments and stakes dotted the barren hillsides. Six months later, the effective discovery of the silver lode was made; Peter O'Riley, Patrick McLaughlin, Emanuel Penrod, and Henry T. P. Comstock split a four-way claim to a vein. O'Riley and McLaughlin probably made the first real finding, while Comstock and his friend Penrod just managed to deal themselves in. Comstock, a local loudmouth, bragged his way into having the section bear his name. Old Virginny, the legend says, was drunkenly staggering home one night with a bottle in his hand. He tripped, the bottle broke, and unwilling to waste the liquid completely, Finney instantly "baptized" the place Virginia. Like the con-

"Of course it is no use for my pencil to try & describe this place — can't do it — big, bustling, noisy city — all in process of creation — streets full of wagons, horses, omnibusses, crowd — sidewalk crowded with rushing crowd — 500 houses now being built, mostly wooden but many brick and stone — Lee, Winall & Sebastian's great circus performing here — . . . lots of gambling saloons open to the public — crowded — Monte, faro, chuckerluck, rouge et noir &c — bands of music in orchestra — just like San Francisco in '49."
— Alfred Doten, *Journals,* Comstock newspaperman, July 1, 1863

tents of Finney's bottle, the news of the great silver strike leaked out to the world.

By autumn the Rush to Washoe had begun, and by the spring of 1860 the roads were clogged with treasure seekers. No wonder; the first assays of the ore showed something more than $3,800 a ton—in days when a ton of "good" ore brought $100. Virginia City and its satellite towns, Gold Hill, Silver City, Dayton, and Empire, became the hub of the western mining world.

Several years of good returns followed. The excitement generated by the mines caused a tremendous influx of people, enough to allow Nevada to become a territory in 1861, and a state in 1864. Annual yields from the mines ran to tens of millions of dollars. All resources were strained from the activity, but a town began to grow on the hills and in the canyons around Mt. Davidson. The mines stretched into the town, and the mills pounded up and down the canyons. The most important of the mills were along the Carson River near Empire.

Technology came to the Comstock in several forms. A mining engineer, Phillip Deidesheimer, invented a method of timbering that helped to prevent the formerly frequent cave-ins of the mines. This "square-set" system remained in use as long as miners worked underground. The need for water in the desert area brought the liquid from the Sierra Nevada in an "inverted siphon" that was a genuine engineering achievement in its day. Methods of cabling later used in San Francisco's cable-car system were invented in Virginia City. Earliest uses of dynamite and of compressed air in mining came on the Comstock. Adolph Sutro, a Swiss immigrant, devised a great tunnel scheme to drain water from the deep mines, where hot water temperatures reached unbearable levels. Sutro's tunnel, begun in 1865 and finished in 1878, was too late for its planned use but is still widely regarded as an engineering marvel.

One result of these technological advances and the expansion of population was an extensive use of the area's natural resources. Timbers for the mines, lumber for homes, and wood to burn in the mills all came from the slopes of the Sierra Nevada, across the

---

"Virginia was a busy city of streets and houses aboveground. Under it was another busy city, down in the bowels of the earth, where a great population of men thronged in and out among an intricate maze of tunnels and drifts, flitting hither and thither under a winking sparkle of lights, and over their heads towered a vast web of interlocking timbers that held the walls of the gutted Comstock apart. These timbers were as large as a man's body, and the framework stretched upward so far that no eye could pierce to its top. . . . It was like peering up through the clean-picked ribs and bones of some colossal skeleton. . . . One . . . cannot well imagine what that forest of timbers cost, from the time they were felled in the pineries beyond Washoe Lake, hauled up and around Mount Davidson at atrocious rates of freightage, then squared, let down into the deep maw of the mine and built up there. Twenty ample fortunes would not timber one of the greatest of those silver mines."

— Mark Twain, *Roughing It*

"They had what they called a boom up on the Carson River, which was located right close to the abandoned power dam. There was an immense chain across the river there, imbedded into the cliffs on each side. The links in that chain were about 18 inches long. . . . It was enormous chain, and had to be very strong to withstand the pressure of wood against the boom. I have seen pictures . . . where that boom was 30 or 40 feet high in the river and the wood was backed up for several miles."

— James Hickey, Carson Valley pioneer

"When the river was high from the spring floods, the wood was put into it and flooded down. . . . Most of it was taken out in Empire, where it was piled in long ricks in the town; later it was taken by train on flatcars to the mills and to the mines. . . . In order to keep the wood in the stream, men were stationed along the river, and they had large pickaroons—that was the name of the large hoe—and they kept the wood in place. One of the liveliest times in my recollections was during the spring wood drives. The town was filled with wood drivers."

— Eugenia Bruns, Empire student, later a school administrator

---

valleys from the Comstock. The timber industry pervaded a large segment of the region. Fuel for the mills came largely from the area of Alpine County (California) above Carson Valley. There, woodcutters worked through the summer and autumn to pile logs along the Carson River and other streams. Then, with the spring flood, the logs washed downstream in the waters. Crews of laborers pulled the wood from the rivers at various places along the way. The practice gained prominence as the "Carson River wood drive." Other lumber came from the area of the Tahoe Basin in the high Sierra. There, trees cut around the lake were freighted across the water from the west side to Glenbrook on the east, then transported to the Comstock.

The result of this activity was that all the virgin forests for miles around fell to the woodsman's axe. As the nineteenth century ended, no mature trees existed in the cutting areas. All had been taken to serve the needs of civilization. Only after the turn of the century did people begin to realize that the forests could provide society with recreation, too, and the cutting of trees diminished. The Tahoe Basin and parts of the Sierra Nevada became destinations for tourists, as well as lumbermen.

Virginia City's boom continued until the end of the 1870s. The town gained a highly sophisticated air. Fine public buildings like the Storey County courthouse, churches, homes, mansions for the nabobs, commercial establishments, and places of entertainment like Piper's Opera House provided a civilized environment. The owners of the great mines became famous capitalists and politicians. John W. Mackay, a poor Irish miner when he arrived in Virginia City, left there the holder of a tremendous fortune to found the Postal Telegraph company. Mackay and his family were also important benefactors to Nevada and later to the University of Nevada. John Percival Jones, a Welsh immigrant and former stone mason, became the superintendent of the Crown Point mill, and then U.S. senator for Nevada. Although completely undistinguished, Jones's career in the U.S. Senate lasted for thirty years (U.S. Senate seats then were awarded by legislatures, in Nevada, almost invariably through corrupt bargains). Jones's other note of fame was that he founded the city of Santa Monica, Califor-

Virginia City

nia. William Morris Stewart, formerly of California, practiced both law and politics on the Comstock. This attorney was prominent in legal affairs and important in the writing of the state's constitution. Stewart also became a U.S. senator in two different eras of Nevada history, the initial one in the Comstock days when he became Nevada's first U.S. senator, and the second during the depression that followed the boom. James G. Fair, like Mackay an Irish immigrant, used some of his Comstock fortune to build a fancy hotel in San Francisco (the Fairmont), and to purchase a one-term U.S. Senate seat. In politics, Fair was disparagingly known as "Slippery Jim." Two other men of Irish descent, James C. Flood and William S. O'Brien, former saloon-keepers of San Francisco, joined the growing numbers of Comstock investors; and when they had made their fortunes from Nevada, they took the money but remained in San Francisco to spend it. William Sharon, one of the kings of Virginia City finance, arrived on the Comstock as a representative of the Bank of California. Sharon, a shrewd businessman, operated the Belcher mine and participated in organizing the company that became the Virginia and Truckee railroad. Like some of the other moguls, Sharon found it easy and convenient to purchase a seat in the U.S. Senate, where he remained without any particular honor for a single term, afterward enjoying the title "Senator" by which people addressed him. A few lesser personages like Lemuel "Sandy" Bowers found riches on the Comstock, but these people were exceptional. The titans of Comstock fame organized the mining companies, made the financial arrangements, and took care of the politics that helped to make the great silver lode produce.

The most important company came into prominence with the second boom that began about 1872. This, the "bonanza firm," was composed of four partners, Mackay, Flood, Fair, and O'Brien. The earlier prospectors, discoverers of the mines, had left the mining business: Comstock died a suicide in Montana; Finney was killed in a fall from a horse; McLaughlin sold out, became a cook, and died a pauper; and O'Riley died insane. The "bonanza kings" developed and exploited

their holdings (the Consolidated-Virginia mines), manipulated their stocks, saw the Bank of California go defunct as a result of Comstock trading, and finally, at the end, drifted away back to California. Only John W. Mackay retained a reputation of respectability from the boom period, using his money to found a communications company and to oversee the laying of the first trans-Pacific cable. Some of the proceeds of Mackay's fortune returned to Nevada after his death in 1902 in the form of benefactions to the University of Nevada, given by his son Clarence: a mining school, an athletics field, a science building, endowment funds, and a statue of John Mackay executed by the great sculptor Gutson Borglum.

The Comstock heyday was surely not all mines, politics, and high finance. Several newspapers, including the long-lasting *Territorial Enterprise*, educated and entertained the populace. The *Enterprise* gave employment to some of the West's most prominent journalists and writers, among them Samuel Clemens (Mark Twain) and William Wright (Dan De Quille). Clemens came to Nevada in 1861 with his brother Orion, the newly-appointed territorial secretary. After a brief stay in Aurora, he moved to Virginia City and was there for about a year. Wright wrote for Comstock newspapers for more than twenty years and authored a now-standard work, *History of the Big Bonanza* (1876), about the boom town. A third newspaperman, not so well known as the others, but ultimately contributing a great deal to Nevada historiography, was Alfred Doten. Doten, a popular writer and a good one, also kept a diary in which for forty years he chronicled the events of the Comstock and the surrounding area. The "Doten Diaries" have become an indispensable source for writers of the history of the era.

Nor did the residents of the Comstock towns lack for other diversions. Piper's Opera House, built early in the boom days and rebuilt and remodeled numerous times afterwards, provided a focus for some of the best theatrical and musical groups of the time. In its more recent incarnations, Piper's has continued to attract both traditional and modern entertainers and their audiences. Houses of worship, especially the beautiful St.

Mary's of the Mountains Roman Catholic church, brought yet another cultural dimension. Street entertainments, ranging from early-day circuses to the late modern camel and ostrich races, have contributed both humor and grotesqueries. The Comstock was a place where even a common prostitute's death evolved into a folk legend. In short, this town that began in the Gilded Age was both typical of its times and extravagant in its amusements.

In the end, the Comstock towns yielded to the inevitable and inexorable cycle of mining: discovery, boom, bust. Fires, national and local financial conditions, sagging metals prices, and a drop in demand for silver following the demonetization in 1873 all depleted the cities and towns. Gold Hill, Silver City, Dayton, and Empire became virtual ghosts. While Virginia City retained a few residents, it also was nearly moribund into the 1940s. A brief experiment with cyaniding the tailings in 1919 left only a picturesque ruin at American Flat. Indeed, after producing more than $350 million, it was over.

Well, it was not quite over. The Comstock towns found, as the population began to shift westward after World War II, that they could attract enough tourists to revive their economy a bit. Piper's Opera House and the Fourth Ward school were spruced up, dangerous buildings fell to wreckers, old buildings received new fronts; museums, antique shops, mansion tours, and other tourist entertainments came into being. A restoration commission formed in 1960 marked various historic sites and worked hard to make the Comstock into somewhat of an outdoor museum. And the tourists came. Promoters devised still more entertainments, including a now annual camel race, commemorating the fact that these desert beasts were once used to carry freight in the region. Still, underneath all the encouragement of tourism, there was a considerable amount of quiet talk that maybe, just maybe, the mines of the Comstock Lode would revive again. If metals prices rose, if technology improved, if a new ledge or vein could be uncovered . . .

And so it happened. In the 1970s, Houston Oil and Minerals Company opened a pit between Virginia City

and Gold Hill, and began to tear into the old mines. Technology of the late twentieth century demands that gold and silver be mined not in the old tunnel-and-shaft manner, but in huge, open pits, destructive, ugly, and highly efficient. Residents of the Comstock towns, historic preservationists, and some history buffs complained bitterly at the loss of some old or historic prop-

---

"Sunday, Jan 20 [1867] . . . Evening we went down town — went to Jule Bulette's to see her body — She was foully murdered in her bed last night by some party unknown — from marks on her throat she must have been strangled & a pillow was over her face when discovered at noon today — smothered . . . Worst murder ever in this City — horrible — about 35 yrs old — prostitute — lived in little house on D st., 3d house from Union st., East side . . .

"Jan 21 . . . At noon coroners inquest on Jule Bulette — At 3 PM funeral of her . . . She was an Honorary member of Va Engine Co No 1, therefore the Co buried her . . . The firemen did not go out to Cemetery — There were 16 carriages loaded with friends & sisterhood of deceased which went out with her, however. . . .

"May 24 . . . The murderer of Jule Bulette is now in the County Jail — He has been trying to sell some of the articles stolen from her on the night of the murder, & this led to his detection . . . His name is John Millan & he has been working at Hall's Pioneer Laundry for some time past . . . This creates deep excitement in this City. . . .

"April 24 [1868] . . . I . . . rode in the carriage with the Drs. McMeans & Green, out to the hanging of John Milleain . . . We stood within 15 ft of him when he dropped — Dropped at 10 minutes of 1 — cut down at 15 minutes past 1, after hanging 25 minutes."

— Alfred Doten, Comstock newspaperman

erties. Still, Houston was merely carrying out the legacy of mining camps. The shades of Mackay, Flood, Fair, Sharon, O'Brien, Comstock, O'Riley, Finney, and their pals were probably dancing in high glee on the flank of Mt. Davidson.

The Pyramid Lake War

The aboriginal inhabitants of northwestern Nevada were Washo and Paiute tribes, hunters and gatherers, with their ancestral properties in the vicinities, respectively, of Lake Tahoe (the Washos) and Pyramid Lake (the Paiutes). At the time of the first white intrusion, the tribes had settled their differences in a series of battles and were living miles distant from each other, having little contact. The Washos were a peaceable group by the time of the Comstock rush; the Paiutes probably would have been also, had they not been provoked by a succession of incidents that became the Pyramid Lake War.

When John C. Frémont met the Paiutes at Pyramid Lake on his first trip of discovery, he found them not unfriendly, willing to offer directions for his journey. As the Comstock boom attracted hundreds and then thousands of people, however, relationships began to become tense. Following some confrontations and minor skirmishes between whites and natives, in May 1860, four men (or three, or seven, according to differing accounts) were found slaughtered at Williams Station on the Carson River. When the station owner made the discovery, he spread an alarm to Carson Valley and Virginia City. Indians were blamed for the attack, said to be unprovoked, although the dead men may have kidnapped some Indian women. Within hours after receiving the news, the residents of western Utah Territory had raised an "army" of 105 volunteers bent on killing all the Paiutes they could find.

The citizen army was completely unprepared for frontier battles. On May 12, 1860, the men marched from the site of present-day Wadsworth, downstream along the bank of the Truckee River, and into a neatly-prepared Paiute trap. More than half the volunteers died in the ensuing fight or in the frantic retreat back to Virginia City. This setback created a panic. The whites decided that the Paiutes must be defeated. The second battle of Pyramid Lake determined that outcome; on June 4, with 160 Indians and 2 whites (of an army of over 700) dead in battle, the Indians deserted their war camps and the soldiers took control. Fort Churchill was erected on the Carson River to ensure that the situation continued. The treaty of peace that brought the conflict to a close was negotiated by Numaga (Young Winnemucca) and U.S. Army General Frederick West Lander. Lander gained the honor of having his name on one of Nevada's counties when the state was organized.

"So up to Virginia City I went in 1932. Virginia City had a student body of some thirty-four to thirty-five students. . . . I went up as a coach and a teacher. . . . I really enjoyed it up in Virginia City, and I enjoyed the people very much. They're the salt of the earth. The town at that time was really down, minewise. There was very little mine activity goin' on and consequently very few families there. But what were there were the real Nevada mining type."

— Jake Lawlor, basketball coach

"There is plenty of ore in the Comstock Lode even now [1965]. Only a fraction has been mined. The process followed in the early days was to mine out the rich ore shoots, which were very formal in shape and size. The adjoining mineralized matter, in which the rich ore shoots occurred, carried low values in silver and gold. I consider these low grade ore bodies to be a national asset. It is a question of economics to mine them, and it's not profitable with the inflated prices of today. . . . The Comstock Lode goes right under "C" street. Still, the south end of the Lode could be mined by open cuts to a certain depth in the area of the Belcher, Crown Point, Kentuck, Yellow Jacket, Imperial group and north as far as the Exchequer mine."

— Roy A. Hardy, mining engineer

In 1874, the Paiutes were given a reservation that included Pyramid Lake and some of its environs. The tribe became self-governing and established a council headquarters at Nixon. There, the Indians lived in relative harmony with the outside civilization. The peace had a single outstanding exception.

Pyramid Lake, the mouth of the Truckee River, is a remnant of prehistoric Lake Lahontan. The only real source of water to the lake is the river, and even that flow is irregular as droughts recur over the years. Evaporation alone in the arid climate takes hundreds of thousands of acre-feet annually. The lake also contained a species of cutthroat trout and a variety of sucker-like fish called cui-ui (pronounced *kwee*-wee), said by the Indians to be a staple in their rather meager diet. In 1903, the U.S. government began to divert some of the Truckee's water to its new irrigation project near Fallon. The lake, which had been receding for thousands of years, began to fall dramatically, a measured 87 feet between 1867 and 1967. Part of the drop was surely due to the diversion from the Truckee.

In the 1940s, a decree of adjudication for the Truckee's waters was filed in federal court. Nobody in the arid West is ever satisfied with water allocation, for this is a place of scarcity. The decree stood, however, until the 1970s, when the Paiute tribe filed suit to have the original allotments set aside in the interest of preserving the lake and its fishery. Water users upstream from Pyramid, the cities, counties, utilities, and irrigation districts, were all named as defendants in the suit. The defendants argued that the decree had been made with the full knowledge of the Indians, and that the upstream users, now in the majority, had firmer rights. The Indians claimed that they had been unrepresented or poorly represented in the original court action; now their fishery was endangered, and the lake continued to drop. No one would predict how the case would end, only that nobody would ever have enough water to fill all needs both of civilization and of a dying fishery.

The beautiful desert lake is a magnet, not just for the Indians whose ancestral home it is, but for travelers from everywhere. The weird rock formations, the gorgeous white pelicans that swirl in elegant formation from Anaho Island National Wildlife Refuge, the fish, the strange desert quiet, all make everyone wish that somehow, somewhere, there would always be enough water to make Pyramid Lake live forever. It will not live forever; nothing does. Lake Lahontan's beaches have dried up all over the Great Basin. But the modern battle of Pyramid Lake may go on yet awhile.

Carson City

W. L. Hall and a few others lived in the valley that eventually held the state capital. They settled there in the backwash of the California gold rush. One day in 1851, the legend says, they shot an eagle, nailed the stuffed trophy to their cabin, and called the place Eagle Ranch. The surrounding area took the name Eagle Valley. Around Hall's cabin and trading post, a small commercial center grew up, serving the westward-moving wagon trains. In 1858, Abraham Curry and some partners bought the Hall holdings, and planned to erect a town there. The village was named to honor John C. Frémont's famous scout, Christopher "Kit" Carson.

Curry claimed afterward that he had foreseen the establishment of a capital city on the site of his ranch holdings. In fact, his plans for the town did contain a "capitol square." When the territory and then the state came into being, the property was ready.

The territorial legislature created Ormsby County in 1861, naming the jurisdiction to honor Major William Ormsby, killed in the Pyramid Lake War. Carson City became the county seat of Ormsby, the territorial capital, and then the state capital. This situation endured throughout the balance of Nevada history. The only exception was that in a governmental consolidation, Ormsby County was abolished in 1969, and Carson City's boundaries became the same as those of the former county.

The borders of Carson City contain some of the state's most interesting geography. Of the county's (city's) 172 square miles, 27 are in Lake Tahoe, and 100 square miles are in the mountains of the Sierra Nevada. Little wonder that this, Nevada's smallest county (in area), was also the nation's smallest state capital (in population). Despite its tiny size, however, Carson City had more than governmental importance. A U.S. Mint established there in 1866 began to turn out coins with the metals of the Comstock. Smaller coins, dollars, double eagles, and half eagles, were minted there until 1879, when the smaller coins were discontinued. The mint closed in 1893 after producing more than $50 million in coins destined to become collector's pieces. The mint building, on Carson City's main street, underwent various changes between 1893 and 1939, when the state of Nevada acquired the structure for a museum. With the establishment of the Nevada State Museum, the place became a permanent attraction for visitors to western Nevada. Owing largely to generous gifts from the Fleischmann family and later the Fleischmann Foundation, the museum gained a distinguished reputation and fine displays reflecting the natural, political, economic, and social history of Nevada.

The capitol building was contructed in 1871. Like other public edifices in the vicinity, it was made of locally quarried stone, and on a traditional design that included a gleaming dome. The state officers and the legislature were housed there until 1971, when the lawmakers moved to a modern new building to the south of the capitol. The governor and other officials retained their quarters in the original building which was fully remodeled and restored in the late 1970s. Only in 1909 did the state provide an executive residence for the governor and his family. The neighborhood surrounding the governor's mansion became an important historic district in the capital city.

Carson had many of the attributes of a busy, central city, almost from its beginning. Two volunteer fire companies, the headquarters of the Virginia and Truckee railroad, stores, hotels, homes, and facilities for cultural events marked the town. Several newspapers published in Carson, including the *Territorial Enterprise,* which later moved to Virginia City, and the long-lived Carson *Appeal,* established in 1865, and still issued in the 1980s. After the Second World War, with all of the West booming from the population influx, Carson City also expanded. Until that time,

State Capitol, Carson City

"This convention happened to be in Reno and Mother was there with Dad. . . . Young Denver Dickerson happened to be in there as a delegate. He was a representative from out in Ely. He was pretty busy and active, and nobody wanted to be Lieutenant Governor, so they offered it to him. When Governor Sparks died then Dickerson became Governor. They built the mansion during his term.

"Mrs. Dickerson was about to have a baby so they thought it would be nice to hurry a bit and finish the mansion so she could have the baby in the mansion. So the paint was hardly dry when the Dickersons moved in there, and their daughter June was born."

— Lucy Davis Crowell, daughter
of Carson City pioneers

"We moved over to Carson City . . . on the last day of June, 1935. . . . We were able to find a house to rent right away. This was an old house built in the late 1860s by Mr. H. M. Yerington. . . . The house was big and rambling. . . . At this time, there were no new homes in Carson City. I learned that the newest building in Carson was at least ten years old, so you had to rent one of the older houses if you expected to live in Carson City."

— Hugh A. Shamberger, state engineer

housing was so scarce that at the change of administrations, the outgoing officials had to move before the new ones could come in. The post-war growth, however, made numerous changes in Carson City, including the loss of its status as the smallest state capital in the United States.

The Carson City of the 1980s is a vital, active government seat and typical Nevada town. Tourism creates a good deal of its economy, and increasing numbers of state buildings reflect the growth of modern bureaucracy. The historic homes, built before and just after the turn of the twentieth century, provide a contrast with the casinos, hotels, and government buildings along Carson Street (the main thoroughfare). The excellent Nevada State Museum gives a focus for the town's pride in its past.

Reno

Before the founding of Reno, the region was agricultural. The first populated areas were several miles south of the Truckee River, in Washoe Valley. There, farms provided hay and vegetables for the passing traffic of gold seekers and emigrants. When the Comstock Lode was uncovered in 1859, commerce increased to include saw mills and ore reduction plants. Within a few years, the Virginia and Truckee railroad provided easy access to the Comstock, new mills arose

along the Carson River, and business other than agriculture became marginal.

The Truckee Meadows was on the emigrant trail along the Truckee River. Wild hay, plentiful water, and a lovely setting at the foot of the eastern slope of the Sierra Nevada provided cross-country travelers with a pleasant respite before the mountain crossing. The Donner party came into the meadows in the late autumn of 1846, and had they decided to winter there, might have survived; instead, the group approached the Sierra, and many perished in the snow. As traffic increased through the Truckee Meadows, a small toll crossing of the Truckee River took advantage of the westering travel. In 1859, C. W. Fuller established a ferry and then a bridge on the site. The bridge washed out, and Fuller's business seemed unstable enough that he sold out in 1861 to a western promoter named Myron C. Lake.

The bridge and ford of the river became Lake's Crossing. Myron Lake established toll roads and built a lodging house and a few other structures to serve the throngs passing through on the way from California over the Sierra to the Comstock. Within only a few years, Lake had amassed considerable wealth and property in the riverside area. Toll collections ran as high as $2,500 a day.

The construction of the Central Pacific railroad changed Lake's Crossing forever. As workers pushed the rails over the mountains, it became clear that a town would be needed on the site of Lake's Crossing. The legend says that E. B. Crocker, brother of an officer of the railroad corporation, wanted to name the place "Argenta" because he liked the prospect of conductors announcing the name through the cars. Crocker lost his wish; post-Civil War patriotism demanded that place names honor fallen heroes. Jesse Reno died in 1862 at the battle of South Mountain and thus gave his name to the coming settlement on the Truckee River and the Central Pacific. The sale of lots took place May 9, 1868; the first train arrived a month later, on June 18. Reno thus, like hundreds of other towns across the nation, was spawned by the railroad.

Myron Lake increased his fortune again by selling

land to the railroad and continuing to operate the hotel and toll bridge. He lost a legal battle over toll collections in 1873, and the bridge became free. By 1880, Lake was nevertheless the most important taxpayer in what became Washoe County. A house he owned (but did not use as a family home) was preserved in Reno as the "Lake Mansion," and a street in downtown Reno retains the name. Lake died in 1884.

When Nevada became a state, the seat of Washoe County was designated as Washoe City, then the metropolis of Washoe Valley. Only three years after Reno arose, the riverside town acquired the county seat, and has kept it since that time. Myron Lake donated land for the courthouse, on the south side of the river—a toll crossing of his bridge from the main part of town. The courthouse was built on the site about the time the bridge became free. The government building remained there, a landmark in a city destined to become a landmark itself.

Reno rather quickly became a city of contrasts. The first building lot sold at the railroad's auction was at the southeast corner of what became Virginia Street (the main street) and Commercial Row (fronting on the tracks). The structure erected there on a plot that went for $600 was a combination saloon and gambling hall; there has never been anything on that lot other than a bar or casino. For nearly a century afterwards, Commercial Row marked the northern border of the downtown gambling district. At the same time, important state politicians and business leaders found that property along the Truckee River presented attractive views and pleasant surroundings. Both north and south of the river, elegant homes and mansions began to dot the streets. Reno became the most important political and financial center of the state, and remained so until past the middle of the twentieth century.

Some of the leaders left their names on sites around the Truckee Meadows: Francis G. Newlands, congressman and senator; George Bartlett, congressman and famous divorce judge; George Nixon, financier, politician, and senator; George Wingfield, financier, banker, and political boss; Patrick McCarran, lawyer, judge, senator, and political titan. These and others

gave an exciting, colorful atmosphere to life in the riverside town. There were some, equally colorful and not so respectable, who brought Reno a reputation as a tough little burg. Among those were William Graham and James McKay, owners and operators of most of the illegal action in town, and friends of some of the nation's most notorious characters of the Prohibition era. McKay and Graham were imprisoned for mail fraud, leaving at least one unsolved murder in their wake. So people on all sides of society brought

"I can remember the streetcars that used to run on the streets of Reno. . . . One would go clear out Second Street to the end of the city limits; another one would go up to the University of Nevada up Sierra Street; and another one would go to Sparks up Fourth Street. Later on, the runs were extended out Fourth Street west to Ralston and up Ralston to the bottom of the hill. . . . And then they ran a separate line out to Moana Springs. That one went out Virginia Street to California and up California to Plumas, I believe it was . . .

"I also remember when I was in Reno in 1910, they had the Jeffries-Johnson fight in Reno on the Fourth of July. . . . Well, I can recall going up and watching Johnson very busily at work sparring and punching at a bag and doing his roadwork and everything, while up at Moana Springs Jeffries was playing cards and drinking whiskey. . . . There was a report my father told me about that Johnson, when the fight was signed, had agreed to throw the bout. . . . That was why Jeffries was not training. The day before the fight, Johnson backed out of the agreement and said the white boy would have to take care of himself in the ring. It was quite a shock to everybody . . . that Johnson won . . . and immediately, they started to try to find a 'white hope.' That's where the 'white hope' in the boxing fraternity came from."

— John F. Cahlan,
son of Reno pioneers

notoriety and fame to Reno. But Reno's first real nationwide recognition did not come from finance, gambling, crime, or politics.

In 1906, Laura Corey ended her twenty-year marriage to the president of U.S. Steel by divorcing him in Reno. The residency requirement at that time was six months. A huge financial settlement and William Corey's position made Reno a dateline for dozens of news stories. In 1920, Mary Pickford engaged Patrick McCarran as her lawyer to obtain a divorce from Owen Moore, and again, news wires hummed with titillating items. The Nevada residency requirement was still six months at the time Mary Pickford decided to leave Mr. Moore and marry Douglas Fairbanks, but legal grounds for divorce were considered very loose in Nevada. In 1927, the legislature dropped the time to three months, and the divorce traffic increased to a status that made it seem important in the local economy. In 1931, on the same day that casino gambling was relegalized, Governor Balzar signed a law making the residency requirement for Nevada divorce only six weeks. Reno then became a mecca for unhappy spouses, for other states and jurisdictions had much stricter statutes for both residency and grounds for divorce.

The divorce trade attracted citizens from all walks of life, but many were also prominent society women and men. The notoriety stemming from Nevada divorces (usually only *Reno* appeared in the publicity) made major news services keep full-time reporters near the Washoe County courthouse. These people, with little enough to do (after all, what can you write about some 1,500 similar lawsuits a year?) began to dream up legends and customs to make the process more colorful. They decided that the new divorcee *always* kissed the pillars of the courthouse when she emerged with her decree, and then *invariably* walked the block to the Virginia Street bridge to throw her wedding ring into the Truckee River. Dozens of news photos documented those activities. The lipstick smears on the courthouse posts and the rings little boys fished out of the river gave credence to the tales. Of course, men hardly ever did anything so undignified

"We used to . . . cover the courthouse. Your tools of the trade were the volume of *Who's Who* and the social registers, the master social register for the cities . . . , and in your office you had the individual social registers for each city. And every divorce, and we were just—oh, we were having them—they had two courts at that point, and there was a divorce every five minutes in both courts all day. They had no time for civil matters, criminal matters, or anything else; they'd have to squeeze those in somewhere. You'd have to go through each divorce. . . . And so you'd have to check every name in the social register or in *Who's Who* to try to stumble onto those prominent people. And—what a peculiar activity!"

— Edward Olsen, Associated Press bureau chief, Reno

"While I was doing [Reno Chamber of Commerce advertising services] for free, I used to go over—to encourage the legends that had been written about Reno by various authors and feature writers. And I used to go over to the Woolworth's store on a dull day and buy a few dollars worth of dime store wedding rings, and then when nobody was lookin', toss 'em in the river off the bridge. And this meant that kids lookin' for crawdads in the summer months would occasionally come up with a ring, and they'd always stand up and hold the ring up, and yell with all their friends, who were doing the same thing, and this would attract the tourists on the bridge, and 'here's a wedding ring that had been thrown off the bridge!' And so it 'proved that it was a true legend.'

"And divorcees kissing the pillars of the courthouse was supposedly an old tradition, and occasionally [with] a little kleenex, I could get a little pink smear on the courthouse pillar—might be what it was supposed to be, and this encouraged a number of people to do it."

— Thomas C. Wilson, advertising agency owner

when they obtained Reno divorces, and anyway, it was considered a mark of chivalry to allow the woman to obtain the divorce. A gossip columnist, a man, Walter Winchell, invented a term for what happened during that era—Reno-vation.

In time, other states adopted more realistic or humane divorce laws, and Reno's traffic diminished. The "guest houses" and dude ranches disappeared or took up other business. Still, in many places "Reno" signified a divorce mill, or conversely, a place where dissatisfied spouses could legally part with a minimum of fuss and bother.

The other law Governor Balzar signed in March 1931 made Reno a magnet for happier people. Casinos had existed since the town's founding, mainly inside a two-block area in downtown Reno. While gambling was supposedly illegal between 1910 and 1931, the business still flourished, but without paying taxes or license fees. Relegalization brought to Reno some of the world's most colorful characters and businessmen, people who transformed the downtown section, and then changed it again. For the most part, these owners were good citizens of Reno and of Nevada, recognizing that their privilege in Nevada was a great benefit to them. More than good citizens, some became community benefactors and outstanding contributors.

Probably Reno needed no other promoters while Raymond I. "Pappy" Smith lived, and no other capitalist pacesetter while William Harrah was alive. Both of these entrepreneurs arrived in Reno in the mid-1930s, each from a carnival-like background in California. Smith founded Harolds Club, and Harrah established a series of bingo parlors and finally two hotel-casinos (one at Tahoe) named Harrah's. Smith enjoyed doing good works for the community—scholarships for university students, special advertising projects, highway promotion, and many charities—while Harrah liked having a place that led all the others in excellent service and appointments. Harrah also found pleasure in a rich man's hobby of acquiring antique cars, a collection that he turned into a museum of great importance.

The Smith and Harrah establishments made the pattern for all other casinos in Reno, some that measured up and some that did not, some that succeeded and others that failed. In the 1970s, with Smith dead and times changing, Reno underwent an orgy of casino/hotel building, a spurt so enormous that four resorts

---

"If there was one thing that distinguished the operation of the club and the casino over and above anything else, it certainly was the big-heartedness of Mr. Smith. As long as I was associated with them, . . . it wasn't uncommon for Mr. Smith personally to make refunds to customers in amounts that were almost staggering. For instance, $350,000 in one particular year was refunded to people who had spent the grocery money . . . or something of that nature. And it was common knowledge around the club that if anyone found themselves in that position or predicament, they were to be sent to Mr. Smith."

— Leslie Kofoed, Harolds Club executive

"When Bill Harrah started to do something he always did it right. . . . He come in one day, and they just finished a bar, and I was very interested in the bar because they were covering it with gold leaf. And I asked the painter or the man that was applying it if that was real gold; he said yes. . . . When they got it laid, then they covered it with some kind of resin to keep it from peeling, and when it got all done it didn't look nearly as well as I thought it would.

"Harrah came in and looked at it, and he said, 'Warren, what do you think of that?'

"And I says, 'Well, it didn't turn out just the way I thought it would. . . .'

". . . 'Well, you don't like it?'

". . . 'Well, no.'

"He turned to the guy, and he said, 'Take it off.' "

— Warren Nelson, Harrah's Club executive

opened the same day. The resulting sprawl and construction expansion changed Reno forever; the new
Las Vegas-style operations never would have prospered at an earlier time, but the new era and the right
people made a difference. Harrah died in June 1978,
and that probably marked the end of an epoch in
Reno's life and entertainments.

If some of Reno's life was gaudy and public, much
was also sedate and educational or cultural. The University of Nevada was established there in 1885 and
opened in 1886. The institution had a rather slow
growth until the late 1940s and early 1950s, when new
buildings, many donated by the Fleischmann Foundation, and a population explosion combined to make the
campus a more distinguished-looking place. The university began in the 1950s to expand its resources, first
with a campus in Las Vegas and then with community
colleges at various locations around the state. Still, the
older campus at Reno retained the atmosphere that
made it seem typically a small-town and friendly
place. The Fleischmann Atmospherium-Planetarium
won a national prize for architecture for a modernistic
design, and the supporters of the university raised
enough money to restore the oldest building on campus, which dates from 1886. Excellent programs in
mining, engineering, journalism, psychology, and the
humanities, along with a new medical school and a fine
library, all in a tree-shaded, traditional setting, demon-
strated the relatively mature character of the University
of Nevada Reno.

Along with the university, other cultural institutions
include private and public art galleries, the nation's
oldest volunteer community theater, numerous old and
new churches of nearly every denomination, a performing arts auditorium at the center of town, and a
convention center of considerable proportion at the
outskirts. The Nevada State Historical Society, with
fine modern quarters and an extensive museum collection, became attached to the university campus. The
ubiquitous hotel/casinos compete with entertainment
of both musical and theatrical variety. The town has
an active musical community with interests and performances ranging from jazz to opera to chamber music.

"Reno was just beginning to be an important
town; 3,500, I think they said was the population
when we came in November of '89. I was delighted
with Reno when I arrived here as a girl. The Depot
Hotel was still in existence. . . . I thought the
Washoe County Bank was quite imposing. The
Bishop Whitaker School was a lovely location and
is still. I wasn't particularly impressed with Reno
High School. In fact, I didn't like it from the start.
Maybe it was because people were beginning to
talk about the University. . . . We located on Lake
Street, and, even though there were just alfalfa
fields in between, that looked to be the growing
school, *the* educational institution."

— Katharine Riegelhuth, university professor

"Blanchfield was quite a pioneer in Reno. He
was a veteran of the English air corps during the war
and he came over to this country and went into this
mail service. A buddy from the air service . . . had
died and they were burying him in the K of P cemetery. It was decided that Blanchfield . . . was to go
and fly over and drop a wreath on the grave when
the thing was over. . . . I was there. He dropped
the wreath and he almost made a bull's-eye. And
I can see that plane—see, it was up above these
trees, making this turn, and it turned and finally got
over near Ralston and just cut down."

— Silas Ross, funeral director

"I remember the island real well. It was full of
willows and just was nothing but an island until
they cleared it off for a runway for Ely. And he had
a biplane, a single motor biplane, and he took off
from this runway, and he just barely missed the
trees at the end of the runway. If he'd hit them,
he'd've gone into the river. Well, he made one circle around Reno and came back and landed. And
that was the first airplane flight I had ever seen."

— John F. Cahlan, son of Reno pioneers

In short, Reno's cultural life matured from the rural delights of the 1860s and the gambling hells of the 1900s to the modern and sophisticated city of today.

Because Reno was always a transportation center, beginning with its position on the emigrant trail, the coming of the railroad, and later with the building of highways and freeways, there has been a continuing interest in that field. In fact, the "Biggest Little City" began initially to advertise its title as a welcome to the first cross-country highway, in 1926. The airport development was equally important, beginning as early as 1911. In that year, pioneer airman Eugene Ely landed on Belle Isle in downtown Reno. This was a small island in the middle of the Truckee River. Local promoters cleared the island of willows and other impediments for Ely's landing. Later, the site acquired bridges across the river and became Wingfield Park. Still later, a regular airfield was developed further out of town, near the corner of Plumas Street and Moana Lane. This site, called Blanch Field, was named for a World War I-era barnstormer, William Blanchfield. Blanchfield was killed in Reno while attempting to drop flowers from a plane onto a grave during a burial ceremony. Among the aviators who landed at Blanch Field was Charles Lindbergh, on a promotional trip with the "Spirit of St. Louis." During the 1930s, Reno outgrew the tiny facility at Blanch Field, and put a golf course on the site. The new airport at Hubbard Field (formerly a cattle pasture) became—with various expansions to the north—the permanent Reno airport. In the 1980s, the newly remodeled and completely modern Reno airport stirred hardly any memories at all of a cleared willow patch in the Truckee River.

Reno has been the subject of hundreds of articles and books, all trying to explain the town's atmosphere or the attitudes of its citizens. None has been fully successful, for Reno is many cities in one, in heavy contrast to other Nevada towns with more single-mindedness. The combination makes it possible to find whatever one seeks there: everything that goes with sophisticated entertainment, surely; but also, a college town, lovely green parks, a financial center, sports and athletics ranging from high school basketball to some of the

best skiing in the nation, and a core population of old-timers or their descendants who will occasionally recall Walter Van Tilburg Clark's *City of Trembling Leaves*, and sort of wish it would all return to something like the 1920s (with all modern conveniences, of course).

The Irrigation Era

As Nevada began its life with agriculture, so it has continued to have a certain amount of that business, despite an arid climate that brings only some eight inches of rainfall a year. That aridity has always presented a challenge to some people. One of the leaders who accepted the challenge was a politician named Francis Griffith Newlands.

Newlands arrived in Nevada at the end of the 1880s. He was the son-in-law of Comstock mogul William Sharon, and the custodian of Sharon's estate matters. Newlands's chosen mission in life was to organize the arid West into a blooming garden. Nevada was then some years into its post-Comstock depression, which lasted until 1900. Newlands was elected to Congress in 1892, and labored for the next ten years to pass a comprehensive act that would bring irrigation works to the dry states. It was assumed then that turning rivers out of their banks into well-engineered canals would solve the problems of lack of rainfall. The Reclamation Act of 1902 was Newlands's monument; the next year, the first irrigation project under federal sponsorship began at what would be Fallon, Nevada.

Before the project was established, perhaps a hundred ranchers in the area were using the Carson River for irrigation. These pioneers used ditches and small dams, working individually or in small companies. Some of the larger owners included Ernest Freeman and I. H. Kent of the Stillwater district. There were some stores and other commercial ventures as well, both at Stillwater and at St. Clair. A mill processed grains raised in the area, using water power from the Carson.

The settlements had begun when cross-country wagon trains stopped at Ragtown. Later, the Pony Express crossed the area, but its stations disappeared with the abandonment of that traffic. So the ranchers and others in the vicinity needed to be fairly self-sufficient, for the roads and railway into the section did not arrive until after the building of the project. Dusty wagon or foot tracks served until the first decade of the twentieth century. The farmers thus had marginal operations, raising grain and hay for livestock and row crops for their families' needs.

Because various assumptions about the water supply combined with similarly untested theories about the soils, the Truckee-Carson Project (later renamed to honor Newlands) was designed to irrigate 350,000 acres in what was then called (rather inelegantly) the Carson Sink Valley. Part of the Truckee's waters were turned into a 30-mile-long canal at Derby, while the Carson River continued to be utilized as it flowed through the area. Lahontan Dam, completed in 1913, impounded these streams.

The combined waters of the two rivers were inadequate; worse yet, the soils of the area, previously unanalyzed, proved full of alkali and salts which made them unsuitable for most crops. The size of the planned project shrunk and then was reduced again; about 70,000 acres was the maximum ever irrigated from the complex system.

Nevertheless, the fine little farming community grew up as a result of the work in the (newly-named) Lahontan Valley. Fallon, the largest town, took the county seat of Churchill County from Stillwater and became the center of a multi-million-dollar agricultural industry. Fallon also attracted a World War II Naval auxiliary air station, which both adds to the economy and gives an added dimension to the society there. Schools, churches, and various businesses mostly connected with agriculture mark one of Nevada's fine agrarian centers. The excellent Churchill County Museum preserves the region's cultural artifacts in one of the best such institutions in the state.

Hazen, the former railhead, became a siding on the Southern Pacific, and finally, almost a ghost town. Hazen's early days were marked by violence and Nevada's last lynching. In the late twentieth century,

however, little at the site recalls those events.

Fernley, west of Fallon in another part of the Newlands Project, remained a small agricultural center until after World War II, when a cement plant built nearby increased its population. Then, in the booming 1960s and 1970s, Fernley became somewhat of a "bedroom community" for Reno businesspeople

---

"The farmers were people that wanted to make a change in life. They wanted to take in the possibility of moving to the west and having a vocation or interest there. They were . . . a high class of people and very industrious. They were nice people to associate with, but there wasn't very much opportunity to become well acquainted, although I guess I knew every farmer on the Project by his first name and vice-versa. . . .

"The social life was not particularly outstanding, simply because the farmers and their wives were too darn busy. Boy, they had plenty to do!"

— Stanley Marean, Newlands Project water master

"The building of the Lahontan Dam and the canals of the Newlands Project was one of the most interesting projects of Churchill County in my lifetime. . . . Some of the old-timers and a good many of the homesteaders were disillusioned, as it did not always come up to their expectations. The homesteaders had a hard time getting their crops to bear as wind blew seeds out of the sandy land. But there were a great many who succeeded. . . .

"Much controversy has taken place since Lahontan Dam was built as to whether it was a success or not, but, of course, we know that the progress and building up of Fallon and Churchill County is due a great deal to the success of the Newlands Project."

— Cecyl Johnson, daughter of Churchill County pioneers

looking for quiet surroundings, and acquired a much different atmosphere from that of its sleepy, farmer days.

The other irrigated district of northwestern Nevada, around Lovelock, had a longer history and equally prosperous agriculture. The Big Meadows on the Emigrant Trail contained plentiful ground water and wild grass in abundance, important provisions for cross-country travelers of the 1850s. Before that time, Peter Skene Ogden, Kit Carson, and John C. Frémont had passed through. George Lovelock, a pioneer immigrant from England, made the first permanent ranch settlement there, and when the Central Pacific rails pushed through, the place was called Lovelock's, reflecting the rancher's donation of the townsite and right-of-way. The little settlement grew until the town was chartered in 1917. At the end of World War I, Humboldt County was divided and the southern part containing Lovelock was named to honor a World War I general; Lovelock became the seat of Pershing County.

Irrigation works existed in the Big Meadows almost from the beginning of settlement there, impounding or diverting the waters of the Humboldt River. John G. Taylor, an important sheep raiser, established what was called the Pitt-Taylor reservoir, but that effort was largely unsuccessful. In the 1930s, the U.S. Reclamation Service built an earthen dam near a former railroad siding called Rye Patch. Rye Patch dam became a significant part of the irrigated agricultural economy of Pershing County and the lower Humboldt River area. In recent years, the reservoir has also become an important recreation facility, and the site of a notable archeological exploration. The town of Lovelock serves all of these interests, maintaining a mostly agricultural and rural atmosphere, with a favorable place on the Interstate highway adding some tourism economy as well.

The Railroads

By any reckoning, the building of the Central Pacific railroad was the greatest engineering and construction achievement of the nineteenth-century West.

"Among my classmates [at the University of Nevada] was Charlie Russell who was the governor of the state and a congressman of the state. Another was Cliff Young who was a congressman and state senator. . . . I've often reminisced over the years, it's rather coincidental that Charlie Russell and Cliff Young and myself were born in the same block in Lovelock. The little community of Lovelock, and all three of us had varying degrees of success with a political career; and interestingly enough, two Republicans, and I was the lone Democrat."

— Alan Bible, former
United States Senator

Beginning in 1863, and extending for nearly the next five years, the rails pushed from Sacramento, California, across the crags of the Sierra Nevada, through the canyons, over valleys and rivers and streams, through good and terrible weather, 138 miles to the Nevada border. The first train entered Nevada on December 13, 1867; the first locomotive steamed into Reno six months later. Passenger service between Sacramento and Reno began in July 1868. The work over the Sierra, consuming tons of material—and the lives of many laborers—took half a decade to complete; from Reno to Promontory, Utah, and the end of the track required less than a year more.

About fifteen miles beyond Reno, the next terminus was Wadsworth, named to honor another casualty of the Civil War who fell at the Battle of the Wilderness. Wadsworth became a bustling little community, containing railroad shops, a depot, hotel, business houses, and homes for railroad workers. Within fifteen years after the coming of the railroad, the population numbered about five hundred. The town served a wide agricultural business in the surrounding area, providing both commercial and cultural activity. A disastrous fire in 1884 nearly erased the small city, but it was quickly rebuilt to better standards than before, with plans for expansion and permanency. It was not to happen that way.

In 1899, the Central Pacific/Southern Pacific underwent a series of organizational changes and reconstructions. Wadsworth was doomed as the new rails bypassed the site. In 1904, the railroad buildings and many other structures were moved to a new town a mile east of Reno called Sparks. By the turn of the twentieth century, apparently enough Civil War generals had towns named in their honor, so the railroad's officers chose the name Sparks to recognize Nevada's governor.

Next on the line as the tracks pressed across Nevada in 1868 was Lovelock, already the site of an agricultural community. Here, the work had been going so fast that the workers ran out of rails. The heads of the railroad corporation thus had time to negotiate a treaty with the local Shoshone Indians that allowed the chiefs of the tribe to ride in the coaches. This arrangement proved beneficial to both the corporation and the Indians; the Shoshones had free transportation and became adept at warning the railroad's workers of hazards like washouts on the line.

The Central Pacific/Southern Pacific continued to serve the transportation needs of northwestern Nevada into the end of the twentieth century. The business changed in hundreds of ways, and highways and freeways nearly eliminated passenger traffic over the rails. Still, the founding of towns, and the continuing economic asset of the railroad gave a special feature to the history of the cities begun along the tracks.

The Virginia and Truckee railroad was established, under various changes of name, as early as 1861. The financial dealing, the engineering problems, and the political activity surrounding the shortline have been the stuff of numerous books. The ground-breaking took place at American Flat in February 1869, with William Sharon as head of the company and Isaac James as chief engineer. The standard-gauge road was conceived initially to serve the freighting needs of the Comstock mines and towns. After just seven and a half months of construction in the Comstock area, superintendent Henry M. Yerington drove a first spike in Carson City, and a locomotive began to operate over the rails. Full service between Gold Hill and Carson City

opened on January 29, 1870. Carson City became the business and maintenance headquarters when the company erected a huge shop and roundhouse building just east of Carson Street.

The V&T soon had an enthusiastic group of promoters wanting a line to Reno. The final spike on that route was driven on August 24, 1872. New discoveries on the Comstock that year made increased traffic between the mines and the main Central Pacific line at Reno even more lucrative. Several years of good returns followed. Numberless passengers, freight shipments, excursions, and historic events marked the advance of the V&T. The rails went to Minden in 1906, making a transportation complex of considerable importance to northwestern Nevada.

Inevitably, the decline set in. The last dividends on the Comstock were paid in 1880. The Central Pacific/Southern Pacific wearied of sharing revenues with the shortline and started building its own branches, most notably a cutoff from Hazen. And finally, people began to find that road or highway transportation was cheaper or more convenient, and the railroad began to die. After 1924, every annual report said that the V&T had a deficit.

The V&T never lacked for supporters and fans. From 1933 to 1937, Darius Ogden Mills used his personal fortune to keep the road in operation. After his death, the V&T went into receivership, and the line to Virginia City was abandoned. The rails in that section were pulled up in 1941 and sold to Japanese scrap dealers. The roadbed deteriorated and became dangerous and, finally, too expensive to repair. After petitions, hearings, and protests, especially from residents of Carson Valley, the V&T went out of business at the end of May 1950.

Many people have now forgotten the narrow-gauge Nevada-California-Oregon Railway. Surveys began early in 1880 out of Reno for a railroad to connect that city with the lumbering districts of northern California and with the Pacific Northwest. The financing of the line was fraught with controversy, but ground-breaking took place in Reno on December 22, 1880, and a first spike ceremony followed in May 1881. The railroad tracks meandered north of Reno, while financiers and directors fought each other to complete the line. Some of these were real fights; at a board of directors meeting in September 1881, two men were shot.

A stage line originating at the Oneida station offered freight and passenger service from the N-C-O as far north as Susanville, beginning in October 1882. Construction and financing remained sporadic. In June 1888, the tracks had reached Doyle, California, about 58 miles north. Further extensions, always financially troubled, continued into the twentieth century until the tracks reached Lakeview, Oregon, in 1912.

Meanwhile, the Western Pacific had emerged as an important competitor for other western railroads, and in 1917 it acquired 113 miles of the N-C-O and then broad-gauged the line. The Western Pacific also took over the Reno depot and shops, and in January 1918, the last narrow-gauge N-C-O train pulled out. The Southern Pacific acquired the rest of the facilities in California in 1926. The Western Pacific suspended passenger service from its Reno depot in 1930. In the 1980s, passenger traffic on the Western Pacific out of Reno had to be first by car to Portola, California.

Nostalgia has served to keep the railroads of northwestern Nevada alive—by way of their artifacts. Some of the Southern Pacific's historic rolling stock was donated for an outdoor museum in Sparks, where it re-ceives tender oversight from the Sparks Chamber of Commerce. The N-C-O—later Western Pacific—depot survives on Reno's East Fourth Street as the office of a liquor distributor. The Virginia and Truckee's cars and engines, often seen in western movies, became objects of great concern by railfans. Some of the stock was scrapped, of course, and so were many other pieces of machinery. Still, the last managers of the road donated some parts to the state of Nevada for display first at the Nevada State Museum, and finally, in the V&T Museum. The V&T Museum, at the outskirts of Carson City, provides railfans and buffs with a contact with the past, and with Nevada's most beloved short-line railroad.

Perhaps because their towns have been there longer than others of the state, the residents of northwestern Nevada seem to be in rather stable condition. Quite satisfied with their existence, and with a lovely setting, they welcome visitors openly, with an acceptance that may seem at first to be overly casual. Despite Reno's gaudy reputation, the glitter of casinos, and the promotion of tourism, northwestern Nevada is a typical bastion of Silver State conservatism. The people here are proud of their heritage, and not excessively anxious about the future.

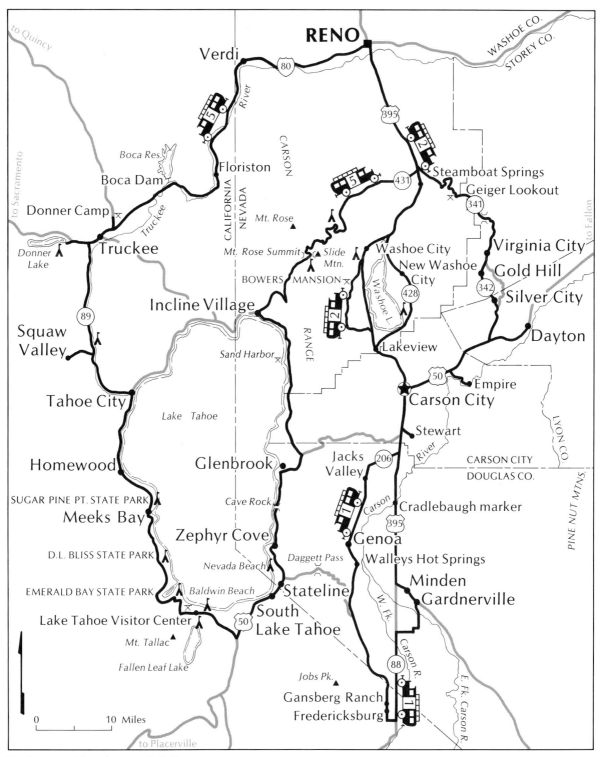

Northwestern Nevada, tours 1, 2, 5

TOURING IN NORTHWESTERN NEVADA

~~~~~~~~~~~~~~~~~~

The tours for this area have been composed not to show every town or site, but to guide travelers to some of the most interesting and accessible natural or manmade features. There are many places of interest more than a day's trip out of the Reno area; if it is possible for you to make such a tour, ask locally—at the Nevada Historical Society, for example—about overnight camping in this section.

As the field of the tours here is fairly compact, and commercial centers are available, picnic or camping gear is not vitally necessary; and yet it is pleasant on a good day to have a picnic. A number of excellent picnic grounds exist in this section.

While travel in northwestern Nevada should not be considered hazardous, tourists are urged to make sure that the vehicle is in good condition, and that extra supplies are available. On warm days, a jug of cool water can be very welcome.

You will surely want a camera along. Some of the state's best scenery and most picturesque structures exist here. Camera supplies are readily available in most communities.

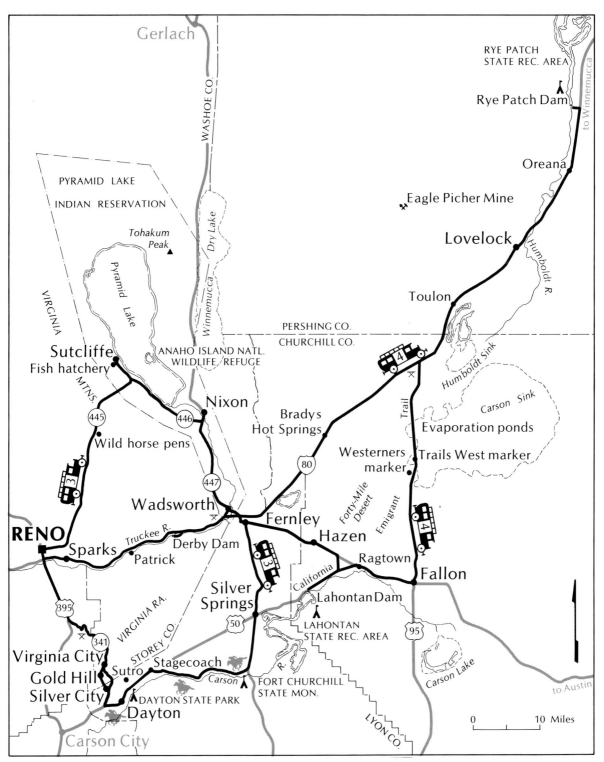

Northwestern Nevada, tours 3, 4

What to see in Reno: The Greater Reno Chamber of Commerce, 133 North Sierra Street in downtown Reno, has maps, brochures, and a guide to a 43-mile scenic drive of the Reno-Sparks area. The drive will display parks, homes, golf courses, cultural sites, and industrial features.

The Nevada State Historical Society, 1620 North Virginia Street, has museum exhibits and research material. There are also some printed materials for sale. Admission is free. All tours in this section begin at the Nevada Historical Society building.

The Fleischmann Planetarium is in the same complex with the Historical Society. The planetarium offers "star shows" on a regular schedule, and contains exhibits about outer space. There is a charge for the star-show presentations.

The University of Nevada campus is directly south of the planetarium on North Virginia Street. The restored Morrill Hall, oldest building on the campus, was built in 1886 and serves as a symbol of the university's past.

The Washoe County courthouse, Pioneer Theater-Auditorium, and Sierra Arts Foundation facility are all near the corner of South Virginia and Court streets. The Arts Foundation ticket center has information about cultural events in the area.

The Sparks Chamber of Commerce and outdoor railroad exhibit are on B Street (the main street) in Sparks.

Harrah's Automobile Collection is on Glendale Road between Reno and Sparks. There is an admission fee.

Take time to drive around downtown Reno, to see the casinos and entertainment offerings. This is really where Nevada's tourist industry began.

TOUR ONE, Northwestern Nevada's earliest settlements: Reno — Carson City — Genoa — Carson Valley and return. Approximately 116 miles round trip. Pack a picnic or plan to visit a restaurant in one of the towns along the way.

Leaving the Nevada Historical Society, head south on Virginia Street (toward downtown Reno). As you drive through the downtown area, you can see these features: in 1.4 miles, cross the tracks and see the city's slogan on the Reno Arch, "The Biggest Little City in the World;" 0.2 miles further, cross the Virginia Street bridge; in another 0.1 miles, the Washoe County courthouse is on the right, Pioneer Theater-Auditorium on the left; 3.0 miles further, the Centennial Coliseum convention center and restored pioneer buildings—the Lake mansion, the Glendale school. Continue 6.1 miles on South Virginia Street, now U.S. 395.

The drive is across the Truckee Meadows. Mt. Rose is the highest peak in the part of the Sierra Nevada you see on the right; the Virginia Range is on the left. From the intersection and traffic light, go straight ahead another 1.7 miles. You will see the sinter mounds and terraces of Reno Hot Springs and Steamboat. These springs are among the most studied in the West. Discovered in 1860, and named "Steamboat" because of the sound of rushing hot water, the site has had several incarnations as a resort. The post office, established in 1880, is still active. The V&T had a station at Steamboat during its heyday as a health spa. Underground waters here are very hot—up to 400°F—while surface temperatures have been measured above boiling. There has been a good deal of geothermal exploration and various industrial uses of the heat, but much of the early-day "health spa" activity has died out. Steamboat is at the left; stay on U.S. 395 into Pleasant Valley.

Drive 4.6 miles to the summit of Washoe Hill, then down into Washoe Valley 0.9 miles to the site of Washoe City. There is almost nothing original here to mark Washoe County's first county seat. Drive 0.4 miles; the Washoe City cemetery is at the right.

Continue driving through Washoe Valley for 1.1 miles. The Winters ranch is at the left. At one time, this site had stables for purebred horses and a racetrack among its features. Drive through the junction, staying on U.S. 395. Washoe Lake is at the left; we usually see water birds along here—ducks, mudhens, terns, geese, occasionally swans, and various long-legged aquatic residents. Drive 1.4 miles beyond the Winters ranch to the ruins of one of the buildings of Ophir, at the left. Ophir was a milling town for the Comstock. A long tramway across Washoe Lake aided transportation; little remains of that now, although at times of low water you can see the route marked by the stumps of old pilings that supported the tram.

Drive 5.9 miles across Washoe Valley to Lakeview. The house of the watermaster for the inverted siphon works is at the right, that pretty Victorian structure. From Lakeview, continue 1.9 miles on U.S. 395 into Eagle Valley, with Carson City visible ahead. There is a historical marker at the right, commemorating the first airplane flight over the Sierra and its touchdown here in the spring of 1919. Continue 0.7 miles and enter the Carson City urban area. U.S. 395 becomes Carson Street. Drive 0.7 miles and arrive at the Nevada State Museum, on the right. Stop here to obtain maps, brochures, and printed and graphic materials to make your trip more interesting and informed.

Take time as well to tour the museum; this is one of the state's treasure houses. Admission is free, although donations are welcome. You will see exhibits of natural history and of the artifacts of the U.S. Mint that once occupied the building. There is a full-scale model of a mine to walk through.

Other features you might enjoy visiting in Carson City include two more museums: the Warren Engine

Virginia & Truckee Museum, Carson City

Company fire-fighters exhibit a block west of the capitol at Curry and Musser streets, and the V&T museum at the south edge of town (1.3 miles south of the state museum, on the west side of Carson Street). You might also like a look now at the historic homes and the governor's mansion along Mountain Street (we will return here near the end of today's tour).

Completing your tour of Carson City, return to the state museum and continue driving south past the government buildings on Carson Street (U.S. 395) for 1.3 miles. The V&T museum is to the right. Drive 1.8 miles, go through the intersection of U.S. 50 and U.S. 395, and stay on U.S. 395. Drive 1.4 miles to the Jacks Valley Road and turn right, toward the Sierra Nevada. The most distinctive peak to the south is Job's Peak; the title honors an early climber with the fine biblical name of Moses Job. Drive 3.4 miles along the Jacks Valley Road, and enter Jacks Valley.

This beautiful valley was among the earliest settled in this vicinity, the German Springmeyer family one of the first owners of a ranch here. Stay on the paved route, driving 1.3 miles. Here is a view of Carson Valley, whose appropriate slogan is ''The Garden Spot of Nevada.'' Continue down into the valley. The road follows the emigrant trail to California; watch for small, yellow T-shaped markers placed along the route by Trails West. Drive 0.9 miles. The James Canyon ranch is at the left. Look here for some exotic livestock: bison, humpbacked Brahma cattle, white French Charolais cows.

Drive 2.3 miles. There is a Pony Express marker at the right, denoting the fact that many historic routes came together here in Carson Valley. Drive 0.2 miles; the Genoa cemetery is at the right. In another 0.4 miles, arrive in Genoa. The courthouse/museum is at the right, Fort Genoa park at the left. There are numerous monuments and markers in this, Nevada's first town. Do take time to visit both the Fort Genoa and the Carson Valley historical society museums. Both have printed material free and for sale, and both have excellent, enthusiastic staffs. The town of Genoa has many picturesque buildings but only limited commercial facilities. Completing your visit to Genoa, return

Genoa

to the courthouse/museum to continue the tour, driving south.

Drive 0.1 miles to the crossroads and stop sign. Go south on SR 206, driving 1.7 miles to Walley's Hot Springs. Here is a resort, pool, restaurant, and historical marker. The place has been a spa off and on since as early as 1862, when David Walley built a hotel here. Walley's hotel was destroyed by fire, and others took over the operation. During Prohibition, this was a famous bootlegger hangout and allegedly the hiding place of badman "Baby Face" Nelson.

Continue driving south 0.7 miles to Van Sickle Station, once the largest hotel on the Carson River emigrant route. The first buildings on the site were constructed as early as 1855 and included a house, blacksmith shop, barns, and stables. The profitable operation brought its owner as much as a thousand dollars

a day during the Comstock boom.

Continue driving south 0.1 miles to the junction, and go straight ahead 0.4 miles to two historical markers at the right, commemorating the historic Daggett Pass (Kingsbury Grade) road and a flouring mill that stood on the site.

Drive south 2.5 miles through this lush ranching country on SR 206, to the marker for Mottsville, at the left. Then drive 0.2 miles to an intersection and stop sign; go ahead on SR 206. Continue 1.3 miles to another junction, and go straight ahead for 0.7 miles to the marker on the right for Sheridan. The hamlets of Mottsville, Sheridan, and others dotted the valley to serve the limited commercial needs of ranchers. From the Sheridan marker, continue 3.4 miles to the junction and turn right onto the Fredericksburg Road (don't miss that turn; it appears rather unexpectedly).

Wood drive on the Carson River, 1890s

This road skirts the west edge of Carson Valley and will show you some of this area's "Pennsylvania Dutch" section. Drive 0.8 miles and cross the California state line. Continue 1.6 miles; here is the Gansberg ranch, owned by descendants of early German settlers. Continue 0.5 miles and arrive at Fredericksburg, the holdings of pioneer Germans, the Frederick Bruns family. The Fredericksburg cemetery is 0.1 miles ahead, on the right.

Continue 0.7 miles to the crossroads, and turn left. Drive 0.2 miles to California SR 88, and turn left again to drive back across Carson Valley. Drive 1.9 miles and cross the Nevada state line; the highway becomes Nevada SR 88. Continue 1.3 miles; this is the Dressler ranch, owned by descendants of a young German textile worker who settled here in the 1860s.

Continue driving across Carson Valley. These fine ranches raise cattle and grow alfalfa, cutting three crops a year in this lovely setting. Drive 1.6 miles and cross the Carson River. Continue on SR 88; the Sierra Nevada rises at the left, the Pine Nut Hills are to the right. The Pine Nuts are the ancestral home of the Washo Indians, who still hold allotments there. Drive 1.5 miles to Centerville, and turn right onto SR 756. Continue 1.8 miles to a fork and bear left toward Gardnerville.

Drive 0.8 miles; Waterloo Lane (and the holdings of the German pioneer Luhrs family) is at the left. Go straight ahead, drive 0.3 miles and cross the East Fork of the Carson River. Drive 0.8 miles and enter Gardnerville.

Proceed to the stoplight. This is the main intersection of Gardnerville's business district. The Basque restaurants are within this block. There are other commercial facilities as well. If you stop here, or tour Gardnerville's interesting back streets, you will find many picturesque sights. Lampe Park, with picnic tables and restrooms is at the south edge of town; the name honors a pioneer German family who were important in the valley's dairy business. Completing your visit to Gardnerville, return to the main street and stoplight, and drive northwest toward Minden (as if you had made a left turn at the stoplight when you arrived there).

Drive 0.7 miles on the main street (it becomes Railroad Street in Minden). The Carson Valley chamber of commerce is at the right. Here is an opportunity to learn more about the valley; there are maps, brochures, and some materials for sale. From the chamber of commerce, continue into Minden, 0.3 miles. To see Minden's historic business district, turn left here, then right and drive 0.4 miles along Esmeralda Street. Here you will see the old divorcee haven at the Minden Inn, a public park with what may be Nevada's last bandstand, and at the corner of Esmeralda and Eighth streets, the Douglas County courthouse and the Douglas County library. The library has an excellent local history collection, an enthusiastic and well-trained staff, and some materials free and for sale. Ask about the (free) architectural tour guide for this area. Minden is on the site of the holdings of the pioneer German Dangberg family and is named for the senior Dangberg's birthplace.

From the corner of Esmeralda and Eighth streets, turn right on Eighth, then drive one block, and turn left to rejoin the highway (Railroad Street). Drive 0.6 miles to the intersection and bear right onto U.S. 395 north. Drive 1.2 miles; there is a historical marker for the Boyd Toll Road, one of several important early routes across the valley. It is interesting to think about these toll roads, and to contrast them with modern, tax-supported highways.

Drive 4.1 miles to the historical marker for Cradlebaugh, at the left. As you cross the Carson River here, picture the stream loaded with thousands of cords of fuel floating here in the water for the wood drive, and backed up into the Sierra foothills.

Drive 3.8 miles to the summit, and leave Carson Valley. Continue on U.S. 395 north, returning now to Eagle Valley. Drive 1.4 miles to the junction with U.S. 50, and stay on U.S. 395 through the stoplight. Drive 0.3 miles and turn right on SR 518; there is a historical marker for Stewart at the right. Drive 0.3 miles to the historical marker for Eagle Valley at the left, and stay on the main road here. Drive 0.8 miles and arrive at Stewart.

These beautiful native stone buildings mark the site of a long-lasting Indian boarding school that served the people of the West until the school closed in 1980. In 1981, the owners and local Indians announced plans for a museum to use the buildings. The historical marker in the Indian graveyard ahead at the left is for the famous Washo basketmaker, Dat-so-la-lee. Return to U.S. 395, 1.1 miles, and turn right toward Carson City.

Drive into Carson City, 2.6 miles to Musser Street (the capitol is on your right), and turn left. Drive 7 blocks (0.3 miles) to Mountain Street, and turn right. As you drive along this historic district, you will see many handsome Victorian homes, all still occupied. After 0.2 miles the governor's mansion will be on your left, the nineteenth-century Bliss house on the right. Drive 0.1 miles to the corner of Mountain and Washington, and turn right on Washington, driving 7 blocks (0.3 miles) to the stoplight at Carson Street. The old V&T depot, now the Masonic Temple, is straight ahead. Turn left on Carson Street, and leave Carson City, driving 3.9 miles heading north.

The historical marker for Lakeview is at the right. Drive 0.2 miles to Exit #42, take the exit, go 0.2 miles to the bottom of the hill and turn right toward Washoe Lake State Park on Eastlake Boulevard. Drive along the edge of this odd lake, which is without much visible support in the form of streams and rivers, 3.3 miles to the entrance of Washoe Lake state park. Here are picnic tables, camping facilities, and a place for boating and fishing.

Leaving the park, return to the entrance and turn left to continue driving north along the lake. As you drive along this highway, you will be able to see one of western Nevada's new suburban sections. Drive 3.1 miles and enter New Washoe City, then continue 4.0 miles along Eastlake Boulevard to the junction with U.S. 395. Turn right (north) and return to Reno, approximately 15 miles.

TOUR TWO, The Comstock Lode: Reno — Virginia City — Dayton — Carson City — Bowers Mansion and return. Approximately 80 miles round trip. Pack a picnic or plan to visit a restaurant for lunch along the way.

Leaving the Nevada Historical Society, head south (toward downtown Reno) on Virginia Street. Drive through downtown Reno, and see these landmarks: in 1.4 miles, cross the railroad tracks and view the Reno Arch, the city trademark; in 0.2 miles more, the Virginia Street ''bridge of sighs;'' and 0.1 miles further, the Washoe County courthouse, on the right-hand side of the street.

Continue driving south on Virginia Street, 3.0 miles; the Centennial Coliseum is on the left. In the complex with the convention center are the restored Lake mansion, and the area's first schoolhouse, from the little settlement of Glendale, east of Reno. Continue driving south; this is U.S. 395.

Drive 6.1 miles. Mt. Rose is the highest peak in the range to the right of the highway; the Virginia Range is to the left. You are driving across the Truckee Meadows. At the intersection and stoplight, turn left on SR 341 toward Virginia City.

Drive 0.6 miles; the old Toll Road (Geiger Grade) is at the right. Stay on SR 341. The Toll Road was once the main route out of the Truckee Meadows to the Comstock. The present route of Geiger Grade (SR 341) is newer, and has been rebuilt several times; it was first paved in the 1930s. The drive affords some of our favorite views of Mt. Rose and Washoe Valley. The hints of minerals in the rocks in the highway cuts show why prospectors in this area could become excited.

Drive 4.1 miles to Geiger Lookout. At the roadside rest is a picnic ground, and wonderful views of the valleys and mountains. Mt. Rose, nearly 10,800 feet, is the highest mountain in this area and directly across Washoe Valley. Slide Mountain is to the left of Mt. Rose, and the Slide Mountain Ski Bowl is visible on Slide.

Continue driving 2.8 miles through this fragrant piñon, sage, and rabbitbrush range to the Geiger Grade historical marker at the right-hand side of the highway. Drive 0.2 miles and enter Storey County. Then continue uphill 1.7 miles to the summit of Geiger Grade. The Lousetown historical marker is 0.4 miles ahead on the left. From that point, drive 1.8 miles and look ahead on the left; here is the beginning of the tailings piles of the Comstock Lode. Drive 1.1 miles and there is Virginia City just ahead. Continue 0.4 miles; there is a roadside rest at the left, with picnic tables and a historical marker.

Virginia City

Drive 0.5 miles and arrive at the Virginia City Visitors' Bureau. Here is a parking lot, and available pamphlets, brochures, maps, and other printed material to make your visit here enjoyable and well-informed. We suggest that you put at least these on your "must see" list: Piper's Opera House and the Storey County courthouse on C Street (above B, the main street), and St. Mary's in the Mountains church, which is visible from almost anywhere in town, below the main street. And do take at least one of the mansion tours. Mine tours are often available, and can be entertaining.

Leaving Virginia City, start again from the Visitors' Bureau and continue driving south on the main street (uphill on SR 341) 0.5 miles to the junction with SR 342, and stay to the right on SR 342. Drive 0.3 miles and enter Gold Hill. As you drive slowly downhill, you can look to the right to see Houston Minerals' recent open cut into the Comstock Lode. There are many historical markers to read as you go. Drive 0.5 miles; the Gold Hill depot of the V&T is at the right. Drive 2.1 miles and enter Lyon County, pass through Devil's Gate, and into Silver City. Continue driving downhill 0.9 miles to the junction with SR 341 (the truck route). The Johntown historical marker is at the left.

Continue driving downhill on the Comstock Highway through Gold Canyon. There is a Pony Express marker after 2.6 miles, and in another 0.3 miles, the junction with U.S. 50. You will return here shortly.

Turn left (east) on U.S. 50 and drive 3.0 miles to the Dayton city limit, and then 0.5 miles further to a junction and a cluster of historical markers and monuments. The rock monument commemorates the Paiute Chief Truckee, for whom the river is named; and the more formal markers note Dayton's early history on the Pony Express trail (when it was called Chinatown), and identify the town as a historic site on the Comstock.

Dayton is an interesting little town, and worth some time to look around. Turn left at the intersection to the business district. The pioneer cemetery is on a hillside to the north of town. The gold discovery site of 1850 is in Dayton on Gold Creek. Gold Creek runs on the east side of Odeon Hall. There are other old structures and a few commercial facilities in Dayton. Completing your tour here, return to U.S. 50, and return west, toward Carson City.

Drive 3.5 miles; the Comstock Highway is at the right. Stay on U.S. 50. Drive 1.4 miles. The Mound House historical marker is on the right. If you are curious about that tall tower behind the marker: the structure is used for making shot for shells. Molten lead is released from the top and forms into balls as the material drops.

Drive 2.8 miles, continuing west on U.S. 50. There is a historical marker for Empire at the left; cross the highway carefully to read it. The gravel plant behind the marker almost conceals the old Empire cemetery.

Side trip: *If you are driving a high-axle vehicle,* and would like to see the remains of old Empire's Carson River mills, go back 0.2 miles toward Dayton and turn right on Deer Run Road. Drive 0.6 miles to the bridge, and go to the left on the dirt road along the river. The road is on some of the roadbed of the V&T, and there are numerous ruins along the route. A drive of 2.0 miles along the river road will take you to the ruins of a cyanide mill and the site of a V&T ''balloon''—a place to turn a train around. The road deteriorates from that point. Return to the Empire historical marker to continue the tour.

From the Empire marker, continue driving west on U.S. 50 for 1.7 miles to Airport Road (a stoplight). Continue on U.S. 50 for 1.9 miles through four more stoplights to the fifth one, at Carson Street in Carson City. Turn left, into Carson City.

Drive 0.2 miles, passing the V&T depot at Caroline Street (on the left), to the Nevada State Museum, on the right. Stop here first for maps, brochures, a fine museum with excellent exhibits of natural history, a mine model to walk through, and many items concerning the building's former status as a U.S. Mint. The museum has a book shop, where you may buy books and pamphlets on Nevada history and archeology, along with photos and slides.

After visiting the museum, drive south along Carson Street to see the state buildings. The capitol is 0.2 miles, the legislative building just south of that. The V&T Museum is 1.1 miles south of the capitol on the

west side of Carson Street. At the V&T Museum, you will find a fair amount of restored rolling stock, nicely displayed.

For a different kind of museum, we recommend the Warren Engine Company's historic presentation on Curry at the corner of Musser, one block west of the capitol. The Warren Engine Company has a long history. In its early days, Carson City had two volunteer fire companies, the Warren and the Curry. The men fought fires as well as they could, but there was a problem at times: they were competing companies, so once in a while a battle would break out at the site of a fire, contesting which company would extinguish it. How many buildings were sacrificed to this competition? Nobody knows. The fireman who conducts your tour of the engine house will be knowledgeable and enthusiastic.

We hope you will take time to drive through the historic district of Carson City, using the materials you obtained at the museum. The governor's mansion is on Mountain Street, surrounded by some very interesting homes.

Completing your visit to Carson City, return to the corner of Carson Street and U.S. 50, where you arrived, and head north on Carson Street (toward Reno). This is U.S. 395.

Drive on U.S. 395, 3.7 miles. As you leave Eagle Valley, you will drive up Lakeview Hill; the historical marker for Lakeview is at the right. The text of the marker explains a bit about the inverted siphon that served the Comstock with water from the Sierra Nevada. Continue on U.S. 395 north, 0.2 miles to Exit #42. Take the exit, go 0.3 miles to the bottom of the hill, and turn left onto Eastlake Boulevard. Drive under the freeway and turn right onto old U.S. 395, which is now SR 429. Drive 1.6 miles to Franktown Road, and turn left.

The drive along Franktown Road will take you through the historical agricultural district where the settlement preceded the discovery of the Comstock. Washoe Lake will be visible across the valley to the right, at the foot of the Virginia Range. The wealthy modern ranchers here raise purebred livestock; we saw sleek Black Angus and French Charolais cattle along with the rather standard Herefords and Holsteins. Drive 4.3 miles to the junction. Look off to the right a few hundred yards; there is the old Franktown station of the V&T. Turn left here and drive 0.8 miles.

Bowers Mansion is at the left. Proceed to the entrance, 0.2 miles. The Bowerses were Comstock millionaires. Sandy was a prospector who struck it rich, and Eilley, his wife, enjoyed spending the money. Their lives were rather tragic after they built this mansion; he died, and then, having spent the wealth, Eilley told fortunes, took in roomers, and finally died insane. Now, the mansion is a nicely-restored monument to the Comstock heyday. The park provides picnicking and swimming, and you may tour the mansion during the season between mid–May and November 1. We recommend the tour; it is well worth the time and small fee involved. The facilities here are operated by Washoe County. Bowers Mansion has been a favorite spot for generations of western Nevada residents. The V&T trains used to stop in the meadow just to the east, bringing people here on excursions.

From the Bowers Mansion turnoff, continue driving north on the highway. Drive 0.9 miles; there is a historic marker at the right for the milling town of Ophir that once was a busy community here. Now only those piles of rocks show as remains of Ophir. Continue 0.5 miles; the turn for Davis Creek park will take you to a camping and picnic site in fragrant pine trees, another favorite of local residents.

Drive 0.4 miles to the junction with U.S. 395 and turn left (toward Reno). Drive 0.3 miles; the house on the right is the former ranch of the Winters family. The forlorn look of the house now gives no hint that one of the area's most active racetracks once existed here on the property of a wealthy politician/farmer.

Continue on U.S. 395 north for 1.0 mile. The Washoe City cemetery is on the left. Continue 0.5 miles; the historic marker and site of old Washoe City is at the right. There are no obvious remnants of Washoe County's first county seat. Continue driving, 0.5 miles. Washoe Lake is to the right. Drive on up-hill, then down into Pleasant Valley.

Continue 4.9 miles. The historical marker for Steamboat Springs is at the right. Read the marker, and smell the hydrogen sulphide—"rotten eggs!" Sinter mounds and terraces, and some steam vents can be seen on both sides of the highway for the next mile or so.

Drive 1.7 miles to the intersection and stoplight. Go straight ahead on U.S. 395, and return to Reno, approximately 10 miles.

TOUR THREE, The Pyramid Lake War: Reno — Pyramid Lake — Sutcliffe — Nixon — Fort Churchill — Dayton — Virginia City and return. Approximately 152 miles round trip. Pack a picnic or camping gear.

Leaving the Nevada Historical Society, head north on Virginia Street (away from downtown), and drive 0.3 miles, turning right on McCarran Boulevard, the second stoplight. Continue 1.7 miles to the intersection with U.S. 395 and Clear Acre Lane; stay on McCarran Boulevard through the interchange, and continue on McCarran. The drive will take you through the north city limits of Reno and Sparks. Drive 2.2 miles to Pyramid Way, and turn left. Pyramid Way becomes SR 445.

Drive 13.0 miles. The drive is across the desert area north of Sparks. Historically, this was grazing land for local ranchers. The road at your right led to an area in the mountains where the rocket engines for the "moon lander" were tested by Rocketdyne Division of North American Aviation; the route now leads to private ranches. Continue on SR 445, driving 2.3 miles to the Old Milk Ranch road junction. Here is another indication of the former importance of this section for farming and ranching.

Continue on SR 445 for 1.6 miles. The Palomino Valley road marks the site of holding pens for wild horses. In an attempt to save, not slaughter, wild horses gathered from the ranges of Nevada, the animals are held here for adoption after a roundup. If you take trips around Nevada, you may see some of these wild horses. Despite what you may have read, they are not mustangs, but strays, the descendants of strays, and animals that have been turned out by farmers as no longer useful. Mustangs as a breed died out many years ago. The wild horses of today are very numerous (more numerous than mustangs ever were), and are regarded by most Nevada ranchers as pests, competing with range cattle for forage.

Continue driving 1.3 miles, and look to the right. The concrete building was the headquarters for Rocketdyne while the moon-lander and other rocket-engine testing was underway. This section is now used for growing alfalfa hay, and for suburban developments for Reno and Sparks.

Drive 7.3 miles and cross the boundary of the Pyramid Lake Indian Reservation. Continue driving 2.1 miles to the view point. In the hills to the right as you drive, some ruins mark the site of Pyramid City, a silver boom camp of 1876. No activity took place there between 1889, when the post office closed, and the beginning of the 1970s boom.

At the view point there is a historical marker, and Frémont's pyramid is visible across the lake. This beautiful view is a favorite of ours—almost everyone's who comes to Pyramid Lake. We hope you will take time to enjoy it.

From the view point, drive 0.8 miles to the junction of SR 445 and SR 446. Keep to the left, toward Sutcliffe. *You will return here later*.

Drive 2.7 miles toward Sutcliffe, then turn left and go 0.5 miles to the fish hatchery. Tours of the hatchery, accompanied by brief, simple lectures on fish biology, are conducted here by members of the Paiute tribe. Here, you will learn about the processes by which the Indians are trying to preserve the Pyramid Lake cutthroat trout and the prehistoric cui-ui (pronounced *kwee*-wee). The best time to come here is in the spring (April and May), when the fish are spawned. We recommend this tour highly, and found it very much worth the hour or so we spent with the attendants.

Frémont's Pyramid, Lake Pyramid

From the hatchery, return the 0.5 miles to SR 445. If you wish to tour Sutcliffe, you will find the tribal headquarters (formerly at Nixon), limited commercial facilities, and some souvenirs for sale. This is a mecca for fishermen; fish smaller than eighteen inches long must be returned to the lake! You must have a permit to fish, which may be obtained from the tribal officer at Sutcliffe.

From the junction of the fish hatchery road and SR 445, return (south) 2.6 miles to the junction with SR 446, and this time bear left, toward the lake, on SR 446. You will be able to see Frémont's pyramid across the lake for several miles of the drive. To the right of the pyramid is Anaho Island National Wildlife Refuge, sanctuary for lovely white pelicans. As you drive, 7.6 miles, notice the strange tufa formations, and watch the sky and the water for whirling pelicans. (You should also be alert for livestock on the highway; this is the reservation's cattle-grazing land as well.)

Look at the lake to the left. Here is the Truckee's mouth, the major source of the lake's water. The flats have been deposited by the river over thousands of years, but have only relatively recently been exposed as the lake falls. Many other evidences of the decline of the water show on the surrounding hills, and even next to the highway. If you stop near one of the beaches, notice the millions of tiny remains of extinct snails. Drive 5.6 miles to the junction with SR 447, and turn left, toward Nixon. *You will return here.*

Drive 0.8 miles and enter Nixon. Services here are extremely limited, as most of the tribal activity has shifted to Sutcliffe. One of the landmarks is just beyond the store, on a small rise to the right. This Episcopal mission church was constructed during the time that Brother David was pastor here. Brother David took that name when he retired as Shakespearean actor Gareth Hughes, and he spent many years ministering to the Paiutes here.

After visiting Nixon, return and follow SR 447 south to see the route of the Pyramid Lake War. Leaving Nixon, drive 0.8 miles; the Paiutes pursued their attackers in May 1860, upstream along the Truckee from here. At the junction with SR 446, stay on SR 447, and drive 1.0 mile. The Indian trail along the river is to your left, on the east side of the river.

There is a paved road at the left. Look ahead, and to the left. There is a bluff and plateau along which the Indian trail ran. Stay on SR 447; the plateau will be visible from the highway from time to time as you drive. Drive 4.5 miles. Here is a historical marker about the War. Look at the valley below and behind the marker; at this place, in the first battle, the whites established an outpost in the wake of their advance in the unlikely event that they might have to cover a retreat. Now continue 8.5 miles on SR 447, and picture the whites of the first battle in a panicky rout up the river, then returning downstream in force two weeks later.

As you come over the rise, look down into the valley that holds Wadsworth. Here at the big bend of the Truckee, the white armies gathered twice for their assaults on the Paiutes, and then marched downstream. Drive 0.5 miles to the reservation boundary, and then continue 0.5 miles into Wadsworth. In Wadsworth, turn left on old U.S. 40 (the I-80 business loop).

Wadsworth has a few picturesque old buildings, left behind when the railroad offices moved to Sparks; commercial facilities are limited. Drive 0.4 miles, cross the Truckee River, then go 0.2 miles to the historical marker for Wadsworth, on the left.

From the historical marker, drive 0.7 miles under the freeway underpass and straight ahead on the I-80 business loop. Drive 0.3 miles to the Fernley railroad underpass, and follow the main road 0.6 miles into Fernley (see Tour Four in this section). In Fernley, stay on the main street for 0.4 miles to the intersection with Alternate U.S. 95, and turn right (toward Carson City and Yerington).

Drive 13.3 miles. You are heading downhill into the community of Silver Springs. To the left, ahead in the distance, is the water of Lahontan reservoir (see Tour Four in this section). Drive 0.8 miles to the crossroads and stop sign. Go straight ahead on Alt. U.S. 95. The vicinity of Silver Springs has been the site of several land sales promotions, at least as early as the 1940s. The town has not developed to the extent that its promoters had hoped. Drive 2.9 miles; the road at the left

Ruins at Fort Churchill

is the entrance to the Lahontan reservoir recreation area. Continue on Alt. U.S. 95.

As you drive 5.1 miles, the Carson River is visible as a row of trees across the valley to the left of the highway. Turn right to Fort Churchill state park, and another 0.9 miles will take you to the park and visitor center. Here are the last remnants of the Pyramid Lake War.

Fort Churchill state park is one of the jewels of the park system. Here is a small museum, with a scale model of the original fort, plaques commemorating the Pony Express trail through this place, and some self-guiding walks both at the museum and in the park itself. In the park, there are picnic facilities, campgrounds, and many opportunities to view the ruins.

Completing your visit to Fort Churchill, return to the park entrance and turn west (not back toward Alt. U.S. 95), and drive on Fort Churchill Road. Drive 0.2 miles, and the pavement ends. The road ahead is wide, graveled, and graded, suitable for any vehicle in good condition with a careful driver. If it has been storming, there may be some muddy spots. The scenic route will take you along the Carson River, through some pleasant ranching country.

Drive 0.5 miles; there is a Pony Express marker at the left. Drive 2.0 miles, and look to the left on the river bank. The public lands marker is for a primitive campground along the river; all land from this point on is private property, and not open for recreation. This drive could provide an opportunity to see some water birds; we saw a whole field full of Canadian honkers. Drive 2.5 miles, through the ranch and vehicle test center, and stay on the main road.

Drive 1.2 miles; the Break-a-Heart road is at the right, but stay on the main road. Drive 2.1 miles; the dam here on the river is used for impounding irrigation water. Continue 3.2 miles, and drive through the Chaves ranch, staying on the main road. Continue 3.0 miles to a fork and a Pony Express marker. Take the right-hand road. As you approach the highway, the settlement to the right is called Stagecoach-Nevada. This land promotion was somewhat more successful than Silver Springs. Drive 1.0 mile to the intersection, and turn left on U.S. 50. (The road that continues across the highway is the historic Six-Mile Canyon road to the Comstock. It is not always passable, so we will take you on the paved route.)

Drive 3.0 miles on U.S. 50 to the historical marker

for Sutro, on the right. A small settlement is visible to the right, against the hills. The Sutro Tunnel access is the most important historic feature there. The tailings piles you see came from the tunnel construction. Despite the existence of the sign just ahead, the place is fenced and posted against trespassers.

From the historical marker, drive west 1.7 miles; there is a Pony Express marker at the left of the highway. Continue 0.4 miles till you find Dayton state park, a left turn off the highway. This is a pleasant picnic spot along the river. Continue on U.S. 50 for 0.3 miles, and enter Dayton. Drive 0.6 miles, and there is a historical marker at the left, just ahead of the intersection. Turn right at the intersection; *you will return here* to continue the tour.

We hope you will enjoy the old town of Dayton. There are many historic or picturesque structures here. Just a block from where you turned, if you turn right again, you will see the Odeon Hall on one side of the street, the old fire station on the other. Gold Creek runs under the road between them; this is very near the site of the first gold discovery in 1850. Completing your visit to Dayton, return to U.S. 50 and the historical marker at the intersection, and continue driving west (toward Carson City).

Drive 3.6 miles, and turn right on SR 341, the Comstock Highway. Drive 0.3 miles, and there is a Pony Express trail marker. As you drive up the Comstock Highway, you will have many opportunities to see both old and new mining operations. We hope you will watch for these, and enjoy a leisurely drive into one of Nevada's most historic sections. Continue 2.5 miles to the fork. Read the sign there, and if you are driving a suitable vehicle, take the left fork, SR 342. Otherwise, stay on SR 341 to Virginia City, 5.2 miles.

There will be numerous historical markers on the drive through the Comstock towns. We hope you will take time to read them. Drive 0.6 miles up SR 342 and enter Silver City. Continue on the Comstock Highway 0.2 miles through Devil's Gate and across the Storey County line, then 1.4 miles to enter Gold Hill. As you drive up the canyon into Gold Hill, you can appreciate the magnitude of the open cut mine to the left of the highway. Drive 0.8 miles; the Gold Hill depot of the Virginia and Truckee railroad is at the left. Continue 0.7 miles, and enter Virginia City; the Fourth Ward school is 0.2 miles ahead on the right. SR 341 joins SR 342 at this point. Another 0.5 miles past the school is the Virginia City Visitors' Bureau, on the left. Stop at the Visitors' Bureau to obtain maps, pamphlets, tour guides, books, and other materials to make your visit to the Comstock pleasant and educational. Completing your tour of Virginia City, return to the Visitors' Bureau and continue north on SR 341.

Drive 3.7 miles up the canyon and through a piñon and juniper forest. The Lousetown historical marker is at the right. Drive 0.6 miles to the summit of Geiger Grade, and continue on SR 341. You will cross the Washoe County line in 1.6 miles. Drive 0.2 miles. The historical marker for Geiger Grade is at the left. The old road was in use into the 1930s; if you think this highway seems a bit steep, picture driving the one you see across the canyon! Continue 2.8 miles to Geiger Lookout. Here is a picnic spot with a splendid view of Washoe Valley below and of Mt. Rose towering across the valley.

From Geiger Lookout, drive 5.7 miles down Geiger Grade (SR 341) to U.S. 395, and turn right (toward Reno). Return to Reno, approximately 10 miles.

TOUR FOUR, Irrigation and transportation: Reno — Derby Dam — Lovelock — Rye Patch Dam — Forty-Mile Desert — Fallon — Lahontan Dam and return. Approximately 280 miles round trip. Pack a picnic or camping gear.

Leaving the Nevada Historical Society, head south on Virginia Street (toward downtown Reno). Drive 1.0 mile to the I-80 access, and head east (left) on I-80. Drive 4.0 miles. As you pass the McCarran Boulevard exit, look to the right of the highway. The huge warehouses you can see for the next two miles along the highway are the result of Nevada's status as a freeport state. The law allows goods in transit to be warehoused here without assessments for property or inventory taxes.

Continue driving east on I-80 for 10.3 miles. The

ride carries you down the beautiful Truckee River Canyon, parallel to the tracks of the Southern Pacific railroad, and roughly along the route of parts of the Truckee River section of the emigrant trail. At the Scenic View there is a historical marker commemorating the Truckee River route. Also in the scene below is the family ranch of late U.S. Senator Patrick A. McCarran; the site is called Patrick.

Drive 9.0 miles to Exit #36, Derby Dam. Take the exit, turn right, and drive 1.0 mile, following the signs for Derby Dam back along the road next to the freeway, to the historical marker and Bureau of Reclamation billboard at the left-hand side of the road. Continue on this same road 0.2 miles through the tiny underpass (its dimensions are barely 8 feet high, 9 feet wide), and 0.1 miles more to view the dam. In this area, when construction on the Truckee-Carson Project began, there was once a tough little camp, where the legend says that there was a murder every day (a ''man in the ditch for breakfast''). Nothing now remains of Derby. You can see the diversion ditch on the hillside below the dam; from this point, the canal carries some of the Truckee River's water thirty miles to the project at Fallon. Return to I-80, 1.2 miles, and continue driving east on I-80 (toward Fernley).

Drive 8.2 miles and cross the Lyon County line. Continue on I-80 for 3.2 miles to the junction with U.S. 50, and stay on I-80. Drive 5.2 miles. The standing water or dry lake to the right (depending on the time of year) is part of the Carson Sink. Here is a demonstration of the nature of the Great Basin. The rivers (in this case the Carson) flow not into larger rivers or to the ocean, but into a system of interior drainage, ending in sinks like this and disappearing into the ground, or, through evaporation, into the dry air. Continue driving east on I-80.

Drive 11.3 miles. Brady's Hot Springs, at the right, was once a famous resort in this area. For many years there were a swimming pool and other recreational features on the site. The springs were on the emigrant trail, but relatively useless to wagon trains because the water was too hot for livestock to drink until after it was gathered in casks and cooled, and because people became ill from drinking the highly mineralized liquid. Exploration drilling and pumping eliminated the surface flows. Geothermal use now is in food processing at the plant you see on the site. The company's investment there amounts to over $4 million.

Drive 18.2 miles. There is a roadside rest here at the junction with U.S. 95. There are shaded picnic tables, garbage cans, toilets, drinking water. Historical markers commemorate the aboriginal inhabitants of this section and the Forty Mile Desert. Continue driving east on I-80, but note this place, as *you will return here*.

Drive 9.6 miles. As you drive, the Carson Sink is behind, the Humboldt Sink to the right of the highway. The Humboldt Range is ahead and to the right, the Trinity Range to the left. At Toulon, a former railroad siding, there has been intermittent milling of ores for the area. Continue on I-80 for 11.6 miles to Exit #105, Lovelock. Take the exit, and drive 0.7 miles to enter Lovelock city limits. Drive another 0.7 miles, turn left at the stoplight, and you will see the handsome courthouse of Pershing County. The Pershing County Library is directly north of the courthouse.

Lovelock has all necessary facilities for tourists. In the courthouse area, there are a historical marker, picnic tables, a children's playground, and a swimming pool. The library has a local history collection and an excellent, knowledgeable staff. Some of Lovelock's annual celebrations are ''Frontier Days,'' a rock and mineral show, and the unique Portuguese fiesta. Recent investigation has shown that a Chinese community at Lovelock once played a significant part in the town's economy and culture. Although little remains on the surface, an archaeological ''dig'' uncovered caches of gold coins and artifacts of an early-day Chinatown. There are some interesting old churches and a Masonic hall within a block or two of the civic buildings, so do take time to drive around this historic town.

Completing your tour of Lovelock, return to the stoplight on the main street and continue east, following the signs for I-80, and take the access road east (toward Elko).

Drive 6.7 miles. The Eagle Picher plant to the left of the highway processes diatomite (diatomaceous earth) from a nearby mine. This is the largest single mineral operation in Pershing County. Drive 7.0 miles to the Oreana site. Oreana was a railroad siding; later a milling operation there treated ores from Rochester, but there has been no substantial activity since the 1920s. Ruins and some occupied buildings are visible near the highway. Rochester, some ten miles away, was a silver mining district and opened in 1912. Some work continued there until World War II. Continue on I-80 east.

Drive 9.3 miles to Exit #129, Rye Patch Dam. Take the exit and follow signs to the dam. Drive 0.7 miles and cross two sets of Southern Pacific tracks. Stay on the main paved road downhill for 0.9 miles to the entrance station of the reservoir. The Nevada State Park System operates facilities here. There are picnicking, camping, boating, and a boat launch, and, of course, fishing. The reservoir was constructed by the Reclamation Service. Although the original intention of the builders was to provide irrigation water for the farmers of the Big Meadow area, a benefit in recreation comes to a wider population. Completing your visit to Rye Patch, return to I-80, and turn west (toward Lovelock).

Retrace your route back to Lovelock, approximately 23.0 miles. Then continue west from Lovelock back to the intersection with U.S. 95, another 22.6 miles. As you drive along this modern freeway, it might be interesting to think of the hundreds of pioneer wagon trains that came this way in a route roughly paralleling the highway. The heat, dust, thirst, and seemingly endless track: fifteen miles might be a day's journey. The beautiful Big Meadow where Lovelock arose was always a welcome place in which to revive for awhile, and to prepare for what still lay ahead.

At the rest area, turn south on U.S. 95 toward Fallon. If you did not read the historical markers before, take time to read them now, so that you may appreciate the nature of the Forty Mile Desert that begins here. Few places in the western United States have a more poignant history of emigrant travel than this stretch.

Drive 3.6 miles and cross the railroad track. Even after the railroad was built through here in 1868, the wagon road remained in use, generally paralleling the tracks. Drive 7.0 miles. The shallow ponds you see at the left of the highway are for concentrating brine gathered from the desert flats—to make table salt.

Drive 6.0 miles, and look to the right, next to the highway. The small, yellow T-shaped marker placed by Trails West shows the route of the emigrants here. Drive 1.2 miles and look again to the right of the highway, a few hundred yards off. A large, concrete monument placed by the Nevada Corral of Westerners stands on the trail across the Forty Mile Desert. Drive 1.1 miles; the dirt road at the right will lead you just over a mile to the Westerners' marker, which is inscribed with an excerpt from the diary of an early traveler through here. The road is rough, but usually passable.

Continue on U.S. 95 for 3.4 miles. A milling plant is on the right. Please observe the no trespassing signs. Drive 7.1 miles to the boundary of the Newlands Reclamation Project, and stay on U.S. 95.

We always enjoy coming upon Fallon's green fields and pleasant shade trees after a ride over the desolate Forty Mile Desert. Little wonder that the early pioneers of this section wanted to cultivate the arid land! Drive 3.4 miles and enter Fallon. U.S. 95 becomes Maine Street. Maine Street was named by Warren Williams, a pioneer here, who wanted the route to honor his native state. Drive 0.5 miles and cross Williams Avenue, staying on Maine for 0.2 miles through the business district. Cross Stillwater Avenue, stay on Maine for 0.5 miles, and arrive at the Churchill County Museum on your right.

If you make no other stop in Fallon, this should be it. This museum is one of the best in the state. There are professionally prepared indoor and outdoor exhibits of artifacts and relics of the early days of this section. The staff is excellent and knowledgeable about the area. Admission is free, with donations welcome. There are some books and pamphlets for sale.

Fallon is the center of an exceedingly interesting historical and geological area. If you have a day to spend here, ask for information at the museum, at the county library (553 South Maine), or at the Chamber of Commerce on Williams Avenue. There are ghost towns, a wildlife refuge, and scars from the faults of a 1954 earthquake, all within a short drive from town. The Churchill County Library has an excellent local history collection with emphasis on the mineral industry, and a well-trained, enthusiastic staff.

To continue the tour, return to the corner of Maine and Williams, and turn west (left) on Williams. As you make the turn, notice the elegant Churchill County courthouse, facing on Williams. Williams Avenue is U.S. 50. Drive now on U.S. 50, leaving Fallon, and go 8.1 miles. If it is the right season of the year (late summer, early autumn), you may see some roadside stands with locally grown melons for sale here. These fruits are a special treat that we recommend highly for breakfast or dessert. The stands are operated by the people who grow the melons, so you may have a chance to meet the local farmers if you stop.

The historical marker for Ragtown is at the right-hand side of the highway. If you look around here, you can appreciate this ending of the Forty Mile Desert trek.

Drive 1.3 miles to the junction with Alternate U.S. 50, and turn left (south) on Alt. U.S. 50. Drive 7.1 miles, and turn left to the Lahontan Reservoir Recreation Area. This is a good, gravel road. Be alert for traffic, as this is a very popular playground. Drive 0.6 miles to a fork and bear right. Drive 0.3 miles and cross the Carson River; Lahontan Dam is visible upstream to your right. Drive 0.2 miles, and go straight ahead; another 0.2 miles will take you to the park entrance.

Like Rye Patch, Lahontan reservoir provides excellent recreation facilities under the supervision of the State Park System. The dam, completed in 1913, impounds the waters of the Carson and Truckee rivers to supply the irrigation needs of the farmers and ranchers of the Newlands Project. The reservoir also contains fish, and there is an environment for boating, camping, picnicking, and relaxing in this pleasant park. Enjoy your visit here, then return to the entrance station, and then to the highway, 1.3 miles, and turn left.

Drive 0.4 miles and cross a canal, then 0.3 miles to the dirt road on the left leading to the historical marker and view point for Lahontan Dam. This place offers an excellent and interesting look at the surroundings. Return to the highway, and turn right (toward Fallon).

Drive 5.0 miles, and turn left on Bench Road. Drive 2.4 miles through one of the western sections of the Newlands project. Here you will see the prosperous hay ranches, cattle yards, and family farms with orchards and gardens that symbolize the economy of this section. Turn left at the highway (now Alt. U.S. 95 & Alt. U.S. 50).

Drive 3.7 miles. The settlement is Hazen; there is a historical marker on the right-hand side of the highway. Hazen was a railhead for the construction period of the Newlands Project, and the site of Nevada's last lynching.

Drive 2.6 miles and cross the Lyon County line. Continue on the highway for 7.7 miles to the junction of Alt. U.S. 95 & Alt. U.S. 50 & U.S. 50. Go straight ahead, staying on Alt. U.S. 50; you will be at the outskirts of Fernley. Drive 1.0 mile and enter Fernley. Stay on the main street through town, driving 0.8 miles. We always enjoy this little jog off the main highway, to see the contrast between old and new in this tiny agricultural community in transition. At the west end of town, bear right on this highway which has now become the I-80 business loop. Drive 0.5 miles, through the Fernley railroad underpass, then 0.2 miles through the highway underpass, and go straight ahead. The Nevada Cement Company plant is on the right as you drive 1.4 miles along this old section of U.S. 40, parallel to the railroad tracks.

The historical marker for Wadsworth is on the right. Drive 0.1 miles and enter Wadsworth. Drive 0.1 miles further and look to the right at the nice old railroad bridge. The old town of Wadsworth is to the right of the highway. Services are extremely limited here.

Drive 0.4 miles to the junction with SR 447, continue straight ahead on the I-80 business loop, and prepare to return to the freeway. Drive 1.4 miles to the I-80 access and take the access west (toward Reno). Drive 1.5 miles. The rest area has picnic tables, garbage cans, toilets, a trailer holding tank disposal, and free overnight parking for campers and trailers (if you can stand the noise of the freeway and the diesel truck idling in the space next to you).

Return to Reno, approximately 30 miles, up the splendid Truckee River Canyon.

TOUR FIVE, Scenery, recreation, and ski resorts: Reno — Verdi — Donner Camp — Donner Lake — Tahoe City — Lake Tahoe and return. Approximately 160 miles round trip. Pack a picnic or camping gear (and swimsuits in summer, skis in winter).

Leaving the Nevada Historical Society, drive toward downtown Reno for 0.9 miles and turn right to take the access road to I-80 west. The ride will take you upstream along the Truckee River, parallel to the Southern Pacific railroad tracks toward the foothills of the West's most splendorous mountain range. Drive 7.5 miles to Exit #5, East Verdi, take the exit, drive 1.8 miles along old U.S. 40, and enter Verdi.

Verdi, a lumbering town that came into existence with the advance of the railroad, was the first settlement inside Nevada as the tracks moved east from California. The forests on the hills around the little camp provided hundreds—thousands—of ties for the tracklayers. Verdi's other claim to notoriety is that it was the site of an early train robbery; some residents want to say it was the nation's *first* train robbery, but it was not. The event took place on November 5, 1870. The criminals stopped the train and removed two cars containing a gold shipment. The railroad's historian points out laconically that, ''The program worked to perfection except that the men subsequently were caught . . . and served long terms in the penitentiary.'' The ''program'' indeed worked so badly that other train robbers found another $300 when the same train reached a spot near Wells later that day.

Now, Verdi contains limited commercial facilities and has become somewhat of a bedroom community for Reno people who like mountain living. Drive 0.4 miles and cross the tracks, then 0.2 miles and bear left into the old Verdi business district. Drive 0.3 miles and turn left onto Bridge Street. Driving another 0.4

miles, cross the tracks and turn right; the historical marker to commemorate the train robbery is at the right as you make the turn. Then continue on South Verdi Road, west toward the mountains. Go through the intersection, driving 0.3 miles, under the freeway, and continue on South Verdi Road. Cross the tracks, then drive 0.1 miles back through the underpass of the freeway, and follow signs to I-80 west. Drive 0.3 miles to the junction, bear right, then take the next left turn at the stop sign. The historical marker for Verdi is at the right, just before you turn. Drive another 0.3 miles and cross the Truckee River, then continue toward the freeway. Drive 0.5 miles and bear right at the fork. (If you arrived at this point all right, you receive five points for following instructions! If you got lost, merely look around for an access to I-80 west.) Now drive along the frontage road next to the freeway for 0.9 miles; rejoin I-80 west at Last Chance.

As you drive, the Southern Pacific tracks and the Truckee River will be to the left of the freeway. Wooden water flumes above the river, and the associated power plants, first built around 1900, were designed to provide the Virginia City mines with the first hydroelectric power needed to operate the huge pumps clearing the shafts of water. Drive 2.0 miles and cross the California state line.

Continuing 5.9 miles, you will see several more power stations and dams along the river. You have already passed Mogul; others are Farad and Fleish (short for Fleishhacker, early owner of the power system). A boon when Virginia City had problems with water in the mines, these installations provide only a minor part of western Nevada's electricity needs now, for the drop in elevation and the flow of the river are too small for a large production.

Floriston is visible to the left of the freeway. This was the site of a paper pulp mill in the heyday of the section's lumbering industry. The freeway passes over the millsite. The ice industry was second in importance to lumbering in this area. Ice ponds along the Truckee provided ice for cold-storage boxes throughout much of western Nevada and eastern California and served the railroad's needs in shipping produce from the Sacramento Valley. Drive 5.0 miles and cross the Truckee River. To the right of the freeway just past the river crossing, you can see Boca Dam and a few ruins of the ice houses where the product was stored (Boca Dam was not part of the ice harvesting; it was built in the 1930s for flood control). Drive 1.7 miles and cross the Truckee River again.

Drive 4.4 miles to the exit for SR 89 (to Sierraville and Loyalton). Take the exit, and at the top of the rise turn right on California SR 89. Drive 3.0 miles and turn right into Donner Camp. Here is a picnic ground and an intensely poignant historic site. Here in Alder Valley, 21 members of the Donner party camped in the late autumn of 1846. The elder Donners and their children, along with several others, were stranded, starving, here in the snow. Only nine of the group left here alive. There is a self-guiding walk around the Donner campsites, and an explanatory billboard at the beginning of the walk.

Following your visit here, turn around and return along SR 89 for 2.9 miles and go over the I-80 overpass. SR 89 becomes SR 267. Drive 0.5 miles and enter Truckee, continue 0.4 miles to the intersection and stop sign, and go straight ahead into the Truckee business section on the main street, Donner Pass Road. Truckee has all necessary tourist facilities, and is accustomed to serving cross-country travelers, first as a railroad town, and later as a place on the interstate highway.

Continue through Truckee, 0.5 miles to the freeway underpass. Stay on Donner Pass Road for 0.8 miles through Truckee's new business district. At the stoplight, go straight ahead, driving 0.6 miles to the next stop sign and again go straight ahead. Drive 0.4 miles to the freeway overpass, and follow the signs to Donner Lake. Another 0.5 miles will bring you to the entrance to Donner Lake state park. Here you will find picnicking, camping, fishing, and a museum where you may obtain information about the area. The park is crowded in mid-summer, and the campground is usually full.

Many people think that the Donner party's tragedy took place here, at what used to be called Truckee Lake. That is only partly true. Among their other errors, the party divided, with some, including the Donners, staying at Alder Valley, and others camping here on the lake shore through the dreadful winter of 1846-47.

Completing your visit here, return to the park entrance and turn east (toward Truckee). Drive 0.3 miles and take the I-80 access road east. Drive 0.9 miles and take the exit for Squaw Valley–Tahoe City, SR 89 south. Turn right at the bottom of the hill, toward Lake Tahoe. Drive 0.5 miles and through the old railroad underpass, then drive 8.1 miles along SR 89 to the sign for Squaw Valley.

The drive here will be up the Truckee River canyon in some of this section's most beautiful forest and recreation lands. There are numerous popular camp and picnic sites next to the river. The Southern Pacific ran a spur along here until the highway removed the need for trains.

Turn right at the Squaw Valley sign and proceed 3.1 miles to the site of the 1960 Winter Olympics, a marvelous place summer or winter to enjoy the high-altitude forests and meadows. In summer the ski lifts run to the mountain tops for enjoyment of the scenery, while in winter the place is extremely busy with snow sports. Completing your visit to Squaw Valley, return to SR 89, 3.1 miles, and turn again upstream toward Tahoe City.

Drive 1.4 miles. This is Alpine Meadows, another popular ski resort and summer vacation-home tract. Continue on SR 89, 3.8 miles. As you drive, in summer, you may see fishermen or rafters on the river; these are popular and pleasant activities here.

As you enter Tahoe City, you will have a first glimpse of the beautiful "Lake of the Sky." *Return to this intersection* after visiting Tahoe City.

Tahoe City is like the capital of this end of the Lake. (That "the Lake" is not a misnomer; most western Nevadans know what we mean when we say "the Lake.") You will be able to see the long pier, a fine public beach, and all sorts of tourist facilities. Near here, Tahoe Tavern served as a destination for generations of travelers. The Tavern Pier had a railroad spur for easy transfer of passengers to and from the steamer *Tahoe*. The Tavern was demolished in 1964, the pier had come down in 1955, and some fifteen years had elapsed before that since the last run of the *Tahoe*.

Returning to the intersection and stoplight, drive across the bridge over the Truckee. Here is the Truckee's source. If you look to the left as you cross the bridge, you will see the gates that control the flow of the river from here. Park near the bridge, and look down from the bridge into the river. You will see many huge, lazing cutthroat trout, providing entertainment for you and other travelers. This place is called Fanny Bridge. You will know why as you watch others lean forward over the railing.

From Fanny Bridge, continue south on SR 89. This side of Tahoe's shore is more popular and accessible as a summer recreation area than a winter one, although there are several fine winter playgrounds. You can see many handsome homes along here, and always, lovely views of the Lake.

Drive 6.3 miles to Homewood. This was a famous early-day resort, dating as a settlement from the 1880s and as a hotel site from just past the turn of the twentieth century. A post office was established in 1909. Continue south for 3.1 miles on SR 89 to Sugar Pine Point state park. Here is a pleasant, well-maintained, fragrant, high-altitude play area with campsites and picnic grounds. Continue from the entrance for 1.8 miles to Meeks Bay resort.

Meeks Bay's pioneer uses included the cutting of hay on its meadowlands as early as 1862. Later, the place was the center of lumbering in the area by the Carson and Tahoe Lumber and Fluming Company, owned by D. L. Bliss. The agricultural uses continued, with cattle grazing in the meadows. The site did not become a resort until all the natural resources had been fully used, in about 1919. Now, Meeks Bay has one of the best beaches on the Lake, and a lovely setting not likely to be invaded again by lumbermen and cattle grazers.

Continue driving south on SR 89 for 4.0 miles to Bliss state park boundary, and then 1.4 miles to the entrance to the park. Here is the Bliss family's gift to westerners, in return for use of the virgin timber of the Tahoe Basin. This park has camping, picnicking, ranger-led activities in season, and lovely surroundings.

From the Bliss state park entrance, continue driving south on SR 89 for 4.2 miles. This will take you through the Emerald Bay resort to Eagle Point. Take advantage of several opportunities along here to view the bay and its romantic little island in the middle. Now and then, people suggest that this highway could be shortened by construction of a bridge across the mouth of the bay. We oppose that. What's the rush?

At Eagle Point campground, you will find high-altitude camping and picnicking and another opportunity to view the mountain scenery. Continue from here for 2.9 miles to Baldwin Beach. As you drive downhill from Eagle Point, you will catch a glimpse of glacial Cascade Lake.

Baldwin Beach resort dates from the 1880s. The "Baldwin" name is that of the famous California and Nevada sportsman-promoter-financier, E. J. "Lucky" Baldwin. Baldwin had a rather raffish reputation, but he did something important for the Tahoe Basin: Baldwin refused to allow lumbering on the property he purchased here, so the only virgin forest in the entire Tahoe Basin is on the former Baldwin estate. Millions of board feet of timber were taken from the rest of the basin to feed the needs of the Comstock.

From Baldwin Beach, continue south on SR 89 for 0.5 miles and cross Taylor Creek, then go 0.2 miles to the Lake Tahoe Visitor Center, at the left. Here is an opportunity to obtain maps and information about the recreation and history of this region.

From the Visitor Center, drive 0.1 miles to the turn for Fallen Leaf campground, another pleasant, high-altitude playground near a beautiful little lake.

Continue driving now, 1.0 mile to the South Lake Tahoe city limit. The scenery, which has been changing to urban rather gradually, will shift more rapidly along here. Drive 1.1 miles to the intersection, and turn left with the stoplight onto U.S. 50 toward Stateline.

On February 14, 1844, John C. Frémont and

Charles Preuss stood on Stevens Peak, about fifteen miles directly south of here, and became the first white men to see Lake Tahoe. Frémont wrote, ''We had a beautiful view of a mountain lake at our feet, about 15 miles in length, and so entirely surrounded by mountains that we could not discover an outlet.'' He underestimated the size; Tahoe is 23 miles long, 13 miles across.

After making the left turn onto U.S. 50, stay on U.S. 50 through South Lake Tahoe, driving 3.9 miles. You can see many recreation sites and views of the

Lake. At Ski Run Boulevard (a stoplight), Heavenly Valley ski resort is at the right. This is a popular place both summer and winter, as the lifts take people to the top for either snow sports or sightseeing.

Continue north on U.S. 50 from Ski Run Boulevard for 1.1 miles, and enter Nevada by crossing Stateline Avenue. Here is Nevada's third-largest casino area (after Las Vegas and Reno). Drive through the casino district, continue north on U.S. 50, and go 0.7 miles to the junction of Nevada SR 207 (the Kingsbury Grade). Stay on U.S. 50 for 1.3 miles, to the turn for

Results of logging at Glenbrook (Tahoe), 1890s

Nevada Beach, and go to the left. Nevada Beach, a fine picnic, camping, and swimming playground, is 0.5 miles from the turn. Facilities are operated by the U.S. Forest Service. Return to U.S. 50, 0.5 miles, and continue driving north.

As you drive 5.2 miles, the highest peak you will see across the Lake is Mt. Tallac. In summer, it has a cross of snow on its facing side. Pass through Cave Rock tunnel, and drive another 3.6 miles.

The turn to Glenbrook is to the left. Glenbrook was once the center of the active lumbering business that served the Comstock. Later, a number of wealthy people, including the yeast-and-gin magnate Max C. Fleischmann, had homes there. Now, except for an old hotel and a small graveyard, there is little to indicate the bustling timber commerce of former years. The historical marker for Glenbrook is at the left side of the highway.

Drive 2.7 miles, and turn left on Nevada SR 28 (toward Incline). Now you are near the north end of the Lake. Drive 5.3 miles and enter Washoe County, then 2.4 miles to Lake Tahoe Nevada (Sand Harbor) state park. Here is an excellent and extremely popular day-use beach and picnic area. This is one of Nevada's most heavily used state parks.

From the entrance to the Sand Harbor park, continue 2.7 miles northwest on SR 28. The Ponderosa Ranch is at the right. The site of the filming of the old TV series "Bonanza," it is now a commercial amusement park.

Continue 1.0 mile. The Incline ski area is at the right. The settlement here is Incline Village, a full-fledged city with all facilities, vacation and year-round homes, and an active community life. Many Incline residents commute to businesses in Reno. Drive 1.4 miles; the Incline Village business district is to the left at the stoplight. Continue on SR 28 from here, 0.5 miles, and turn right on SR 431 (the Mount Rose Highway), toward Reno.

Drive 3.6 miles to the scenic overlook on the right. Here is your last really good opportunity to view the "Lake of the Sky" on this trip. Drive 3.3 miles to the Mount Rose summit. There is a rustic campground at the right for lovers of high altitude—about 9,000 feet at this location.

Continue 0.1 miles. There is a historical marker for the Mount Rose weather observatory at the right. This commemorates the work of Dr. James E. Church, inventor of a method for measuring the water content of snow and thus predicting summer runoff.

Continue driving downhill for 2.3 miles. Mount Rose is the high, rocky peak straight ahead as you came over the summit. The Mount Rose ski area is at the right. Not much happens here in the summer, but in the wintertime, the huge parking lot is jammed.

Continue downhill, 1.0 mile. The right turn will lead you to the Reno Ski Bowl, Slide Mountain Ski Area. Here, as at other similar resorts, the lifts run both summer and winter. The lights of the Slide Mountain ski runs are visible at night from Reno.

From the turn, continue downhill on SR 431, 1.3 miles to Sky Tavern ski resort. As you drive, the view to the right is of Washoe Lake and Washoe Valley. The Virginia Range is across the valley. Sky Tavern is a peaceful place in the summer, a busy one in winter. These resorts have little need to manufacture snow, a rather uneconomical practice in an area short of water.

Drive 4.3 miles. On the hill to the left here at Galena Creek, the area's skiing promotions began. In the 1930s there was a ski jump, with the outrun about where the Highway Department's building is now. Continue downhill on SR 431. From here, the vegetation changes dramatically from the pine, fir, and cedar forest you have enjoyed for most of this trip to sagebrush and other typical desert plants.

Drive 7.4 miles to the intersection with U.S. 395, and turn left toward Reno. Return then to Reno, approximately 10 miles.

NORTHEASTERN NEVADA

NORTHEASTERN NEVADA

From the beginning of recorded history, most travelers have first entered Nevada via its northeast section. This huge region, larger than several eastern states combined, encompasses much of the Silver State's typical history, scenery, and activity.

Exploration

The first white men in northern Nevada were the explorers and trappers of the Hudson's Bay Company, led by Peter Skene Ogden. They came in 1826 and several more times until 1830, seeking fortune in beaver furs and incidentally making the area known to others. In 1828, entering what would be Nevada, Ogden proceeded to a spot near the site of present Denio, then worked his way south to the stream later known as the Humboldt River. On this same journey, Ogden's party trapped for furs and explored the Humboldt east to about where Elko later arose. Ogden called the river "Unknown;" it was destined to have other titles— Ogden's, Mary's, St. Mary's—until some seventeen years later, when another adventurer gave it a permanent name. The next year (1829), Ogden's group further explored the environs of the river, finding the trapping somewhat disappointing in the barren climate, and ultimately determining that the river ended in a sink. Ogden receives credit for discovering the Humboldt River and for exploring it from source to sink. This activity had great importance for the region; the river became one of the West's most significant pathways and landmarks.

The Hudson's Bay Company kept trappers in the area for only a little while longer. The dry climate and uncertain streams made the effort mostly unprofitable, as few animals of the quality needed could survive. Other companies of fur hunters included those under Joseph Work and the American Joseph Walker. Walker was one of the most important explorers of the West, for he pioneered the trail that became the principal overland route to California.

Another of the early explorer-mappers of the northeast section was John C. Frémont. Frémont had been in the Great Basin before he traversed the northeast in 1845, but those trips had not touched this area.

Frémont led his men on a journey from Bent's Fort, Arkansas, across the mountains and deserts to Salt Lake, planning to examine the then-unknown portions of the Great Basin. To the west, they could see only desolate wastes—75 miles of salt desert. On the horizon was one small peak, and the party headed for it. When they arrived, to find good water and grass for their animals, Frémont called the little mountain "Pilot Peak," a name it retained. Pilot Peak also kept its welcoming character for cross-country travelers, from pioneer days through the era of super-highways.

Frémont's group determined at the same time that the Buenaventura River was a myth. Long before explorers entered the Great Basin, map makers had inferred, from no evidence beyond wishful thinking, a huge river flowing across the Basin, through the Sierra Nevada to the sea. The Buenaventura appeared on several documents and in assignments to explorers until the fable finally—along with the river—disappeared.

On this same journey, Frémont blazed a trail that became a wagon road across Nevada's northeast to California's gold fields. A year later, a promoter named Lansford Hastings followed the trail, but lost a significant portion of it; he devised what he called a "cutoff" from the road, and started to proclaim its advantages. A group of emigrants believed Hastings's hyperbole and tried to follow the cutoff. These, the members of the Donner party, took the byroad to disaster, for it was no shortcut, and the delay cost the lives of nearly half the company. Taking the Hastings Cutoff caused the party to lose the landmarks of the regular overland trail, travel an extra 180 miles across Ruby Valley, spend time looking for Overland Pass near the southern end of the Ruby Mountains, all making a tragic alternative to the easier, but still tough route through the present site of Elko.

The explorations basically established the trail—later road—across the Great Basin. Several early emigrant parties, beginning as early as 1841, crossed the mountains and deserts going to California. The first of these, the Bidwell-Bartleson party, had planned to float down the Buenaventura River and brought along boats to do so. These and other items were abandoned in Toano Valley when the party discovered that the river did not exist except on maps. Other emigrant trains followed, led by the famed Joseph Walker, among others. In 1846, the Donners crossed, and by the time gold was discovered in California in 1848, the road was relatively well known although still not an easy track. The waters of the Humboldt and other streams kept men and livestock moistened, and the grasses kept cattle alive. The road beyond the Humboldt was neither as manageable nor as fertile as that through northeastern Nevada; many graves and mounds of abandoned personal effects testified to terrors encountered.

All of these activities of exploration and travel before 1848 were trespasses upon foreign territory. The Treaty of Guadalupe Hidalgo with Mexico remedied that problem and the United States expanded to encompass a huge portion of the American West. California's gold discovery increased traffic immeasurably. Late in the twentieth century, ruts of the old wagon roads are still visible from the northeastern corner of Elko County (the Nevada state line), up to Little Goose Creek, down Rock Springs Creek, and into Thousand Springs Valley. An early county road paralleled the historic track. Today's travelers along Interstate 80 might see remnants of the trail between Deeth and Carlin, near the city of Elko, and on west of Carlin. Other sections of the trail can be reached on foot.

The area had an indigenous population composed mainly of Shoshone Indians. The tribes remained relatively docile during the early white incursions, but when the traffic increased, so also did native resentment. The Shoshone, Paiute, Bannock, and Goshute peoples were mainly hunters and gatherers, and apparently even occasionally cannibals. With the advance of white civilization, the inevitable conflict developed, and with the usual result. First, military forts or camps were established: Forts Ruby, McDermitt, and Halleck, and Camp Floyd came into existence to protect whites against irritable or hostile natives. In time, reservations for the Indians were also established at Duckwater, Owyhee, and McDermitt. A "treaty of peace and friendship" between the Western Shoshones and the United States government in 1863 was also subject to the customary misinterpretations and violations, and did not change the basic Indian-White relationship of conquered-to-conqueror. The headquarters for the Shoshone and Paiute groups in the late twentieth century are at Lee and Owyhee in Elko County and at McDermitt in Humboldt. The most active of the Shoshone companies calls itself the Te-moak (or Temoke) band of Western Shoshone in honor of one of the great chiefs.

The reservations of the tribes or bands became mainly undistinguished little rural centers, devoted to marginal business and agriculture. Because handicrafts of the sophisticated, tourist-oriented type did not become highly developed among Great Basin natives, the trading post that marks southwestern, and some northwestern, American Indian reservations is nonexistent at most Nevada tribal headquarters.

The military forts and camps died out, the buildings and other facilities abandoned as Indian-White conflicts subsided. Even the ruins remaining seemed as insignificant as the battles themselves, and as inevitable in their decay as the outcome of those struggles.

The modern development of the northeast began after Nevada gained statehood in 1864. The most important event in the history of the nineteenth-century West was the building of the railroad. This engineering and construction marvel ended the West's physical, social, and economic isolation, and also the need for many other types of travel and communication. The Pony Express and the cross-country pioneer wagon train gave way to machinery. The Pony ceased its traverse of Nevada in October 1861 when the telegraph made message service quick, but the need for package mail and freight and passenger service continued. The railroad met these requirements. The construction of the Central Pacific across the Great Basin in 1868 and 1869 marked the beginnings of the state's important northeastern railroad centers: Winnemucca, Battle Mountain, Carlin, and Elko.

Winnemucca

Winnemucca, on the south bank of the Humboldt River, was inhabited perhaps as early as 1850; it was first known as French Ford or French Bridge—an important crossing of the stream. Two Frenchmen, Joseph Ginacca and J. A. Algaur, owned toll facilities there. The first permanent residents probably came a decade later. Ginacca, celebrated as Winnemucca's founder, was the originator in the 1860s of a grand scheme known as the Humboldt (or French) Canal. The canal was designed to move water along a 90-mile route, roughly parallel to the river, from the Humboldt at Preble (near the present site of Golconda), to the reduction mills in the area of the Star Mining District. Mill City was laid out in prospect of this development. Stock promoted by a San Francisco corporation and French speculators raised about $100,000. After only about 28 miles of the canal had been excavated, the project was abandoned. The mines never produced enough ore to justify the large mills that had been planned, and the Humboldt's small flow probably could not have turned the machinery in any case. The plan for a ditch fifteen feet wide and three feet deep stopped unfinished after passing through Winnemucca. No water flowed in the planned slough, except briefly in the 1890s for a promotional development near Golconda.

With the organization of Nevada Territory, nearby Unionville became the seat of Humboldt, one of the first fourteen counties in Nevada. But the advance of the railroad brought real status to Winnemucca.

This enormous construction marvel began at Sacramento, California, in the fall of 1863. Across the Sierra Nevada, over the deserts and hills of the Great Basin, marched armies of workers using untold tons of equipment and materials. On September 16, 1868, the tracklayers of the Central Pacific reached the outskirts of Winnemucca, and soon the locomotive "Champion" entered the town to a great welcoming celebration. The settlement became more lively, and was named Winnemucca to honor a great Paiute chief. Soon the trappings of a city appeared, and in 1872, Winnemucca became the seat of Humboldt County.

In another few decades, Winnemucca gained still another major railroad. The Western Pacific, unique for its twentieth-century design and construction, also began on the West Coast, extending nearly a thousand miles to Salt Lake City, Utah. The WP lacked the romance and somewhat original character of the Central Pacific, but it did serve some previously uncovered areas of the West. The Western Pacific tracks reached Winnemucca in 1907, and a separate railroad station was built to welcome the new trains. Floods and other disasters on the WP later forced the company to share trackage with the Southern (Central) Pacific in other sections, but Winnemucca continued to maintain the two identities.

The industries of the immediate Winnemucca area historically involved mainly livestock and agriculture. The fertile riverside lands suited these purposes ideally. The town also served from its beginning as a supply center for mines and other activities nearby.

George Stuart Nixon was Winnemucca's leading citizen prior to the turn of the twentieth century. He began his career in California as a telegrapher on the Central Pacific, later moving to Nevada in a similar capacity. Energetic and ambitious, he founded the First National Bank in Winnemucca, built an impressive home above the main part of town, owned the local newspaper (the *Silver State*), and was generally regarded as an important patron of the arts in the little railroad town. Nixon gave the money that built the Nixon Opera House (later turned into a motion picture theater) and also donated funds for the building of the Winnemucca City Hall. Nixon was first a candidate for U.S. senator in 1894. In 1900, he extended a friendly hand to a young cowboy from Lakeview, Oregon, and thus was formed the financial combination of Nixon and George Wingfield. They became the kings of Tonopah and Goldfield (see Southwestern tours). Nixon was elected U.S. senator in 1904, and moved his base to Reno—where he built a mansion. Winnemucca's distinguished benefactor died in 1912.

Nearly three quarters of a century later, a few people who had failed to appreciate Winnemucca's historical sense proposed to tear down the old Nixon building in favor of a new city hall. They were astonished to find that Winnemucca residents revered Nixon and the old buildings enough to circulate petitions that at least temporarily halted their plans. The city's officers and the chamber of commerce continued to occupy the Nixon building, along with an art gallery, while promoters of progress tried other tactics. Some spoke darkly of Winnemucca's reputation for being "remodeled" by fire.

Phil Tobin was another notable citizen of the Winnemucca area. A popular rancher, Tobin served a single term in the Nevada legislature, gaining fame as the man who introduced the law for Nevada's gambling.

Like most railroad towns, Winnemucca had an important Chinese section, or Chinatown. The settlement resulted from the thousands of Chinese laborers discharged after the building of the Central Pacific. Winnemucca, by local admission, treated the Orientals shabbily. As in similar communities, the Chinese were "fair game" for pranksters and worse. The Chinatown section was razed in 1955, and by the end of a century of maltreatment, local citizens averred that it would be a "miracle" if a Chinese were found in Winnemucca. Nonetheless, a certain amount of sentimentality caused the erection of plaques to the memory of the Chinese laborers in Winnemucca's Pioneer Park, in 1969.

A more successful ethnic minority in Humboldt County is composed of Basques. Soon after the turn of the twentieth century, these former residents of the Pyrenees immigrated to the northern Nevada area to labor on ranches and especially to herd sheep. They worked on ranches for local flockmasters, and later acquired bands of their own. Winnemucca became a center for Basque gatherings; hotels and restaurants of the sort unique to the West appeared there. Not at all

incredible was the tale that young Basque herders, speaking no English, were routed only to "Winnemucca, U.S.A." from their ports of embarcation in Spain. At the end of the twentieth century, Winnemucca proudly proclaims its Basque minority in promotional materials, and its citizens enjoy performances by Basque dancers or weight lifters at festival time.

Winnemucca's place in western American history was secured when it became the site for the last of the great western bank robberies. This was no ordinary event, however; the robber was Butch Cassidy himself, along with Harry Longabaugh (the "Sundance Kid") and other members of the "wild bunch." The bunch came into Winnemucca on September 19, 1900, helped themselves to something more than $32,000 from the First National vault, and took off out of town toward Golconda, riding first stolen horses and then their own. Posses trailed them as far as Wyoming before losing track of the last of the Old West bank robbers. The outlaws celebrated their victory over Winnemucca by sending the bank president a formal studio photo of themselves dressed as respectable businessmen.

Winnemucca retained its status as seat of one of Nevada's largest counties. Then, during World War I, Lovelock to the southwest, also a railroad town, began to grow, threatening to take the county seat. The state legislature solved the problem in 1919 by cutting away the southern half of Humboldt County, creating Pershing County (named for a great World War I general), and leaving Winnemucca with the courthouse for Humboldt. Lovelock took over as the seat of Pershing County (see Northwestern tours).

A later promotion, more successful and profitable to Winnemucca than the Humboldt Canal, was the "Winnemucca to the Sea Highway." Starting as early as 1922, "Fritz" Buckingham, resident of Paradise Valley, began to talk about the need for a shortcut across northern Nevada to the Pacific Northwest. For decades, he made speeches about this necessity, without notable results until after the second World War. Then, with the entire West booming, Buckingham began again, this time with the cooperation of people in California and Oregon. In 1947, he led a delegation to Alturas, California, seeking support. In 1949, a gathering in Winnemucca of representatives of the northern California and southern Oregon region was sponsored by the Humboldt County Chamber of Commerce. Enthusiasm was beginning to build, but money was needed for the highway in Nevada, and that apparently was not forthcoming.

Buckingham was elected to the state legislature, serving in the 1957, 1959, 1960, and 1961 sessions, sponsoring resolutions and appropriations for his highway. At last, in September 1962, celebrations along the route marked the connection of northern Humboldt County with the towns of Lakeview, Klamath Falls, and Medford, Oregon, and Crescent City, California. The Highway to the Sea was done. Then in 1964 a flood washed an enormous redwood log onto the beach at Crescent City, and the citizens there sent it to Winnemucca to mark the end of the cooperative project. The log, with appropriate inscriptions, was placed at the center of Winnemucca, becoming the town's trademark for a successful and beneficial job completed, a monument to civic pride.

Winnemucca became significant in other ways during its modern era. Stockraising and a vital potato-growing industry provided an excellent economy. The advance of modern highways made these aspects profitable. The building of a SAGE radar station on the top of Winnemucca Mountain brought briefly a military presence of some 150 officers and staff. The base (SAGE Heights) at the foot of Winnemucca Mountain was abandoned along with similar installations all over the nation, but civilians took the housing, making an attractive suburb. The town of Winnemucca remained largely wedded to livestock and the railroad's business, but promotion of other economy continued. In the 1960s, Winnemucca hired a consultant to prepare a master plan, aiming at growth in commerce as well as a more attractive community. The result was mixed; in 1980, only something under 10,000 people lived in all of Humboldt County. But the residential sections had many attractive homes, and the business district

contained all of the usual Nevada amenities—casinos, nightlife, and supplies for the surrounding agricultural and mining communities.

Unionville and Mill City

The colorful mining history of Humboldt County began in 1861 with discoveries of gold and silver in the Humboldt Range, near what became Humboldt House, Unionville, and Star Canyon. The next year, 1862, findings of precious metal ore brought settlement of Dun Glen. The rock proved not fabulously rich, although numerous prospectors and miners sought their fortunes in the Humboldt mines. Several mining districts were organized, but the towns themselves, with the exception of Unionville, were transitory. In the late twentieth century, the only important traces of the antique mining districts are at Unionville and Mill City. Although Mill City once had saloons, a hotel, a post office, and a blacksmith shop, only ruins mark the spot of this formerly prosperous site. Expectations of a terminus for the Humboldt Canal died with the mining excitement. Nearby gas stations retain the name "Mill City."

Unionville had a longer existence, discoveries having been made there before Nevada became a territory. Promotion brought on a rush, the building of the town, a newspaper, school, cemetery, and the county seat for

---

"Unionville consisted of eleven cabins and a liberty pole. Six of the cabins were strung along one side of a deep cañon, and the other five faced them. . . . It was always daylight on the mountain tops a long time before the darkness lifted and revealed Unionville.

"We built a small, rude cabin in the side of the crevice and roofed it with canvas, leaving a corner open to serve as a chimney, through which the cattle used to tumble occasionally, at night, and mash our furniture and interrupt our sleep."

— Mark Twain, *Roughing It*

Humboldt. Dozens of colorful tales of Unionville entertained generations of westerners. The truth was, however, that it never amounted to very much, except in the minds of its residents or promoters. Less than $3 million was produced from the ores of the Buena Vista district there. Railroads bypassed the site, and so did superhighways. The miners moved away, followed by the businesspeople. Some seekers after peace and quiet, refugees from city bustle, moved into Unionville toward the middle of the twentieth century. They established homes there, often in or on the foundations of Unionville's original structures. The result was some interesting architecture. In the late twentieth century, a few dozen staunchly loyal Unionvillers remained, but they did not earn their livings from the mines of Buena Vista, nor did they maintain any facilities for travelers to their beautiful canyon oasis.

Paradise Valley and McDermitt

Paradise City (originally Scottsdale, later Paradise Valley) was more important and populated than Winnemucca in the 1860s. Peter Skene Ogden passed through the valley on his journey in the fall of 1828. Not a mining community, but a farming settlement, the place was homesteaded as early as 1863. By the mid-1860s, a sizable group of farmers and ranchers had harvested good crops of hay and grain. But the Paiute and Bannock natives proved troublesome to the farmers, and in 1864 two settlers were killed; other deaths followed in the next four or five years. The white vengeance on the Indians took the customary course.

These conflicts were never referred to as "wars," but only as "troubles," giving them perspective with larger and more significant events. The worst of the battles occurred in 1865, when a Paiute chief named Black Rock Tom led his warriors against the settlers of northern Humboldt County. Fort Winfield Scott was established in Paradise Valley, and Fort McDermitt succeeded the abandoned Fort Scott. Ironically, Fort McDermitt was destined to become the headquarters for a local Indian reservation. No Indian-White battles of note took place in Paradise Valley after 1865, although the military remained at Fort McDermitt for another two and a half decades.

The ranchers of Paradise continued a peaceful life after the end of the Indian troubles. Cattle and sheep ranching made the place a social and economic center for the immediate area. Mexican vaqueros set the local style for taking care of livestock. The town grew up to service the local commerce around the ranch of C. A. Nichols. Charles Kemler built a hotel there in 1866. An adobe brick factory supplied construction needs, and a brewery added to the economy. Paradise grew produce for the surrounding mines, but cattle raising was the chief occupation there in the early days. Later, sheep raising, with Basque sheepherders, also became important. At its peak, the population of Paradise was probably under three hundred people.

The Paiutes and Bannocks, too, pursued a quiet existence on their reservation at Fort McDermitt. A boarding school was established there in 1889. The natives, especially after the second World War, began to integrate their activities with those of the surrounding populations, working in mines and small industry. The reservation in the last decades of the twentieth century seemed typical of similar installations anywhere in Nevada or in the American West.

Paradise Valley gained some attention in the 1980s, under intensive study by a team from the Smithsonian Institution which was making investigations of the lore and folkways of American rural communities. The result of the study, along with a printed report, was an exhibit of more than two hundred artifacts or reconstructions of items—clothing, ranch implements, cooking utensils, and recreational materials—from Paradise Valley in the Washington, D.C., Museum of History and Technology. At the end of the exhibit, the items were shipped to Winnemucca for display there. One of the buildings in Paradise, dating from the 1860s, received recognition as a site on the National Register of Historic Places.

The great Cordero mine near McDermitt provided another focus for working out Nevada's modern history. Some eleven miles west of the town of McDermitt, the Cordero was the largest mercury mine in the

United States after it opened in the 1950s. Production varied according to national metals policies and the needs of supply and demand, but the place remained an important adjunct to the economy of this district.

Golconda

Golconda began largely as a spa or health resort, owing to its hot springs. When the railroad reached there in October 1868, Golconda already had a history as the site of the beginning of the Humboldt Canal. A little mining had taken place there, but that was mostly on a small scale, and when the rails arrived, Golconda (despite its optimistic naming for a royal city of India) was already declining.

But Golconda had other cycles of activity. During the late 1890s, many eastern American and European mining companies had engineers and prospectors in the American West, very actively in the Great Basin. One of these, a firm of Scots from the Glasgow and Western Exploration Company, took up some claims in the Golconda area, and began busily to promote the mining of copper. A new company, the Adelaide Star Mines, Ltd., took over Golconda and some other properties in the general area. A new quarry provided material for building foundations, a town was designed, and a smelter said to rival Anaconda in Montana began work in 1897. By the next year, 1898, there were six hotels and a general store, seventy men working at the smelter, and fifty more in the mine some twelve miles south. People speculated that the population might soon reach 10,000.

These plans and activities continued for a few years, but the ores proved unstable, and the smelter, after undergoing several redesignings and rebuildings, was finally abandoned. After 1916, the machinery was hauled away and Golconda returned to its former small-town status, but with a few more mine dumps. At its height, the place had a population of perhaps 500 people, a narrow-gauge railroad (the Golconda and Adelaide), and a weekly newspaper among its economic features. Nearby hot springs helped to create the health resort; a hotel stood on the site until it burned in 1961.

"This property was in the Potosi Range in Humboldt County out of Golconda. I reported on it as being 'elephant hunting ground,' as it had a very large vein but the values were practically nil (about $2.00 per ton). It was decided to go ahead and do some work by driving a cross-cut tunnel about two hundred feet below the croppings and see what the vein looked like at that elevation. When intersected, the vein at that elevation was all ore. And from that day to this (1965) the mine has been in ore. . . .

"The Getchell Mine comprised an area of approximately twenty-two thousand acres. . . . There was a company town of about eighty cottages, plus a boarding house and twelve small bunkhouses. I lived at the Getchell Mine while building the plant, but later I made weekly visits."

— Roy A. Hardy, mining engineer

The economy in the vicinity of Golconda did not end, however. In the 1930s, an engineer discovered what he called "elephant hunting ground" a few miles to the north, and the Getchell mine was born. The Getchell, largest and most profitable of the Getchell Mines group, produced gold and, during wartime, large quantities of tungsten from an adjacent ore body. The company milled at the site, cyaniding gold and making tungsten nodules. In its first two years, the Getchell mine produced nearly $5 million. The gold mine was converted to an open pit operation in 1961, and a new ore treatment plant shipped its first bullion the next year. The Getchell mine closed in 1967.

In the 1980s, other mines operating in the area included a huge open pit and mill a few miles south of Getchell, owned by the Pinson Mining Company. The Pinson owners called theirs the "most modern gold plant in the world," and predicted a profit from a $17.5 million investment. Like all others, however, the future depended upon the vagaries of the international gold market; meanwhile, the businesspeople at nearby

Winnemucca and Battle Mountain enjoyed the bonanza. The building of boomtowns at mining camps went out of style with the coming of superhighways, so Golconda was unlikely to develop into a city again. The site of Adelaide, once an adjunct to Golconda, was engulfed in the mining boom of the 1980s.

Battle Mountain

Battle Mountain might have adopted as its slogan, "Persistence Pays." From the time the rails reached there in 1868, until the fall of 1980, residents campaigned to have Battle Mountain named the county seat of Lander County. That honor went to Austin, in the southern end of the county, until finally the people of the older town abandoned the fight to the northerners. Originally, in fact, no real townsite was laid out at Battle Mountain. The settlement was to have been at Argenta, several miles east. Then in 1870, mineral discoveries in Copper Canyon south of Battle Mountain brought a rush to the district, and the town was born. The site took its name from historical recollections of an Indian battleground nearby.

Soon, businesses sprouted on the main streets of Battle Mountain, with pioneer merchants and hotelmen J. A. Blossom, L. D. Huntsman, and A. D. Lemaire becoming established. Huntsman's hotel was soon a gathering place for settlers of the surrounding districts, Blossom's lumberyard supplied building needs, and Lemaire and Sons sold general merchandise. A series of fires, in 1877, 1878, and 1880, obliterated much of the early building, but Battle Mountain's hardy pioneers persisted and reconstructed their town.

Within a short time, owing mainly to the prosperity of the mines in the Canyon, Battle Mountain became a veritable railroad center, with the Nevada Central's narrow-gauge tracks heading toward Austin beginning in 1880, and the Battle Mountain and Lewis railroad completed in 1881. The Western Pacific also came to North Battle Mountain in 1907, and like Winnemucca's arrangement, enjoyed separate facilities until the two giant railroad corporations joined trackage.

One of Nevada's most delightful folklore items involved Battle Mountain's transportation facilities. A company calling itself the "Reese River Navigation Company" sold stock in a grandiose scheme. A prospectus advertised that ores from the Austin area would be loaded aboard barges for floating down the Reese River to the railhead at Battle Mountain. Thousands of people bought stock in the fraud, not knowing that the Reese River was an extravagantly named creek or rivulet, occasionally heavy-flowing, but also often dry. In any case, no barges from the Reese River Navigation Company ever appeared on the Reese River, and the only profit went to the phony promoters.

Battle Mountain continued to serve as the center of supplies and society for the mining camps of Copper Canyon. There was a transfer station between the narrow- and standard-gauge rails, and stage lines branching off into the surrounding desert regions. Silver and copper shipments from Lewis, Galena, Copper Basin, and Copper Canyon busied freighters and merchants.

Inevitably, the mining declined, and so did the little camps. The buildings were moved away or fell down, the narrow-gauge railroads went out of business, and soon little remained. One mine, however, refused to die easily; this was the famous Betty O'Neal, about twenty miles southeast of Battle Mountain. The "Betty" was owned by L. W. Getchell before the turn of the twentieth century. About 1920, his son, Noble Getchell, bought the property and operated it successfully for years.

Noble Getchell built an enormous mill to process the ores of the Betty and became one of the wealthy and prominent men of Lander County. In 1923, the county's voters sent Getchell to the state legislature as their senator; he held the post over the next eighteen years, even though he gave up his residence in Lander County.

Getchell also made the Betty O'Neal more than a mining company by hiring a semipro baseball team. The young men of the team—university students—supposedly worked at the mine, but actually their job was to win ballgames for the Betty. Finally, of course, the veins of the Betty played out, the mill decayed, the ballgames ended, and Getchell's place in the legislature went to one of the grandsons of A. D. Lemaire. In the 1980s, with the northeastern section undergoing a new mining boom, the Betty remained fenced around with unfriendly "no trespassing" signs. Only the most optimistic prospector really expected to hear "Play ball!" there again.

In 1967, new explorations took place in the old Copper Canyon area, this time by DuVal Mining Company. DuVal's activities were an economic boon to the Battle Mountain community, bringing new schools, new homes, and a new sewer system. This prosperous operation, and its resultant increase in population for northern Lander County, probably played a role in the awarding of the county seat to Battle Mountain, when the election was held in 1980.

Battle Mountain always meant more than railroads, mining, or politics. The center of an enormous cattle-ranching empire founded by W. T. Jenkins, Battle

---

"Mrs. W. T. Jenkins, the widow of a prominent flockmaster, is a business woman of marked ability. She owns a small ranch in Buffalo Valley and three in Jersey Valley and counts her sheep on a thousand hills, and in at least two valleys. She cuts in Jersey Valley, about 250 tons of hay, but her home ranch is in Lander County. . . . Jersey Valley and Antelope Valley . . . is the winter range for fully 150,000 sheep. On one of her Jersey places she runs quite a bunch of cattle."

— Allen C. Bragg, newspaperman
Humboldt County, 1905

"The State Public Service Commission has approved a proposal by the Nornev Demonstration Geothermal Co. to build a 10-megawatt electric power plant, harnessing the energy of the Beowawe geysers near the boundary between Lander and Eureka counties about six miles west of Beowawe."

— *Reno Evening Gazette,* October 28, 1981

Mountain's prosperity has been diversified. Jenkins immigrated to Lander County from Wales in 1873. He established a cattle-and-sheep outfit with headquarters at Battle Mountain and began to expand. Jenkins died in 1899 before seeing the fruition of his work, but his wife Edith, an exceedingly sturdy and determined pioneer woman, carried on the ranch and increased its holdings, until 1918. One of their daughters, a graduate of an exclusive finishing school in San Francisco, inherited the place when her mother died. The daughter, Nevada's celebrated rancher-socialite Louise J. Marvel, found her talents in running the livestock operation.

The Jenkins-Marvel outfit became the largest of such holdings in northern Nevada, spreading into five counties and influencing the markets for meat, wool, and hides. In 1962, Louise Marvel was designated Nevada's "Cattleman of the Year," a unique appellation, and the first time it was ever given a woman. The Marvel family continued to live in headquarters at Battle Mountain, selling some 500,000 acres of the enormous ranch property in 1964, but holding its envied position among Nevada's native livestock owners.

Beowawe

On a quiet morning, it used to be that one might stand near the old station at Argenta and hear a peculiar roaring sound. On the horizon to the east, steam would rise. The geysers of Beowawe were rumbling in the earth.

The railroad tracks of the Central Pacific went through what became a tiny settlement and supply center for nearby mining districts. In the 1880s, there were a few buildings and about sixty residents in Beowawe, and that situation stayed nearly the same over the next three quarters of a century. In the 1950s, some discussion took place concerning the possibility of constructing a state park and recreation site around Beowawe and the picturesque geysers. The decision, however, was that the place was too isolated for proper care, and the geology too fragile to allow many visitors. That verdict was destined to have a very adverse effect on the area. Geothermal exploration and vandals had, by the 1980s, virtually eliminated the geyser effects at the site.

Just east of Beowawe lay a site known from earliest days as Gravelly Ford, a landmark on the emigrant trail and crossing of the Humboldt River. Near Gravelly Ford, as the railroad workers of the 1860s graded for the track, they found a grave in their pathway, bearing the name of Lucinda Duncan. Carefully, the remains were removed and the grave was relocated to a small knoll away from the tracks. The traincrews and others then began to spin tales about the supposed occupant of the burial. They called it the ''Maiden's Grave'' and paid homage to the woman they decided must have been a beautiful young girl. Twentieth-century research has suggested that this interpretation was in error, but the romance of the Maiden's Grave seemed more attractive than giving obeisance to a middle-aged housewife. Into the late twentieth-century, the grave remains freshly tended and the old-time story persists.

Carlin

Carlin is at once Elko County's oldest organized town and one of its newest. The place had a few settlers before the rails arrived there in December 1868. The town was first called ''Chinese Gardens,'' designating the earlier residents who established vegetable plots there to serve the cross-country traffic. The Orientals labored on the railroad and later worked at laundry or cooking, providing an important economic segment to the railroad town. Knowledge of their cultural activities there has disappeared. Carlin (like several other sites along the railroad) received its name in honor of a Civil War hero; this time it was General William P. Carlin.

With the advance of the railroad, the townsite was laid out and homes and businesses grew up along the tracks and on the bank of the Humboldt. A school district was formed in 1869, but no classes were held until 1871 because of a rather colorful series of incidents surrounding the first teacher hired in the town. The young man first employed turned out to be a fugitive from an abandoned wife and family, a situation not tolerated by mid-nineteenth-century society. Still the cul-

tural amenities came into being, including a town library.

Carlin served as an icing station for cars of the Pacific Fruit Express, and eventually held a roundhouse, shops, telegraph office, and other typical railroad services. Ice was harvested in pools nearby on the Humboldt River, where winter temperatures reached $-50°F$.

One of Carlin's early scandals involved the grisly murder of a local resident by a couple named Potts. The owner of a house sold by the Pottses believed the place haunted, and investigation turned up a mutilated corpse. The Potts couple was tracked to Rock Springs, Wyoming, arrested there, and hanged in a public ceremony in the jailyard at Elko, in June 1890. Mrs. Potts had the distinction of being the first woman legally executed in Nevada.

Carlin was kept alive through the early and mid-twentieth century mainly by the activities of the Southern Pacific railroad. Train crews laid over there, a clubhouse provided entertainment, and some buildings were constructed or replaced. A minimal amount of placer mining gave mainly recreation, and little profit, to a few prospectors. Then came 1965, and a new era both for Carlin and for Nevada mining.

The Newmont Company began exploration of the old Lynn mining district north of Carlin. The area had been sporadically mined and promoted since the early 1900s. By 1967, the Carlin Gold Mine was the second-largest producer in the United States (after only the famous Homestake of South Dakota). The results of this activity—tens of millions of dollars from the open-pit mine—increased tax revenues in both Eureka and Elko counties, and expanded employment in the entire region. The gold mine was estimated to have twenty years of life; its unusual open-pit style of gold mining has provided a colorful landmark, which persists into the 1980s.

Elko

The rails of the Central Pacific reached Elko on a cold day near the end of December 1868. The place was probably named to recognize the local wildlife.

Another version, however, has a Shoshone Indian replying to a railroad worker's enthusiastic hyperbole on the coming of the iron horse with a grunted apparent vulgarism that sounded like ''Elko.''

The sale of lots took place on January 15, 1869; Elko became the seat of a new county of the same name in March that year. The first election, which counted 1,097 votes, took place in May. The *Elko Independent* started publishing on June 19. The red brick courthouse was completed in December. These rather quickly developed trappings of a county seat masked the fact that Elko was an exceedingly tough little frontier town, complete with gunfighters and a vigilance committee that worked unsuccessfully to keep order. Gambling hells and houses of prostitution became prominent within weeks after the arrival of the rails. Chinese laborers, discharged from railroad work crews, formed a colony south of the Central Pacific

tracks, giving a little Chinatown—and a source of coarse amusement for whites—to the growing city. Elko's Chinese population proved somewhat more stable than that of Winnemucca. The Orientals of earlier days left compatriots in the area, prominent members of the community especially in the restaurant business. Elko seemed destined indeed to tie its fortunes to the railroad and to transient society. Fortunately for eastern Nevada, that destiny changed, aided by a fire in 1870 that forced the rebuilding of Elko on a sturdier basis than the tent-and-shanty town that preceded it. A brickyard below the town provided molded mud blocks which proved satisfactory and relatively permanent.

The 1873 legislature, apparently impressed by Elko's boasts of growth and prosperity, designated the town as the site for the state university. The institution, like Elko itself, failed to attract large numbers of

Commercial Street, Elko, ca. 1910

"Pete Itcaina was a sheep man, one of the biggest sheep men in the West. . . . Pete Itcaina, at one time, either owned or had rights to drive his sheep from Wells clear down to the winter feeding grounds in southern White Pine County. . . . And he was a millionaire . . . multimillionaire, most of the time, I guess. He wore high bib overalls. . . . He couldn't express himself very well. . . . And there are many, many stories told about Pete Itcaina. . . .

"Pete Itcaina went into the Silver Dollar Club in Elko . . . and stood at the bar, and put a dollar down. And the bartender looked at him, and . . . he stood there and waited, and finally pounded on the bar, and the bartender said, in effect, '. . . I'll get around to you when I'm ready.' This made Pete Itcaina very, very angry. And he went out and went over . . . and bought the Silver Dollar, and fired the bartender. This actually happened."

— Paul Leonard, Elko newspaperman

people, and within only a decade the school moved to Reno.

Despite its excellent location, and early dreams for expansion, Elko did not become large. By 1900, fewer than a thousand people lived there, the Southern Pacific was threatening to close its facilities, and Nevada mining—the state's most typical industry—was apparently in death throes. Elko would not die, however, for a number of good economic factors still existed there.

The vastness of Elko County, like that of the rest of the Great Basin, held a few minerals, so mining and exploration profited a number of entrepreneurs. But the open spaces also contained excellent grazing lands for cattle and sheep, a fact recognized by numerous hardy pioneers. Huge holdings were amassed by the livestockmen; L. R. Bradley, George Russell, and William Moffat became prominent in Elko County and

in the state of Nevada. Exceedingly successful, these archetypal owners of some of the largest ranches in the United States shaped the course of their county and of Nevada. Lewis Rice Bradley, cattleman, became governor of Nevada in 1870, and his family and descendants continued to influence ranching and politics for decades to follow. Russell, partner in Bradley's and other operations, gave Nevada a merchant-ranching-political family as well. Moffat became one of the wealthiest and most prominent beef shippers in the West, with ranches in four counties, a meat-packing company in Reno, and a landmark home in that city.

Nearly as important as the cattle kings were the sheepmen. Sheep had been trailed through the northeast section of the state for years, by both tramp herders and local residents. Late in the nineteenth century and after the turn of the twentieth century, however, many of the sheepmen found themselves in conflict with the cattle grazers. Cattlemen claimed that sheep ruined the range with sharp hooves and destructive grazing habits; sheepmen refuted that argument, but did not defuse it. Some famous battles between the two factions took place, occasionally with bloodshed the outcome. This, despite the fact that some of the larger ranches (like the Jenkins outfit) kept both sheep and cattle on their ranges.

The Forest Service acted first to restrict overgrazing by sheep. Then, in 1925, the Nevada legislature enacted a stock-watering law that required that livestock could be ranged only on owned or leased land. In 1934, the Congress made that concept a national policy with the Taylor Grazing Act. The sheep and cattle wars virtually ceased, and the numbers of sheep in Nevada declined from hundreds of thousands to only tens of thousands.

Sheepherders of Nevada came from numerous ethnic backgrounds; Mexicans, Greeks, Chinese, and native whites all herded the woollies of the Great Basin. However, Basques constituted Nevada's best-known ethnic group of sheepmen. The Basques of Elko County were genuine pioneers, settling there in the late 1800s. The Spanish Ranch, in Independence Valley near Tuscarora, was the home of Pedro and

Bernardo Altube, Basques from the Spanish province of Vizcaya. The Altubes were not only noted sheepmen (and wealthy ones at that), but became so well known for their heritage that Pedro was designated "The Father of the Basques in America." The Altubes brought Basques and Mexicans to the area, young men who worked a while, then either returned to their native countries or purchased lands and sheep of their own.

A second Basque sheepman, Pete Itcaina, was also a colorful and locally famous character of the Jarbidge area. Itcaina (pronounced it-*china*) was especially known for a hot temper and a large fortune. He grazed his flocks and participated in range wars in three northern Nevada counties.

These and other Basque herders and owners left a colorful heritage in northeastern Nevada that was recognized locally, but seldom mentioned outside the region. In the 1960s, the University of Nevada established a center for the study of Basque peoples worldwide, and within a few years, Basque culture had begun a significant revival. The attention of serious scholars to the unique Basque language and interesting customs, and the realization of this ethnic group's unusual physical attributes gave the people a new identity. People who had claimed French or Spanish heritage to avoid the common rural Nevada epithet "dirty basco" now enjoyed a renewal of pride. Basque festivals, featuring native food, dancing, and contests of strength, drew thousands of Basques, scholars, and interested citizens. No such affair is more famous, colorful, or widely attended than that in Elko, held annually in July.

The influence of the cattle barons and sheep owners made Elko County best known for this aspect of its economy and society. The railroad came to serve the beef business, instead of the other way around. No towns of any size grew up around Elko, and residents began to speak pridefully of their distance from other urban centers—in hundreds of miles from Reno, Salt Lake City, or Boise. These distances and boosterism helped the livestock business to pervade the entire northeastern corner of Nevada. The rodeo, cowboy-ing, shootouts, and the trappings became the entertainments in Elko. The Garcia Saddle Company, famous all over the world, started in Elko and prospered there until the 1930s. In short, Elko was Nevada's archetypal cowtown. Beef, lambs, wool, and hides dominated the economy, society, politics, and casual encounters. Then in 1931, the Nevada legislature made an important change in the rather narrow atmosphere. Legalized casino gambling came permanently to the state that year, and new faces began to appear in Elko.

The family of Newton Crumley, which had gained a foothold in Nevada by owning hotels in Goldfield, had moved to Elko to found one of the state's important hotel-casinos, the Commercial. The Commercial Hotel began as a crude wooden boarding house; various owners improved it, and when the Crumleys purchased it in 1925, the rate of improvements increased. By 1931, the place was one of the landmarks of Elko, but the Crumley management had made it one of the monuments of Nevada.

Nevada's fabulous hotel-casinos started out, after legalization, as carnival-type establishments, lacking the amenities that today's tourists take for granted. Bare floors, eye-shaded dealers, and mainly masculine customers marked these early places. They did not serve food, and only a few served liquor; the business was gambling for money. By 1940, food service had begun to appear and bars had become an adjunct to gambling. But nobody thought of entertaining customers in other ways until Newton Crumley, Jr., did. Crumley brought outstanding floorshows into the Commercial Hotel, and Nevada's tourist industry changed forever.

On April 26, 1941, Ted Lewis, then one of the nation's "big-name" nightclub performers, made his first appearance at the Commercial, and "show biz" had come to Nevada. This beginning in Elko, a mere cowboy hangout, was destined to make Nevada the "show business capital of the world," a reputation that surely would never die. The fact that it all began in Elko was sometimes forgotten by newcomers to places like Las Vegas, but Newton Crumley's fame in Elko

County was secure. From that example, too, casino owners found that the shows, far from distracting customers from gambling, only enhanced their business— the more people in the audience for the show, the bigger the take at the tables. By 1946, entertainment was a fact of casino life in Reno and Las Vegas.

The Crumley operation was more than that, however. The family was truly devoted to the betterment of Elko. Each performer's contract forbade "off-color" jokes and songs, and moreover each group had to give a show outside the casino atmosphere; the Old Folks Home, the school children, a nearby wartime air base, and the School of Industry all benefited from this policy.

Newton Crumley, Sr., died in 1946, Newton Crumley, Jr., in 1962. The hotels (by then there were two, the Commercial and the Ranchinn) changed hands and policies. Elko County's historian designated Newton Crumley, Jr., as "the man who did more for the community of Elko and northeast Nevada than any other individual." That probably was true; he did almost everything there: developed a well-known ranch at North Fork that he eventually sold to Bing Crosby (the "Honorary Mayor of the City of Elko"), served as the county's state senator, had a distinguished World War II military career, won election to the University of Nevada Board of Regents, and endlessly promoted Elko County's wonders to any receptive audience, even after he left Elko for Reno in 1957. His death in a plane crash finished a life of remarkable achievement for Nevada.

Elko County contains many local and national landmarks. Almost unnoticed by historians is its highly significant position as a transportation and communications hub. The first transcontinental trails, wagon roads, railroads, and highways all met in this northeastern section. In the twentieth century, as wires began to crisscross the country, Elko County was the site in 1914 of the setting of the last telephone pole in Pacific Telephone and Telegraph Company's end of the cross-country line. The same year, the last connection on the transcontinental telephone lines was made in Elko County near the Utah state line. The inaugura-

"It was very interesting, and made for interesting reporting, . . . the decision of Newt Crumley, Jr. . . . to bring big time entertainment to Elko. Well, I went to the hotel one day, and . . . I learned that they were going to bring Ted Lewis and his band and floor show to Elko. . . . And of course, this booking of Ted Lewis made quite a big news story, and really shook the town; and everybody said, "What is that Newt Crumley thinking of? He'll bankrupt himself and his father, paying somebody like Ted Lewis to come in. . . .

"So, Lewis came, and of course, just absolutely *jammed* the Commercial showroom . . . every night, it was just, you couldn't get in, and wondered where all the people came from. . . .

"And when they announced, after Ted Lewis, and perhaps another one or two, that Paul Whiteman was coming, it was not only disbelieving in Elko . . . I got a telegram from . . . the editor of *Variety*. . . . So, anyway, my deathless prose appeared on page one of *Variety*. I sent the story about Paul Whiteman and all. And, of course, in *Variety*'s headlines, it said something about 'Whiteman Goes to Stix,' or something along that line, and . . . not having been in the business very long, it was really quite a thrill to hit the front page of *Variety*."

— Paul Leonard, Elko newspaperman

tion of transcontinental telephone service was in January 1915, with Elko playing an important role. As airmail service began in the 1920s, the pilots used the highway through Elko as their guide. When night flying and then passenger service evolved, it was made possible by a mountain-top beacon system that led across Nevada through Elko; one of the beacons still exists at the Elko airport. As communications became more sophisticated, the first transcontinental buried cable passed through Elko, with a repeater station constructed there in 1942. In 1952, when microwave made television and instant transmission possible, a station to carry signals was built on Adobe Hill, just north of Elko. Finally, in the late 1970s, a transcontinental coaxial cable, capable of carrying tens of thousands of conversations simultaneously, crossed through Elko County, and a facility to service it was built near Elko. Thus Elko has indeed served as a vital link in all sorts of transportation, from emigrant trail to Interstate 80, and also in every kind of communication from rather primitive telephones to the most complex electronic transmission. Few other sites in the United States have continuously served so many functions to keep the American people talking and moving.

Despite its many modern attributes, Elko continued in the 1980s to serve the interests of livestock and the railroaders. All of the most important cultural aspects of the area are representations of ranch life in one form or another. Nevada's great mineral industry touched this district only peripherally, but the towns spawned by mining are among the state's longest-lasting and most colorful.

Tuscarora

The first mining town of any duration in the northeast was Tuscarora. Discovered in 1867, Tuscarora held the record for 65 years as highest-producing and most important mining camp of the section. Indeed, for nearly a decade (1875–1884), Tuscarora had more population and significance than Elko, and Elko nearly lost the county seat to the mining camp.

The real origins of the discovery are lost to history, but brothers John and Steve Beard usually receive credit for finding gold on the site. The two prospected for a few years in the attractive region, and enjoyed their find. Then in 1871, W. O. Weed discovered silver, and a great rush brought a town to where only the Beard shack had stood. Tuscarora acquired a post office in 1873; by 1876, it was the biggest town in Elko County. The largest ethnic group was composed of Chinese, laborers released from the railroad building. They began what became the largest Chinatown in Nevada, and gained the appellation ''Little Shanghai'' for the settlement. Opium dens, a joss house, and

gambling halls dotted the colony's street. Chinese in Nevada—like those all over the West—were considered fair game for rowdy whites, so they suffered endless indignities with considerable stoicism, but Chinatowns seldom lasted very long.

Tuscarora did not last, either, despite determined efforts by miners and prospectors of at least three different eras to keep the mines going, or to revive them. Tuscarora's mines gave forth their last ore about 1932; the highest figures estimated for the camp's production are $54 million. Still, its history is revered by Elko County residents, who recall their grandparents talking of Tuscarora's pounding mills, Masonic hall doings, newspaper office, volunteer fire departments (two), mercantile establishments, pioneer water system, or the randy entertainments of Little Shanghai. Although Nevada underwent still another great mining boom in the 1980s, Tuscarora remained little changed from its quiet ways and genteel decline.

Mountain City

Copper mining came to Elko County at Mountain City–Rio Tinto. The site of the discovery was on the north fork of the Humboldt, where in 1869 Jesse Cope uncovered silver chloride ore. Cope's find and its publicity caused a rush to the area, and the founding of what became Mountain City. Soon, gold placers were working in the district, and there was a population of perhaps 3,000. Inevitably, the gold and silver were depleted, and despite determined efforts by another generation of prospectors, Mountain City declined and died, leaving no visible remains.

Then in 1920, S. Frank Hunt, one of Nevada's most famous and interesting geologist-engineers, prospected in the Mountain City district. Hunt was a true professional, not a bonanza seeker. For more than ten years, he persisted in his search for the ore that he knew must be there. Financing came from various benefactors and even from the sale of penny stocks on the streets of Elko.

In February 1932, Hunt struck a body of 40 percent pure copper ore, and the fabulous Rio Tinto mine was born. The Mountain City Copper Company (International Smelting) built a company town at the mine site with all the facilities that the old tent-and-shanty settlement had lacked. Nearby, "new" Mountain City had a bank, telephone exchange, movie theater, schools, a newspaper, and even trees to help put the town back in the limelight. Patsville, at the foot of the road to the mine, had saloons and other entertainments for the miners of the company town.

Inevitably, of course, the mine eventually seemed exhausted. When it closed in the late 1940s, the Mountain City district had produced more than $23 million in gold, silver, and copper. The company town also died and became one of Nevada's "ghosts" until revived by a new rise in metals prices in the 1980s. S. Frank Hunt's memory lived. He gave substantial sums of money to the University of Nevada's Mackay School of Mines, establishing a foundation to assist younger people who will persist in the way he did to bring mineral fortune to northeastern Nevada.

Scenic Areas: Jarbidge, Ruby Marshes, Lamoille

The third of Elko County's mining camps was Jarbidge. The name came from the Shoshone Tsau-haubitts (or Ja–ha-bich). The Shoshones believed Ja-ha-bich was a cruel giant who caught and ate the natives. This legend, along with enormous, eerie rock formations in Jarbidge Canyon, kept the Shoshones—indeed almost anyone else—from camping or living there at least until the mining discoveries of 1909. Of course, there were prospectors among the early cross-country travelers, but none made an effective discovery until July 1909, when D. A. Bourne set off the rush with news of a gold mine. Within a few months, Jarbidge was a camp of perhaps 1,500 people.

The winters in Jarbidge are terrible. Residents claim that the season lasts fully nine months. The first prospectors therefore suffered horribly in the winter of 1909-1910, and by May 1910 the population had declined to a few hundred. For all of Jarbidge's active mining period, probably no more than 300 people lived there. The town never amounted to much as a mining camp, in any event. The silver and gold shipments ended in 1932, except for a small cleanup opera-

Jarbidge Canyon

ion in the 1930s; probably the total production did not exceed $10 million. But Jarbidge had other reasons for fame.

The last stagecoach robbery in the United States occurred at Jarbidge. Although other towns in the area were served by railroad or even trucks by then, in December 1916 Jarbidge had only a stagecoach for transportation to and from the outside world. Although the weather was—as usual—terrible, Fred Searcy tried to fulfill his duty to bring the mail to Jarbidge. When searchers found Searcy's frozen corpse and ripped-open mail sacks on the road, they started to look for a culprit. A man named Ben Kuhl was arrested and convicted; he continued to maintain his innocence through 27 years in the Nevada State Prison. The money he was supposed to have stolen, some $4,000, never was found. The crime was probably minor in the annals of law enforcement; its notable feature is only one: it was the last of the old-time stagecoach heists.

Lamoille Valley

Despite its lack of population and wealth, Jarbidge maintained a magnetic effect on northern Nevadans and others. The canyon is startlingly beautiful in sunny months, covered with aspens and dozens of varieties of wildflowers and shrubs. Deer, wild sheep, and other mammals live there, along with many bird species. The U.S. government has declared some of the vicinity a Wilderness Area, to be enjoyed by outdoors enthusiasts. The streams are said to be full of fish, and in the fall, the hills full of game birds. But indeed, the winters are long, and cold, and wet, and quiet.

A second, somewhat more accessible recreation area of the Elko vicinity is the Ruby Lake National Wildlife Refuge. In the general area of the former cattle ranches of Tom and William S. Short and Albert Hankins, the site became known as ''Ruby Marshes'' to local residents. Excellent fishing, boating, and camping made a popular playground of a formerly quiet cattle-grazing property. In the late 1970s and early 1980s, the federal government attempted to impose new restrictions on boating and other types of recreation at Ruby Marshes. An angry demonstration by fishing and water-sports enthusiasts, and strong political support from the Nevada congressional delegation, forestalled the move; Ruby Marshes remained one of Elko County's popular attractions.

The third scenic marvel of Elko County is the area of Lamoille. In a small, lush valley in the shadow of the splendorous Ruby Mountains, Lamoille is among the most attractive little towns in Nevada. Settled in the 1860s by stock raisers, the place has wonderful beauty. The town of Lamoille gained a post office in 1883, and people there, ranchers and townspeople alike, found a satisfying rural life. The Elko-Lamoille Power Company developed electricity from the creek there in 1913, but left the site relatively unspoiled. In the 1930s, the Civilian Conservation Corps (CCC) graded a road into the valley, providing the first access beyond the farm tracks. In 1947 the road was oiled, making it only a few minutes' drive from Elko and opening Lamoille Valley's attractions to wider groups of travelers. In 1965 Lamoille Canyon was declared a U.S. Scenic Area; the Forest Service constructed facilities, paved the road, and developed campgrounds. The life of Lamoille Valley, formerly supremely insular, changed forever, but the scenery remained, magnificently grand.

Wells

As the railroad had brought development and status to Elko and its vicinity, so also did the rails cause the founding of Wells. The place had been known to cross-country emigrant trains, for uncounted hundreds of wagons stopped there in the meadows and at the pools to refresh their animals and to prepare for the 300 miles ahead down the Humboldt River trail. The site was first called Humboldt Wells in February 1869, but the Central Pacific did not establish a town there until September, when a boxcar served the commercial needs of passengers and freight shippers. Eventually, Humboldt Wells became a division point on the Central Pacific, but the place had a slow growth.

The first permanent building—a log cabin saloon—was celebrated on Christmas Eve, 1869. The next business, a livery stable, opened in 1870, and in 1871 one of the town's longest-lasting and prominent merchants, Morris Badt, opened a general merchandise store. Badt and Cohn (later M. Badt & Co.) served the community of Wells for a third of a century. The general merchandise store grew to include freight shipping, financial negotiations with outside bankers, and finally, a bank.

Wells survived mining rushes in the surrounding area, good times and depressions, fame from its history, and notoriety from its bordellos. As one of the first Nevada cities across the border with Utah, and a good stopping place on both I-80 and U.S. 93, Wells continued to enjoy moderate prosperity into the late

Presbyterian Church, Wells

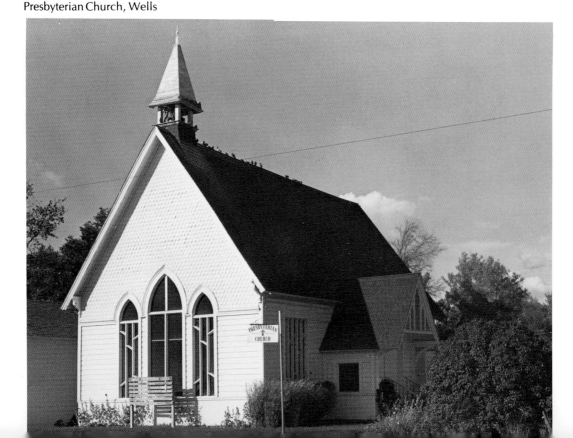

"As I knew the business . . . , my father acted as sort of a fiscal agent and banker for many, many of the ranches around Ruby, Clover, and Starr valleys. He paid their taxes, he paid their insurance. . . . He paid the interest on their land contracts. . . . And my father paid their interest and kept them up and saw that none of them went delinquent.

"Besides that, they would draw little checks on little slips of paper, and send them in with one of their laborers who would help them with the haying or something, say, 'Pay John Jones a hundred dollars.' It was so irregular and sloppy . . . that finally the business issued regular bank books addressed to M. Badt. And finally . . . the bank examiner came around and said, 'You people are running a bank without a license; you'll have to get a license for a bank.' "

— Milton Badt, Elko County pioneer
(son of Morris Badt)

"Well, I went out to Wells, and rented a house—I was getting married that spring. . . . There was one tree in the community. So I went up to the McCuiston ranch about fifty miles east of Wells and got some black willow trees, and planted them around the school. I guess I got about fifty trees and planted them. Some of them prospered."

— Earl Wooster, schoolteacher,
later a school administrator

twentieth century. The place would probably never become a major city, and the population remained at only a few hundred, but Wells has a special and secure place in the history of the westward movements of both the nineteenth and twentieth centuries.

Metropolis

It must have been easy, a bit of a lark, to sit in a New York office in 1909, look at maps, and dream about reclaiming the American desert out West. After all, there were some projects underway, including one at Fallon, Nevada, where the desert was—according to the propaganda—apparently beginning to bloom. Why not put something like that on the Humboldt River? All one needed in this situation was a map and some drawing paper, and look! a model city on the Humboldt!

The next few steps: incorporate the Pacific Reclamation Company, open an office in Salt Lake City, and start to talk the Mormons into buying lots or farms at—let's call it "Metropolis," that sounds grand enough. Raise some money quickly, and put up some fancy buildings so the town will attract enough people to recoup the original investment.

A few problems developed with this grandiose scheme. A pleasant and solid-looking city grew up on the site of Metropolis, and a fair number of people took up plots of ground. But farmers who already owned rights to Humboldt River water filed suit in 1912, pointing out the error in usurping their precious fluid. Eastern promoters had acted without knowing the facts of western water laws. The courts agreed with the Humboldt farmers, and before long the Pacific Reclamation Company was in bankruptcy. A long drought completed the ruin. Houses and other buildings were moved away, the railroad spur was abandoned, and the desert took over the fancy buildings that were left. Local ranchers eventually used the empty basements for a garbage dump. In the end, it seemed clear that no amount of promotion would ever revive Metropolis, probably Nevada's only agricultural "ghost."

Elko County's historian fittingly summarized the ambience of the northeastern corner of Nevada:

"Northeast Nevada is not just a geographical location . . . but a place where the spirit of the west still lingers. It is a severe expanse of desert country, and each man, woman and child has more than a section of land (640 acres) in which to stretch. . . . One of the west's last frontiers, the western mood lives and tarries, unwilling to fade; . . . sham has no place in this section of Nevada. A land of rigorous climate and rough terrain, the country has . . . a condensation of all that the Old West represented."

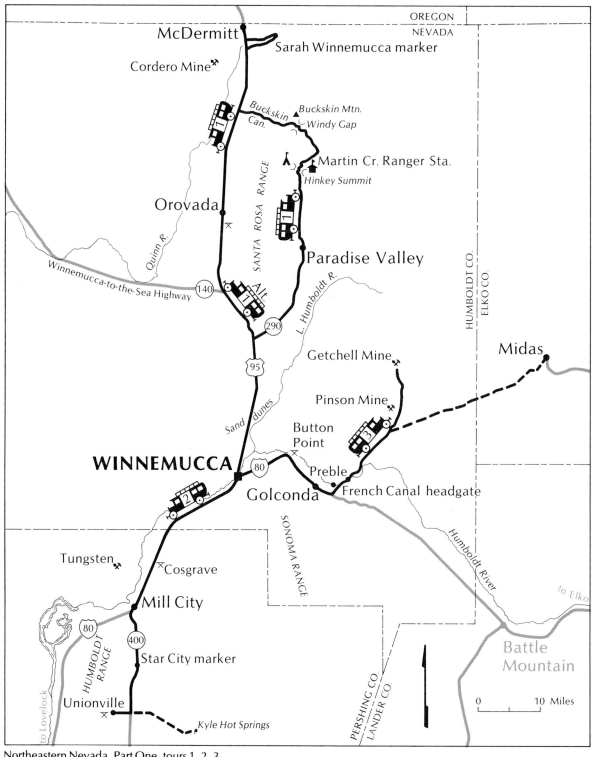

Northeastern Nevada, Part One, tours 1, 2, 3

TOURING IN NORTHEASTERN NEVADA

PART ONE

For the convenience of the traveler, we have divided the tours in this section into two parts: trips out of Winnemucca (Part One), and trips out of Elko (Part Two). The expanses of this section are so large that it seems impractical to expect the uninitiated to traverse them without this sort of guidance.

Tours are designed not to show every facet of each town of the region, but rather to lead the traveler to accessible and attractive sites that seem typical of the section's history and scenery. Travel here should not be considered dangerous, but it is always prudent to check the vehicle for safety and a full fuel tank. We have recommended picnic lunches for most of the tours, especially in the back country. You will surely want to take a camera, for you will see some of Nevada's best scenery.

What to see in Winnemucca: The commercial areas of Winnemucca have all necessities, including restaurants, grocery stores, shops, banks, gas stations, gambling casinos. Ask locally about the Basque restaurants.

The Humboldt County Library is on Fifth Street, across Bridge Street from the courthouse. The library has a small local history collection and a knowledgeable staff.

The Humboldt County Museum is off Maple Street (cross the bridge) on Jungo Road. The collections there consist of relics and artifacts of the area, exhibits prepared by local volunteers, and some photos and documents. The museum is free, but the volunteer staff welcomes donations. Hours are limited; check for a convenient time.

The Chamber of Commerce is located in the Nixon Building. Stop there for maps and brochures about the surrounding area. The "Winnemucca to the Sea" marker is next to the Nixon Building and will serve as the starting place for all tours in this section.

The remnants of the French Canal may be viewed above the cemetery at the west edge of town.

The Nevada Rodeo, one of the last authentic Old West celebrations, is held annually on the Labor Day weekend.

TOUR ONE, Land of the Cowboys and the Indians: Winnemucca — Paradise Valley — McDermitt and return. Approximately 177 miles round trip. Bring a picnic.

Start at the "Winnemucca to the Sea" marker at the intersection of Winnemucca Boulevard (the main street) and Melarkey Street, and turn north on U.S. 95. Drive 0.6 miles to the intersection of U.S. 95 and Jungo Road. The Humboldt County Museum is visible to the left; if you have not stopped there, you should.

Continue on U.S. 95 for 2.3 miles. Here is a good spot to observe the meander of the Humboldt River, and the conformation that makes this crooked stream one of North America's longest rivers.

Continue driving 5.3 miles to the sand dunes. The dunes are still moving eastward; the Nevada Highway Department sends crews following windstorms to clear the road and to help the dunes to move on.

Continue to drive north on U.S. 95 another 14.0 miles, and turn right on SR 290 to Paradise Valley. This is ranching country; watch for livestock and avoid damaging cattle or your car. Stay on the paved road; the dirt roads lead to ranches. Drive 12.7 miles to

---

"A large area a few miles north of Winnemucca is covered with sand dunes formed since the disappearance of Lake Lahontan. This belt of drifting sand extends westward from the lower part of the Little Humboldt Valley to the desert between Black Butte and the hills, and is about forty miles long from east to west, and eight or ten miles wide. The dunes are fully seventy-five feet thick, and their steeper slopes are on the east side, thus indicating that the whole, vast field of sand is slowly traveling eastward. This progress has necessitated a number of changes in the roads of the southern part of the Little Humboldt Valley during recent years. In some places in this region, the telegraph poles have been buried so deeply that they have to be spliced in order to keep the wires above the crests of the dunes."

— *Guidebook of the Western United States,*
Part B, the Overland Route (1915)

"Gearhart Miller owns 400 acres of patented land six miles south of Paradise. His home shows thrift and is an exceedingly pleasant one. His stock yards are full of this year's crop of hay. . . . He has a garden, where all kinds of vegetables are grown for ranch use. In ordinary years he threshes 5,000 bushels of wheat, barley and oats. He milks cows enough to furnish the ranch with milk, cream and butter. . . . Mrs. Miller is a model housewife and the interior of her pretty home is one of the pleasantest I have ever had the pleasure of visiting."

— Allen Bragg, newspaperman (1905)

the Miller ranch road, then continue 4.1 miles into the town of Paradise Valley; the historical marker is across the street from the post office.

Paradise Valley has very limited facilities: a saloon, mercantile store, barber shop(!). The attendant at the Humboldt National Forest ranger station will give maps and information about local roads. Firemen's Park has picnic tables, children's playground, and restrooms. There are two picturesque pioneer churches dating from the 1890s. Enjoy a tour of the town of Paradise Valley; the people are friendly, but not eager to give unsolicited information. The Micca building in the old section is on the National Register of Historic Places. Completing your visit here, look for the road sign in the old section that directs to Hinkey Summit, turn right, then left; the road heads north into the beautiful Santa Rosa Mountains.

Note: *The road ahead is forty miles of graded dirt. The way is safe, and suitable for all cars with careful and adventurous drivers. If this description does not fit you, return south to U.S. 95, turn right toward McDermitt, and pick up the tour's text a few paragraphs below.*

From the sign for Hinkey Summit, drive 3.2 miles, where the pavement ends. Drive straight ahead; ignore the road on the left. Drive 4.6 miles; you will see a cattle guard, National Forest Boundary, trash receptacle, and the crossing of Indian Creek.

Continue 7.3 miles to the summit. The drive takes you through volcanic formations, striated lava, rhyolite pillars, and spectacular views. The road was built by the Paradise CCC camp men in 1938. The vegetation is typical of the sagebrush country, and so is the wildlife. We saw ripe elderberries and chokecherries in mid-August and sighted several red-tail hawks, ravens, doves, a coyote, and some jackrabbits. This country is not deserted!

This area is historic as well as scenic. Here, until 1908, tramp sheep bands ranged uninhibited by regulation. Here also, cattle still graze on what seems like open range—but is actually under federal and state reg-

Winnemucca-to-the-Sea marker

ulation. This is genuine cowboy country, even in the late twentieth century. Remember that cows have the right-of-way on dirt or paved roads. Along this route are several ranch line shacks and a few summer residences.

Continue 1.8 miles to the sign for Martin Creek ranger station and the Lye Creek campground. The campground is 1.5 miles on the left. There are picnic tables, drinking water, toilets, and semi–primitive camps in aspen groves, at an elevation of 7,400 feet. In the fall, this is somewhat crowded, deer-hunting country.

From the Lye Creek/Martin Creek crossroads, drive 2.2 miles. Look across the canyon and see the terraces of sheep trails, remnants of overgrazing in this area. Because overgrazing is not a myth, the organization of the Humboldt National Forest—at the petition of local residents—in 1908 brought regulation of grazing to this vicinity. In 1934, the Taylor Grazing Act brought similar regulation to other public lands, and tramp sheep bands and free cattle grazing ended.

Drive 2.7 miles to the sign for U.S. 95, and turn left. Drive 2.8 miles. The peak ahead is Buckskin Mountain, the formation on its flank is called Buckskin Slide. There is a small mining operation on the facing side, active from time to time.

Drive 1.1 miles to Windy Gap, and bear left. The road starts down from this point. Enjoy the view of several miles of hairpin turns below. Continue 5.0 miles to the National Forest Boundary.

Drive 2.7 miles to the ruins of a mercury milling operation. Here is a fine commentary on the vagaries of the mining business. This mill, probably built in the 1960s to retort mercury, along with trucks, now rusting in the weather, cost its builders many thousands of dollars. When the price of metal drops (any metal— gold, silver, mercury), it is not even worth picking up the pieces. The electrical equipment was removed, and the rest is abandoned to scavengers and vandals.

Drive 5.1 miles to the highway, U.S. 95, and turn right toward McDermitt. You have seen the cowboy country; now come and see the Indians.

If you decide to take the paved highway (U.S. 95): After returning to Highway 95 and the Paradise turnoff, turn right (north) toward McDermitt. Drive 9.3 miles to the junction of U.S. 95 and SR 140. Here is Winnemucca's link to the sea. Services are very limited on the throughway, as you can note from the sign just a few feet from the intersection on SR 140: Next Gas, 69 miles. Continue on U.S. 95 toward McDermitt, and drive 10.5 miles. The rest area here has picnic tables and toilets. The plaque commemorates a group of CCC men who died fighting a forest fire nearby. Drive 2.0 miles through Orovada, a ranch center. Continue 16.4 miles on U.S. 95 to the Buckskin Canyon Road. (This is where you would have rejoined U.S. 95 if you had taken the dirt road over Hinkey Summit.)

Drive 9.9 miles on U.S. 95 to the Fort McDermitt historical marker. Turn right here to tour the reserva-

tion. The road circles the Fort McDermitt reservation for 13.1 miles. The tribe does not sell anything of native culture on the reservation, but the trip is interesting. There are a modern community building, a small hospital, and many neat residences. The children are bused off the reservation for school. The historical marker for "Princess" Sarah Winnemucca is on the circle drive.

The homes here, built on a similar design, are the result of a federal program that allowed members to participate in a "self-help" project to upgrade housing on western Indian reservations. Reservation residents engage in marginal agriculture, raise livestock, and work in the surrounding area in mines and industry. This is a rather typical Nevada reservation, a monument to the actions of both victors and vanquished in a long-gone conflict.

Returning to the highway via the circle route, turn right toward the town of McDermitt, and drive 2.5 miles. McDermitt has tourist facilities in limited quantities—food, restaurants, gasoline, bars, casino, curio shops. An antique jail is next to the post office.

McDermitt grew up to serve the commercial needs of the fort, and then the state line traffic. It now stands as a tourist's first opportunity to engage in Nevada-style recreation when entering the state from the north.

If you wish to visit the Cordero mine, ask locally about receiving permission and for directions.

Return on U.S. 95 to Winnemucca, 74 miles south of McDermitt.

TOUR TWO, Scenes of the 1860s: Winnemucca — Mill City — Unionville and return. Approximately 96 miles round trip (add 20 miles for a side trip to Kyle Hot Springs). Bring along a picnic.

Starting at the "Winnemucca to the Sea" marker at the intersection of Winnemucca Boulevard and Melarkey Street, drive west on I-80 for 11.2 miles to the Rose Creek overpass. Up to this point, the highway parallels the meandering Humboldt River and both the Southern Pacific and Western Pacific tracks. Here, the WP turns west into northern California. Continue 7.8 miles to the Cosgrave roadside rest. Here are picnic tables, drinking water, toilets, garbage cans, phone, and an information kiosk. Trailers are allowed to park free overnight (but it could be next to an idling diesel).

Continue driving 2.3 miles, and look across the tracks to the west, on the hillside. There is the mining camp of Tungsten. During periods of need for strategic metals, or of high prices, Tungsten becomes a busy place. Ore was first discovered after World War II, and a company town and mill were built on the site. Tungsten closed down when prices fell and the government quit stockpiling in the 1950s, but some activity resumed in the 1980s. The place is strictly an industrial operation; no services are available.

Continue 6.4 miles to Exit #149, for Unionville. Turn toward the tracks to see the ruins of Mill City. Drive along the dirt roads, noting the adobe foundations and the remains of the huge mill next to the tracks. There is a considerable amount of trash here, most of it from a later period. Remnants of Mill City are now mostly on private property; collecting of anything except photographs is not recommended.

Return to the paved road and go south on the route marked SR 400 toward Unionville. Drive 9.0 miles to the Star City marker. Note that you are driving through cattle country along this road and stay alert; a half-ton of beef can do terrible damage to your car and could ruin a pleasant day. The side road to Star City is not suitable for passenger cars; there is less to see there than the marker indicates, for a good deal has happened since the marker was placed in the 1970s.

Continue 7.4 miles to the Unionville historical marker, and turn right on a good, graded gravel road, up into a canyon of the Humboldt Range. Unionville proper—homes and ruins—is less than three miles ahead. Near the western end of the settlement is the Pershing County Youth Park. Here are picnic tables, barbecue stoves, shady trees, a historical marker ("Reunion in Unionville"), and when we were there, a resident family of mule deer.

The park is on the site of one of Mark Twain's cabins. Some of Nevada's oldest towns claim to have a cabin that the famous writer occupied at some time. Unionvillers believe that this one is authentic.

This quaint little settlement has several picturesque and photogenic ruins. The setting is a desert oasis in a beautiful canyon with trees, a stream, and flowers in season. The place is not deserted; people live here year-round in old houses or new ones. There are no commercial facilities—no food, gasoline, supplies.

Vandalism has taken a toll of both material and spirit in Unionville. People never leave homes and property unguarded, and although they express hospitable welcome to tourists, they are necessarily—and understandably—wary of strangers. We were told of shoot-

Unionville

ers and "collectors" who had damaged both property and people, and—somewhat hilariously—of a would-be collector whose four-wheel-drive truck got irretrievably stuck and who received only advice from the locals.

About four miles beyond the Youth Park, further up the canyon, are scenic primitive camping and picnic sites on BLM land, and the remnants of an ancient ice pond. If you are driving a high-axle vehicle, the road is safe; it is not recommended for passenger cars.

Following your tour of Unionville, return to the paved road. Turn left on SR 400, drive 16.4 miles to I-80, then return to Winnemucca, approximately 28 miles.

Side trip: Across the pavement as you leave Unionville and the historical marker, a graded road continues to Kyle Hot Springs, about ten miles away. The place is usually deserted, although one of Nevada's county sheriffs is alleged to have dumped drunks there to "dry out," during the 1940s and 1950s. At Kyle Hot Springs there is a sort of "hot tub" arrangement and a kind of sauna, both enclosed in shacks. If you like that activity in a desert setting, it's pleasant. We do not recommend the facilities: your hot tub at home is safer, for this water and sauna are very hot, and there is no guard. If you take the side trip, return to this intersection, then to I-80, and to Winnemucca via I-80.

TOUR THREE, Twentieth-century mining: Winnemucca — Golconda — Getchell Mine and return. Approximately 85 miles round trip (add 56 miles for a side trip to Midas). Bring a picnic lunch, and some folding chairs (there are no picnic tables on this trip).

Starting at the "Winnemucca to the Sea" marker at the corner of Winnemucca Boulevard and Melarkey Street, take the first access to I-80 east, and drive 10.0 miles to the Button Point rest area (Exit #187). Here are the only picnic tables you will see today, toilets, garbage cans, barbecues, drinking water, trailer hold-

ing-tank disposal station, and free overnight parking for campers and trailers. Three historical markers decorate this place. The first, at the entrance to the rest area, explains that Butch Cassidy's horse grazed here, waiting for him to reach the ranch to change from the stolen horse to his own. Other markers commemorate Frank Button, for whom the point is named, and the exploration of the Humboldt River. Return to the freeway and continue east.

The highway generally follows the Emigrant Trail. The Osgood Mountains are on the north, Sonoma Range to the south. Drive 6.5 miles to Exit #194, Golconda and Midas; turn left into Golconda. At Golconda, there are a pioneer cemetery, limited commercial facilities, post office, and ruins of the early mining era. The town is occupied. We noticed a great blue heron residing on the town reservoir.

To see the headwaters of the French Canal: From the Golconda historical marker, take the road just west of the marker, heading to the railroad tracks (this is Guernsey Avenue). Drive 0.4 miles to the tracks and turn right. Drive 2.1 miles along the south side of the railroad track, keeping right at all crossroads, then look to the left next to the river. You will see a few ruins and an antique concrete structure holding water gates, the Canal headgates. There is a dam of more recent vintage nearby on the river, with auto bodies acting as riprap. Return to the Golconda historical marker.

Drive east from the marker on SR 789 toward Pinson and Midas, 6.0 miles. Here is a double crossing of the Western Pacific and Southern Pacific tracks; the site is Preble, headquarters for the building of the Humboldt Canal.

Continue on SR 789 for 9.7 miles to the end of the pavement. Go straight through the intersection to the left, on a good, graded dirt road. Here begin the sophisticated-looking mining operations of the 1980s. The Milchem mine on the left began development about 1980. Drive 3.6 miles; the Pinson plant is on the left, marked by many blue tanks and structures. When built in 1980, this was claimed to be the most modern gold plant in the world. The process was described by the chief mining engineer prior to the opening: "Out of five million tons [of material hauled], you get roughly 600,000 tons of ore. When the ore comes to the mill it is ground up and the gold is taken out of it in some mystical, magical way metallurgists like to keep secret." A newspaper writer called it "a technological Disneyland of crushers, belts, and screens" consisting of "a combination of the latest American and South African technology."

View the Pinson mine from a distance unless you have made prior arrangement for a tour. A combination of heavy trucks, a short season, and uninvited visitors makes operators quite nervous.

Drive 4.5 miles and look straight ahead to the "elephant hunting ground" of the great Getchell Mine. Mining engineers must find such places by using a sixth sense. Now that *you* have found it, drive up past the mill, 1.5 miles, through the gate to the residence of the caretaker. There, ask permission to visit the works, receive some advice on what to see, and sign the waiver and release that absolves Getchell Mine, Inc., from damage to yourself or your car. Then visit this fascinating place. (Please *do* start the visit with the amenities; the caretaker will find you anyway, and will seem a good deal more friendly if you make the first move.)

The mining operation closed down in 1967, the main works were dismantled and sold, and the great pit filled with water. Now the major activity is by specimen collectors, cattle grazers, and coyotes. The area abounds with interesting rocks, including getchellite, which occurs only here. Following your visit to the Getchell Mine, return 9.6 miles to the crossroads at the end of the pavement. If your day is near its end, return to Winnemucca by retracing your route to Golconda and thence to I-80, approximately 32 miles.

Side trip: If you would like to see one more twentieth-century mining camp, come along to Midas. At the crossroads at the end of the pavement, Midas is a sharp left turn, and then a drive on 28 miles of good, graded gravel road.

The town was founded in 1907 as Gold Circle; its name was changed to Midas in 1908. A small settlement, mostly wooden shacks, grew up around the Elko Prince mine there. The population probably peaked at about 2,000; production was somewhat under $2 million until the 1980s. The camp declined rather quickly after about 1920, although mining continued on a reduced scale. The school, business houses, and homes were boarded up and deserted; only the post office hung on until 1942. By 1950, fewer than a dozen people lived at Midas, dreaming of a revival in the metals business. The 1970s and 1980s brought some realization of the dream, but Midas itself changed markedly.

In this somewhat backwater location (the next nearest town is 40 miles away by dirt road), the place has now become a bustling, noisy, littered camp of travel trailers cheek-by-jowl with the old shacks. Cattle graze in the yards. The bar at the center of town remains as the meeting place, social hall, and information exchange, with almost no other commercial facilities in sight. At the new mining boom's inevitable end, Midas will probably revert to a town of early twentieth-century shacks—just as soon as the travel trailers pull out.

Completing your look at Midas, return to the crossroads at the end of the pavement for SR 789 (28 miles), and return from Golconda to Winnemucca on I-80.

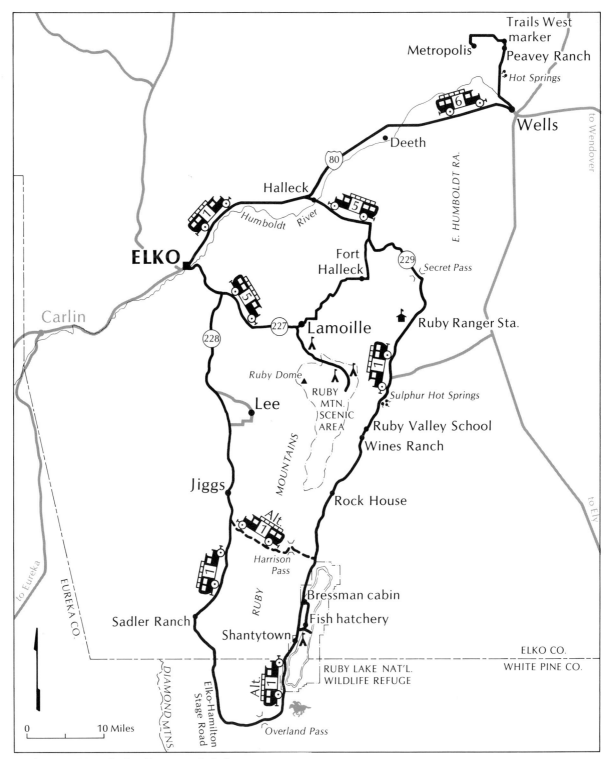

Northeastern Nevada, Part Two, tours 1, 5, 6

TOURING IN NORTHEASTERN NEVADA

PART TWO

The trips in this section are designed for people touring out of Elko. The purpose of the tours is to show some of the most attractive scenic and historic spots in an exceedingly interesting section. We have not tried to lure travelers into areas unsuitable for ordinary passenger cars—unless that caveat is set out at the beginning of the text for the tour. The tourist should understand that distances are huge in this section, so the vehicle must be in good condition and full of fuel at the start of a trip. If extra equipment (beyond the merely prudent supply of food and extra water) is required, we have indicated that. Do take your camera; the scenery in this section is among the most magnificent in the entire state of Nevada.

Travel in this section may be somewhat limited during the winter. We suggest saving the dirt-road trips for late spring, summer, and fall. If it has been storming, check at the Humboldt National Forest office or with some knowledgeable person before starting on a dirt-road tour. Many people in Elko are quite accustomed to driving long distances in the back country, so the Forest Service, BLM, or county sheriff's officers are likely to keep up on road conditions.

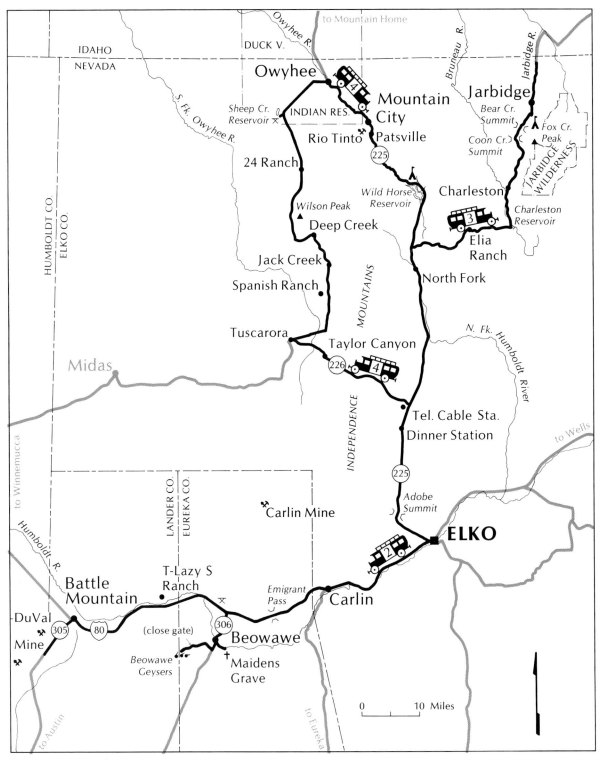

IDAHO
NEVADA

to Mountain Home

Owyhee R.

DUCK V.

Owyhee

Sheep Cr.
Reservoir
INDIAN RES.

S. Fk. Owyhee R.

Mountain
City

Rio Tinto   Patsville

225

24 Ranch

Bruneau R.

Jarbidge R.

Jarbidge

Bear Cr.
Summit

Coon Cr.
Summit

Fox Cr.
Peak

JARBIDGE
WILDERNESS

Charleston

Charleston
Reservoir

Wilson Peak

Wild Horse
Reservoir

Deep Creek

Elia
Ranch

Jack Creek

Spanish Ranch

North Fork

HUMBOLDT CO.
ELKO CO.

Tuscarora

Midas

MOUNTAINS

Taylor Canyon

226

N. Fk. Humboldt River

to Wells

INDEPENDENCE

Tel. Cable Sta.

Dinner Station

225

Carlin Mine

Adobe
Summit

LANDER CO.
EUREKA CO.

to Winnemucca

Humboldt R.

ELKO

2

Battle
Mountain

T-Lazy S
Ranch

Emigrant
Pass

Carlin

DuVal
Mine

305   80

(close gate)

306

Beowawe

Beowawe
Geysers

Maidens
Grave

to Austin

to Eureka

0   10 Miles

Northeastern Nevada, Part Two, tours 2, 3, 4

What to see in Elko: The Northeastern Nevada Museum is on Idaho Street, near the eastern edge of Elko. This, one of the best local museums in the state of Nevada, has professionally prepared exhibits of relics and artifacts of the region, photos, documents, slide shows, and traveling displays for the annual photo contest. This is a "must see" for anyone touring around Elko. There are also free and low-priced brochures and books about the area. All the tours in this section begin in front of the Northeastern Nevada Museum.

The Elko Chamber of Commerce has a tourist information center on Idaho Street, just east of the museum. Here are free brochures and a friendly staff. Ask for a city map to help you in seeing Elko.

The Elko County Library is at 720 Court Street. The holdings include a small local history collection. The staff is helpful and enthusiastic.

Take advantage of your visit to the library to drive along Court Street. This is the town's historic district, containing several Victorian structures.

Elko has all tourist facilities, grocery stores, casinos, bars, shops, and many friendly people. Ask locally about the Basque restaurants. The park next door to the museum has a children's playground. There are also golf courses, swimming pools, a beautiful new convention facility, and the Elko Community College (the university system's first community college).

TOUR ONE, The Ruby Marshes country: Elko — Halleck — Secret Pass — Ruby Marshes — Jiggs and return. Approximately 161 miles round trip via Harrison Pass; approximately 172 miles round trip via Overland Pass. Fill the vehicle with fuel, pack a lunch, bring your bird book.

Leaving the Northeastern Nevada Museum, drive east on Idaho Street to I-80 east (toward Salt Lake). Drive 18.6 miles to Exit #321 for Halleck and Ruby Valley. Leaving the freeway, drive 0.4 miles to the Fort Halleck historical marker, on the right side of the highway. Continue 0.7 miles to Halleck, a railroad siding and post office. This area's early settlers included the family of Mathias and Christine Glaser, who took

up a ranch a little west of here in the 1870s. The Glaser descendants still live on the family property, and use Halleck as their address.

Continue 8.0 miles to the Starr Valley road, on the left. Go straight ahead. Drive another 2.1 miles; the road to Lamoille is on the right. Continue straight ahead on SR 229 toward Secret Pass. (See Tour Five in this section for Lamoille.)

The Secret Pass route in the Ruby Mountains is one of the alternate roads on the Emigrant Trail. Peter Skene Ogden came this way in 1828. The Bidwell-Bartleson emigrant party of 1841-1842 most likely used Secret Pass. If the Donner party of 1846 had crossed Secret Pass, instead of missing it, they might have gone to California in time to outrace the devastating winter in the Sierra Nevada.

Continue on SR 229, driving 9.6 miles to Secret Pass summit. Here at 6,457 feet elevation are lovely views of Ruby Valley. Stay on the paved road; side roads lead to ranches and private property. Watch for livestock on the road, as this is cattle country.

Continue 7.4 miles. The Ruby guard station of the Humboldt National Forest and the National Forest access road are on the right. Look to the left, across the valley. About there, in the summer of 1846, the Donner party entered this valley, saw the steep and rocky Ruby Mountains as a barrier, and turned south to try to circumvent this wall of stone.

Continue 7.8 miles, through the ranch holdings of the Neff company. Notice the outbuildings of adobe and native stone; these are very old ranches. The junction of SR 229 comes in from Wells to the left; do not turn, but continue now straight ahead on SR 767. Drive 2.1 miles, and the pavement ends. The road ahead is adequate for any vehicle. Drive 0.8 miles, and look to the left. This is Sulphur Hot Springs, as you might have guessed from the odor of hydrogen sulphide. At 205°F, the water here has the hottest spring temperature in Elko County. The springs probably rise from a fault. Some researchers believe that this spring was used for cooking by the Bidwell-Bartleson party.

Drive 2.1 miles; do not take the road from the left, but go straight ahead, over the cattle guard. Drive 2.3

miles; here is the Ruby Valley school. The ranch with the stone and brick buildings is the Gardner ranch. Drive another 0.3 miles, past the Ruby Valley community center, on the right. Begin to look for large birds, residents of the Wildlife Refuge at Ruby Marshes. On a day in late summer, we saw flocks of turkey vultures and a group of eight sandhill cranes. Continue driving through the Wines ranch, 5.7 miles; do not take the road to the right, which leads to a ranch.

The Wines family has lived in Ruby Valley since 1865. The ranch at one time encompassed many facilities including a flour mill. Ira D. and Margaret Wines, the early settlers here, had a family of twelve children. Some of their descendants still live in this beautiful valley or elsewhere in Elko County.

Drive 1.5 miles to the crossing of Overland Creek. In another 0.7 miles, there is a rock ruin on the right hand side; the road to the left leads to a ranch. Drive on 1.5 miles to Rock House, a small, limited commercial center. Continue 1.8 miles. Here is a stone farmhouse, built by an early settler who had time and talent to cut and dress stone.

Drive 7.1 miles to the junction (on the right) with Harrison Pass road. If you are driving a passenger car, note this intersection as *you will return here*.

The Donner party, struggling along here in the foothills, also missed this opportunity to cross the Ruby Mountains, although the route had been explored the previous year by a party led by Joseph Walker. Continue straight ahead across the cattle guard toward the Ruby Lake Wildlife Refuge.

Drive 0.3 miles to the boundary of the Ruby National Wildlife Refuge. We enjoyed watching the birds and animals in this area. Drive another 5.7 miles and look to the left. Here are the ruins of the Jacob Bressman cabin, stone ruins of barns behind the cabin, and Bressman's grave on the hill overlooking Ruby Valley. Bressman and his family members settled here about 1880, and he died in January 1896. Look at the road next to the cabin; *you will return here shortly*.

Continue now 1.6 miles to the refuge headquarters. Here is information about the birds and other wildlife on the refuge. The attendant will give you free pam-

phlets about the refuge, a bird checklist, and regulations governing the area. Ask about a walk to the cave behind the station. The Donner party camped on this site. In 1939, a CCC camp was constructed just north of the headquarters. The forty men housed there helped to build the dikes for the refuge.

Return now to the Bressman cabin, and take the road out onto the dikes of the Wildlife Refuge. The road is suitable for any vehicle, and circles to the important viewing places. Follow these directions on this trip of about nine miles: at the first turn, keep right; at the second, keep left; at the third, keep left; at the fourth, turn left; at the fifth, go right. You should end near the refuge campground. The campground has spaces for tents or trailers, with drinking water available. The Gallagher Fish Hatchery, a trout facility, is nearby and tours are available there. The fish hatchery tours are informal, and exceedingly interesting.

Completing your tour of the refuge and its facilities, from the campground entrance, drive south 1.1 miles to Shantytown. This place has very limited facilities, including regular (no other) gasoline and a small grocery store. Only two families stay here through the winter, but they have a good deal of company in summer.

Continue south on the main traveled road 6.7 miles to the boundary of the Ruby Lake Wildlife Refuge. Go straight ahead, not to the ranch or the RV park. Drive 2.1 miles to the Pony Express marker for the Ruby Valley station. The Pony Express station's building has been preserved in front of the Northeastern Nevada Museum in Elko. At the marker, the road forks.

Decision: *The Overland Pass road to the west is adequate only for a high-axle vehicle. If you are driving a passenger car, sports car, or motor home, return north to the Harrison Pass road and take that route to Jiggs.*

Returning to Harrison Pass junction, turn left and head uphill. Drive 3.4 miles to the summit. The road is dirt, well-maintained, easy to drive. This is a popular recreation area for people from Elko. As you reach the summit, enjoy a look from the 7,248-foot elevation back at Ruby Valley and ahead to Huntington Valley.

Drive down the grade, where you may enjoy the greenery along Toyn Creek—aspen groves, willows, wild roses. In 6.3 miles, reach the Humboldt National Forest boundary. Drive 1.2 miles, and the pavement begins. Drive 3.5 miles to the junction with SR 228, and turn right for Jiggs, 3.0 miles ahead.

If you take the Overland Pass route, bear right at the Pony Express marker. Drive 1.0 mile to the National Forest boundary, cross the cattle guard, and stay on the main traveled road.

Drive 2.0 miles to Overland Pass summit. Take a minute to appreciate the historical significance of this spot. The Donner party passed here, with their worst trials still ahead, in 1846. The Pony Express riders went through this place in 1860-1861. Fort Ruby was on this spot; nothing remains to mark its existence.

Drive west 2.8 miles, staying on the main road, and cross the cattle guard. Continue 2.0 miles to a fork in the road and a Pony Express marker. Go to the right. The mountains ahead are those of the Diamond Range.

Continue 1.6 miles, crossing a cattle guard, to the intersection. Turn to the right. This is the historic Elko to Hamilton stage road. Continue on the main road for 3.2 miles to Pot Hole Spring, a reservoir, spring, and cattle trough. Continue 5.1 miles, staying on the main road to a fork, and bear left. You have ended your trip on the Elko-Hamilton stage road, but there are some miles ahead. Go 3.6 miles to the junction with SR 46, and go straight ahead (not to the left). Drive 1.6 miles. This ranch once belonged to Nevada Governor Reinhold Sadler. The buildings are abandoned, but the ranch is not.

Continue on the main traveled road. Some of the ranches are abandoned, and some have absentee owners. We saw a great many turkey vultures and a few golden eagles along this route. Drive 14.1 miles, and you will meet the road from Harrison Pass. The pavement and SR 228 begin here. Drive north toward Jiggs.

Drive 2.9 miles from the intersection, and enter Jiggs. This place was once the headquarters for the sheep and cattle ranching operation of the Hylton family, and an entertainment center for ranchers from Diamond and Mound valleys. Originally, the settlement was called Skelton, later Hylton. For some reason now apparently lost to history, the Post Office Department named it for a comic strip character in 1918. The post office and some very limited facilities remain. Continue through town, north on SR 228.

Drive 13.8 miles. Here is the sign for Lee, the headquarters of the Te-Moak Shoshone band. This is the smallest of the northeastern section's Indian towns. At Lee, there is a very limited store, post office, livestock yard, tribal office building, and several residences. The people engage in agriculture along the well-watered valley of the south Humboldt. The drive to Lee is 6.1 miles each way.

From the intersection, continue driving north on SR 228 for 13.0 miles to the junction with SR 227, turn left, and return to Elko, approximately 7.0 miles to the northwest.

TOUR TWO, Railroad towns and hot spots: Elko — Carlin — Beowawe Geysers — Maiden's Grave — Battle Mountain and return. Approximately 178 miles round trip. Bring your lunch, or plan to visit a restaurant in Battle Mountain.

Leaving the museum, drive west on Idaho Street to the I-80 access west, 5.2 miles. Drive along through the canyon for 12.5 miles. Notice the pillars of the Adobe Range; these wind-shaped formations are common in this section. This will bring you to the highway tunnels.

From the tunnels, continue 3.7 miles to take the Carlin Exit (#282), and drive into Carlin, 1.8 miles to the historical marker on the right-hand side of the road at the intersection. The paved road to the north leads to the great Carlin (Newmont) gold mine. *No visitors are permitted on the property during mining operations without prior arrangement.* Tour this interesting little railroad town. Most of the older buildings are on the lower side of the tracks. Carlin does not cater very much to tourists, but has some facilities. There is a park (Richard Clark Perry Memorial Park) at the west edge of town. The park has picnic tables and shade trees, along with a ballpark that indicates that the park is mainly for local use. Completing your tour of Carlin, return to the historical marker, leave via the I-80 West access, and drive 11.8 miles to Emigrant Pass.

This is a very historic site, although there are no facilities now. The place was a welcome spot on the Emigrant Trail of the 1850s. During the 1940s, some crooked gamblers had what was called a ''zoo joint'' in the area, using animals as lures to draw tourists into their establishment. This activity led to considerable notoriety, a political scandal, and revisions in Nevada gambling control procedures. One of the side effects involved the dismissal of the superintendent of the state police, who apparently assisted the zoo joint operators.

Drive 8.0 more miles, and take Exit #261 to Beowawe. Stay on paved SR 306 to Beowawe and Crescent Valley. Drive 5.7 miles, past the Horseshoe ranch, a big cattle outfit, and into Beowawe. Take time to look at this quaint old railroad siding town. From the tracks, drive past the fire station, school, and church, 1.8 miles to a sign on a dirt road to the Geysers. Turn right. The road is suitable for all vehicles with careful drivers.

Stay on the main graveled road as you drive over the hill and into the valley. Drive 2.8 miles; note the mining on the left. Avoid side roads to mines or ranches. Drive 3.3 miles; here is a gate to open, *and then close*. Drive another 1.2 miles to one of Nevada's hottest hot spots, the Beowawe Geysers. Explore the area carefully on foot, or drive up onto the sinter terrace *if* you have a high-axle vehicle. Many of the biggest geysers have been lost to geothermal experimentation and exploration. In 1977, vandalism effectively ended the high-shooting hot water streams. Still, this is one of the most active geothermal areas in the Great Basin. The water is extremely hot, and the fumaroles still rumble. On a cool morning, you will see plenty of steam. Do not look for a swimming pool. The area is still under consideration for industrial development.

Return 7.3 miles to the pavement of SR 306 (don't forget to close that gate at 1.2 miles). Turn left, toward Beowawe.

Drive 0.3 miles on the pavement to an unmarked dirt road, and turn right. Drive 2.2 miles along the road, crossing a cattle guard and watching for live beef on the road. Look up to the right for a large cross marking the cemetery, and drive 0.2 miles. Here is the ''Maiden's Grave,'' and a pioneer cemetery that has served the valley for a century. Lucinda Duncan's resting place is marked by a huge cross on the knoll. After visiting the cemetery, return to the paved road, through Beowawe, and back to I-80 west, 7.2 miles.

Maiden's Grave, near Beowawe

After entering I-80 west, drive 1.9 miles west to the Beowawe rest stop. Here are picnic tables, garbage cans, toilets, water, and free overnight parking for trailers, campers, and diesel trucks. The historical marker in the rest stop parking lot commemorates the cattle industry of this area. Drive 10.2 miles; note the T-Lazy S ranch to the right of the highway, one of the largest beef outfits in this section.

Continue on I-80 for 14.2 miles to Exit #233, Battle Mountain; drive into Battle Mountain and explore this quaint but busy little railroad/mining center.

You may view the DuVal mining operation only from a distance. If you wish to do so, turn south on SR 305 in the center of Battle Mountain, drive approximately 8.0 miles, and look to the right of the highway. The DuVal company has workings all along the old Copper Basin–Copper Canyon deposits. The "ghost towns" of the nineteenth century have mostly disappeared under this operation.

The Reese River Valley, through which you are driving, is the one that the Reese River Navigation Company promoted. If you drive about 20 miles down the valley, the Reese River crosses the highway, and you will see the folly of investing in the scheme. Return to Battle Mountain, take the I-80 east exit toward Elko. Return to Elko, approximately 74.6 miles.

TOUR THREE, The Jarbidge stage: Elko — Jarbidge and return. Approximately 229 miles round trip. Fill the gasoline tank, pack a lunch or camping gear.

Note: *The road to Jarbidge Canyon is graded and graveled, suitable for most vehicles in good condition with careful drivers. However, this is not for the novice dirt-road traveler: the track is narrow and the grades in places exceed 15 percent. This is also not the road on which to take your big camper, motor home, or travel trailer. But the scenery marks this as one of the half-dozen or so most beautiful sections of Nevada, so let your driving skill be your guide.*

Leaving the museum, drive west on Idaho Street to SR 225 at the edge of town. Turn right (north). If the weather has been unsettled, stop at the Humboldt National Forest Headquarters and inquire about the Jarbidge road. Here, you may also obtain a map that will help you to enjoy the trip. The HNF office is on your right, just past the turn.

Drive 11.6 miles to Adobe Summit. Then continue down SR 225 for 14.5 miles to Dinner Station. Here was an important stop on the stage line. Travelers on the roads of this section were able to break their trips here before going on to Elko, Jarbidge, or Tuscarora. The original buildings from the 1870s were wooden; the stone ones were built after a fire in the 1880s. The place is now occupied as a ranch. The white paint covers masonry of native stone.

Drive 3.5 miles to a dirt road on the left, and look for a concrete building. This structure is one of two in Nevada that serve as the entrance to an underground telephone-cable power station and repeater (the other is at the edge of the Black Rock Desert). This coaxial cable, which was laid in the mid-1970s, provides part of the Bell System's transcontinental long-distance facilities. The small building visible gives little clue to the expansive equipment rooms below.

Drive 0.7 miles to the junction of SR 225 and SR 226; keep going straight ahead on SR 225. Continue 23.5 miles to North Fork. North Fork was once a stage stop and commercial center. There was a post office in the 1880s, and later a hotel and saloon, grocery store, and school. The place also was the center for the ranches owned by the Crumley family, and later sold to Bing Crosby. The post office went out of business in 1944, before the Highway Department built its maintenance facilities here.

Drive 3.9 miles to a graded dirt road, and turn right toward Jarbidge. Continue 13.0 miles to the Elia ranch. As you drive through this active livestock grazing area, notice the barren character of some of the land. There are many signs of early-day overgrazing, including the terraces caused by sheep trailing. Continue 8.0 miles to the intersection. There is a view of the Charleston reservoir straight ahead. Turn left. The road to the right leads to the Bruneau River, and eventually—in about 50 miles—to I-80 and the ranching community of Deeth.

Continue 2.6 miles. The abandoned ranch here was begun by the Prunty family. Continue 3.0 miles; this is the Walker ranch, not abandoned. Drive 0.8 miles to a fork in the road. Take the right-hand fork; the left one leads to ranches and private property.

Drive 0.5 miles. Here is the site of old Charleston. Nothing remains of this former tough and lawless little mining center, except for a modern ranch house on the site. Continue 0.9 miles to the Humboldt National Forest boundary. Heed the Forest Service warning signs, and stay on the main road. Drive 5.6 miles, and enjoy the mountain view. The red mountain is Fox Creek Peak; the one that appears to be of solid rock is apparently unnamed. The road to Jarbidge leads along the side of these peaks.

Continue 5.5 miles to Coon Creek Summit. Here the vegetation changes from nearly all deciduous trees to a mixture with conifers. You may enjoy the wild flowersg and wild country, as we do. We saw a pair of eagles playing a game of ''lazy 8'' here. Drive another 2.8 miles to Bear Creek Summit, and along Bear Creek Meadows. Then drive another 4.5 miles down to the crossroads at the bottom of the canyon and turn left for the Jarbidge townsite.

We always enjoy the ride through this beautiful and historic canyon; Jarbidge is 1.8 miles ahead. In Jarbidge during the summer months there are gasoline, a limited grocery store that doubles as a museum, post office, bar, cafe, ranger station, and hotel of sorts. The population in summer and in the deer-hunting season may reach 200. In the winter, both population and temperature are about zero. Camping and picnic grounds spread all along this stretch of the Jarbidge River. The Pine Creek campground has beautiful, primitive sites. If you plan to hike in the Jarbidge Wilderness, check with the ranger in Jarbidge.

Drive north down the canyon about 7.0 miles to see the columns and palisades that could have provided a basis for the legend of the giant Ja-Ha-Bich. On a bright day near the end of summer, when the aspens

had begun to turn golden, we saw blooming golden rod, fireweed, yarrow, asters, thistles, rabbit brush, and mulleins. The clematis vines contain their strange and lovely white plumes. We found ripe elderberries and bright red rose hips. We kicked a flock of chukars out of the road, and watched ravens at play in the wind currents.

Return to Elko now, approximately 115 miles. You may enjoy the view from the opposite direction.

TOUR FOUR, Cattle country: Elko — Tuscarora — Owyhee — Mountain City and return. Approximately 212 miles round trip. Make sure you have a full gasoline tank, and pack a picnic.

Leaving the museum, drive west on Idaho Street, and take SR 225 north at the western edge of town. Pass the airport, cross the I-80 freeway, and continue into the Independence Mountains ahead. Drive 11.6 miles to Adobe Summit. Continue 14.5 miles to Dinner Station. This was a stop on the Elko-Tuscarora stage line, where hungry travelers could be fed before facing another long journey across the deserts.

Drive another 4.2 miles to the intersection with SR 226, and turn left toward Tuscarora. Stay on the paved road; side roads lead to ranches. Continue 16.5 miles; at this place in 1981, Petrochem Company was drilling an experimental oil well. Drive 1.2 miles through Taylor Canyon (a bar and cabins), then another 0.3 miles and make a left turn on a graded dirt road to Tuscarora. Drive 0.8 miles, and look on the sidehill ahead; there is Tuscarora. Continue 4.7 miles, and turn right to Tuscarora.

Tuscarora's facilities are very limited, but the town is a very interesting place to visit. There are no commercial establishments here on a regular basis. On the street behind the post office is a pottery school operated by the Parks family. Visitors are welcome to see this establishment with its hand-made kilns that fire the products made from local clay.

The museum in Tuscarora, operated by the Phillips family, is open most of the year, unless they decide to leave for a while. The museum has a small admission charge. There are displays and exhibits of Tuscarora relics and photos, and mineral and gun collections. The proprietors also sell picture postcards of Tuscarora's early days and a Tuscarora cookbook that belongs in your collection. The town itself has some picturesque ruins, a pioneer cemetery, and only a few people—friendly residents who will cheerfully answer your questions.

When you have finished your tour of Tuscarora, return to the road on which you arrived; at the two brick chimney ruins, turn left (east) on a good gravel road. Drive 4.4 miles and cross the Owyhee River; you are driving through Independence Valley, one of the important cattle ranching sections of Elko County.

Continue 1.6 miles to paved SR 226, and turn left. While we crossed Independence Valley in late summer, we saw golden eagles, blackbirds, ravens, magpies, doves, and a little barn owl. Continue 6.0 miles, and look to the left; there is the old Spanish Ranch founded by Pedro Altube. Drive along SR 226, and take time to admire the cattle ranches founded by pioneer hard work, now carried on by commercial operators who fly in on their private planes to check on resident caretakers. Do also watch for livestock on the road; much of this is open grazing country.

Continue 11.1 miles to the intersection at the end of SR 226. This is the site of the old town of Deep Creek, but there are no signs of it except for mine dumps on the sidehills. Turn left on the graded dirt road toward Owyhee.

Drive 5.8 miles to the sign for Wilson reservoir, and go straight ahead. You will be continuing for several miles now through the holdings of the Petan Company, much of which formerly belonged to the pioneer Basque Garat family. The Petan Company was founded by C. H. "Pete" Jackson and his wife Ann; the "Petan" is a combination of their first names. The Jacksons were not native to this area, but they loved it through a long and prosperous ranching career. Drive 2.1 miles; note the aspen groves on the side of Wilson Peak, which dominates this landscape. Drive 2.9 miles; the Petan Company headquarters are on the left.

Drive 3.6 miles; there is a side road to the right, but go straight ahead. Continue 1.2 miles; the Petan

Company's 24 ranch (formerly the Garat home) is on the right. This is Elko County's most important, historic and prosperous cattle land. Continue driving 8.2 miles, and enter the Duck Valley Indian Reservation. You will be on this Shoshone-Paiute installation for several miles. The reservation overlaps two states, and is considered one of the more progressive organizations of its kind in the West. As you drive, Sheep Creek Reservoir will be visible ahead. Drive 1.9 miles to the entrance of the reservoir camping and picnic grounds. Here are a variety of facilities for fishing, boating, semi-primitive camping, and a trailer holding-tank dump. We enjoyed watching the water birds on the shoreline.

From the reservoir turnoff, continue 7.3 miles to the beginning of the pavement, and keep to the right. As you drive, watch for grazing livestock, and stay on the main road. Side roads lead to private property.

Drive 2.9 miles on the paved road to the stop sign at SR 225, and turn left into Owyhee. Owyhee has some commercial facilities, an Indian hospital, and gas stations. We saw only one handicraft shop, a leather-worker. The cemeteries are 2.4 miles through the town, one on either side of the highway. Return to the intersection with SR 225 where you entered. Drive south on SR 225 toward Mountain City and Elko. This is a beautiful and easy drive up the Owyhee River canyon.

Drive 11.9 miles to Mountain City. In the 1980s, the mining boom changed this sleepy little town into a hustling commercial village, complete with a casino to serve the traffic from Idaho.

Drive 2.5 miles to the site of Patsville. Here was Rio Tinto's "whoopee town," escape from the uniformity of the company town at the mine. The great Rio Tinto is exactly a mile up the dirt road. Here was S. Frank Hunt's dream come true. The dream came true a second time in the 1980s, as the place reopened following a rise in metals prices. Visitors are not welcome at Rio Tinto while the mine is in operation.

Continue 13.3 miles up the canyon of the Owyhee, and you will enjoy one of the section's scenic areas; stop at the view point of Wildhorse Dam. Along the lake are campgrounds and picnic sites, but few other facilities. This is a very popular fishing lake for Elko County and Idaho residents, and the fish are said to be huge.

Drive along the lake, continuing on SR 225, 17.4 miles to North Fork. This site that now serves as a Highway Department maintenance station was once a busy settlement serving stockraisers with a school, saloon, and grocery store. The adobe building once housed a soda fountain. The Crumley family and then Bing Crosby had ranches at North Fork.

Return now to Elko, 54 miles south, viewing the expanses of Nevada's greatest cattle region.

TOUR FIVE, The Ruby Range: Elko — Lamoille — Halleck and return. Approximately 96 miles round trip. Elko County has some of the most spectacular scenery in the West. Pack a lunch or camping gear.

Leave the museum, driving west on Idaho Street to Twelfth, turn left, cross the bridge and follow signs for SR 227 and SR 228. Drive 1.3 miles to the junction and turn left. Drive another 3.2 miles to Elko Summit. Here is the first view of the Ruby Mountains, which you will enjoy during this tour.

Continue another 2.1 miles to the junction with SR 228, and go straight ahead on SR 227; this is not the time to take side roads. Continue on SR 227 for 4.7 miles, and go straight ahead through the Spring Creek crossroads. Drive another 2.0 miles to the next Spring Creek crossing, and again, go straight ahead on SR 227.

Drive 5.5 miles to the Lamoille Canyon Road. Turn right. The views from the 13.5-mile road into the canyon offer mountain splendor at any season (don't try it in the winter). There are campgrounds, picnic areas, and view points with signs for the entire length of the drive. The most important features of the canyon are those having to do with its glacial origins. The Forest Service has prepared informative plaques; take time to read them. At Avalance Overlook information site (a mile from the far end of the canyon), look for beaver dams and lodges.

At the end of the 13.5-mile drive is the trail head area. Here are long and short hikes into the high moun-

tains, where you may enjoy glacial lakes and gorgeous scenery.

Completing your visit to Lamoille Canyon, return to SR 227, and turn right; drive 0.6 miles to the Lamoille Valley historical marker. At Lamoille, you will find limited services and an interesting rural community.

From the historical marker, drive east through town 0.5 miles to the Presbyterian church, and turn left on a graded dirt road. Drive through this typical Nevada ranching country for 3.3 miles, to a road coming from the right. Stay to the left; the road goes to a ranch.

Drive 0.6 miles; keep right at the intersection. As you drive, the view to the west is of the huge fertile Humboldt River valley that holds Elko and its environs.

Drive northeast for 2.4 miles, and go left at the fork; the right-hand road leads to a ranch. Drive another 2.2 miles, and bear to the right, across the cattle guard. Drive another 1.6 miles, across John Day Creek, to the sign for the Soldier Creek Road; go straight ahead. Drive 1.1 miles to the Fort Halleck site marker, a stone pillar with a metal plaque. Any ruins of the fort would be in the grove of trees behind the marker, on private and fenced land.

From the Fort Halleck marker, drive north for 6.4 miles on the main traveled road to the junction with SR 229, and turn left toward Halleck. Drive 2.0 miles. The road to Starr Valley leads to ranches; stay on SR 229. Continue 8.9 miles to Halleck. Here is only a post office and railroad siding that serves the surrounding ranches, which must seem very isolated at times. Continue 0.8 miles to the Fort Halleck historical marker, on the left side of the road. From the marker, follow signs to the I-80 access road toward Elko (west). Return to Elko, 20.0 miles.

TOUR SIX, Towns that water built: Elko — Wells — Metropolis and return. Approximately 130 miles round trip. Pack a picnic or plan to visit a restaurant in Wells.

Leave the museum, take the first access road to I-80 east, and drive 50 miles to Wells. Wells has all facilities for travelers. Take time, too, to drive around this little railroad village. The street fronting on the railroad tracks is especially picturesque. Here are numerous historic buildings, recalling Wells's long-time status as a travel stopping place.

In Wells, turn north at the intersection of Sixth (the main street) and Lake Avenue. Cross the railroad tracks, and turn left on Eighth Street. After 0.3 miles, the pavement ends. Drive straight ahead, parallel to the tracks, 0.3 miles to the Humboldt Wells historical marker on the right-hand side of the road. Drive another 0.4 miles, cross the cattle guard, and the pavement starts again.

Drive north along the paved road for 4.8 miles, and look to the right for hot springs in a small mound. The springs here occur along a fault line, and are not considered especially hot, although they do not freeze over even in very cold winters. Continue north 3.3 miles through the Peavey ranch, and where the road curves sharply to the left in 0.4 miles, look off the pavement straight ahead to the yellow trail marker. This marker, placed by the Trails West organization, indicates that this area was one of the first watering spots on the Nevada section of the California Trail.

Continue west 3.5 miles to the end of the pavement. The road is adequate for your passenger car. Drive another 0.8 miles, and turn left. Drive 1.5 miles, and look ahead to the ruins of Metropolis. The place has been completely abandoned since the 1950s, and this is what is left of the Pacific Reclamation Company's pipe dream of an agricultural paradise on the desert.

Return to Wells, and then to Elko via I-80, approximately 65 miles.

Lincoln School, Metropolis

EAST-CENTRAL NEVADA

Ruins at Cherry Creek

EAST-CENTRAL NEVADA

In contrast to sections with more diversified history, the east-central region belongs almost exclusively to the minerals industry. No large lakes, no long-flowing rivers mark this section. There is a small amount of agriculture, mainly in the valleys separating the several mountain ranges that cross Nevada. These features, along with an official Scenic Area and two state parks comprise the landscape of the White Pine region. The history of this section, however, is among the most colorful and interesting of all. The climate is healthful, if dry. And the Scenic Area stands as a world-famous and remarkable attraction.

Exploration

Before mining began here, White Pine was just a pathway to somewhere else. Jedediah Smith, first white man to traverse the Great Basin, crossed this area along what later became part of the Overland (Simpson-Egan) Trail. Subsequently, United States government surveyors came through the area, mapping for wagon roads. The earliest of these, Howard Egan, surveyed a cutoff from the more northerly Emigrant Trail in 1855. In 1859, the Army's Captain James Simpson drew the maps for what became the Simpson-Egan route. This early road crossed from east to west: Spring Station, Antelope Springs, Spring Valley, Schell Creek, Egan Canyon, Butte Station, through Ruby Valley, and Jacob's Well. When the Pony Express was established in 1860, the riders generally followed this historic Simpson-Egan trail. Ruby Station, the Pony relief stop, was probably the first building in White Pine County. Another main way-station for the Overland Telegraph was also in Ruby Valley. But the first genuine settlement in the area came with the ore discoveries in the west-central part of what became White Pine County.

Treasure Hill

In October 1865, a group of prospectors from Austin came into what was later named the White Pine Mining District. Their finds of copper, lead, iron, and antimony were large enough that a Philadelphia concern started production by forming the Monte Cristo Mining Company. The company sent a superintendent to Nevada and took over development in 1867, building a mill to process the materials. The same autumn, a discovery on Treasure Hill changed the history of eastern Nevada.

A. J. Leathers, a blacksmith, had an Indian friend named Napias (silver) Jim. Jim showed Leathers a piece of rich ore from which the blacksmith produced a button of silver. The price of the white metal then was $1.32 an ounce, and the mine that Napias Jim had showed Leathers became the Hidden Treasure mine, the ore assaying from five hundred to eight hundred dollars a ton. Within a short time, T. E. Eberhardt had a horn silver mine, with ore at eight hundred to a thousand dollars a ton. A third operation, the Keystone, showed a material that looked rather like putty—nearly pure silver at fifteen to twenty thousand dollars a ton! By the spring of 1868, Nevada's shortest, most intense mining rush had begun. Treasure Hill was a magnet for every boomer, promoter, card shark, merchant-capitalist, prostitute, and prospector in the West. Three cities came into being: Hamilton at the bottom of Treasure Hill, Treasure City on the hillside, and Shermantown and Eberhardt adjacent to one another on the foot opposite Hamilton.

Hamilton was the largest of these. Beginning as a tent city with more saloons than lodging houses, the place soon had substantial quarried-stone buildings, mills, graded streets and sidewalks, and other trappings of a real town. Hamilton became an incorporated city in 1869, and the same year, after the legislature created White Pine County, the county seat. Probably a peak of 4,000 people lived there, although it was widely claimed that there were 10,000.

Treasure City's rise was nearly as rapid and picturesque. A bank, Wells Fargo office, hotels, homes, and amusement places made this the second-largest town in White Pine, with a population of about 2,000. Shermantown, where huge mills processed the ores, had about a thousand people. Nearly half the population of White Pine County was foreign-born, the majority being from Ireland and Great Britain. The boomers and promoters seemed never quiet about the marvelous prospects of Treasure City's mines, Shermantown's great mills, and the riches of the town of Hamilton. Five different stage lines kept the streets busy with freight from the Elko area—and the saloon-keepers happy.

Before long, scientific mining engineers, both American and English, began to examine the mines that prospectors had claimed inexhaustible. Their findings disappointed the residents of White Pine, who had not wanted to believe that the discoveries were deposits, not veins. Adding to the town's problems, real-estate speculators had become too active, driving lot prices beyond the reach of prospective residents. Prohibitive freight rates drove away some businessmen. A miners' strike, bad weather, bank failure, and general business doldrums began an exodus from Treasure Hill in 1870. A group of young Hamilton businessmen formed the "Order of Deserted Lovers," recognizing the departure of numerous female residents.

The boom was really ended by 1871. In the summer of 1873, Alexander Cohn lighted a fire that nearly destroyed the part of Hamilton that was left, hoping to collect a little insurance on his losses. The exodus from Treasure Hill increased after that; Hamilton disincorporated in 1875. Soon, the county treasury had only $1.75 to meet bills of $3,000. The first White Pine borrasca was underway. Treasure City's vaunted mines played out by 1878, and the town was deserted. The courthouse in Hamilton burned in 1885, and the county seat moved to Ely in 1887.

English financiers, interested early in the mines of Treasure Hill, held on for nearly two decades, trying to develop the area on an industrial scale; but even-

tually, in 1893, even that effort died. The towns of Treasure Hill became ghosts. White Pine's historian observed that those towns produced more excitement than money, and that was true; during its entire boom period, and later attempts at development by the English companies, the yield from Treasure Hill was less than $10 million.

Although they were ghosts, the settlements did not lack callers. One of the favorite pastimes of Nevadans—and of visitors to the state—became that of exploring the deserted camps. These hobbyists even invented a new term, and "ghost-towning" became the weekend or vacation activity for hundreds and then thousands of tourists. Nell Murbarger, a newspaper writer, published *Ghosts of the Glory Trail* (1956), with colorful tales and directions for getting to the old camps. Again, the traffic increased, and the equipment of the ghost-towners expanded and improved. Rock picks, shovels, chain saws, and finally metal detectors were part of the everyday luggage in the back of the pickup truck. Piece by piece, stick by board, brick by block, and even grave marker by tombstone, the White Pine ghost towns disappeared. Concurrently, the garages or backyard treasure piles of Nevada and the surrounding states filled. Visitors to Hamilton in the 1940s found the remains of the elegant Withington hotel, a mill, and Wells Fargo office, and several boarded-up houses there. Treasure City's bank vault and bank walls were still in place in the 1950s. By the 1960s, the traffic was so heavy, and Hamilton so barren, that the old ghost-towners would not have recognized it. Other ghost-town guides, more complete and extensive than Murbarger's, helped to clear out the last of Hamilton, Treasure City, Shermantown, and Eberhardt. This activity all aided the prospectors and miners who brought on the mining boom of the 1970s and 1980s. Then, the flanks of Treasure Hill were dotted by mobile homes and travel trailers, equally as hodge-podge as the tents and shanties of the early days. Bulldozers, power shovels, and graders supported the new miners. And the mining companies and their representatives, goaded by dreams of $23,000 ore, were equally as optimistic about the prospective returns from the mines of the White Pine District as their predecessors had been (they also had security guards, with side-arms to prevent claim-jumping or high-grading). Good, graded roads to the high-altitude camps marked the new prosperity of these industrial concerns. But somehow, it just was not the same.

Ward

All mining camps have a similar pattern: discovery, publicity, bonanza or boom, decline, and finally, borrasca, or final bust. White Pine's towns followed that design faithfully, from the 1860s into the last of the twentieth century. The next of the fabulous and famous discoveries of White Pine was known as Ward. Silver, lead, and copper deposits in the Egan range southeast of Hamilton were discovered by Thomas F. Ward in 1872. The Martin White company of San Francisco took over development in 1875, and began a boom.

The difficult ores of the Ward district made life hard for workers and developers alike. The first industrial construction reflecting that fact was six charcoal (or coke) ovens built in 1875. Trees were cut in the surrounding hills and hauled to the site of these furnaces in order to produce the charcoal used in smelting the ores. The White group built a mill-smelter that was finished in 1877; it used coke from the ovens. A second mill was constructed in 1878, but neither of these proved successful at dealing with the complex materials. In 1879, the mill was closed—apparently for repairs—and someone, perhaps for vengeance, fired the hundreds of bushels of charcoal stored in the kilns. The fire left the kilns standing but effectively ruined at least one of them for further coking.

Ward had all the trappings of a typical mining camp, including a blacksmith shop, city hall, school, restaurants, saloons, stores, and a newspaper. But the area was unsuitable for a town, being on uneven ground; the weather at over 8,000 feet elevation was severe, the ores proved more and more difficult to process, and the place declined quickly. A fire in 1883 destroyed several buildings. A booster claimed that 2,000 people (probably half that) lived in Ward at the peak; by 1886 there were only twelve registered voters there, and two years after that, none. Less than a quarter million dollars worth of ore was reported to official sources.

The ruins of Ward came apart rather soon, owing in part to weather, and partly to "ghost-towners." Still,

Ward Charcoal Ovens State Monument

the great charcoal ovens, the largest of their kind in Nevada, stood to guard the area east of the town. Their picturesque and rather eerie presence became an eastern Nevada landmark. With the establishment of the Park System, the state assumed ownership of the ovens, established a picnic area, and graded the road. In the 1980s, the charcoal kilns provide an interesting, if somewhat unusual, stopping place for tourists. Nearly indestructible, and possessing a marvelous acoustic quality for singing of campfire songs or for the shouts of children, the coke ovens of Ward serve a purpose for which they were never designed.

Cherry Creek

While Ward was still booming, Cherry Creek arose. The first discoveries of gold and silver in what became that town were made in 1863 by a company of soldiers. These were largely ignored, and a mining district was organized only in 1872. The development of the mines was rather slow until 1880 when the population peaked at about 1,500. The most important mines were the

---

"Dancing, of course, was the social activity. And, the social life of the early days was done on a much nicer scale than it's being done now. There were dances held in Cherry Creek in the upstairs hall there. It was about the only two-story building that I can recall. There was a store, a general merchandise store, and a post office on the first floor, and upstairs was the dance hall. . . .

"Now, there was a little sociability aside from the dance, too. There were two saloons in Cherry Creek. One of them had the reputation of selling 'fighting' whiskey and the other 'loving' whiskey. It depended upon where the menfolk congregated. . . . As a rule, the people were very, very sociable and followed the amenities of the day."

— Charles Gallagher, photographer
and state legislator

Teacup (or ticup, a Shoshone word for biscuit), Exchequer, and the Star, the latter being the largest and longest producer. A townsite was laid out as early as 1873. The name of the town probably derives from the wild cherries or chokecherries in the area of the Egan range where the mines were discovered.

The first buildings in Cherry Creek came prefabricated, as it were, from the abandoned town of Schellbourne: a printshop that became a general store, a hotel, and restaurant. By 1874, several hundred people lived in what was presumed to be a thriving camp. The usual Chinatown with its customary facilities formed part of Cherry Creek. Besides being a mining town, Cherry Creek devoted itself to entertainment. The pioneers and historians of White Pine all recalled dances, literally dozens of dances at Cherry Creek Hall (later Williamson Hall). Even the terrible fire of 1901, which occurred long after Cherry Creek had officially declined, did not stop the dances. People went to Cherry Creek dances from everywhere within traveling distance until there were no more dance floors or musicians there.

Inevitably, the mines played out. A financial panic in 1883 and the closing of the Star mine the next year meant the end of Cherry Creek's prosperity. A brief bid for the county seat in 1885 (after the courthouse fire in Hamilton) failed, and the status went to Ely. Cherry Creek's mines produced a little less than $4 million, mostly during the boom, and a bit during a cleanup operation in the 1930s.

Taylor

Directly across the valley from Ward, discoveries were made at what became Taylor. Silver was found there, and a mining district was organized in 1873. Taylor developed and declined rather quickly, but it briefly became the largest town in White Pine County. A Wells Fargo office, saloons, a school, opera house, stores, and a newspaper office made it a lively community, but not a particularly colorful one. A White Pine historian declared that the most violent event there was a pushing match between two men who disagreed on the qualifications of President Grover Cleveland. Taylor's life was short—only about eighteen months. The Monitor and Argus mines proved not very productive, even though an English company tried to develop them commercially. Probably the population peaked at 1,500, and the place was quickly deserted after 1886. Production amounted to less than a million dollars in the nineteenth century. Ghost towning in the mid-twentieth century took care of most of Taylor's remains, and then bull-dozers in the 1980s erased the rest.

Osceola

The last of the important nineteenth-century mining camps in White Pine was Osceola. This camp, somewhat isolated from the others in the Snake Range, had an unusual development. Osceola was strictly a gold camp, and a hydraulic one on the California model at that. Western travelers could recall seeing the Mother Lode gold camps of California, with high piles of washed gravel to mark their rise and decline. Osceola's environs resembled that. Gold was discovered at Osceola in the summer of 1872, and a mining district was organized that autumn.

A twelve-mile-long gold-bearing quartz belt yielded gold dust and nuggets for ten years, from 1876 to 1886; the largest nugget was said to be worth $6,000, with gold at $20.67 per ounce. Osceola was no boomtown. Development was systematic, with a water system being designed by a man named Hampton. Three hundred men were employed to dig the water ditch around the mountain to near the base of Wheeler Peak. Timber for the flumes was harvested locally. While it was not a boomtown, Osceola did contain most of the usual amenities, including a long-lasting mercantile store owned by the Marriott family. Among the better-known mine owners and operators was E. J. "Jot" Travis. A favorable location on well-traveled roads made Osceola a good stopping place.

Eventually, of course, the best years were over. One after another, the buildings decayed or burned, and the families who had lived there died out. Ghost-towners

took care of most of the relics. Despite the excitement of gold in this remote location, Osceola produced less than three quarters of a million dollars. The remains of the great ditch continued to mark the vicinity of Wheeler Peak at the end of the twentieth century, while the scars of the hydraulic mining marked the hillsides.

Livestock and Agriculture

The agriculture of White Pine supplied the mining towns, and created a certain amount of economic activity. If the agriculture was marginal, it was important at least to a strong segment of the population. Indeed, the food and fiber produced in the section often provided nearly the only business activity there.

Before the turn of the twentieth century, the largest amount of land in use in White Pine County—over 4.7 million acres—was devoted to grazing livestock; about 12,000 acres were utilized for crops, primarily hay, but also potatoes, grain, and eventually row crops. These activities were mainly in Steptoe, Spring, and White Pine valleys, where pioneer ranchers established homesteads or small empires. The climate of east-central Nevada did not support large amounts of fruit or tender vegetables, and this segment of the industry never did develop. Livestock included cattle, sheep, hogs, and poultry—typical meat animals to supply the mining camps. The most numerous animals were sheep; many of White Pine's livestockmen trailed woollies through the northern section of the state. Indeed, with the dying out of the mining camps, and until the great copper boom of the twentieth century, the sheepmen were the economic kings of White Pine.

Some of the barons of White Pine's ovine trade were John Tippett of Antelope Valley; William McCurdy, who had holdings near Tippett's; John Weaver, the Parrish family, and G. Georgetta of Deep Creek; A. L. Parker of the White Pine Mountain area; and Thomas Nelson, the first of the northern Nevadans to use Chinese sheepherders and camptenders. The old-timers of Cherry Creek recalled these Chinese, regarding them somewhat as a curiosity of the livestock business. Among the first sheep owners in White Pine was the famous Howard Egan, whose name marks numerous sites in the county; he was not really in the sheep business, nor did he have them for long, being a surveyor by trade, but he successfully sold animals in the Overland trade in the 1860s. Many cattle ranches of White Pine had sheep as well, although this fact is overlooked by the romancers of the Old West, whose cattlemen and sheepmen invariably had blood feuds and shootouts.

Still, the cattlemen were better known. One of the big outfits of White Pine was the Adams-McGill combine. Jewett Adams (once governor of Nevada) and W. N. McGill formed a cattle partnership that lasted for twenty years. McGill himself, after an early career as a surveyor and miner, established a fine ranch in 1886 that became a landmark in central Nevada. With partners or alone, McGill ran both cattle and sheep in three counties. At one time in the 1890s, he was the largest taxpayer in White Pine. The ranch site was destined to become something other than agricultural; in the twentieth century, after several years of smelting in the town named in his honor, the dusty, talc-like waste from the smelter buried McGill's former ranch.

A second large owner of land and cattle in White Pine was Abner C. Cleveland. Cleveland came to Nevada in the 1860s, residing first in Washoe County, where he served, among other things, as a county commissioner and assemblyman. After moving to White Pine, he served there as state senator. Cleveland was responsible for building a toll road north from Hamilton during its boom years. In 1873, he purchased a large ranch in Spring Valley and went into the cattle business. Becoming prominent in that place, Cleveland was an important state politician as well, and a candidate for governor in 1894 and in 1902. The Cleveland ranch remains a landmark of the beautiful valley; even after it changed owners, the place was known by the Cleveland name.

Other men and their families had ranches in the valleys of White Pine, but the major industry was mining, so their names are not prominent in history despite

their contributions. Among these men were Henry Comins, miner, businessman, three-term legislator, and rancher of eastern White Pine; and W. C. Gallagher, rancher of Duck Creek. Comins Lake and Gallagher's Gap remain to mark their memories. One man who was apparently a farmer on a truly marginal scale left his fame in another way; his name was Absalom, or "Ab," Lehman.

Lehman's place was in southeastern White Pine County. He farmed there from about the 1860s until he died in 1891. Because the place was small, Lehman had time on his hands; one day—perhaps as early as the 1870s—he stumbled onto a natural marvel. He found a limestone cave of glorious beauty and began to explore it. In the early 1880s, Lehman took friends, neighbors, tourists, and publicists into the cave, first as adventure, and then for fees. As the fame of the place spread, the cave was also recognized by scientists as having various unique qualities. By 1922, Congress had made the site a National Monument; in 1933, the National Park Service took over and began to develop the area.

Under various government agencies, Lehman's

"Ab Lehman of Snake Valley reports that he and others have struck a cave of wondrous beauty on his ranch near Jeff Davis Peak. Stalactites of extraordinary size hang from its roof, and stalagmites equally large rear their heads from the floor. A stalactite weighing six hundred pounds has been taken from the cave and planted beside the monument erected by Ivers to mark the spot where he observed the last transit of Venus on Lehman's ranch. . . . The cave was explored for about 200 feet when the points of stalactites and stalagmites came so close together as to offer a bar to further progress. They will again explore the cave armed with sledge hammers and break their way into what appears to be another chamber."

— *Ward Reflex*, April 15, 1885

Lehman Cave

cave became an exceedingly well-preserved geological phenomenon, despite the fact that tours were conducted all year by guides there. Near the end of the twentieth century, much of the cave is as Lehman and his friends left it, and tourists continue to enjoy it.

The district surrounding Lehman's cave also has marvelous natural beauty. The second-highest peak in Nevada, Mount Wheeler, stands at 13,058 feet, in the Snake Range, inviting campers, travelers, and climbers to its heights. The place has been declared a National Scenic Area, placing it under the protection of the federal government. In the 1950s and 1960s, a movement was underway for National Park status for the Wheeler Peak Scenic Area and Lehman's cave. This activity came to nothing, owing to lack of support (or outright opposition) in eastern Nevada. National Park status seems unneeded to enjoy the outdoor wonders of this section of White Pine.

Preston and Lund

Mormons (Latter Day Saints) were among the first settlers in Nevada; they were not early, but were very active for some time in White Pine. The church purchased hundreds of head of livestock for some of its communicants in the Duck Creek area and elsewhere, with the customary understanding that the church would profit from the arrangement. Then came the great "white winter" of 1889-1890. All over northern Nevada, livestock died, frozen or starved to death. Every farmer and rancher had a horror tale of cows standing frozen in fields, of sheep frozen under several feet of snow, of horses frozen in their stalls, and finally, of spring floods on the streams backed up with swollen carcasses. This great natural disaster hit every ranch with its terrors. Oddly enough, it caused the building of two of Nevada's Mormon communities.

In 1887, after decades of enacting other statutes against Mormon practices, Congress passed the Edmunds-Tucker Act, prohibiting the Mormon Church from making business arrangements with livestock producers and ordering their stock expropriated. Animals were taken at government fiat by non-Mormon ranchers. Most of the cattle died in the "white winter." Then, yielding to national pressure, the Mormons renounced their unpopular plural marriage practices in 1890. In return, Congress decided that the Edmunds-Tucker Act was inappropriate and perhaps unconstitutional and repealed it in 1893. Federal authorities ordered the livestock returned to the former owners; understandably, the new owners stalled. As the anti-polygamy strictures of the Mormons endured, the government forced the issue in 1896, demanding that the confiscated livestock be returned. Unable to turn over the animals, the non-Mormon ranchers were forced to give up their land. On those ranches, in 1898, the Latter Day Saints began a colonization. The Tom Plane, Maddox, and McQuitty ranches formed the core of the colony, with additional land purchased from Adams and McGill. They called the place the Georgetown Ranch. There the colony stayed until

Preston School

1902, when the copper companies wanted the land for a smelter and paid the colony $35,000 for it. East Ely was built on the site. The Mormons then needed to move.

The LDS church sent the Georgetown residents, colonizers, and missionaries to the White River district with recruits from Utah to lead the settlement. Two small agricultural communities grew out of this effort: Preston, and six miles south, Lund. Each was named for a Mormon leader: Anthony Lund, a member of the church's governing body, and William Preston, a bishop. All through the next three quarters of a century, the LDS continued its presence and the farmers and town settlers enjoyed their lives there. The tiny communities changed hardly at all, except for the installation of twentieth-century conveniences; they stood in contrast to the rowdier mining camps of White Pine.

"One time a 'Sky Merchant' arrived at the ranch, hoping to bring some of us wild ones to God. . . . He got all of the boys to kneel beside their chairs and then began with an elaborate prayer. He prayed for the crops, the cattle, the food, the pigs that were for the kill on the morrow, the weather, the moon; in fact, the prayer was so lengthy that Chris . . . drew from his pocket a plug of . . . chewing tobacco and whispered to me, 'Here, for Christ's sake, take a chew and pass it on; maybe we can steady our nerves until he's through.' Once he slowed down and we thought he'd stop, but he spit on his hands, rubbed them hard together and began again. The tobacco made its rounds, and the evening's revival meeting was a lively topic of conversation the following day as we scraped the hogs."

— Cowboy on the Tom Plane ranch, quoted by Effie O. Read, *White Pine Lang Syne*

Ely

Ranching and outdoor recreation would never have profited White Pine as mining did. The real history of the area belongs to the mineral industry, and especially to copper.

The early history of the Robinson mining district resembled that of almost any similar region in Nevada. Prospectors found gold, silver, lead, zinc, later manganese, but essentially copper. The ores were low grade, and the technology of the 1870s did not permit development of the copper deposits. There was only a small furnace built in 1873 by the Selby Copper Company of Ohio at what was then the only settlement in White Pine County, Mineral City. The operation proved unsuccessful and shut down within a short time. Still prospectors doing assessment work on previous discoveries managed to continue showing copper ores in considerable quantities. In 1888, the local newspaper contained a comment on a large copper belt in the region, and the writer claimed that only capital was needed to develop industrial operation. There were mills crushing the rocks, but the material required smelting. Smelting, being more sophisticated, is therefore more expensive. The necessary capital was not forthcoming during the nineteenth century, although there was a fair amount of optioning and trading during the 1890s. Thus the district was reasonably well known and explored by 1900.

In September 1900, two young miners drifted into Ely. They had between them the magnificent sum of seventy-five cents, but they also had the promise of jobs at the Chainman mine. Their names, destined to become a part of Nevada's most productive mining district, were Edwin Gray and David Bartley. Somehow, the local newspaper received and printed a rumor that they were capitalists there to make large investments, so they were given considerable freedom to investigate various properties in the area. Gray and Bartley made the most of their privileges, and soon were the holders of options on a couple of promising-looking copper outcrops. Their previous experience in copper mining had been in Shasta County, California.

That year, 1900, marked the twentieth of a long economic depression in Nevada. The Comstock, largest-producing district in the state, had long since died out; the White Pine rush had brought disappointment and decline; the Reese River "excitement" had been mainly that, not money. In short, the time was right for something new to happen in Nevada. It was not an accident that mining was about to enjoy a revival.

All over the central part of the state in the late 1890s and at the turn of the century, eastern capital was paying for mineral exploration. Philadelphia and New York speculators spent many thousands of dollars in wages for engineers and prospectors to investigate the old mining districts, or to find new ones. In the case of the Robinson District, Mulford Martin of New York and a group led by the "copper king" himself, William Clark of Montana, had people on the ground. Martin's men had made extensive drillings and shafts, and Clark had personally visited the Robinson district before Gray and Bartley arrived.

In this atmosphere, it was probably inevitable that, given the mineral deposits' existence, someone would make a substantial discovery. It fell to the young miners, Bartley and Gray, to do just that. As the two worked on their optioned claims, they tunneled into good, low-grade copper ore, averaging about three percent. Given the technology of the time, this was not enough to cause a rush by financiers. A local merchant, William B. Graham, helped them to hold onto their options with a grubstake and loans over the next two years.

Copper was not an easy metal to extract. The processes were expensive, big plants would cost huge amounts, Ely was far from transportation centers where reduction operations existed; the problems seemed endless. And yet, the ore seemed good and potentially profitable.

In 1902, Mark Requa appeared. The son of a pioneer Comstock miner and industrialist, he was looking for investments in central Nevada, and already owned the Eureka and Palisade railroad. Within a short time, he had put together the White Pine Copper Company, capitalized at half a million dollars, and with its main assets the Ruth group of claims that Bartley and Gray had been developing in company with a few others.

Requa and his partners began to plan for development of the prospects. They needed to work on the ore, to find ways of determining its content, to make transportation of the ores economical, and finally, to design an industrial complex for reduction and smelting. The successful completion of these chores brought to Requa and his partners a certain amount of attention from the financial community, particularly in this case the Guggenheim concern. The Guggenheims literally moved in on Requa, and although he was briefly employed by the company over which they gained control, by the end of 1906, the Nevada Consolidated Copper Company announced that Requa had "retired." Nevada Con took over development, financing, and operation of the important copper mining business in White Pine.

In the fall of 1906, crews began preparing a benchland above the McGill ranch to accommodate a mill and smelter. Water came from a pipeline to Duck Creek into a system of five reservoirs with a storage capacity of over 260 million gallons. The first concentrator in the smelter was completed early in 1908; at that time more than 14 million tons of ore had been extracted from the Ruth group of claims discovered and worked by Gray, Bartley, and others. While all of eastern Nevada had a noisy celebration, the smelter shipped out the first load of blister copper on August 7, 1908. All through the eight years since the young miners walked into Ely with seventy-five cents between them, many thousands of dollars had gone into development of the mines. The next year, 1909, Nevada Con shipped $6.5 million worth of copper from the district. This figure was due to be exceeded many times over the next seventy years. The Robinson District proved to be Nevada's richest deposit.

The mines themselves, initially begun in the traditional tunnel-and-shaft style, were opened to pit development at about the same time. By 1916, two huge holes near Ruth were combined into a single excavation and named the Liberty Pit. The process involved stripping off the over-burden to expose the low-grade ores. Then roads—actually terraces—spiraled around and around the hole, and enormous steam shovels (later electric ones) loaded equally huge trucks, which then took their material to the railroad nearby. The ore body was truly tremendous, seemingly unending. The mine itself became somewhat of a tourist attraction.

The Kennecott Copper Company took over the operations in 1933, buying out the Nevada Consolidated. The pit mining continued, eventually to encompass three separate excavations. In time, even the low-grade ore seemed to be playing out, but the end came for added reasons. In the 1970s, the federal government, under provisions of the ''clean air'' act, imposed standards in the area. The Kennecott operators claimed that their mining process did not allow compliance with the standard; the government said it had to, or the mine must close. The mines closed in 1979. Kennecott, fearing for safety of visitors, shut off access to the former tourist view points. In the early 1980s, no traffic into the pit areas was allowed, and guards enforced the prohibition. Water, formerly pumped out of the lower depths, was allowed to make lakes of the pits. One of Nevada's great visitor magnets had gone, and Kennecott officials seemed unlikely to lift the restrictions. But it was heady while it lasted.

Nevada's richest mining district spawned not just copper, but also several towns of varying sizes and descriptions, a railroad that seemed full of romance to its aficionados, and a colorful landscape. Ely, of course, developed into a cosmopolitan little city, acting as a service and commercial center for the surrounding area. A favorable position on what became two U.S. highways provided a certain amount of trade in the city.

The county seat status at Ely also kept a number of bureaucrats and politicians in business. A rather short-lived promotion by the Nevada Consolidated to bring ''company town'' status to what was called Ely City resulted in construction of several buildings and offices on the townsite. This promotion lasted until about the end of 1908; the place was renamed East Ely, and the site declined somewhat, with several semi-deserted streets. In 1931, when Nevada legalized gambling, several establishments moved their games from the back room to the front, and others opened. In short, Ely provided commerce, business, and a political center for eastern Nevada. Politics was largely Democratic, in reflection of the labor contingent at the mines. Two newspapers, the *Daily Times* and the *Record*, had long histories, and interestingly, each was owned or operated by a state senator and then governor of Nevada: Vail Pittman at the *Times* was Democratic state senator for one term, and governor from 1945 to 1950; Charles Russell, his competitor at the *Record*, was a Republican state senator, and succeeded Pittman as governor. The two papers merged later. With the closing of the mines in 1979, Ely suffered somewhat of a depression, but retained enough population to continue serving a varied clientele.

McGill

The copper corporations, seeking somewhat more control over their employees, built company towns that had more permanency than East Ely. The smelter at McGill, under construction near the McGill ranch in 1906, caused a few people to begin a tent city near the site. By the end of 1908, with the earlier Ely City plan at an end, the company built some fifty concrete houses for its skilled employees, and then rows of low-cost units for others. These were rented at attractive rates to the employees, and the company town for the smelter had begun. The workers there appreciated the low-cost living arrangements and found everyday life quite pleasant at McGill. By 1910, nearly 2,000 people lived there, and several commercial establishments (rather limited in the number of places of traditional mining-camp entertainment) existed. The jail was directly adjacent to the saloon, an arrangement that company officers believed would serve as a reminder of the need for propriety. The company also built special facilities for the recreation of the workers—a gymnasium, library–reading room, a clubhouse with bowling alleys and swimming pool, and other encouragements for outdoor sports for which the company donated equipment. Police and fire protection, along with emergency medical facilities were part of the company arrangements.

McGill's need for labor attracted people literally

"We built sheds of material that was simply—it wasn't scavenged—you went and got it. There was no problem with it. You simply took what you needed. Eventually the company would let you have dirt for a lawn. This was all free. You didn't buy paint . . . You went down and asked for a requisition, and they gave you the paint to paint your house. . . . You could get almost anything you wanted this way. . . .

"[McGill residents] weren't poor people; they were well cared for across the board, but they didn't have a lot. They owed money, and maybe this is why they had as much as they did. They could go down and buy anything—you owed for it [at the company store], and there was no hesitation arranging credit. In fact, there was one theory that if you owed money you wouldn't be fired because they had to get their money out of you. . . .

"I went to work for [the company] at fifteen. My job was to clean up around the ore cars, on the top floor of the roasters. Wages were $3.10 per day, and this wasn't bad for a fifteen-year-old kid. . . . [The company] did remarkably well by most of the children who wanted to work. Some would go to work cleaning bricks. . . . This was a dusty job, and . . . if this was wet with sulfuric acid it would irritate skin, would burn your clothes and so forth. . . . [I]t was just making work for the kids."
                           — W. Wallace White, former McGill resident

---

from all over the world. The United States was then receiving what was generally called the "new immigration," people from southeastern Europe and Asia. McGill was soon divided into sections: Greek Town, Jap Town, Austrian Town. The "whites" lived in lower, middle, or upper townsite, according to their stations at the plant. These distinctions extended in social arrangements as well, and took some time to die out, but after World War I's xenophobias, and after a generation or two, if your name ended with -ovich, -poulos, or -anaka, hardly anyone took special notice; intermarriage became relatively common and the old separations between nationalities mostly erased themselves. The smelter stayed open, even after the local mines closed, processing ore from other states.

Ruth and Kimberly

The settlements at the mines were constructed by the company as well. Ruth and Kimberly, named respectively for the daughter of one of the miners and for one of the mining engineers, grew up at the sites. Ruth had the first building in the district, a stone cabin built by Gray and Bartley. In 1903, Mark Requa constructed two board-and-batten houses for his own family. After the organization of Nevada Consolidated, by 1905, Ruth had bunkhouses, a boarding house, post office, and a first-aid station/hospital. The place did not grow as rapidly as McGill, for the company officers lived at the smelter town. In fact, the original settlement died out quickly, buried under overburden. The company town was laid out in 1910; employees could rent a two-room house for $8 a month, and the corporation paid for lights, water, and heating fuel.

In time, a home considered palatial in those days was built for Walter Larsh, the mine general manager. Commercial establishments—a meat market, grocery store, poolhall-saloon, and similar necessities grew up. Ruth was considered a favored place to live or visit; a Labor Day celebration in 1912 drew a crowd of 4,000. By the 1980s, with the mines closed, no celebration was in order, and one probably would not attract *four* people.

Kimberly came into being, and then into prominence as another of the company towns. The original claims around Pilot Knob were owned by, among others, W. A. Clark, the Montana copper king. A post office was established in 1905. This, the oldest of the White Pine copper districts, dating from the 1870s and 1880s, soon after it joined the Nevada Consolidated group, had the sameness of geography that marked the other company towns: rows of neat houses, company-sponsored businesses and recreation, and no place to blow off steam. By the 1980s, Kimberly no longer needed such recreation; it had disappeared under the exigencies of the copper mining business.

"Whoopee Towns"

If the company towns had little sophisticated recreation, their satellites suffered no such lack. The colorful names included Smelterville, Rag Dump, and Riepetown. These places had houses of prostitution, saloons, poolhalls, dancehalls, in short, the needed amenities for rough mining camps. They made huge profits for their promoters and were the sites of endless police problems. One description probably fitted all, if one allowed for varying proportions. A White Pine historian wrote:

Rag Dump, a hell on earth, was just north of McGill. It received this name because most of its buildings were of canvas and calico. The riff-raff following the Ely boom easily made their way to Rag Dump, and it outdid all other places for moral ugliness. There were gunmen, desperadoes, scoundrels, obscene women . . . The . . . sporting houses allowed boys under sixteen years of age to enter and join the painted Jezebels in booze drinking and incubation of disease. (Effie O. Read, *White Pine Lang Syne*.)

Riepetown was probably not much better. After a fire there in 1917, company pressure almost succeeded in having the place abandoned, but promises of good behavior from Riepetown residents led to county assistance for improved fire protection and the town was rebuilt. Then Riepetown returned to its old ways. Finally, of course, the whoopee towns died; legalized gambling, modernization of other surrounding towns,

"Each ethnic group . . . had their own national holiday, and that's when all the trouble used to be. The Greeks would have a national holiday, and the Austrians and the Italians would always be there to try and stop them. The same with the Austrians. . . . They used to put on the big celebrations, and the others would all gang up on them, because, I think, they were in the majority . . . particularly at the mines. And whenever they had a holiday, you could look for one or two killings at pretty near every one. . . . I was a young man, and we used to go up [to Riepetown] and watch the celebrations sometimes. They never bothered anybody that didn't enter into the activity. You could watch it, and you were perfectly safe in watching it."

— Lester Hilp, druggist

"Rag Town and Rag Dump and Steptoe City and Smelterville were all just little places off-limits around McGill where the McGill supervision did not extend. They were not rough. They were places where if you wanted to go if the McGill clubs were closed, you could go out there. Or, if you wanted to perhaps carry on a little bit wilder than it would be permissible in the other saloons, those little towns were open. . . .

"I remember . . . a songstress in Dick Riepe's saloon. She was accompanied by her mother. The mother sat there with her knitting all the time while her daughter was singing. She usually sang songs by request. . . . Before she left, she gave a concert to the public in one of the motion picture theaters here. It was a very beautiful, delightful thing, attended by everybody, as a social function. Well then, things deteriorated and it got so women were singing in all of the saloons."

— Charles Gallagher, photographer, state senator

and then the closing of the mines ensured their demise. By the early 1980s, Riepetown was a mere collection of trash and cement foundations. Rag Dump had disappeared years before, and Smelterville simply dissolved into the desert.

The Nevada Northern Railway

The Nevada Northern Railway completed the industrial complex of mines, mills, and smelters in east-central Nevada. The line was promoted by old residents and newcomers alike. After a few years of discussion, the Nevada Northern was incorporated on June 1, 1905. Within two months, surveyors had completed their work of laying out a course from Cobre (Spanish for copper) on the Southern Pacific to the north, into Ely. Grading and construction of the standard-gauge road began almost at once, beginning at Cobre, south to Currie, through Cherry Creek, past McGill, into Ely, and out to the mining districts. As the rails advanced, the citizens developed considerable enthusiasm for celebrating "Railroad Days" when the road reached certain points. Some of the most memorable of those festivals were held in Cherry Creek and Ely.

The Nevada Northern reached Cherry Creek on July 4, 1906, and Railroad Day plans came to fruition on the 16th. Mark Requa made a speech in which he prophesied large-scale mining in the district, and state senator W. C. Gallagher saluted the fulfilled promise of a long-planned facility. The copper company and the railroad moguls treated Cherry Creek residents to champagne, and then the crews continued working south.

Ely's "Railroad Day" came at the end of September. A special train from Salt Lake City brought various dignitaries, while others from the west brought Nevada Governor John Sparks and U.S. Senator Francis G. Newlands. A copper spike made from local ore was driven by Requa. The politicians and capitalists made speeches, glowing with pride and promise about the future of the mines, the towns, and the railroad. Miniature copper spikes were distributed to the crowd.

W. N. McGill had prepared a huge barbecue in trenches dug on the courthouse lawn, and so the celebration began. Two dances entertained the crowds. However, the main feature was the availability of liquid refreshments; the railroad's historian observed, "All in all, the event was best remembered by those concerned as Ely's one big drunk."

The Nevada Northern continued through Ely along Garden Street (it had originally been planned for Aultman, the main street, a design vetoed by local citizens), a depot was built in East Ely, the rails reached the mines and put on ore cars, passenger service to McGill started in 1908, and the line was done. In 1920, the Nevada Consolidated Copper Company put on its own locomotives and crews to operate the trains from the mines to the smelter at McGill. The advance of technology brought diesel and then electric engines to the line.

The railroad donated some of its outdated equipment to the White Pine County Museum, which displays it proudly. The road continued to operate, too, even after the shutdown of the mines, carrying fuel to the smelter and ore from other locations for processing there, then hauling concentrates out. The Nevada Northern became a wholly owned subsidiary of the Kennecott Copper Corporation in 1939.

With the single exception of the displayed steam engine at the Museum, which was donated there in 1959, the other steam locomotives were all scrapped in the 1950s. When the mines closed in 1979, the trains no longer ran there, although the company, ever-optimistic about reopening, left the rails in place.

In the late twentieth century, the Nevada Northern is one of the state's most successful shortlines, providing dividends to stockholders and profits to operators. It enjoys the distinction of being the last shortline railway in Nevada, and one of the last in the West. It stands as an interesting reminder of the copper towns of eastern Nevada.

The east-central district was Nevada's most productive and profitable mining complex into the last quarter of the twentieth century. The area contributed more monetary wealth than any other metals complex up to that time. Copper mining lacks the romance of silver and gold, but Nevadans have had reason to appreciate this contribution to their economy, and reason to grieve at its decline. The people who came to prominence in White Pine were often among the state's best citizens, and they maintained a strange solidarity of association. This cohesion spawned ''White Pine Picnics'' in all sorts of out-of-the-way towns in Nevada and elsewhere. There is something about this colorful and interesting section that especially means *home* to several thousands of people.

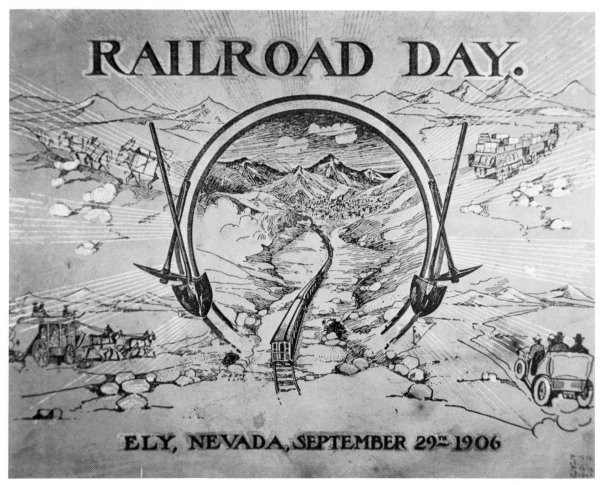

Souvenir program from Ely's Railroad Day

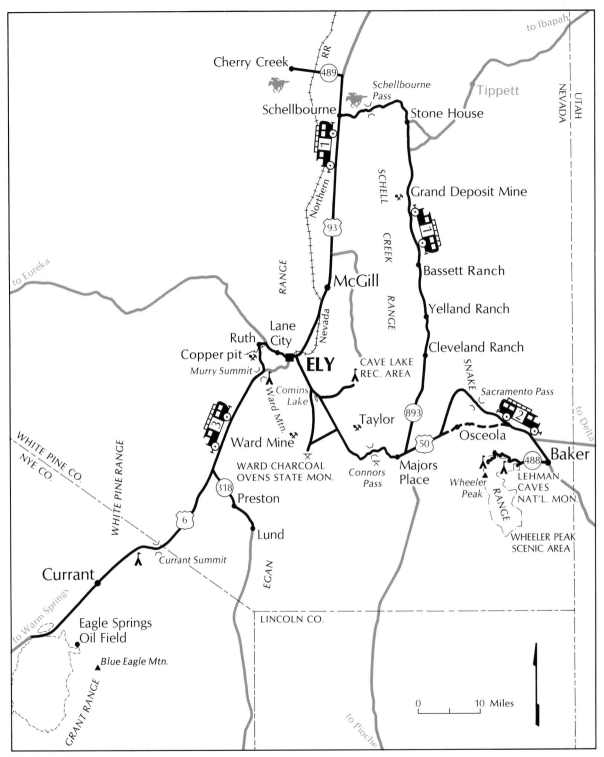

East-Central Nevada, tours 1, 2, 3

TOURING IN EAST-CENTRAL NEVADA

———✦❈✦———

The tours in this section have been prepared as a suggested method for seeing the east-central section of our state. There has been no particular effort to lead travelers into every cranny of White Pine, but rather to show several of the most attractive and accessible features, both natural and manmade.

To begin your tour, make sure that your vehicle is in good condition, that the gasoline tank is full, and that your camera is ready. Specific suggestions for additional supplies or equipment may be contained in individual tours. All the trips begin on Aultman Street, in front of the Museum/Information Center.

What to see in Ely: Stop first at the Museum/Information Center at 2000 Aultman Street. The museum displays include relics of the early days of White Pine County. Also available are maps, brochures, directions for reaching local attractions. Take advantage of these materials to drive around the Ely-McGill area to see the railroad and copper towns. The drive to McGill is only twelve miles and is well worth the time to see the smelter and the neat company-town houses. No tours are available at the smelter.

The railroad station in East Ely is an attraction for railfans nationwide. There are usually some Nevada Northern cars in the switching yard behind the station, available for photographing. As this is a working railroad and not a museum, tourists are advised to use caution in approaching the facilities.

Ely has all necessities for tourists—motels, hotels, restaurants, casinos, grocery stores, golf course, swimming pool, and the Bristlecone Convention Center. Ask locally about the Basque restaurants. The White Pine County Library has a local history collection, along with a knowledgeable staff. The library is located in the county complex on Campton Street (above Aultman), near the park and swimming pool.

TOUR ONE, Early White Pine: Ely — Spring Valley — Schellbourne — Cherry Creek and return. Approximately 164 miles round trip. Pack a lunch.

Leave the museum, driving east on Aultman Street, and turn right (south) on U.S. 93 & 50 & 6. Drive 7.2 miles to Comins Lake, on the right-hand side of the highway. Named for Henry Comins, this reservoir is a popular recreation site. Continue 6.2 miles to the historical marker (on the right-hand side of the highway) for the Ward Mining District (see Tour Three in this section). Continue 0.6 miles to the Taylor historical marker, on the left side of the highway. Look at the mountains behind the marker; there is a large, modern development of the old Taylor district underway by the Silver King Mining Company. Do not approach working mines without prior permission. We saw two golden eagles playing on the highway here on a summer day.

Continue 8.1 miles to the Connors Pass rest area. Here are picnic tables, pit toilets, no water.

Drive 4.7 miles to the junction of U.S. 93 with 50 & 6, Major's Place. Bear left here, onto U.S. 6 & 50, then drive 1.9 miles to the next junction, and turn left onto SR 893. You will drive the length of the beautiful Spring Valley, with the Snake Range on the right, Schell Creek Range on the left of the highway. Continue 15.2 miles to the access road for the Cleveland ranch. The ranch buildings are in the grove of cottonwood trees on the right. This is still a working ranch, no longer owned by the A. C. Cleveland family, but retaining the name. Continue 6.6 miles; this is the Yelland ranch. The Yelland family is a pioneer group in this area, and donated the land on which the Ely airport is located. Continue 8.2 miles; the old ranch here is that of the pioneer Bassett family.

Continue driving 9.9 miles to the end of the pavement. The road ahead, while unpaved, is suitable for all vehicles with careful drivers. Drive 0.3 miles; ignore the road from the right, and continue straight ahead. In another 0.4 miles, look to the left against the hill, and see the remains of the Grand Deposit mining camp. This was an installation of the post World War II period, when tungsten was in great demand. The mining camps of the 1950s did not develop the sophistication of those before the turn of the twentieth century, since good roads to metropolitan centers existed nearby.

Continue driving 7.6 miles. There is a road to the right to Tippett. This is the historic headquarters of the sheep-raising business in this section of eastern Nevada. The road also leads to the Goshute Indian reservation. Continue straight ahead, 1.2 miles to the crossroads, and keep going straight.

Drive 3.4 miles. Here is another road to Tippett and Ibapah (Utah). Go straight ahead, past an abandoned stone house on the left. From this point, you will be climbing out of Spring Valley. We saw ducks and other water birds on the pond in the meadow formed by Spring Valley Creek here.

Continue driving 3.8 miles to the Pony Express marker, keep going straight ahead on the main road.

East Ely railroad station

You will be made aware of the presence of the Pony Express all through this area. Continue up the grade 5.2 miles to the summit of Schellbourne Pass. A "sportsman" with a high-powered rifle succeeded in nearly obliterating the reinforced concrete Pony marker on the left side of the road. The Pony Express trail led down the canyon from this point. Continue on the main road.

Drive 2.1 miles, and here is the view of the Schell Creek Pony station and the site of Fort Schellbourne. This historic site is mostly unmapped, and the ranch is privately owned. The proprietors do not know which of the old buildings (if any) served the Pony traffic and the later horse soldiers.

Drive 0.3 miles to the sign for the Schellbourne ranch, and here is another Pony Express marker. For the great "Pony Express Re-ride" at the Pony's centennial in 1961, various organizations marked the trail at one-quarter mile and mile intervals. Continue 0.8 miles. From the Pony Express marker on the right-hand side of the road, a portion of the Pony trail and old wagon road is visible, leading across the valley below. Continue 2.6 miles to the highway, Schellbourne historical marker, and roadside rest; turn right (north) on U.S. 93.

Drive 0.7 miles; here is a Pony Express historical site marker on the right-hand side of the highway. Continue 5.3 miles to the junction with SR 489, and turn left for Cherry Creek. Drive 4.6 miles, and cross the Nevada Northern railroad tracks at the Cherry Creek siding. We found the Nevada Northern buildings here to be photogenic. Continue 3.7 miles to the Cherry Creek historical marker, on the right-hand side of the road as you enter the town. The only commercial facility here is a bar—and it's not always open. The town is picturesque; there are some ruins of the 1870s and 1880s, and later. Cherry Creek is occupied, not a ghost town. There are two cemeteries; ask directions locally if this is your interest. Enjoy looking about this historic old entertainment center.

Leaving Cherry Creek, start at the historical marker, drive 8.3 miles to the junction with U.S. 93, and turn right (south) toward Ely, and return to Ely, approximately 45 miles.

TOUR TWO, Recreation areas and natural wonders: Ely — Ward — Lehman Cave — Wheeler Peak — Osceola — Cave Lake and return. Approximately 180 miles round trip if via highway; approximately 177 miles round trip if returning through Osceola. Pack your lunch, *and a jacket* (even if it's a warm day).

Leaving the museum, drive east on Aultman Street and turn right (south) on U.S. 93 & 50 & 6. Drive 5.8 miles to the Ward turnoff, and turn right; the turn is not well marked, and there is no sign, only a stone monument from which some collector has taken the plaque. The road is good, graded, two lanes wide.

Drive 7.2 miles; the road to the Ward mining district is at the right, but drive straight ahead. Look to the right on the hillside, to see modern mining activity that has destroyed old Ward. The place is very active in the early 1980s and there is a guard at the entrance to the mill site.

Continue 1.9 miles; there is a side road from the left, but stay straight ahead. *You will return here* after visiting the charcoal ovens. Look ahead: the ovens are visible to the right. Drive 1.0 mile, and make a right turn to the Ward Charcoal Ovens State Monument, 0.5 miles ahead. Enjoy the sights and sounds of these nineteenth-century stone masonry structures.

After visiting the ovens, return north 1.5 miles to the intersection and turn right toward the highway, 5.0 miles ahead. Turn right on U.S. 93 & 50 & 6 and drive 0.5 miles; here is the historical marker for Taylor. Look behind the marker in the hills; the Silver King Mining Company has extensive works here. Continue driving on U.S. 93 & 50 & 6, 8.1 miles to the Connors

Pass rest area. Here are picnic tables, pit toilets, no water. As you drive across Connors Pass, enjoy the view of the Snake Range and splendid Mount Wheeler, Nevada's second-highest peak. Continue 4.7 miles to the junction at Major's Place, and bear left onto U.S. 6 & 50, driving straight across the valley toward the mountains. Drive 1.9 miles to the junction with SR 893, but stay on U.S. 6 & 50. The road is lined during the summer with pink bee-spider plants in bloom.

Drive 5.9 miles to the Osceola historical marker. *If you return via the side road to Osceola, you will come back to this spot.*

Continue on U.S. 6 & 50, 12.0 miles to Sacramento Pass. This is a good place to enjoy Mount Wheeler, on the right. Continue 10.4 miles, toward Baker, and turn right onto SR 487; drive 5.2 miles to the crossroads in Baker, and turn right on SR 488 toward Lehman Cave and Wheeler Peak. Baker has limited gasoline and grocery facilities.

Continue on SR 488 to the Lehman Cave Visitor Center, 5.6 miles. Here is where you will want to wear your jacket and visit the calcite marvel that is Lehman Cave. The National Park Service conducts tours on the hour, and the activity is fun and educational for anyone in reasonably good physical condition. The Visitor Center also has for sale books and pamphlets on the history and natural history of the cave and the surrounding area. Take time to see the ten-minute film before going on the tour of the cave; this will give a better understanding of what you will see underground. (Incidentally, if you are a spelunker, the Monument does not advertise it, but there are available special cave tours—not of Lehman's cave, but of another nearby— for these hobbyists. You need to make arrangements in advance and pass a test to demonstrate your ability to crawl through small spaces. Ask the ranger at the reception desk, or write to the Superintendent of the Lehman Cave Monument, Baker, Nevada 89311.)

Leaving the Visitor Center, drive back down the entrance road 0.7 miles to the intersection and turn left for Mount Wheeler. This is a good, paved road, but steep, so your vehicle needs to be in good condition.

You should also be aware that the road rises to above 10,000 feet in altitude, and affords wonderful views of the valley below. Drive 4.9 miles to the historical marker for the Osceola ditch. There is a 0.6-mile (round-trip) self-guided hike to see the remnants of the water trough; remember that you are in very high altitude, and do not try to do this quickly.

Leaving the historical marker, continue uphill 6.9 miles to the Wheeler Peak campground and the trailhead for hiking the paths. Here are developed campsites, tables, barbecues, drinking water, and pit toilets. This is an excellent place to see the famous natural features of eastern Nevada. The bristlecone pine trees are among nature's oldest living things, and the limestone formations around this high peak are most elegant. If you are planning to hike, again, be aware

that the campground elevation is above 9,000 feet. You should also know that summer thunderstorms here can be sudden and violent.

After visiting the Wheeler Peak area, return downhill 11.8 miles to SR 488, and turn left (toward Baker). Drive 4.9 miles to Baker, turn left on SR 487, then go 5.2 miles to the intersection with U.S. 6 & 50. Turn left, toward Major's Place. Continue on U.S. 6 & 50 for 7.8 miles to the Osceola turnoff.

Alternate return via Osceola: This road is graded, dirt, and adequate for all vehicles in good condition and with careful drivers. *Do not attempt this route in winter or in bad weather.*

Turn left at the sign for Osceola, and stay always on

Bristlecone forest near Wheeler Peak

the main traveled road. Side roads lead to private property. Drive 4.8 miles to a junction and bear right; the road to the left leads to an unattended AT&T microwave station. Continue 0.2 miles to the summit and a cattle guard; stay on the main road. Continue 1.2 miles to Osceola. Although you will see a good many ruins, some of the houses, including that of the Marriott family, are still occupied. Enjoy the picturesque sights, but be aware that someone is probably guarding the property. Drive 0.5 miles; there is a mill ruin on the right. Drive 0.5 miles; there is some of the gravel remaining from hydraulic mining, across the canyon. Continue 0.2 miles to the pioneer cemetery. Then continue on this main traveled road 3.3 miles to the historical marker and U.S. 6 & 50.

If not returning via Osceola: From the junction of U.S. 6 & 50 and the Osceola turnoff, return to the Osceola historical marker via U.S. 6 & 50, 13.7 miles.

From the historical marker, drive 7.8 miles to Major's place at the junction with U.S. 93, and continue on U.S. 93 & 50 & 6. Drive 18.9 miles to the turn for Cave Lake, and turn right. The road is a good, wide, graded gravel route. Follow the signs, 6.7 miles to Cave Lake State Park. Enjoy the elegant limestone formations along the way. At Cave Lake State Park, you will find a campground, lake fishing, boating, and picnic facilities. Hunters find big game (deer and elk) in season. *There may be no drinking water*, as the system has some development problems. This is a good camp spot; big trailers are not advised.

Return to the highway, 6.7 miles, following your visit to Cave Lake. Turn right to return to Ely, approximately 7.1 miles.

TOUR THREE, Past, present, and future resources: Ely — Ruth — Preston — Lund — Oil Fields and return. Approximately 160 miles round trip. Pack your picnic lunch.

Leaving the museum, drive west on Aultman Street to Highway 50 West. The highway parallels the Nevada Northern Railway tracks up Robinson Canyon. Drive 3.4 miles to the ruins of Lane City. The mine dumps here are from the great open pit excavations; the equipment yard is ahead on the left.

Continue 2.5 miles; there is a historical marker on the left side of the road at the junction. Turn left for Ruth. The mine dumps here are more of the overburden cleared from the copper pits. Drive 0.5 miles; stay straight ahead at the junction. Continue 0.7 miles, and turn left. Drive through New Ruth, along Sunshine Street. Here, you will find very limited facilities, since the town has mostly closed down with the end of mining. The post office is the only consistently active operation. Drive 0.3 miles, and cross the railroad tracks; continue 0.9 miles to a junction and bear right. The road is no longer maintained as a paved highway. For its own protection and yours, the Company is serious about preventing casual tourists from visiting the pits, so everything on the roadsides is closed. *Take this warning seriously, and do not trespass.*

Continue 1.2 miles; here Old Ruth begins. Stay on the paved road, and in another 0.4 miles notice the main Old Ruth ruins on the right. Caretakers stay on or near the property. Look up over the top of the town; the white "bubbles" are the NASA missile tracking station on Kimberly Mountain. Continue on the paved road.

Drive 2.1 miles to the junction with Highway 6, and turn right (toward Tonopah). Drive 0.1 miles to the left turn for Ward Mountain campground. The site is one-third of a mile, a lovely spot amid piñon and junipers, with water, picnic tables, ball park, drinking water, pit toilets. After enjoying this spot, return to the highway.

Continue on U.S. 6 (toward Tonopah) for 17.6 miles to the junction with SR 318. The drive is over Murry Summit, with the high limestone peaks and ridges of the White Pine Mountains appearing on the right. At the junction with SR 318, turn left toward Preston and Lund. Drive 6.0 miles, into the beautiful fertile valley chosen by the former residents of the Georgetown ranch for the new colony. Drive another

0.6 miles to the Preston turnoff, and turn right, into town.

There are no commercial facilities in Preston. Enjoy exploring, and notice the old Preston school, built in 1915; the church, constructed in 1912; and the pioneer cemetery. At the church, 0.6 miles from the Preston cemetery, take the fork to the left. Drive 2.0 miles, and turn left on the paved road. Drive another 0.3 miles, and turn right onto SR 318.

Continue 2.9 miles, and enter Lund. This prosperous agricultural community serves the valley with a few commercial facilities—gasoline, limited grocery store—and with educational establishments for the area. There are only a few really old buildings; the log corrals and fences show a sturdy and economical population. The Lund pioneer cemetery is at a right turn 0.3 miles beyond the town entrance.

Return to the highway, and turn left to return to Lund; go back through Lund on SR 318. Drive 5.6 miles to the Preston turnoff, and continue ahead and rejoin U.S. 6 in 6.0 miles. We saw golden eagles playing along this road.

At the intersection with U.S. 6, turn left (south, toward Tonopah). You are driving across the White River Valley. The ranches here support hay and cattle. The White Pine Mountains, on the right, gave the county its name.

Continue 14.0 miles to the Nye County line. Leaving the valley floor, the road climbs again into piñon and juniper forests. Drive 5.4 miles, over Currant Summit to the Currant Creek campground. Here are picnic tables, garbage cans, limited trailer space, pit toilets.

Drive 3.8 miles; this is old Currant, built before the new highway was constructed, and abandoned then.

Continue 4.7 miles to Currant. Here are some services, a cafe, gasoline, a bar, and a motel. Stay to the left at the intersection, and now drive across Railroad Valley on U.S. 6 to see Nevada's first, most famous and productive oil field. Discovered in the 1950s by William Pennington, the place has been working on a small scale for about thirty years. ''Railroad'' is a fairly common place name in Nevada; the appellation was usually given during the 19th century by people who thought they could imagine (or intended to promote) a railroad across level sections like this one. Drive 10.5 miles from Currant; the road to the left leads to some of the original oil discovery sites at Eagle Springs. This field will never rival the Teapot Dome, or some of the richer fields in Wyoming, but the equipment you see at work here is adding to U.S. domestic fuel supplies. Continue on U.S. 6 for 2.6 miles to the refinery, newly constructed in the 1980s. Drive another 0.9 miles, and turn around, returning via U.S. 6 to Ely, approximately 64 miles.

Railroad Valley oil operation

CENTRAL NEVADA

Austin, ca. 1890

Austin, 1981

CENTRAL NEVADA

The central area of Nevada has some history of early exploration and of surveyors and mappers, but little of trappers or emigrant travelers. The several north-south mountain ranges impeded regular traffic. Paiute Indians there remained largely undisturbed by settlers. John C. Frémont passed through the area in 1845, and in 1859 Captain J. H. Simpson surveyed for what eventually became the Overland Route. Thus for some years the region remained virtually unknown. The first real trail blazed across central Nevada came with the Pony Express.

The "Pony" began as an overland mail and express carrier from St. Joseph, Missouri, to Sacramento, California. The line was inaugurated on April 3, 1860, and ran until October 28, 1861. The Pony's purpose was to provide the fastest possible service across the vastnesses of the American West; until that time, the only mail route had no stations beyond Salt Lake City. With the decision to start the Pony Express, the firm of Russell, Majors, and Waddell needed 500 horses, 190 changing stations, and some 80 experienced horsemen. The average ride was $33\frac{1}{3}$ miles, each man using three horses on the route. The riders had to be men of good character; they promised (for their wage of $120 to $125 per month) not to swear or drink, not to fight with their associates, and to be faithful to their duties as carriers of the mail.

The procedure of the Express carriers involved riding mustangs, transporting the mochila (or pouch), and galloping alone across the desert. At first, riders were heavily armed with two revolvers, a long knife, and a rifle; this artillery was soon replaced by a single revolver, thus enabling them to carry more mail. For a few months, from July to October 1861, the Overland Stage paralleled the Pony's trail, competing by carrying passengers as well as mail. But the Pony's true end came in October 1861 when the telegraph provided near-instant message service across the continent. Despite the romance of adventure and genuine heroism of the Pony riders and their company, the venture was a financial failure. At the end, the expenses considerably outweighed the income, but despite its handling of the mail, the Pony never received Congressional assistance. Still, the sense of high adventure continued to live on. As the Pony Express stations decayed or fell away, the American people—especially those in the West—tried to keep the spirit alive.

Nevada contained 27 Pony stations, with two more just across the border in California. Some of the important sites in central Nevada include (from east to west) Diamond Springs, Sulphur Springs, Roberts Creek, Grubb's Well, Dry Creek, Simpson Park, Reese River, Dry Wells, Smith Creek, and Cold Springs. No other section of the state had so many. Preservation, archeological study, and the centennial "reride" kept several of the stations known into the late twentieth century, with some being marked for historical significance.

Austin

Genuine settlement came to central Nevada, like that of other sections, with the discovery of minerals. Some prospecting had occurred as early as 1857, but lack of good ore and Indian troubles ended the work. Appropriately enough, the first major discovery was made by William Talcott, a former Pony Express rider who had settled at Jacobsville. Someone named the place Pony Canyon. In May 1862, Talcott had lost some horses, the legend says, and in searching for them, accidentally stumbled over a rich outcrop of greenish ore. Assays proved the material to contain rich deposits of free silver. As usual, the assayer in Virginia City, to whom the samples had been sent, told a friend and then some others, and the rush to the Reese River country began. Pressed by politics and the increase in population, the territorial legislature carved out Lander County, naming it for a famous western military figure, Frederick West Lander.

Lander County came to bear the name "the mother of counties." The area was so large (fully a third of what was then Nevada Territory) that when other towns grew up and started competing for county-seat status, the lawmakers simply cut off a chunk and thus created a new county. Some of the beneficiaries of this fertile generosity were Elko, White Pine, Eureka, and Nye counties.

Jacobsville was the first permanent settlement in what became Lander County, but Austin quickly developed into the most important town there. Jacobsville was even briefly the county seat, but an election held soon after the designation of Lander County gave the honor to Austin. Other settlements—not really towns—grew up in the surrounding area as the rush began: Clifton, Kingston, Amador, and a few more. Austin claimed the largest population, as many as 10,000, although the true figure was probably closer to 2,000.

The rush followed the usual pattern. Tents and shacks sprinkled the hillsides of the Toiyabe Range. The winter was terrible, and people suffered dreadfully, but they stayed to maintain a hold on their claims. Within a year after Talcott's discovery, there were stores, hotels, saloons, cabins, and other facilities at both Austin and Clifton. The two towns competed for trade, with Clifton enjoying an advantage in that it was on flat ground while Austin lay in the sharp little Pony Canyon. Austin won, for its businessmen were offered free ground for their establishments in the townsite in return for assisting with the building of a road to the flat below the city. Within a short time, a good, graded road stretched up the canyon, and Clifton was only a stop on the way to Austin.

By the summer of 1863, Austin contained all the trappings of a busy mining camp: a traveler found two hotels, two stores, five saloons, two meat markets, a bakery, a livery stable, two lawyers, "two ——— houses," a dairy, Wells Fargo office, and a printing office among its commercial establishments. The printing office was that of the *Reese River Reveille*, destined to become Nevada's longest-publishing newspaper, as it began in May 1863. A school opened

that fall, and the Bank of Austin was operating before winter.

The boom continued. Some of the ore reportedly assayed at $22,519 per ton (with silver at about $1.32 per ounce). Up to 75 mines operated in the Reese River district during the boom years to about 1870. The greatest of all was the Austin Silver Mining Company, which produced more than $11 million.

If Lander was the "mother of counties," then Austin was surely the father of mining camps. If Austin's mines seemed to be declining, then prospectors went out from there to find other deposits, ledges, and lodes. Settlements developed from these rather far-flung activities included Ione, Hamilton, and Eureka, all of which quickly became county seats. Several smaller towns as far away as Pioche were born the same way.

No boom could go on forever, and Austin's was no exception to that rule. The mines played out, and the place settled into a genteel decline. Still, Austin gave a number of institutions to Nevada history and folklore. The town had a secure place in the state's affections for these, the famous "Gridley flour sack," the Sazerac Lying Club, and the "sagebrush linnet," Emma Nevada.

Reuel Gridley was a grocer who owned a fine stone building above the center of Austin. At the time of the

---

"George gives hard old acct of Reese. . . . people at Reese sleeping out around the hay yards, under the lea of the houses and all sorts of places — houses all very temporary affairs, tents — sage brush & mud shanties — very few lumber houses — only 2 houses got floors, viz the International Hotel and a hurdy gurdy house — this was at Austin — devil of a place — money scarce, except among gamblers & speculators — everybody poor — grub scarce & dear — 6 mills there, but only one at work, a 5 stamp . . ."

— Alfred Doten, *Journals,* Comstock newspaperman, October 29, 1863 first mayoral election in 1864, Gridley and a local physician, H. S. Herrick, made a wager on the outcome. If Gridley's candidate (a southern sympathizer) won, Dr. Herrick would tote a 50-pound sack of flour up the main street to the tune of "Dixie." On the other hand, if Herrick's man (a Union stalwart) won, then Gridley would carry the bag along the same path to the tune of "John Brown." Gridley furnished the flour, and decorated the sack with ribbons and flags. Herrick's Union man won, and the town enjoyed a huge celebration with bands playing, speeches shouted, and liquor free-flowing in every bar. The parade ended near the edge of town, where Gridley made a short speech, offering to sell the sack of flour for $200, the proceeds to go to the Sanitary Fund (the Civil War version of the Red Cross).

The idea seemed so good that Gridley and the sack then went on the road, finally as far as the St. Louis World's Fair, and in nine months or so, he raised thousands of dollars for the Sanitary Fund. The events made Austin and its grocer world famous, and the little store in Pony Canyon became somewhat of a national shrine. Gridley himself left Austin after his feat, and died in California in 1870. The marker on Gridley's grave in Stockton commemorated his accomplishment for the Sanitary Fund. The sack of flour eventually reposed in the Nevada State Museum.

The Sazerac Lying Club was the invention of Fred Hart, editor of the *Reese River Reveille*. Mourning the lack of news, even in a mining-boom town, Hart took to "reporting" events he said occurred in the Sazerac saloon. No story was too absurd to appear under Hart's byline, nor was any tale too tall to be accepted at the Sazerac. Eventually, the fables were gathered into a book that Hart edited, providing latter-day readers with a glimpse of mining camp humor that, while rough, bigoted, and occasionally profane, was probably typical of its day. *The Sazerac Lying Club* became a classic of Nevada literature and a basic source book of authentic American western humor.

Also among Austin's prominent citizens in the 1870s was the family of Dr. Wixom. The Wixoms had

"We do not lie for greed or gain, nor do we tolerate that class of liars who by word of mouth deceive their fellow-men for selfish or wicked ends. No, members of the Club, while we permit a range of thought extending far away into the most distant depths of the realm of the impossible and the improbable, we do not stoop to the lie of deceit; we ask no man to place implicit belief in our lies—but if any man does so believe, he sustains no injury. . . . The first lie of the evening is now in order, and I hope members will restrain their narrations within the bounds required by our constitution and by-laws.

"These remarks being duly applauded, the President, by virtue of his rank, was called on for the first lie. This is a synopsis of what he said, and it is on the records under the title of

Oozed Into Him

"While on a recent journey to San Francisco, he shared a section in the sleeping car with one of the Comstock bonanza kings. The monarch occupied the upper berth, and the President . . . the lower one. When the latter arrived in San Francisco he felt a peculiar heaviness in his body and limbs, his arms and legs especially being so weighty that he was hardly able to control their motions. He visited a prominent physician, who . . . told him he displayed symptoms of metallic poisoning, and advised him to go to the Hammam, a bathing establishment . . . and get 'retorted.' He accordingly went to that institution and . . . when his pores began to open, silver oozed out of his body. . . . Altogether, he cleaned up a bar valued at $417.92. . . . He says the silver must have oozed into him from the bonanza king in the berth above, that night on the sleeper."

— *The Sazerac Lying Club*

a daughter, Emmy, who began in her early childhood to exhibit considerable talent in singing. She was much in demand, as they used to say, for performances at church and social affairs. Emmy Wixom apparently made her first public appearance at the age of ten at Christmas services in 1870. There was no suitable teacher in Austin, so Emma Wixom trained under various tutors in California, and then, under the patronage of Marie Hungerford Mackay (wife of the Bonanza king), in Paris. She adopted "Emma Nevada" as her stage name, and under that title gained international fame as a gifted soprano. Emma Nevada made numerous appearances on stages all over the world, each duly reported to the Austin papers. Every article, of course, pointed out her origins and early life in the little mining camp.

In 1885, Emma Nevada made two West Coast tours, with appearances in San Francisco. Dozens of people from her home town made the train trip to the coast to witness her triumph there. In the Fall that year, Emma Nevada returned to her home state, performing on December 4 at Piper's Opera House in Virginia City, and then two days later at Austin's Methodist church. It was her final visit to the scene of her childhood; Emma Nevada made a farewell tour to the West in 1902 and died in England in 1940.

Austin was not all mines, business, and entertainment. The town contained three large brick churches, two of them with pipe organs. The Methodist church was built by rather unusual arrangements. The minister, J. L. Trefren, wanted an edifice for his flock, but the people were "stock poor;" that is, they owned mining stocks, but had no money. Reverend Trefren decided to accept the stock and use it for collateral to build his church. Trefren gathered up the stock certificates donated by his communicants, organized the Methodist Mining Company, and went to New Hampshire, his native state, with the papers. He was able to stir enough interest there in Nevada mines to sell the stocks. The stocks were sold on installments, and before all the payments were made, the boom collapsed, leaving the church with a substantial debt. Eventually

the building was paid for, but in mid-twentieth century it was falling into disrepair; the other two pioneer churches in Austin had apparently lapsed in activity, so the Methodist was the only enduring house of worship there. Mrs. Belle Roberts, the last surviving member of the original congregation, acquired the property and took as her own the project of restoration. She raised the money for repairs to the church and then donated the building to the Lander County Historical Society. This unique building, the only one of its kind in Nevada built by a mining company, continued to serve the little community. Two other pioneer churches also underwent restorative measures, and the three together form an attractive part of Austin's scene.

At the end of the boom, the miners moved away. The newer camp of Eureka, some seventy miles east, took their attention. A fire in 1881 obliterated many substantial structures, and other blazes engulfed most of the rest. Austin's decline continued until only a few hangers-on resided there, serving each other with food, gasoline, or other small commercial facilities, or with governmental ministration. In 1954, novelist-historian Oscar Lewis wrote the town's biography, and recalling the *Sazerac Lying Club* and the gaiety of the Gridley affair, named it *The Town That Died Laughing*—although it was really a long way from dead at the time. Austin retained its status as county seat until Battle Mountain (to the north) claimed the title in 1980. A favorable place on a national east-west highway also helped to keep the grim reaper away. As the twentieth century neared its end, Austin continued its refusal to die, but hardly anyone would again call, as they had in the 1860s, "Ho! For the Reese River!"

Austin Transportation

Austin's favorable place on a trans-national highway was not accidental. The place had always promoted transportation facilities, and with considerable finesse. Of course, the townsite was on the original Simpson, or Overland, route. Beyond that, however, was the building of the railroad to connect with the Southern (then Central) Pacific to the north. This was the famous narrow-gauge, shortline Nevada Central Railway. Its promoter was M. J. Farrell, secretary of the Manhattan Silver Mining Company, and Lander County state senator. At its 1875 session, the Nevada legislature authorized Lander County to subsidize a railroad in the amount of some $200,000 in county bonds. The important limitation was that the road be built into the city of Austin within a five-year period. Farrell went diligently to work, but it was about three years before he could interest the Stokes family of financiers in underwriting the project. The route was staked in the summer of 1878, but no rails were laid until the summer of 1879.

The boom was essentially over by the time the railroad began to push rails south toward Austin from Battle Mountain. The financing had been extremely complicated, and the construction process proved equally complex. The deadline of February 9, 1880, was approaching, and the rails still were not near enough to assure that the claim for the $200,000 subsidy could be exercised; the road had to be within the Austin city limits. Versions of the rest of the story have the Austin city council expanding the city border to meet the tracklayers; at any rate, at ten minutes before midnight, the tracks were 900 feet into Austin's limits— expanded or not. The town went wild over this example of nineteenth-century technology and industry, and Austin had a connection to outside world transportation. General Ledlie, who had supervised some of the final construction phases, was honored by having one of the stations bear his name. A small local line known humorously as the "mule's relief" also connected to the Nevada Central.

By 1884, the Nevada Central was in bankruptcy. Anson Phelps Stokes took the road back from its old owners and tried to reorganize the company. At the same time, the mines continued to decline, and Stokes also took over the Manhattan Silver Mines, calling the new company the Austin Mining Company. He directed the reshuffling and reconstruction of several mines and industrial sites, until he turned the job over to his son, J. G. Phelps Stokes, in 1897. The younger

Stokes so enjoyed his prospects that he built a towering castle at the edge of Austin to use as a residence while he was there.

Nonetheless, in Austin's continuing slide, after about 1911, most of the mining there ceased. The railroad was almost fatally hit by the disastrous Humboldt River flood in 1910, and then in the 1920s highway transportation began to supercede the rails. The glamor of the horseless carriage overshadowed that of the iron horse. The last train ran on February 2, 1937, and by 1938 the Nevada Central was dead, abandoned that year by state order. Eventually the rails were removed, and a graveled road took their place. The 90-mile trail became SR 8-A and later SR 304; it was paved in 1952.

In the 1930s, people began to use their autos for vacation trips, and the "Lincoln Highway" that led through Austin helped to make the town into some-

---

"This road is a great one. The engine is a little larger than a wheel barrow, & the cars are curiosities. There is one good passenger car on the road, & it was put on for our especial benefit today. The road is narrow gauge & is in good condition. We . . . got over the ground in pretty good shape. It was very funny to see some Indians with their . . . bright blankets wrapped around them sitting on top of the coal on the tender. They always ride there."

— Tasker L. Oddie, letter to his mother, February 10, 1898

"PM I rode on the street motor, 'Mules' Relief' for the first time—was the only passenger—rode through to the extreme upper end of the track . . . —Just completed there today, & this was 1st trip of motor over it, so I was the first & only through passenger on the road— . . . The whistles blowed in honor of the occasion, & we had couple of kegs of beer to treat the boys."

— Alfred Doten, *Journals,* newspaperman, July 10, 1884

what of a tourist attraction. Local boosters extolled Austin's charms across the country, aided by the Lincoln Highway Association and its slogan, "See America First." In time, the Lincoln Highway was designated U.S. 50, and Austin's tourist business benefited somewhat. Still, Austin was not destined to become a town of flashy casinos or similar allurements. The traffic for the mining boom of the 1980s hardly changed Austin's ways, except to make it more difficult to find a seat at the bar.

Eureka

The Lincoln Highway that served Austin also led east to Eureka. There, the area had been prospected as early as 1864, but the complex lead-silver ores resisted successful processing until 1869. In that year, Eureka township was platted, and the place became a stop on the stage route. The village grew rather quickly, from three or four cabins in 1869 to about 9,000 people at its peak in 1878. The legislature obligingly carved a portion of Lander County off to make Eureka County in 1873. The town of Eureka became the county seat, an honor it retained.

Still, until 1869, there were probably fewer than 100 white people in what became Eureka County. Paiute and Shoshone natives were the only inhabitants. A group of prospectors from Austin discovered the mines and, after a few unsuccessful attempts to develop them, gave up in favor of more complicated processing. Between 1869 and 1872, as many as sixteen furnaces were built to reduce the ores, principally from the mines of Ruby Hill. The smoky town of Eureka gained a dubious reputation as the "Pittsburgh of the West." Eventually, the number of smelters was reduced to two. The plants, one at either end of the town, produced lead fumes in sufficient quantity to poison the air of the little canyon, resulting in sickness and death to numbers of Eureka residents before the furnaces closed. Slag heaps of enormous proportions began then, and a century after the end of the last run at the smelters, remained to decorate the landscape.

The mines of Ruby Hill provided grist for the smelt-

"In the first flood in Eureka, I believe way back in the seventies, there were seventeen lives lost. But after the first flood, it made that big ditch, as they all call it, in the back, and that relieved a lot of the water coming down the canyon. But it was always the same. You always watched the clouds in the summertime. After a hot spell, you get a lot of thunder and lightning. As the clouds broke on this side, as we called it, which would be the north of Prospect Mountain, then look out, we might get a flood. If it broke on the other side, we didn't care."
— Peter Merialdo, Eureka County Recorder

ers at Eureka. The Richmond and Eureka Consolidated, the Jackson, Phoenix, and KK Consolidated all had rich deposits. The miners who lived in the settlement there numbered perhaps 900 at the peak of population. They came from all parts of the world—Italy, England, Cornwall, Mexico—and enjoyed their national customs in Eureka County. A Cornish glee club, for example, entertained at all sorts of functions.

Charcoal for the smelters came partly from the area of Fish Creek, where a group of Italian charcoal burners used pits (or ricks) for reducing wood to charcoal. The Italians, somewhere between 600 and 800 in population, had a fair-sized industry there, cutting wood (mainly piñon from the surrounding hills), burning it in the pits, and then hauling the material by wagon to the smelters at Eureka. This important activity provided fuel at a maximum rate of about 16,000 bushels of charcoal per day for the smelters. A charcoal pit could produce between 2,800 and 3,300 bushels from a hundred cords of green wood, the result of denuding ten to twelve acres of forest land. By 1874, the hills around Eureka for a radius of 20 miles had been stripped of trees for the charcoal business. By 1878, the average hauling distance from the production site to the smelter had grown to 35 miles. Obviously, the economics of the situation required that prices for charcoal ought to rise. That fact of life was lost on certain users of the material, who, in the summer of 1879, decided to cut the price they would pay.

Understandably, the Charcoal Burners Association took offense at the fiat of the smelter owners, and a hundred or so of the members issued a statement declining to deliver any more material until the issue was settled. The mainly Italian burners were poor and ignorant, perhaps, but they recognized a challenge when they found one. Some charcoal wagons were unloaded, others dumped. The smelter owners' response was to call the job action a "riot" and to ask for military assistance.

The governor called up the local militia. Owners and burners took up arms and exchanged threats. Finally, with the dispute at an impasse, on August 18, 1879, a sheriff's posse of nine men rode the thirty miles out of Eureka to the burners' camp in Fish Creek Valley. In the confused confrontation that followed, five of the carbonari died, and several others were taken to jail. And so ended the celebrated Charcoal Burners War. The affair became an international incident, investi-

gated by U.S. and Italian diplomatic authorities, and eventually the U.S. government paid reparations to families of the dead. One of the posse's deputies claimed in later years that the Italian he killed that day returned to haunt him.

A more important result of the "war" was a further decline in Eureka's already slumping population, business, and industry. Within another year, production had begun to slip markedly, and 1888 was the last year during the nineteenth century in which the figures reached a million dollars. The smelters lasted a few more years, processing ores from outside the district; the remaining one closed in 1891.

Still, Eureka had a wonderful heyday. Immigrants from all over the world made it a colorful and exciting place on national days. Four churches filled the town's religious requirements. At one time, nine cemeteries existed, holding remains of people of many nationalities and fraternal and religious persuasions. An opera house was the center for social and cultural events unmatched in Nevada except perhaps at Virginia City. Five volunteer fire companies and two militia groups provided exciting activities for young men.

Political and business figures among the residents of Eureka included at least two governors of the state and three congressmen. The governors, John Edward Jones (1894–1896) and Reinhold Sadler (1896–1902) had the distinction of being the state's only elected immigrant governors; Jones was from Wales and Sadler from Prussia. One of the congressmen, George Cassidy, was also the editor and publisher of the long-lasting *Eureka Sentinel*. Another of the congressmen, Thomas Wren, was the author of a standard history of Nevada. The third congressman, George A. Bartlett, was better known later as one of the important divorce lawyers and judges in Reno.

Reinhold Sadler's home and mercantile store dominated a section of Eureka. The two-story brick house stands on a hill overlooking the town; on its lower floor was an entrance to a tunnel that led to the store on the street below. These arrangements, not rare in Eureka, stemmed from the little city's peculiar geography of

---

"Among the prominent buildings lately erected, and now under process of construction, can be mentioned the International Hotel, Jackson House, 'Sentinel' building, and Opera House, each being handsome two story brick structures, to say nothing of the many elegant private residences that adorn our town. There are two banks, namely, Paxton & Co., and the White Pine County Bank, both of which are doing a prosperous business.

"A magnificent court-house, to cost $53,000, is now in process of construction. This building will be one of the finest county buildings on the coast, and will certainly be a matter of laudable pride to all the citizens of the county."

— Lambert Molinelli, *Eureka and Its Resources* (1879)

streets terraced up the canyon hillsides—and severe winters that left several feet of snow on the roads. As late as the 1960s, tunnels and caverns existed for exploration under the streets of Eureka.

The *Eureka Sentinel* began publication in 1870. Longer lasting than either of the other two papers, the *Eureka Leader* and the *Ruby Hill Mining News*, the *Sentinel* has educated and entertained the people of central Nevada for over a hundred and ten years. Although it is no longer printed in the historic building where it began, the *Sentinel* seems healthy in the early 1980s. The picturesque building constructed in 1879 became a landmark, a historical site, and finally, a museum. The Eureka Sentinel Museum, in the same structure that housed the printing of the newspaper, opened in 1982, in time to greet a new mining boom.

The mineral excitement of the late twentieth century brought important changes to Eureka. Reworking or new discoveries of gold, silver, lead, and molybdenum caused a genuine boom, destined to last while metals prices remained high. A new high school, a casino, spruced-up buildings along the main street, and traffic jams when shifts changed at the mines all marked the modern town. Still, important buildings remained from earlier days—the Opera House ("The Movies"), the courthouse built in 1879, the Sentinel museum, the Sadler home, and a few others. The boom even spurred restoration of the historic Jackson House hotel. The local historical society recognized the importance of the old structures and designed a walk-through tour; they have a free pamphlet for anyone requesting it.

The Eureka and Palisade

By many accounts, the most important adjunct to the industrial complex of Eureka was the narrow-gauge Eureka and Palisade railroad. When it seemed clear that the ores of Prospect Mountain could indeed be smelted, various promoters began to work for a railroad that would meet the Central Pacific, which ran across the state to the north. The company was organized in November 1873; grading began on the three-foot-wide roadbed which would stretch 84 miles from Palisade to Eureka. Financiers after 1874 included Bank of California moguls D. O. Mills and William Sharon. Across the flats and up the hills, over Garden Pass, and finally into Eureka the tracklayers worked. On October 22, 1875, with Eureka decorated with flags and the citizenry appropriately loaded with alcohol, the great celebration took place. The road was destined to hold a strong part in the economy and affections of the people of central Nevada.

The railroad proved prosperous through more than a decade, through mine excitements and shutdowns, through smelter openings and closings, strikes, and a disastrous snow blockade in 1889-1890, until finally in 1893 the E&P suffered its first deficit. By 1900, the little railroad was in receivership, and a new company was organized on the carcass of the previous one.

The reorganized line began in 1902 with Mark Requa at its head. The main business for the next several years was hauling from the mines to the smelters at Salt Lake City. Requa also tried to promote his plans for expanding into the copper districts newly developed at Ely. Then in 1910, not financial, but physical tragedy struck. The Humboldt River had one of its great floods and washed out the line, destroying eleven miles of track. This rare and huge wet-mantle flood inundated and destroyed great sections of inhabited and pasture land along the Humboldt; a similar crisis did not occur again until 1952. In 1910, a lake extended south from Palisade (the northern terminus) for more than thirty miles. In that little town, the roundhouse and shops stood in water five feet deep. The Southern Pacific and Western Pacific connections did not escape either; their tracks and tunnels all got soaked under the deluge. On April 2, 1910, the owners announced that the Eureka and Palisade was suspending operations. There were apparently no takers for an offer of a bargain sale.

The suspension dragged on until the Spring of 1911 when George Whittell, a major stockholder in the road, came up with the necessary cash and found himself the owner of the E&P. Fully a year elapsed before Eureka had train service again, and the re-opening celebration almost equaled that of 1875. The company inaugurated tri-weekly, daily-except-Sunday trips along the 90-mile stretch, and struggled along for several more years. Then, during the World War I period, John E. Sexton was placed in charge of the Eureka and Palisade, and a new era began. Sexton's name continued to be identified with the road—attached to it, even—for historians and railfans ever after.

Sexton's antics as manager of the Eureka and Palisade became legends. In a rage because of some regulation causing what he thought was subservience to the great Southern Pacific, Sexton parked an E&P train across the SP's right-of-way, and declined to move until the dispute was resolved to his satisfaction. Forced by another regulation to carry supplies he thought inappropriate for the E&P, he put a large shipment of butter next to the engine's boiler for the duration of a trip. No slight was too small to require retaliation, no regulator too big for a challenge. Sexton's management nonetheless brought the railroad slightly into the black during his tenure, but then highways and trucklines began to take away the rail business. Finally, there was simply no profit in continuing; Sexton died and his successor lacked the necessary drive, and the road was abandoned on September 21, 1938. A paved highway, SR 278, serves to connect Eureka to the cities in the north.

Palisade fared no better. Even before the 1910 flood, Palisade had begun to decline. A fire in the summer of 1902 destroyed most of the buildings in the north end of town. Two hotels burned in that conflagration, and only strong work saved the E&P facilities then. The 1910 flood washed away a store, the jail, and eight houses, the ruins of which lodged against a bridge downstream and backed up more water. Two more bridges washed away, including the E&P trestle. A fire in July 1910 took out six more buildings, and another in the summer of 1927 destroyed four of the last five locomotives. After the abandonment of the railroad, there were a justice court and a few other facilities at Palisade, but finally even the post office closed in 1961. In the last of the twentieth century, little remains except some shade trees, a cemetery, and sagging foundations to mark the terminus of one of Nevada's great shortline railroads.

Livestock and Agriculture of Central Nevada

In the most fervid mining excitement, there were always a few people who turned not to the pick and shovel, but to the riata, shepherd's crook, or plow. These producers of food and fiber supplied the mining camps; some became wealthy, some went broke, but they furnished necessities that miners could not provide for themselves. The agriculture and livestock business of central Nevada was necessarily marginal, owing to the dry climate and lack of irrigation sources, but the operators were diligent.

The year after the discovery of mines in Austin and Eureka, there were only about 3,800 cattle and just over a thousand sheep in all of Lander County. Within ten years, the combined figure for Lander and Eureka had increased many times to nearly 24,000 cattle and almost 42,000 sheep. The numbers are probably low, for county assessors—the sources for information— routinely underestimated their headcounts.

In the same decade, the areas under cultivation in the two counties increased correspondingly; hay and grain were needed for livestock feed. When Lander County comprised about a third of the entire Nevada Territory, it had about 8,200 acres devoted to fodder crops, and a decade later (by then it was considerably smaller), there were still 2,400 acres in hay and grain. Eureka County had about 1,900 acres in the same commodities. Considering the severe climate and small markets, it took some diligence to plant orchards in the valleys; Lander County reported more than 500 fruit trees (apples and plums), and Eureka somewhat under a hundred.

The important sections of central Nevada devoted to these businesses included Big Smoky Valley south of Austin, and Diamond Valley northwest of Eureka. There, the farmers and ranchers developed wells and ditches from tiny water sources. This activity continued into the twentieth century on a marginal or subsistence basis, mainly in family farms. The Bureau of Land Management tried during the 1940s to change the desert's botanical environment by experimenting with large plantings of crested wheat. This grass was expected to flourish in the arid climate and thus enhance the cattle grazing industry. The results of that experiment were mixed.

Then, about the mid-twentieth century, a change occurred. Large livestock producers moved into Smoky Valley, and in Diamond Valley a large underground lake was found to exist. The Diamond Valley development, beginning in 1957, proved both dramatic and profitable. With the activation of water wells tapping the lake, real estate sales increased, and so did Desert Land entries. Now, no longer isolated or economically deprived, Diamond Valley land has become more productive for both meat and fodder, a new financial ad-

junct to central Nevada. The beautiful valley seems destined to develop at last into an important agricultural complex to supplement the uncertain economy of a district too heavily devoted to minerals.

Visitors to central Nevada will find that the residents there are friendly and hospitable, but that, unlike people in other parts of the state, they cater very little to tourism. Central Nevadans are justly proud of their heritage; right now, however, they are exceedingly caught up in the exigencies of their exciting daily lives. History is in their past and in their experience; but this year there is a mining boom, and business to be done.

TOURING IN CENTRAL NEVADA

The tours in this section have been designed so travelers can visit and enjoy some of the section's historical and scenic sites. The trips are not meant to be comprehensive for the entire section, but rather as a sampling of what is available in an interesting region.

While travel in central Nevada should not be considered dangerous to people or vehicles, the prudent tourist will take care before leaving on a trip to make sure that the fuel tank is full and that the car, truck, or cycle is in good repair. We have included some special caveats if roads are unsuitable for any vehicle. You will surely want to take a camera, for the tours have some photogenic places to visit. We have recommended picnics where we thought it appropriate; it may be hard to find a restaurant open in a ghost town!

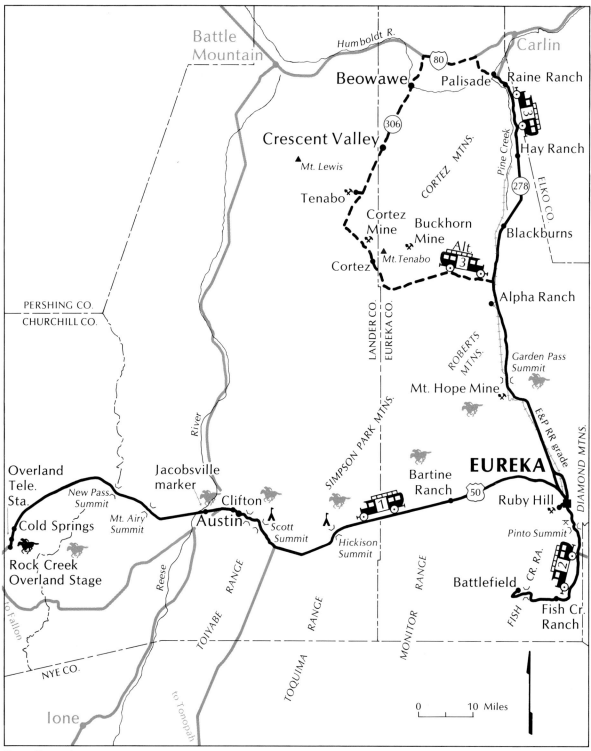

Central Nevada, tours 1, 2, 3

What to see in Eureka: Stop first at the assessor's office in the courthouse at the center of town to obtain a free copy of the Eureka walking tour guide. This four-page pamphlet contains both historical and economic information about the area, and a map of the town. The walking/driving tour is highly recommended; it will show most of the outstanding features of this little city.

The courthouse itself is worth a second look. Well-maintained since 1879, it is in exceedingly good condition. All the county officers maintain quarters there. All of the tours in this section begin in front of the courthouse.

The Jackson House hotel, across Main Street from the courthouse, was restored in 1982. Originally the Jackson House, it was known in a long interim as the Brown Hotel. Now, the place serves as a historical landmark in a historic town.

The *Eureka Sentinel* building, on Monroe, a block south of the courthouse, serves as the Eureka County museum. The museum, opened in 1982, contains an outstanding exhibit of antique printing presses and is destined to become a magnet for printing historians.

The Eureka County library opened in December 1981. It is on Monroe, directly behind the courthouse, facing north. The handsome new structure replaced a basement facility.

Eureka has all tourist necessities. Reservations for lodging are recommended.

TOUR ONE, Remnants of the Pony Express and Overland Stage route: Eureka — Austin — Cold Springs — Rock Creek and return. Approximately 250 miles round trip. Pack a picnic or camping gear, or plan to visit tourist facilities in Austin.

Leaving the courthouse, head northwest on Main Street (U.S. 50). Drive 3.3 miles on U.S. 50 to the junction with SR 278. Watch for golden eagles along this way; over the years we have seen many of them perched on poles or soaring along on thermals, looking for a tasty rodent or unlucky rabbit for dinner. At the junction, stay on U.S. 50, and drive 11.8 miles across Diamond Valley's south end.

The Roberts Creek road is at the right. There was a Pony station 15 miles north of this spot. Nothing identifiable of the Roberts Creek station remains; the site is on a private ranch. Continue on U.S. 50, 9.3 miles. The Bartine ranch house (abandoned) is on the right.

Continue driving 6.7 miles. The road to Bean Flat is at the right. There was a Pony station called Grubb's Well, 8 miles north of this place. Nothing remains on the site, which is on a private ranch. Continue 1.2 miles; there is a rest area at the right. Drive 4.9 miles, and enter Lander County.

Continue driving, 6.9 miles to the Dry Creek ranch road, on the right. A Pony station called Dry Creek was 4 miles north of this place. The ruins, if any exist, are fenced on the property of the Dry Creek (Damele) ranch. The ruins of an Overland Stage station are 2.9 miles up the road. The remnants there consist of a pile of rocks that once was a wall, and bits of trash, thoroughly sifted over by vandals and collectors. Continue

Eureka County Courthouse, Eureka

Stokes Castle, Austin

from the intersection on U.S. 50, 1.3 miles to the Hickison Petroglyph Site, and turn right. The recreation site is 0.8 miles up the road.

At Hickison recreation area, there are picnic and camping facilities, pit toilets, and a short, self-guided walk from the parking lot to view the petroglyphs (ancient rock writings). The site is closed in winter but maintained the rest of the year. Return to the highway, 0.8 miles, and turn right toward Austin.

Drive 0.5 miles. There is a historical marker at the left, describing the petroglyphs located nearby. Con-

tinue on U.S. 50 and drive 11.4 miles. The view is of Monitor Valley as you descend. The rugged and beautiful peaks of the Toiyabe Range are ahead; the Toquima Range is on the left, Simpson Park Mountains to the north of the Toiyabes. The road to the area of the Simpson Park Pony Express station is here. The site was about five miles north. Although the area was in active use for longer than the Pony Express, into the era of the Overland Stage, nothing visible now remains at the place, which is on a private ranch. Drive 0.9 miles to the junction with SR 376, and continue on U.S. 50.

Drive 5.0 miles. The Bob Scott campground is on the right. Here are campsites for campers and trailers, picnic tables, drinking water and flush toilets during the summer season; it is closed in winter. The campground is in a shady grove of fragrant piñon trees. A fee is charged for camping in this place, which is maintained by the Forest Service.

From the campground road, drive west 0.1 miles on U.S. 50; there is a historical marker commemorating the surveyors of this section on the left. Continue 3.8 miles to Austin summit. A terrible range fire in the summer of 1981 destroyed much of the vegetation here. The fire was an environmental disaster, causing fears of later damage by erosion and flash floods.

Continue now down Pony Canyon for 2.1 miles and enter Austin. Drive 0.4 miles to the historical marker on the Gridley Store, on your right. We hope you will enjoy visiting this interesting and historic little town. There is a public park with picnic tables and a children's playground, restaurants, motels, gasoline stations, and grocery stores. Stokes Castle is south of the highway on a steep, winding road near the west edge of town. The pioneer cemeteries are on the west edge of town. There is a historical marker for Austin's churches 0.5 miles downhill from the Gridley Store, on the right side of the main street (U.S. 50). Completing your visit to Austin, return to the Gridley Store to resume the tour.

From the Gridley Store, drive downhill (west) on Austin's main street for 1.2 miles to the historical marker for Austin, on the left side of the highway.

Look in the valley below and behind the marker; this is the site of Clifton. A few picturesque ruins are out of sight below the cliff; remnants of the Nevada Central railway may be seen in the valley.

From the Austin historical marker, continue west on U.S. 50. The junction with SR 305 is 0.3 miles ahead, and just beyond that, the pioneer cemeteries of Austin. Continue on U.S. 50 for 5.4 miles to the historical marker for Jacobsville, on the right-hand side of the highway. The foundations referred to on the marker may be those of the Overland Stage station. The Pony Express station that was near this site has disappeared. Continue on U.S. 50 for 1.6 miles, and cross the Reese River (the trickle here is somewhat extravagantly called a *river*). Continue 0.7 miles to the Pony Express Trail marker. As the trail crosses the highway from this point, you may think that you can see the original Pony tracks. You should know, however, that the trail was marked and then traversed in the "reride" that celebrated the Pony's centennial in 1961.

Continue 9.3 miles to Mt. Airy summit. The Dry Wells Pony station and later the Overland Stage station were nearby. Dedicated researchers have been unable to pinpoint the exact location. Drive 6.0 miles and cross New Pass summit. Drive 2.4 miles to the historical marker and site of New Pass station on the Overland Stage route. Active concurrent with the Pony Express, the station served traffic in this area until the water supply ran out. Please remember that these ruins are protected by federal and state antiquities statutes.

Continue 12.6 miles, downhill through the canyon on U.S. 50 and into the Edwards Creek Valley. The Clan Alpine Range is ahead in the distance. The historical marker for Edwards Creek Valley is on the left. Drive 6.8 miles; there is a Pony Express Trail marker at the left, and in 3.8 miles, another Pony Express marker on the right. The Cold Springs settlement here at the left near the marker serves traffic through the area, much as the old Overland Stage stops did. Drive 1.5 miles, and look to the right; there are the ruins of an Overland Telegraph station. In 0.2 miles, there is an information kiosk and the trailhead for a one-and-

one-half-mile walk to the site of the Cold Springs Pony Express station, one of the largest ruins on the Pony trail.

From the Pony Express kiosk, the Rock Creek Overland Stage ruins are 0.2 miles ahead on U.S. 50. Here is a historical marker, and a good place to remember your trip through Pony Express country.

Return to Eureka, approximately 123 miles via U.S. 50.

TOUR TWO, The charcoal industry of the 1870s: Eureka — Fish Creek — Ruby Hill and return. Approximately 70 miles round trip. Pack a picnic and wear good walking shoes, as this is a trip that will encourage you to be out of the car.

Leave the courthouse on Main Street (U.S. 50), heading south and then east. Drive 0.8 miles. There is a rest area at the left, and a historical marker for Eureka. Continue on U.S. 50.

As you drive through this area, notice the piñon-juniper forest here. This is all second growth; during the charcoal era, the trees were all stripped from the hillsides around Eureka for more than thirty miles in all directions.

Drive 3.2 miles. There is a rest area on the right-hand side of the highway, with picnic tables and garbage cans. Continue 0.8 miles to Pinto summit, then continue downhill into Little Smokey (Fish Creek) Valley. Drive 5.2 miles to the junction with SR 20, and turn right toward Fish Creek. From here, you might imagine that you are following the route of a posse of angry deputies and businessmen with horses and wagons, planning nobody-knew-what, except to force the Charcoal Burners Association to deliver fuel to the smelters, and failing that, to effect arrests of recalcitrant carbonari.

Drive 7.9 miles along SR 20 to a fork in the route. Go to the right on a graded gravel road. The road is adequate for all vehicles with careful drivers, but not recommended for wintertime travel. Stay on the main traveled road. Continue 0.3 miles to the next intersection, and go to the right. Fish Creek ranch is visible ahead. Drive 2.0 miles to the next fork, and go to the left, not toward the ranch.

Drive 2.9 miles. There is a road at the right, but go straight ahead into the Fish Creek Range. Stay on the main road. These hills were once heavily wooded with piñon and juniper trees; most of what you see here is a hundred years old or less.

Drive 3.8 miles. Look to the left on the hill. There is a small kiln, and next to it, a pit for charcoal production. You may see the pit by walking up the track toward the kiln. Drive another 0.1 miles and look to the left. A rock dam holds an antique burning pit. The ground here is littered with bits of century-old charcoal.

Drive 0.6 miles; there is a burners' campsite on the right. Here, too, the ground is covered with blackened wood chips. We picked up a handful for souvenirs. Drive another 0.6 miles to the summit, and continue downhill. Watch for charcoal pits alongside the road; there is one in 0.7 miles, on the left.

Now you are entering the area of the Charcoal Burners War. The angry posse probably came this way. Drive 2.1 miles. There is a faint road on the right, the track perhaps followed by the posse to the burners' camp. *The road is suitable only for high-axle vehicles with careful drivers.*

If you wish to see the ''battlefield,'' turn right here on the faint road, and drive 0.4 miles to the fork. Take the right-hand fork, and drive 0.9 miles to the site of the ''war.'' There is literally nothing to mark the tragedy that occurred here. Some wood cut more than a century ago, and some lumps of charcoal are the only remnants on this historic site. Return to the main road. Now you might imagine that you follow the wagons carrying the dead Italians back to Eureka.

Drive back to the summit, 2.8 miles, then 10.3 miles to the SR 20 intersection, and 7.9 miles north to U.S. 50. Turn left on U.S. 50, and return toward Eureka.

Drive 9.2 miles, and enter Eureka. Drive 0.4 miles along Main Street (U.S. 50). Here is a slag heap and the ruins of a smelter that used the charcoal produced in the Fish Creek hills. Look at the mountain behind

and to the right; a chimney for the smelter once lay there, spewing lead fumes. Continue on Main Street, 0.4 miles to the courthouse and turn left. Drive uphill on the paved street; this is the main road to Ruby Hill, SR 604. Stay on SR 604.

Drive 0.5 miles to the junction. Stay on the main SR 604. This route leads past some of Eureka's historic cemeteries, clearly visible from the highway. The drive also gives great views of Diamond Valley, to the west and north.

Drive 0.8 miles; there is a road at the right. Stay on the main highway, and drive into Ruby Hill. The place is now mainly a milling site. The mine is visible as a headframe as you drive up the grade. Here is the source of the lead-silver ores of this district. Continue 1.1 miles, and you arrive at the mine gates and the end of SR 604. Turn around here, and prepare to return. A portion of the old town of Ruby Hill is visible on the hill ahead after you make the turnaround. The mine and mill are still active and guarded, so observe the ''no trespassing'' signs, and return downhill on SR 604, 2.4 miles to the courthouse.

TOUR THREE, Route of the Eureka and Palisade: Eureka — Palisade and return. Approximately 170 miles round trip. An alternate return includes a ghost-town tour via Beowawe—Crescent Valley—Tenabo—Cortez; it will add approximately 60 miles to the round trip. This trip will be especially interesting for railfans. Pack a picnic.

Leave the courthouse on Main Street (U.S. 50), heading northwest (downhill). Drive 0.4 miles to the junction with a paved fork and go to the right (north). The road leads along the former site of the Eureka and Palisade depot and shops. Drive 0.6 miles and look to the left to see the bed of the E&P. Continue on this paved road; side roads lead to ranches or to dead-ends. Drive 3.4 miles to a fork in the road; take the dirt road to the left, which follows the route of the E&P across the Diamond Valley. Drive 1.2 miles to a junction. The roadbed is clearly visible to the left. Be alert for cattle grazing here; hitting one could spoil your day.

At the junction, turn left and drive 0.7 miles to a ranch. The road crosses the E&P route just beyond the turn. This is a fine view of the roadbed.

Passing the ranch, SR 278 is just ahead; drive 0.4 miles and turn right on SR 278. Drive 0.7 miles; the airport road is at the right, but go straight ahead. Now the highway will roughly parallel the route of the E&P across Diamond Valley. The Diamond Range is on the right, Simpson Park Range on the left. You may see some wild horses along here; these are not the mustangs of romantic fame, but descendants of domestic horses turned out or escaped from farmers. Local ranchers regard these wild ones as pests and competitors with cattle for forage here. Drive 8.6 miles; the E&P roadbed crosses the highway. Drive 3.0 miles to the Diamond Valley historical marker, on the right side of the highway.

Drive 1.3 miles to the junction, and stay on SR 278; the E&P is visible along the left side of the highway. Drive 2.4 miles; there is a Pony Express Trail marker, a reminder that easy travel on a paved highway is a modern-day luxury.

Drive 0.6 miles. There is a sign pointing to the Mt. Hope mine. This is one of Eureka County's old silver mines; the 1980s saw a newly developing molybdenum operation on the site, under the control of Exxon. Visitors are not needed there.

Continue 1.5 miles, and look to the left of the highway; there is a structure of the E&P, stonework and a wooden culvert. This is one of the few remaining such structures on the entire route of the little railroad.

Continue 1.7 miles to Garden Pass. There was once a station of the E&P near this site. We saw some beautiful, big hawks playing here, looking for some unfortunate field mouse for breakfast. Continue 12.2 miles on SR 278; the road to Alpha is at the left. Once a station on the E&P, the building is now a private residence. Continue driving on SR 278. As you traverse this cattle-ranching country, remember that beef animals are bred for meat, not intelligence, so if you see them near the road, don't expect them to understand that they must get out of your way. Just proceed carefully.

Drive 5.2 miles. There is a road at the left with a sign for the Buckhorn mine. The Buckhorn is a gold mine, under active development in an older district by the Bethex Corporation. Tourists should not approach working mines. Continue on SR 278, and drive 10.7 miles.

The site here is Blackburns. Once the location of a station on the E&P, later a gasoline station and cafe, it is now abandoned. As late as 1960, the road on which you have been driving had only a thin paved surface, and this place was a welcome sight which marked the beginning of improved highway. Continue on SR 278; the E&P roadbed is visible from time to time to the left of the highway as you drive 13.4 miles toward Palisade and into the Cortez Mountains, to the Pieretti Hay Ranch. An E&P station near here was called Hay Ranch. Diamond Valley was covered in its early days by wild hay, some of which still exists.

Drive 4.8 miles to the sign for Pine Valley. Continue then 4.9 miles to the Bispo ranch, then 2.1 miles along Pine Creek, and look to the left side of the highway. There is a washed-out bridge on Pine Creek. In 1910, a great wet-mantle flood covered Pine Valley, through which you have been driving, for 30 miles. The channel you see was 1,000 feet wide in places.

Drive 1.9 miles. The Raines ranch on the right has an old railroad building on the site, but it was probably hauled in. Continue 1.4 miles to the historical marker for Palisade, on the right. Go into the turnaround to read the marker, then turn back to the highway and follow the sign for Palisade. Drive 1.0 mile on a dirt road, crossing a cattle guard, to a ranch. Then pass the ranch, and go up the grade; both Southern Pacific and Western Pacific tracks are below. Continue 0.5 miles to the bridge, and cross the Humboldt River. *Note this spot and plan to return here.* Just across the bridge, there is a junction; go to the right.

At the next fork, bear left, then to the right at the next intersection, and you may enjoy a tour of the ruins of old Palisade, the terminus of the railroad. Across the tracks, you can see the formations that gave Palisade its name. A brief ride up the canyon will display the palisades and the Humboldt River. Return to bridge.

If you have enjoyed the railfan tour, and wish to see it from the opposite direction, simply retrace your route back on SR 278, then on U.S. 50 to Eureka, approximately 84 miles.

Alternate return, ghost town tour: If your vehicle is in good condition, and you would like an adventure through some of the area's ghost towns, follow this route. At the bridge, do not recross the river, but instead turn and go along the dirt road leading downstream, then off to the right into the hills. The route is adequate for all vehicles with careful drivers, but somewhat twisting and steep in places. Drive 0.2 miles to a fork, and bear right, up the canyon. Stay on this main traveled road.

Drive 2.0 miles to the first summit, and continue on this main route. Drive another 0.4 miles to the second summit. Avoid side roads, which lead to dead-ends or to private property. Continue 0.7 miles to a junction and go straight ahead; the left-hand road leads to the private property visible below, and eventually, to an active iron mine.

Continue 3.2 miles to the paved intersection. Follow signs for I-80 and Battle Mountain; take the freeway access toward Battle Mountain. Drive 2.1 miles; avoid the Emigrant Pass exit, and continue 8.0 miles. The Tuscarora Mountains are on the right, Cortez Mountains on the left. This freeway parallels the Emigrant Trail. Take Exit #261 for Beowawe and Crescent Valley, SR 306. As you drive, the highest mountain visible in the distance to the right of the highway is Mt. Lewis.

Continue 4.7 miles along paved SR 306; the Horseshoe dude ranch is on the right. Continue 0.8 miles and cross the bridge, then 0.3 miles and cross the tracks and enter Beowawe. (For Beowawe's history, see the Northeastern Nevada tours.)

Continue on SR 306, 13.4 miles across Crescent Valley to the little settlement of that name. The beautiful peaks of Mt. Lewis will be visible occasionally on the right, beyond the Shoshone Range.

Crescent Valley has limited facilities, groceries,

gasoline, a bar. Continue driving 1.6 miles on SR 306 across the valley to the Lander County line. Drive 2.1 miles; there is a Highway Department gravel plant. Continue 3.5 miles to a crossroads, and go straight ahead on paved SR 306. Drive 1.2 miles, and there is a dirt road at the right, with Tenabo visible as a collection of buildings on the hillside. Visit Tenabo if you like, 1.5 miles up the dirt road.

Tenabo was a silver camp of the twentieth century. A rush began there after discoveries in 1907. With a peak population of about a thousand people, the place had numerous commercial establishments, and became a valley center. A mill operated for about three years, when the ore ran out. The post office closed in 1912. Later, some gold discoveries and even a dredging operation existed, producing some profits, but the town did not revive. An active mine exists, however, in the 1980s, without an apparent need for commerce in Tenabo. All of the buildings are deserted.

Return to the highway, and turn right (south). Drive 3.2 miles to a fork, and go to the left on a paved road to the Cortez mine. Drive 0.8 miles to an intersection, and stay to the left on the paved road. As you drive across the valley and into the Cortez Mountains, the big gold mine is ahead on the left. Drive 5.4 miles to the intersection. View this high technology gold mine from a distance; do not visit working mines without prior arrangement. Cortez mines began as a silver lode in the 1860s, and silver mining was sporadically profitable from that time until the 1930s, when the price dropped. In 1969, with the advance of technology to deal with low-grade gold ores, the place revived to what you see here. The town itself, however, has no such life.

Now turn right on a good, gravel road into the Cortez Mountains, through Cortez Canyon, and drive 2.7 miles. You can see the remnants of mining operations all over the hills here on the range to the left. There is a rock ruin on the left, a little smelter; the ruin on the right may have been a residence. Inside the smelter, the rocks show signs of melted material; check for snakes before crawling in.

Drive 2.3 miles on the main road; avoid side roads. As you near the top of the canyon Mt. Tenabo is on the left. At the intersection, turn to the left to see the ghost town of Cortez. Note this place as *you will return here*. Drive 1.0 mile to Cortez, and enjoy a look at the ruins. Then, return to the intersection (1.0 mile), and turn left (south) toward Austin, on a good, graveled road. Drive 3.2 miles to the Eureka County line.

Continue on this same road for 4.8 miles to a junction and turn left (east) toward Buckhorn and SR 278. Drive 2.7 miles to the summit, and a fork in the road. Keep to the right on the road straight across the valley, and drive 9.6 miles to another fork. Bear to the right; the left-hand road goes to the Buckhorn mine. Continue on the main road; side roads lead to mines and other private holdings. Drive 2.2 miles; there is a road on the right, but go straight ahead. Drive 0.1 miles and cross the stream in Denay Valley. Continue 2.2 miles to an intersection. Here, go straight ahead, downhill across Garden Valley, 1.0 mile to the crossing of Henderson Creek. Drive 0.1 miles to the junction, and go straight ahead (uphill) on the main road. Drive 3.3 miles, and here is SR 278. Turn right, toward Eureka, and return to Eureka. It is 39.7 miles on SR 278, to the intersection with U.S. 50, then a left turn and 3.5 miles on U.S. 50 to Eureka.

Tenabo

SOUTHEASTERN NEVADA

Northbound from Pioche on U.S. 93

SOUTHEASTERN NEVADA

Southeastern Nevada has at once the rowdiest and the most sedate history of any section of the state. Here, the followers of the mining frontier met the society of the Mormon missionary. In the end, oddly, these antithetical agglomerations decided that they could share both government and each other's company.

Early Settlers

Despite the appearance of good meadow land and a fair water supply, this southeastern section remained unvisited by explorers and wagon trains, with the single exception of the 1849 Death Valley Jayhawkers party. Paiutes roamed the area, hunting and gathering among the piñons and junipers. No great roads were planned to go through Meadow and Pahranagat valleys, no cross-country travelers took wagon roads this way to California's gold fields, no explorers or mappers or trappers voyaged about southeastern Nevada. The first use of the water by whites was probably in 1849. The first pioneers came only in 1857, when a group of Mormon missionaries explored the area, engaged in some marginal farming in Meadow Valley, and then, discouraged from their efforts by official church disapproval, departed the next year. They left no permanent settlement behind.

What actually started the confrontation between the Mormons and other residents of the area was the existence of silver ore in considerable quantities. In 1863, according to the legend, an impecunious Indian visited a missionary named William Hamblin, then living at St. George, Utah. The Indian had with him some good-looking rocks that he called something like "panagari" (silver); he suggested that Hamblin pay to see the source. Despite Governor Brigham Young's expressed disapproval of mining, Hamblin accepted the bargain and soon located the Panacker claim. The site is in Meadow Valley, a rough north-south stretch of about fourteen miles long by a mile wide, connecting at its southern end with the Meadow Valley Wash. The wash is a pleasant little stream, which soon provided enough water for local needs.

In March, Hamblin and a few other men formed the Meadow Valley Mining District. They began the customary mining practice then, hauling the ore to Salt Lake City that spring. But hostile Indians plagued the operation.

Meanwhile, and unrelated to the mining developments, although possibly in response to an enthusiastic description of the area written by Hamblin, a contingent of Mormon missionaries and settlers arrived in May 1864. The coming of this group, under the leadership of Francis Lee, signalled the renewal of LDS activity in southern Nevada (still then a part of Utah Territory). They established a colony at Panaca. A similar settlement was made in Eagle Valley, northeast of Panaca. A third colony, Callville, on the Colorado River (see Southern Nevada tours), completed what the LDS church leaders hoped would be a commercial complex. This dream was doomed by both politics and mineral developments.

The Indian troubles continued to cause problems for both miners and settlers. They took time off from other activities to construct an adobe fort in Eagle Valley, hoping to hold off the natives. Soon, soldiers from California were on the site, supposedly to protect the colonists, but, according to a government report, they "spent their leisure, when they were not killing Indians, in locating mines." Eventually, of course, the Indian troubles were solved in the usual way, a combination of force and persuasion.

Before long, other prospectors drifted into the area and staked claims, many of these overlapping previous ones. In 1869, a banker-capitalist, F. L. A. Pioche, acquired several of the earlier prospects and with others formed the Meadow Valley Mining Company. The center of the district in the Highland Range was named Pioche. Shortly afterwards, William H. Raymond and

John H. Ely, who had been mining in Pahranagat Valley, also moved into the Pioche section with the Raymond and Ely Company. Soon, the so-called Ely District become southern Nevada's most important nineteenth-century silver producer.

Still, politics remained to cause problems. The Nevada legislature asked, and in 1866 the Congress granted, an additional degree of longitude on the eastern border—a loss to Utah. The Mormons in the section declined to recognize this change in their seat of government and refused to pay taxes to Lincoln County and to Nevada, thus precipitating a conflict. In the end, after extensive surveys, the Mormon settlements were declared in 1870 to be in Nevada, but their leaders decided that, rather than shift their allegiance to the Silver State, they would leave it. As with the Muddy Valley towns (see Southern Nevada tours), the Mormon villages of northern Lincoln County were largely depopulated. More than twenty families had lived in Spring and Eagle valleys; by 1880, most of these had gone, leaving only a handful in what had been planned to be the foundation of the Latter Day Saints in southern Nevada.

"An interesting aspect of that production is that Grandfather and Father together always took the choicest of the lumber and sawed it up in convenient sizes, set it aside to cure under the most favorable circumstances for the construction of caskets. . . . The frontier area, of course, was totally dependent on the local resources for taking care of their own dead. . . . Whenever there was a death in town, immediately after you could hear the whine of saws and the pounding of hammers in a little shop that was just across the street from where we went to grammar school. We were always aware by the sound, if for no other reason than that it meant there was a death."

— Elbert B. Edwards, Panaca pioneer

Panaca

Only Panaca, with its population of a few hundred, remained as an outpost of the LDS church. This, the oldest surviving town in eastern Nevada, served the area as an agricultural supply center. In 1866, the Mormon church declared the "mission" status there revoked and elevated it to a ward. The Mormons continued to cultivate their fields and to sell produce to miners who had no time to grow their own. A school, small grocery and mercantile stores, a church, and modest homes on wide, shady streets marked Panaca's beginnings and also its history. The place never has had more than a few hundred residents, but it serves as a symbol of Mormonism's early efforts in southeastern Nevada.

Descendants of pioneer families of Panaca recall the important events of life there: taking grain to be ground into flour on what seemed an elaborate excursion to Enterprise, Utah; extra people around the town at hay harvest time; vandalizing the remnants of ghost towns, or playing mildly rowdy tricks on Halloween; the celebration of Pioneers Day, July 24; athletic competitions between school or town teams of Panaca and Pioche. These all appear as the sorts of activities that marked any farming community or Mormon village.

Workers in Panaca also engaged in cutting timber to supply the Pioche mines or for housing in the region, an activity that substantially reduced the wooded character of the hills in that section. The farming and ranching, with its center at Panaca, was initially quite successful, and the community, although small, prospered. Years of drought and overgrazing, however, took a heavy toll. Farming on a commercial scale eventually became economically marginal. The residents and descendants of the earliest settlers remained, however, and became well known in southern Nevada, and some gave their names to landmarks: Bunker, Leavitt, and several families of Woods, Lees, and Edwardses. One of the latter, William H. Edwards, claimed the distinction of being the first white child born in the valley.

When the shortline, narrow-gauge Caliente and

Pioche railroad came in 1907, it did not make great changes in Panaca's life, although it ended the town's extreme isolation while the railroad endured. The road was never profitable and was plagued throughout its ten-year life with political and financial intrigue. And when U.S. Highway 93 was built, it bypassed Panaca, leaving the little town a mile from the main road. The result was to place Panaca in a state of suspended animation, or historical inertia. This condition continued into the 1980s, making Panaca into almost a showplace of pioneer days.

Pahranagat Valley and Hiko

The western side of the Meadow Valley Wash contained the first developed mines of Lincoln County. The Pahranagat Valley, bordered by the Hiko Range on the east and the Pahranagats on the west, had good water and a meadow-covered floor. Mount Irish, in the Pahranagat Range, became the site of the early rush. There, in March 1865, prospectors discovered silver, and by that fall a small boom had developed. Early the next year, 1866, the by-now expanding population requested county government. Prospectors continued to pour in, especially from Austin, where times had become dull.

Four little towns came into existence at the mines of Mt. Irish: Logan City, Crescent, Silver Cañon, and Hiko. Of these, Hiko had the longest existence. By 1868, there were a post office, stores, and a courthouse. The latter building marked the success of petitions for local government; Hiko had been named the county seat.

The Pahranagat mines gained added prominence with a visit in 1866 by Nevada Governor Henry G. Blasdel. The governor nearly lost his life in crossing the uncharted deserts of Nevada in the trek to Pahranagat, inspecting the newly created Lincoln County and its government. Blasdel also discovered, as others would soon do, that the mines of Pahranagat had been over-sold. The furnace and mill constructed by developer William Raymond generally failed to perform adequately. Some ore was shipped to Salt Lake City, but this also proved disappointing.

Eventually, something less than a million dollars came from the Pahranagat mines. This district was neither one of the best nor one of the easiest to develop in the southeastern section. Hiko rather quickly gave up the county seat to the leading town of the Meadow Valley District; in 1871, Pioche assumed the role. There had been very little exercise of government in the county up to that time, so Hiko did not lose much except status. The election for changing the county seat told the story, with the following vote: for Pioche, 501; for Panaca, 54; and one each for Las Vegas (still a part of Lincoln County) and for Meadow Valley.

If Hiko lost the county seat, it retained a certain amount of commerce and a good deal of charm. Although by the 1980s it was only a collection of farms and a post office, Hiko had served for many years as the center for a ranching district. Cyril Bastian, one of the owners of extensive properties there, was a highly respected legislator for ten sessions, for some of which he served as speaker of the assembly. When reapportionment of the legislature came in the 1960s, Lincoln County lost a delegate, and one of its most distinguished representatives.

A second, and perhaps better-known feature of the Pahranagat Valley is a national wildlife refuge surrounding the lakes there. Full of natural springs and swamps, the place provides a home for dozens of varieties of waterfowl, and an outdoor classroom for naturalists.

Pioche

Five or six hundred million years ago, the area around Pioche was covered by an inland sea. Scientists have found here fossils of trilobites, brachiopods, jellyfish, and sponges, showing the nature of the section's early geologic history. During later times the area was heavily forested, and then the trees also became fossilized or petrified. Great forces thrust up the mountain ranges. Important mineralization came with these early times, and it was minerals that brought prospectors into the environment in the 1860s.

In 1869, as it became clear that the Pahranagat mines had been overestimated, the Raymond and Ely company, looking for new prospects, built a new mill at Bullionville, a short distance south from the discoveries at Pioche. The rich ores at Pioche, and the possibility of having the materials milled nearby, brought on one of the state's greatest mining rushes. From 1870 to 1873, Pioche was one of the busiest and toughest mining camps in the entire American West. With the movement of the county seat from Hiko to the newer town, there occurred a series of events that made Pioche's place secure in Nevada's history. It was not a tale full of honor.

The needful thing for a county seat has always been a courthouse. Pioche was no different, and plans were laid rather quickly for the construction of the building. Just over a year after the announcement of the first rich mines at Pioche, the blueprints were drawn and bids accepted for construction of a courthouse; $25,000 worth of bonds were sold at a discounted rate of $20,000 to raise the money. The county's tax resources did not develop the necessary cash, and the county commissioners were required to issue scrip in lieu of payments of money for salaries and materials. The looseness of this practice allowed the sheriff, as tax collector, to enrich himself considerably. The courthouse was built within the year, but the monetary problems continued.

The commissioners issued more bonds, and then more scrip. Within four years, they had plunged the county almost irretrievably into debt. During the 1880s and 1890s, with the courthouse bonds still outstanding, the county was forced to suspend school for lack of money. The citizenry apparently took no special notice of these difficulties, and cheerfully allowed their own taxes to run delinquent. Still, the courthouse debt compounded itself, by 1881 to over $300,000, and with no payments having been made on the principal. The amount was nearly one-half the county's assessed valuation. In 1890, the county tried to default on the debt, but was overruled by the state supreme court; the amount outstanding at that time was near $400,000.

Eventually, the state legislature tried to bail out the embattled county, but was unsuccessful; and by 1907,

"While the excitement continued in and about the mines there were even worse things going on among the law-and-order men who were supposed to keep the bad element down. . . . The Sheriff's office . . . was considered worth forty thousand dollars a year. All other things were in proportion. . . . The story of Lincoln County and the removal of the county-seat from Hiko to Pioche and the building of the Pioche court house I remember very well . . . It is not a story of which to be proud. It was steal, steal, early and late, and keep on stealing. That was the main point in Lincoln County affairs. It is now forty years since I first came to Lincoln County, but I remember very well the main points."

— Charles Gracey, mill superintendent,
Nevada Historical Society Report (1908)

the amount was up to $650,000. The county issued new bonds at that time, and in 1938—just in time for a new courthouse to be constructed—liquidated the indebtedness incurred in the 1870s. Of some assistance in the payment was the 1909 division of the county in two, with the new entity—Clark County—assuming part of the indebtedness.

Did the courthouse really cost a million dollars? That claim is widely made, and it might have been close. Lincoln County's historian puts the amount at about $800,000. The 1938 courthouse building was completely paid for in 1973, and since that time, Lincoln County has scrupulously avoided overwhelming itself with debts. The old courthouse stands as a monument to earlier days, when it represented "steal, steal, early and late." In the 1980s, plans were underway to reopen the building as a museum, ending its long vacation from Lincoln County political life.

But Pioche always symbolized more than politics. During its boom years, the place was reckoned the wildest, rowdiest, most deadly town, full of rough

Pioche's "million-dollar courthouse"

characters—a man's town, if he could stay alive. Pioche counted more than forty murders in its first five years; legend says that as many as seventy-two people were killed before there was a natural death in the place, a claim unsupported by a careful count. Still, the cemetery maintained by the residents of Pioche contained interesting evidence of the town's violent past.

Pioche endured the usual boom-bust cycle of mining camps. By the end of the 1870s, fires and floods had repeatedly ravaged the town, and miners began to leave for richer ground. Water rose in the mine shafts, and times were bleak.

Brief revivals occurred, and sudden rushes, but essentially Pioche's days as a mining camp had ended.

W. S. Godbe caused one of the revivals, demonstrating his faith in the district by constructing a huge smelter and mill just north of Pioche. The smelter was productive only for a couple of years in the 1890s, but it made a picturesque landmark for the desert landscape.

Pioche had a few more ups and downs. There was a small boom in the 1930s, spurred by the coming of inexpensive power from Hoover Dam. The power project was exceedingly important to all the Lincoln County towns. The settlements had been without public utilities since their founding; private generators took care of minimal needs there. Then, an enabling act of the legislature and the New Deal's Rural Electrification program allowed the organization of power districts. Construction of a line from Hoover Dam began in 1937 and was completed in 1938.

The coming of "cheap" power allowed the mines to reopen, and the demands of World War II industry kept them open for the duration of the conflict. When the Korean War began, the mines—especially manganese and tungsten—reopened, only to close again at the end of another war. The opening and closing of the mines explains the varieties of buildings in Pioche. There, one sees the architecture of several eras of history—and the dumps of at least three mining booms.

The boom of the mid-twentieth century enriched Pioche to a fair degree, for the town was on a main road and the mining camps were outside the city. Moreover, by the 1950s the character of mining booms had changed; companies no longer built what they expected to be cities, but depended instead on existing centers. Manganese, tungsten, zinc, and lead produced during the 1950s seemed perhaps unromantic, but the economic assistance helped to keep Pioche alive. After 1957, and the end of government support programs for tungsten, Pioche began another slide.

In the 1980s, with nearly the entire state of Nevada undergoing still another mining boom, Pioche seemed

left behind. Some local citizens talked of "maybe" this mine or that reopening, but clearly Pioche had entered the stages of maturity that marked her a "grand old lady" of Lincoln County. Off main lines of both highways and railroads, unsuitable geographically for real estate development, the county seat of Lincoln contained an interesting past and a few apparently contented residents. They even gave up their pretence of attracting tourists to the "boot hill" cemetery, allowing the markers to disappear or decay.

When the U.S. Air Force proposed in the late 1970s and early 1980s to plant MX missiles in the desert near Pioche, a few people speculated that the town might boom again, or metamorphose somehow into a great, new, modern metropolis. When the Air Force plans were cancelled, those who had bought real estate on these speculations were disappointed, but the long-time residents had seen booms and busts before; this was merely another of those. Most were simply relieved not to see another boom.

As the twentieth century neared its end, Pioche remained about as it had for the past quarter of that century, somewhat out of the mainstream, but committed

Godbe mill, Pioche

to retaining certain aspects of modern life, and equally committed to holding other such aspects at bay. The county-seat status kept a few people employed, and the cultural activities represented in museums and historical societies or businessmen's clubs seemed sufficient for a static population.

"This was in a period of about 1936 to 1938. And at that time, there was no local power as such in Lincoln County. They had little power plants in both Pioche and Panaca and Caliente, but they were locally-produced power. And when the mines did the production there from steam, they kept power for the town 'til about ten, ten-thirty. When they would go off the air, as it were, when they stopped producing power, why, the lights would blink twice and then they gave you about ten minutes to either get another—light, kerosene lamp, or a gas lamp—and then the power would be turned off. And so, the mines did not have enough power to really do the mining that was necessary."

— Louie Gardella, Agricultural Extension Agent

"Yeah, I guess Pioche generally has got a reputation of having been a rather wild camp. And there were a lot of stories when we were operating down there generated from these Saturday night dances and things like that. Even during the '30s, I guess, to some extent. But there weren't so many working you see, then. It was when the big crew came in. And there was excitement later on in the '40s when we had lots of men. The Ely Valley mine was goin'. The Caselton mine was goin'. The Prince mine was going, and the Bristol was going. . . . There were at least 600 people employed in the mines. So of course, with that number, there didn't have to be over a small percentage that was raisin' hell to generate a lot of pretty good stories."

— Paul Gemmill, mine superintendent

Bristol

Northwest of Pioche during the 1870s, while Pioche was enduring its decline, the miners of the Jack Rabbit district believed that they had struck rich silver ore. In the same general area, on the opposite side of the Bristol Range, miners at Bristol were trying to process ores with a newly built mill and smelter. For awhile, it seemed that they might indeed be correct, and that Lincoln County would have a new boom district; they were wrong. The complex ores of this end of the county resisted the primitive processing methods of the furnaces of that day. Both of the small districts had only a little output, except for publicity and promotion. Bristol even had a newspaper for about six months. The major remnant of these efforts was a row of three native-stone charcoal ovens at Bristol Well. These had provided fuel for the furnace that failed to accommodate the silver ores of the Bristol Range. Occasionally, the mines of Jack Rabbit or Bristol were opened, producing a fair amount during the post-World War I era, most recently operated by a Canadian firm. But modern methods proved as unsuccessful as earlier ones; the silver mines of Lincoln County have disappointed many experimenters. The total output of the Bristol and Jack Rabbit districts was in excess of $5 million, but other installations in the area were more profitable.

Delamar

Men thought that Delamar in the Meadow Valley Range would revive Lincoln County's mining industry. Gold ore was discovered there about 1892 and was reported to be of good quality. It took a promoter-capitalist named J. R. Delamar to make the boom work, however. Within two years after his takeover, there were more people in Delamar than in Pioche. Through the years of good returns, Delamar's town seemed to pour gold from its rocks; in fact, there were five years with over a million dollars' worth a year. The town attained a rather sophisticated character, with stores, saloons, homes, and a newspaper, along with several gold mines. The April Fool was the largest producer.

As most mining camps are inevitably doomed, Delamar was doubly so. The miners there used dry power drills, creating horrendous dust. As they drilled into the mine walls, the dry dust flew and the men inhaled the stuff. Before long, the miners began to gasp and die, victims of ''miner's con''—silicosis or consumption. Breathing the fine dust kicked up by the drills literally blocked their lung passages. The town of Delamar began to have a reputation as a ''widow maker.'' The tailings piles below the mill proved as dusty and dangerous as the mines themselves. Soon the town was dead, and the mines closed in 1909. Delamar became a ghost town on Nevada's southeastern desert.

Then the vacationers and collectors and hobbyists came. The buildings of Delamar began to come down, stick by stone, until only ruins were left. Wartime scrap drives took care of the metals. In the 1970s, there were a few picturesque ruins of walls standing, and an identifiable mill. At that time, the graveyards were still intact. By the early 1980s, the place existed only in people's memories or imaginations: a few holes where

foundations had been marked the former building sites, and ghouls and grave-robbers had about erased the cemeteries. Delamar was fine for its promoters, deadly for its workers, and eventually, merely a spot on the desert where once a town could have been. And the dust of the tailings pile blew endlessly over the flat.

Caliente

Caliente's history parallels not so much that of mining camps, but more that of the Union Pacific railroad. When Senator William Clark decided to build the Salt Lake to Los Angeles line, and started to do so in 1900, Caliente was staked out as a division point for switching, changing trains, and watering the steam engines. Around that beginning a pleasant little city grew up, not a mining boom camp and never a particularly prosperous ''whoopee town,'' but giving a stable and businesslike air among the more ephemeral settlements.

Originally, the place was called Culverwell, marking the ownership of a ranch nearby by a family of that name. The railroad itself was the subject of tremen-

Railroad depot at Caliente

dous controversy between two competing companies, with Clark finally victorious. Culverwell became "Calientes." When the post office was established in 1903, the *s* was dropped, and Caliente was born. The population tripled from 1902 to 1904; 33 registered voters in 1902, 105 by 1904. Mostly, the people worked for the railroad in various capacities, and lived in rather standard little railroad-supplied houses. By 1910, Caliente was the largest town in Lincoln County, with 1,755 residents. While Pioche might grow and subside, Caliente stayed about the same. The big events were those having to do with the railroad: floods and washouts, train derailments, the coming of diesel to replace steam, the eventual closing of the shops and roundhouse with the latter development, and, in the 1980s, the laying of a new track as the result of increased rail traffic.

The division point at Caliente vanished with the advent of modern technology, and the residents of the town have adjusted to that event. The city government took over the ornate railroad depot and remodeled it slightly to accommodate offices. The fancy architecture of the depot fitted nicely with a local branch library that displayed in an "art room" the works of local painters.

As Caliente looked forward to its next century, the citizens there seemed satisfied with an existence that, although it depended upon the vagaries of the railroad, reflected the rural atmosphere of a town that cared little for mining. A small amount of real-estate speculation took place around Caliente when the Air Force announced that it would put MX missiles nearby. The cancellation of the Air Force plans, however, seemed to bring little grief or even disappointment to Caliente residents, who said they would go ahead with designs for a new condominium-golf course development anyway—and enjoy it themselves. A favorable place on a U.S. highway, splendid recreation areas nearby, and a sort of calm outlook on life made Caliente's future seem as solid as its past.

Caselton and Prince

Not all the mining camps of Lincoln County came with the 1870s, nor did they all have the boom-and-bust cycle that plagued the others. In the 1930s, the Combined Metals Reduction Company, a well-capitalized and experienced organization, moved into the old mining district that had been the Prince. The Prince had produced nearly $8 million between 1910 and 1938. Now, aided by newly available electric power from Hoover Dam, Combined Metals modernized the plants, built mills, and made an industrial complex at the site. Not precious metals, but zinc, lead, and manganese came from this production. When the federal government began in the 1940s to stockpile strategic metals, the Caselton plant was ready. In the 1950s they produced tungsten as well.

When the Basic Magnesium plant got underway at Henderson (see Southern Nevada tours), Combined Metals participated in that operation. In 1950, with the mill built at Caselton to produce manganese, the development was hailed as an outstanding event in Nevada mining history. The Caselton installation continued through the boom of the 1950s to produce industrial minerals and a few rare metals and nonmetallics—beryllium, perlite—along with its steel hardeners.

In the mid-1950s, with mining all over the state slowing as the boom subsided, the Combined Metals outfit processed its tailings, cleaned out its old stopes, and, in 1957, with metals prices on the way down, closed. All through its life, however, Caselton was an exceedingly important contributor to Lincoln County's life and economy. Not so visible, and certainly not as colorful as the silver or gold camps, the Caselton-Prince gave more to the county than almost any other. In fact, despite its industrial character, the residents of Lincoln County spoke fondly of Caselton's past, and, in the 1980s, repeated rumors that some "outside capitalist" was about to unwater the shafts and tunnels to bring the Caselton-Prince back to life. It would take more than money, however, for water did indeed fill the holes, the mill and its equipment rusted, the miners' homes and cabins would take more than mere refurbishing. Technology had outmoded almost everything on the site. A nearby lime plant took over some

"1957 is when the mine closed for lack of profitability . . . and that's *known* ore that's sittin' there and blocked out, see? So, time is such an important factor that some of the proposed government mining legislation would kick you out of the property . . . They even propose that when the ore is mined out the property should revert to government ownership, you know, you'd have to say that the Caselton was mined out when it closed down. . . . And so it was mined out. But, then when the price comes up, it's not mined out any more. But even then it's not ready to operate, because it's gonna take a tremendous effort to get back in, rehabilitate adits and tunnels and raises, and retimber, get a crew trained and developed— . . . And yet, you could say, on paper, you can say it would be profitable, see?"

— Paul Gemmill, mine superintendent

"[I]n 1933, I moved to Moapa Valley and Caliente, Nevada to take over the operation of the Civilian Conservation Corps camps, then engaged in construction [of] facilities at the unofficial park sites in Clark and Lincoln counties, and performing flood control work at Panaca. . . .

"When the 1935 legislature was in session in Carson City, I prepared and steered to passage the act of March 28, 1935, creating a state park commission; also legislation establishing by law as state parks, the Valley of Fire in Clark County, Cathedral Gorge, Beaver Dam Wash, and Kershaw-Ryan Park. At that time I became well acquainted with [Governor] Richard S. Kirman, who appointed me as one of the five state park commissioners. I was duly elected chairman."

— Thomas W. Miller, State Park
Commission Chairman

of the usable houses. Still, with a better price for manganese, it might . . .

State Parks

Nevada is justly famous for excellent outdoor recreation. Lincoln County, probably more than any other subdivision of the state, exemplifies this aspect. Within only a few miles of each other are these state parks and recreation areas: Kershaw-Ryan State Park, Cathedral Gorge State Park, Beaver Dam Wash State Park, and Echo Canyon State Recreation Area. It is no accident that these facilities came to Lincoln County, for although more spectacular scenery and a broader financial base might exist in other sections, Lincoln County and southern Nevada had supporters who gave tirelessly to promotion of the outdoors there.

James G. Scrugham was southern Nevada's earliest outdoors advocate. As state engineer, Scrugham discovered the beauties of the scenery. As a scholar, Scrugham also had a special respect for the history and geology of the area and was able to put his feelings into concrete form. During his tenure as state engineer, Scrugham traveled widely through the southern section, calling attention to the antiquities and natural wonders there. He was a member of the first group to suggest the building of a dam on the Colorado River. He was responsible for the excavation of the Lost City ruins (see Southern Nevada tours). And Scrugham worked endlessly for the protection of Nevada's outdoors attractions. When he was elected governor in 1922, Scrugham continued from a new power base to support preservation of special sites in southern Nevada, and he worked for organized state action to carry out this purpose. Later, when he was in Congress (1933–1942), Scrugham was responsible for gaining appropriations for CCC work in Nevada, with much of the money devoted to developing the state's park and recreation areas. No other county benefited so strongly as did Lincoln.

Thomas W. Miller was Scrugham's friend and equally avid supporter of outdoor recreation. Miller was given charge of the CCC camps in Lincoln County, and in that capacity he carried out numerous assignments having to do with park development. The Valley of Fire (see Southern Nevada tours), Cathedral Gorge, and Kershaw-Ryan state parks had special attention from both Scrugham and Miller in their separate capacities. Miller's CCC position ended with the New Deal programs, but he also served for many years as chairman of the state park commission.

During the World War II period, the parks were nearly lost, owing to lack of money and minimal attention to maintenance. Governor Charles H. Russell, elected in 1950, heard pleas on behalf of restoring Nevada's outdoor recreation and supported a program of rehabilitation and expansion. The 1955 legislature restored the park commission and created a professional staff for overseeing the installations. Since that time, new parks and recreation areas have been organized in Nevada, including the Echo Canyon park in Lincoln County. Thomas W. Miller was honored with plaques and sites bearing his name in the Valley of Fire and Cathedral Gorge parks. Oddly, however, southern Nevada seems to have forgotten that the first supporter for preservation of the outdoors there was James G. Scrugham; no parks or monuments bear the name of the real father of the Nevada State Park System.

Lincoln County's state parks are particularly attractive and well kept. The jewel of the group is the earliest, the Kershaw-Ryan park, in a tiny, oak-and-vine-covered canyon near Caliente. The most spectacular scenery is undoubtedly at Cathedral Gorge, where wind and weather form the sandstone into wonderful shapes. The Echo Canyon area offers the best fishing in the group—indeed, some of the best fishing in southern Nevada, outside of Lake Mead. Beaver Dam Wash rounds out the group with its wild and rather primitive camping and hiking enticements.

All of the parks serve the deer-hunting crowds in the Fall and the fisherpeople in the Spring and Summer; at any time, travelers can enjoy especially good facilities in lovely surroundings. As the parks have matured, so also have the staff members, who now offer expert knowledge in the natural history of each area as well as a special dedication to the system and to the touring public. Nowhere in the Park System are these attri-

"We spent a lot of our time over in what is now the Cathedral Gorge State Park. . . . We were possibly fifteen or sixteen years old at the time. We would go home with stories of what we had seen, then we got a camera and took pictures. . . . Finally, we carried so many stories home that our fathers became interested and went out with us on occasion. We took them into some of the unknown areas. They became very enthused. Uncle Will was at that time president of the Panaca Commercial Club . . . Father was one of the directors and they took advantage of tours of every politician through the state and had us show them through. It was in this way that I got acquainted first with such people as Governor Jim Scrugham. . . .

"On one occasion, I was called out of school to go serve as a guide for a party that was headed by Governor Jim Scrugham. He had in with him at that time, Dr. Mark Harrington, the archaeologist who at that time was doing exploratory work in the buried city in Moapa Valley. . . . We gave them the deluxe tour."

— Elbert B. Edwards, Panaca pioneer

butes so manifest as at the parks of southeastern Nevada.

From its evangelistic or violent beginnings, Lincoln County has evolved into one of the quietest sections of Nevada. The people of the southeastern region find enjoyment in calm and pleasant surroundings. If a mining boom should touch down in this area again, undoubtedly the residents would accept that as easily as they accept their present tranquility. Still, a traveler seeking solace from the jangle of everyday life elsewhere might well hope that the mines stay full of water and that the lakes and reservoirs stay full of fish.

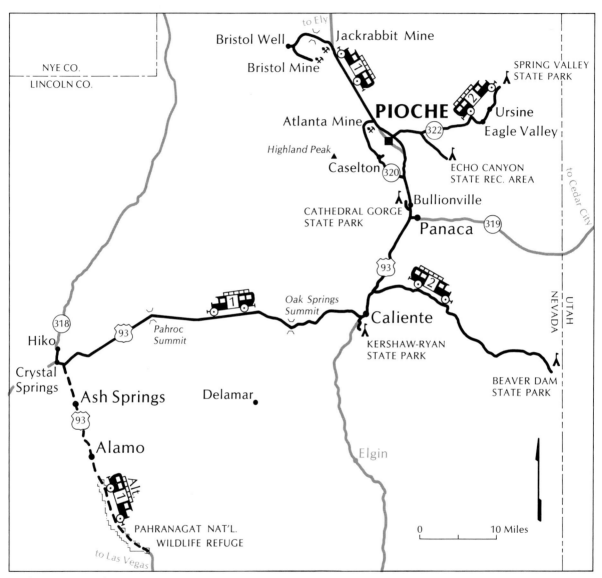

NYE CO.
LINCOLN CO.

to Ely

Bristol Well
Bristol Mine

Jackrabbit Mine

SPRING VALLEY
STATE PARK

PIOCHE

Ursine
Eagle Valley

Atlanta Mine

322

Highland Peak

320

Caselton

ECHO CANYON
STATE REC. AREA

Bullionville

CATHEDRAL GORGE
STATE PARK

Panaca

319

93

318

Hiko

93

Pahroc Summit

Oak Springs Summit

Caliente

KERSHAW-RYAN
STATE PARK

UTAH
NEVADA

to Cedar City

Crystal
Springs

Ash Springs

93

Delamar

Elgin

BEAVER DAM
STATE PARK

Alamo

Alt.

PAHRANAGAT NAT'L.
WILDLIFE REFUGE

to Las Vegas

0   10 Miles

Southeastern Nevada, tours 1, 2

TOURING IN SOUTHEASTERN NEVADA

———⟨∞⟩———

Touring in this section of the state is exciting and pleasurable, but the distances between sites can seem tremendous. We advise, therefore, that before undertaking any of the trips, you check your vehicle carefully and make sure that you understand the text of the tour directions fully. Traveling here should not be considered hazardous, and our directions will carry a tourist into some of the most easily accessible sites. Still, prudence dictates following the warnings.

You are especially encouraged in Southeastern Nevada to take along camping gear. Here, you will find some of the best outdoor recreation in the state in picturesque surroundings. You will also want a camera, of course, for the historic sites and scenery lend themselves to that activity.

The trips begin in front of the Lincoln County Museum on the main street of Pioche.

What to see in Pioche: Stop first at the Lincoln County Museum and library on the main street. Here, you will find relics, artifacts, minerals, and memorabilia from Lincoln County's earlier days. The museum attendant is knowledgeable about the area and its lore. There is a small amount of printed matter for sale at the museum. The tours in this section begin in front of the museum.

A second museum in the "million-dollar courthouse" is in the planning stages in the early 1980s; an exhibit of historic photos there is open to the public, but the hours are limited. The courthouse is on a side street near the Lincoln County Museum and is visible from almost anywhere in town.

The "new" county courthouse is north (downhill) from the museum. Ask in the district attorney's office for a brochure about the area. The old engine on display in front of the courthouse is a relic of the Pioche and Bullionville railroad.

The pioneer cemeteries are at the north edge of town, past the courthouse.

Pioche has adequate facilities for tourists, but in limited quantities. Reservations for lodging are recommended. Take time to drive around the town, for it contains many older structures from earlier days.

TOUR ONE, Historic towns of southeastern Nevada: Pioche — Bristol Well — Bristol mine — Caselton — Panaca — Caliente — Hiko and return. Approximately 200 miles round trip (with a 54-mile side trip to Pahranagat National Wildlife Refuge). Pack a picnic or plan to visit a cafe in Caliente.

Beginning your tour at the Lincoln County Museum on Main Street, drive north (downhill) a half block to the junction with U.S. 93, and turn left onto U.S. 93. Drive north along U.S. 93 to enjoy the views of the Highland and Bristol ranges. Drive 2.3 miles; the road to the Atlanta mine is on the left. Go straight ahead on the main paved highway. Continue 1.0 mile to a crossroads and sign for Caselton-Prince; stay on U.S. 93. Drive 10.3 miles to the historical marker for Jack Rabbit, on the left side of the highway, and turn left, cross the cattle guard, and bear right (toward Sunnyside) on

a graded dirt road. The road is adequate for all vehicles with careful drivers.

Continue 1.2 miles. There are side roads right and left here, but go straight ahead toward Bristol Well. You are advised to stay off the side roads in this area, as they lead to dead ends or to private property. Continue 2.1 miles and cross Bristol Pass, elevation 6,149. Continue 3.0 miles to a fork in the road. Go to the right toward Bristol Well. Note this intersection, as *you will return here.*

Continue 1.0 mile to a fork in the road, and bear left. The Bristol Well settlement ruins show to the right, and the charcoal ovens are visible ahead to the right. Drive 0.3 miles to the green sandstone charcoal kilns. North of the ovens are the slag heap and remnants of the settlement of Bristol Well, which in the 1890s had a population of about 400. The ovens here were built and operated for awhile after 1880 to supply smelting fuel for the ores of the Bristol Mine. The piñon and juniper trees you see around this place are all second growth; the native trees were cut to feed the charcoal industry. The cemetery, a mile south of here, had only one remaining headstone in 1981. We found some ancient sea-bed coral in our walk around. Explore the area, and then return to the fork in the road, approximately 1.3 miles back.

Pioche business district

At the fork in the road, this time go to the right, toward the Bristol mine. Stay on the main road; side roads are chancy. Drive 3.1 miles to the border of the Bristol property. View the mine and its works from this point, and turn around in the space provided. Do not violate "no trespassing" signs or try to approach mines without prior permission. The Bristol was still worked in the 1970s, and could open again. Return to the main road, 3.1 miles. At the fork in the road, keep straight ahead to the right, and retrace your route to Highway 93, 6.3 miles. At U.S. 93, turn right toward Pioche.

Drive 10.3 miles, and turn right on SR 320, a paved road toward Caselton and the Prince mine. Look to the left on the mountain for a view of the Atlanta mine. Drive 3.0 miles to a junction of three roads; take the middle one. The roads on either side go to private, guarded property. Continue 2.4 miles to the signs for Caselton Heights; stay on the paved SR 320. To the left at the junction is Sierra Chemical Company's lime operation; some of the workers live at Caselton Heights. Drive 0.6 miles, and take the left fork to see the Caselton mill. Drive 0.4 miles, and the pavement ends at the Caselton mill. Observe the "no trespassing" signs; there are caretakers on the property. But the mill is photogenic! Turn around here and return to the highway, 0.4 miles.

At the junction with SR 320, turn left, and enjoy a view of Meadow Valley to the right as you drive 4.6 miles to the junction with U.S. 93. Turn right (toward Caliente).

Drive 3.9 miles to the Bullionville historical marker, on the right-hand side of the highway. There is a small cemetery on the knoll above. Continue 0.2 miles to the sign for Cathedral Gorge State Park. Stay on the highway (see Tour Two in this section). Drive 0.9 miles and turn left to Panaca on SR 319. Panaca is 0.8 miles ahead.

Panaca's commercial facilities are extremely limited, consisting of a gasoline station, small grocery store, post office. The historical marker, 0.3 miles ahead, is opposite the school and the LDS church. Panaca's main economic and cultural ties are with

Utah; Cedar City is 82 miles east. Do enjoy a drive around this historic village, and see the many interesting old homes and other buildings. This is the place to appreciate the hard pioneering environment endured by the Mormons of this community.

Return to U.S. 93, 1.1 miles, and turn left (toward Caliente). The highway parallels the tracks of the Union Pacific, Caliente's—and southern Nevada's—transportation lifeline through this lush and beautiful Meadow Valley. Drive 3.9 miles. In a building at the right of the highway is the office of the *Lincoln County Record*. The *Record* began publication as the *Ely Record* in September of 1870, at Pioche. Two years later, it was called the *Pioche Daily Record*. Before long, the paper became a weekly, reflecting the hard times of the area, and finally, in these days, it maintains an office in the building you see here.

Drive 9.1 miles and enter Caliente. This is the metropolis of southeastern Nevada. All services are available, if somewhat limited in quantity and style. Caliente, besides being a transportation center, is also the site for the state training school for delinquent girls. These young women learn vocational skills at the center and attend Lincoln County schools. (A similar facility for boys is at Elko.) The historical marker is 0.8 miles beyond where you entered the town limit, on the railroad right-of-way. Return to this place to continue the tour, after you finish your visit to Caliente.

Besides having necessary commercial services, Caliente has scenery worth investigating. Drive around the old residential sections of the town, and do go by the depot. If the library is open, you might enjoy the art gallery (the library's hours are limited). Return then to the historical marker, and drive south on U.S. 93, 1.2 miles to the south town limit.

Bear right and go west along U.S. 93 through the elegant canyon of the Meadow Valley Wash. Here are high cliffs, sandstone pillars and formations in many colors. The formations change with every storm and season. The road ascends to Oak Springs summit, and then leads down to Delamar Valley.

Drive 6.8 miles. There is a roadside rest with picnic tables, garbage cans, and free overnight parking, but

The "rolling rocks" of Pahranagat

no water and no toilets. Continue 3.1 miles to the Oak Springs summit.

After passing the summit, you may notice that the piñon and juniper have given way to another type of Nevada desert vegetation, the Joshua tree. Drive 6.8 miles; the historical marker for Delamar is on the left side of the highway.

The road to Delamar, behind the sign, is not suitable for ordinary vehicles, and the site of the old town has become filthy and dangerous. We cannot recommend a tour through there. Continue west on U.S. 93.

You will be driving toward the border of the Las Vegas Bombing and Gunnery Range and the Nevada Test Site. You may see fighter pilots from Nellis Air Force Base practicing aerobatics and military maneuvers. We saw a golden eagle doing as well as the fighter planes!

The road drops down into the Pahranagat Valley, where the center was Hiko, early county seat of Lincoln County. In the hills surrounding the valley are strange stone formations that inspired Dan De Quille, a famous western writer, to write a mock serious piece about the "rolling rocks of Pahranagat." The article brought fame of a sort to this out-of-the-way spot in southeastern Nevada. The boulders, De Quille averred, had a strange magnetic relationship to the valley floor, and on some mysterious inner command, they rolled down—and up—the valley's sides. Do you believe that? A lot of people did, and then refused to *dis*believe it when De Quille proclaimed his hoax.

Drive 24.2 miles, and you will see a view of Pahranagat Valley, a green spot on the desert. Drive 1.4 miles to the junction of SR 375 & U.S. 93. Turn right onto SR 375. Drive west another 0.6 miles to SR 318, and turn right toward Hiko. Just past the junction on the left, next to the trees, is the historical marker for Crystal Springs.

Drive 3.9 miles. The office of this Wildlife Management Area is on the right. The area was named to honor Nevada Senator Key Pittman, coauthor of the Pittman-Robertson Act, which supports federal assistance to sections like this one.

Drive 0.7 miles. The brick ruins on the left are all that remains of Hiko. At one time, Hiko contained homes, mills, and business houses. Some of the remnants were used by local ranchers, and others simply decayed into the valley floor. The historical marker for Hiko is 0.2 miles further, on the left. The little cemetery behind the marker is the private plot of the Castles family.

Return 5.4 miles to the junction of U.S. 93 and SR 375 and turn left (northeast) on U.S. 93 to return to Pioche, approximately 68 miles.

Side trip from this point: If you wish to see the Pahranagat Lake Wildlife Refuge, instead of turning toward Pioche, follow the signs for the drive to Ash Springs and Alamo. The Wildlife Refuge is approximately a 54-mile round trip from this point, all on paved roads. Follow these directions:

From the junction, drive south on U.S. 50 for 5.0 miles to Ash Springs. Here are gasoline, groceries, a cafe. Drive 7.4 miles to the Alamo historical marker, at the right-hand side of the highway. This is the edge of Alamo; if you wish to tour the town, drive down to the right.

Drive 3.5 miles to the upper end of Upper Pahranagat Lake, and the boundary of the Wildlife Refuge. The southern boundary of the Wildlife Refuge is 11.0 miles from this point. You can drive along the edge of the lakes and look for water birds, or view them from the highway. There are viewpoints and picnic facilities every few miles for the entire distance. When you reach the lower end of Lower Pahranagat Lake, turn around, and return to the junction, and then to Pioche, about 95 miles.

TOUR TWO, Southeastern Nevada state parks: Pioche — Cathedral Gorge — Kershaw-Ryan — Beaver Dam — Spring Valley — Echo Dam and return. Approximately 167 miles round trip. Pack a picnic or camping gear.

Leaving the Lincoln County Museum, drive south (uphill) on Main Street to the junction with U.S. 93, and turn right (toward Caliente). Drive 7.5 miles to Miller Point, and turn right off the highway. The view point for Cathedral Gorge is 0.4 miles from the turn. The name honors Thomas W. Miller, first chairman of the Nevada State Park Commission. At Miller Point, there is a fine view and photo spot for Cathedral Gorge, interpretive plaques, a brief natural-history walking tour, and picnic tables, toilets, and garbage cans. After visiting here, return to the highway, 0.4 miles, and turn right.

Drive 1.9 miles; the Bullionville historical marker is on the right. Continue 0.2 miles, past the marker, and turn right to Cathedral Gorge State Park. Drive 0.8 miles to the fork in the road, and turn left; the campground is 0.7 miles ahead. At the campground, there are sites for trailers, tents, and campers in a shady area, along with water, showers, toilets, and beautiful views of the Gorge. Completing your look at the campground, return to the fork in the road, 0.7 miles, and turn left for a driving view—and opportunities to walk and touch—in the main scenic area of Cathedral Gorge. The red and yellow sandstone formations provide interesting and colorful scenery, and every storm changes their shapes. After visiting Cathedral Gorge, return to the highway, 0.8 miles, and turn right toward Caliente.

Drive 13.9 miles and enter Caliente. This little railroad community has all necessary services for tourists. The public offices, including the county branch library and an art gallery featuring the work of local artists, are in the depot building. (The historical marker is 0.8 miles beyond the entrance to the town, on the left side of the main street on the railroad right-of-way.) Drive through Caliente on the main street, 1.3 miles to the entrance for Kershaw-Ryan park, and turn left. The park is 3.0 miles from the turn.

Kershaw-Ryan state park is a cool, green, quiet little canyon site, a gem in the State Park System. Here are picnic facilities, drinking water, showers, toilets, campsites for campers or tents or trailers. After enjoying Kershaw-Ryan, return 3.0 miles to the highway and turn right on U.S. 93. Retrace your route through Caliente, driving 6.4 miles to a right turn for Beaver Dam Wash state park.

Beaver Dam is a semi-primitive campground in a beautiful, juniper-piñon forest/canyon location. Trail-

Cathedral Gorge State Park

ers and big campers are neither recommended nor allowed. This most remote of all Nevada state parks is at the end of 28 miles of graded dirt road. With the stated exceptions of trailers and big campers, the road is adequate for vehicles in good condition and with careful drivers. If you have a pet along on this trip, we advise keeping it under control at Beaver Dam. There are resident families of skunks—friendly and curious, but if disturbed, ruinous for a good day or evening! Return to U.S. 93 to continue your tour of state parks.

Turn right on U.S. 93, driving 16.4 miles north, staying on the truck route at the turnoff, avoiding Pioche; continue 2.8 miles to the junction of U.S. 93 and SR 322, and turn right (east) toward Ursine.

Drive 1.2 miles. There is a dirt road at the left; keep straight ahead on the paved road. Continue 2.8 miles to the intersection, and go straight ahead toward Ursine on SR 322. Continue 5.2 miles; stay straight ahead, and do not go on the dirt road to Rose Valley on the right. Drive 5.2 miles to the Eagle Valley fort historical marker, on the right. Here is a list of the earliest settlers sent by the Mormon Church into this area as colonists, along with a brief account of their problems with the Indians. Stay on the paved road, around the outskirts of Ursine. Notice that this is cattle-grazing country, and be alert for animals on the highway. That's a fine excuse for a slow drive up this beautiful canyon!

Drive 3.2 miles and arrive at Spring Valley State Park. Here is a fishing haven—a lake, boat ramp, camping, a fish-cleaning station, and information about the fishing on the bulletin board. Other facilities in this lovely desert lake setting include picnic tables, toilets, a trailer sanitary station, and a telephone. There are car pull-outs and places to stand fishing all around this lake. After your inspection here, return to the park entrance, and retrace your route along SR 322 for 13.5 miles and turn left onto SR 86 toward Echo Dam. As you drive, notice the red sandstone formations, and the view of Highland Peak as you head north.

On paved SR 86, drive 7.7 miles to Echo Dam park. This is an enjoyable place to camp or picnic. There is lake fishing; camps for tents, campers, or trailers; toilets, water at all sites, covered picnic tables. Occasionally, the water behind Echo Dam disappears almost overnight; nobody really knows why, and that phenomenon does not destroy the prospect of pleasant activities here. Finishing your visit to Echo Dam, retrace your route to SR 322, and turn left toward Pioche, with the view of Mt. Wilson to the right of the road as you drive. After the turn, return to Pioche, approximately 4.0 miles.

SOUTHERN NEVADA

Petroglyphs in Clark County

SOUTHERN NEVADA

The area now comprising southern Nevada began its settlement not like the rest of the state for economic reasons, but from religion. No other section of the state had so many early missionary pioneers or so heavy a religious impact.

Explorers and Early Settlers

The first white people in the area that then belonged to the Spanish Empire were priest-explorers, spying out what became the Old Spanish Trail. This road led from Santa Fe, New Mexico, to the missions of southern California. Fr. Francisco Garcés is thought to have entered the Las Vegas Valley in 1776, looking not only for a route along the Colorado River, but also for prospective converts. A second journey that same year by Fr. Silvestre Velez de Escalante failed to traverse the Great Basin. The importance of these trips in 1776 was twofold: first, the approaches to the trail were marked out for future travel, and secondly, because they failed fully to explore the area and relied on legends told in a tongue they did not completely comprehend, the Spanish travelers made significant errors on their resulting maps. From these explorations came the myth of the San Buenaventura River, crossing the Great Basin to empty into the Pacific Ocean. For the next seventy years, trappers, mappers, and explorers searched in vain for the great rivercourse that crossed the West to the Pacific. Not until John C. Frémont came into the Great Basin in the 1840s was the legend finally killed. After 1776, in any event, the Spanish had little interest in developing colonies in the deserts here.

In 1821, the section came under the domination of Mexico, but the Mexican government seemingly thought it not valuable enough to explore or develop. In 1826, Jedediah Smith traveled along the Colorado River but apparently did not approach *las vegas*. In 1830, finally, people began to come into the Las Vegas valley, but they were travelers, not settlers. The 1,200-mile-long Spanish Trail became a relatively active road after traders from Santa Fe brought a pack train through the area in 1830-1831. The first of this travel extended from the junction of the Colorado River and the Las Vegas Wash. The traffic continued until about 1848, with various revisions of the route. A shorter version of the road led by a trail from the Colorado River in Utah, into Nevada along the Virgin River, and then across the desert to Las Vegas, passing near the present site of Bunkerville.

A second road was opened in 1847 across the southern area, this leading into what was eventually called Death Valley. The plan was to mark out a way for Mormon travel between Salt Lake City and California, and to avoid the high passes of the Sierra Nevada by going south. So great were the hardships and so frequent the disasters that few people used the route after the first trials.

Still, people traveled across the Old Spanish Trail, and they had to stop somewhere; "las vegas," the marshy plain or meadows, seemed like a good camping spot. By the 1850s, the Mormon authorities had decided to colonize this section of New Mexico, and therefore sent out a party of missionaries to settle at Las Vegas in the summer of 1855.

"We found Las Vegas to be a nice patch of grass about half a mile wide and two or three miles long, situated at the foot of a bench 40 or 50 feet high. The valley faces east, and a pretty clear stream of water, about the size of a common millrace, comes from two springs about four miles west of our location."

— George W. Bean, missionary-interpreter, letter, June 24, 1855

The group went quickly to work, laying out a fort, farms, and irrigation works, and planting crops. The land was not exactly hospitable; no satisfactory wood for building was available, although there was firewood that could be used later. At that time of year, the water in canteens heated to scalding. Eventually, mountains twenty miles and more away were found to have timber, and construction began. The adobe fort, about 150 feet square and 14 feet high, took shape. And the mission objective, to convert the Indians to the faith of the Latter Day Saints, seemed to be succeeding. Perhaps more disinterested observers thought the natives' response could be laid mainly to kindly treatment and an enhancement of their rough and primitive diet.

Troubles arose at the capital of the theocracy in Salt Lake City; and then, following the general disappointment with the settlement south of the Great Basin, in September 1858, the Mormon colonists departed. They left very little behind. However, they were destined to try again to colonize other sites nearby. The water rights of Las Vegas Valley were acquired by a local agriculturalist, O. D. Gass. Gass and his family lived in the old fort building. With only a few other ranches in the area, Gass became a prominent political figure in Arizona after his place was declared to be in that newly organized Territory. Nevada acquired this southern section from Arizona in 1867.

In 1882, the old Las Vegas ranch came into the hands of Archibald and Helen J. Stewart, and another nearby was owned by the Kyle (or Kiel) family. These two families, both with colorful and interesting histories, continued to live in the area, raising produce to sell to miners and travelers through the section. The Kyles gave their name to local landmarks, and Helen J. Stewart presided over the most important ranch site in the valley. In May 1905, all of that changed.

Meanwhile, other settlements had been erected by the Mormons in their colonizing efforts. One of these, Callville on the Colorado River, was designed and built by Anson Call as a supply base for Mormons and other travelers along the stream. Begun in 1864 as an experiment in dealing with the Colorado River naviga-

tion trade, the place was busy for only a few years, and by June 1869 it was abandoned—probably with the prospect of a cross-country railroad taking away the commerce. The walls of the storehouse at Callville stood on the site for more than fifty years, only to be covered by the waters that came with Lake Mead. Callville Bay retained the name.

The Muddy River

Other settlements arose along the reaches of the Muddy and Virgin Rivers. Because they had received promising reports on the possibilities of agriculture along the two little streams, the Latter Day Saints felt optimistic about chances for establishing an agrarian empire there. These leaders came into the Muddy (Moapa) Valley in January 1865 at the command of the church's council. The towns were named Overton, St. Thomas, and St. Joseph; others were supposed to follow when needed. The sites overlooked the river in the general area where, hundreds of years before, Pueblo and Basketmaker tribes had established their own villages. The land was drained, and a fair agricultural economy grew up. Markets existed both in Utah and locally.

All the towns were planned in advance, with wide streets, church square, schools, and houses. Still, the church authorities and settlers alike had reckoned without the severities of southern Nevada's soil and climate. St. Joseph never had any substantial buildings except for a fort. Overton was destined to grow in other directions, and St. Thomas had yet another fate. In 1870, Brigham Young pronounced himself dissatisfied with the Muddy River Valley developments and withdrew much of the church's support.

Just a few years previous, the settlements had become part of Nevada. The residents there did not agree with the survey, asserting that they were in Arizona, and therefore owed no taxes to Nevada. By 1870, with a new survey completed, Lincoln County began to press the Muddy Valley residents for payment of back taxes. The church authorities and the settlers petitioned national and state legislatures for forgiveness of these levies, but were refused. At a meeting in Salt Lake

City in December 1870, the settlers decided to leave Muddy Valley, and did so, beginning in February the next year. Within a short time, Daniel Bonelli, operator of a ferry concession where the Virgin flowed into the Colorado River, was the only Mormon resident left. The others—as many as 600—abandoned their homes and fields, most to return to Utah in the area of Glendale and Mount Carmel.

The loss of this stable population was a heavy blow to southern Nevada's economy. The valley became an outlaw haven, home of cattle rustlers and horse thieves, while the houses decayed and orchards and vineyards died out. The Mormons, however, did try again to colonize the section. In the 1870s, Bunkerville and Mesquite came with a new migration, and old St. Joseph was reborn as Logandale. Again, these tiny communities formed an agrarian backbone for southern Nevada, but it was never quite the same as it had been before 1871.

The sites of the older towns were destined for great change. In the 1930s, with the building of the great dam on the Colorado River at Black Canyon, it became necessary to plan in a different direction. St. Thomas would be inundated by the waters of what was called Lake Mead behind the dam. At the same time, the remnants of the Pueblo culture lay along the banks of the river, in the path of the rise of the lake. For several years, beginning in the late 1920s, various private citizens, later the CCC and the National Park Service, and some local public agencies started to try to retrieve the artifacts of the ancient culture. Governor James G. Scrugham, acutely aware of the values of the relics, called on Mark R. Harrington, archaeologist of the Southwest Museum to investigate the site. The result of this work was that Harrington and members of the staff of the Museum of the American Indian in New York examined the artifacts and saved many of them from the waters of the artificial lake. Moreover, they established the importance of the area for archaeological study.

A museum was built at Overton by the CCC and others and was eventually taken over by the state of Nevada. The Overton or ''Lost City'' museum stands as a monument and repository for the early people of the Muddy and Virgin valleys. The site is more than thirty miles in length, and although much of it was covered by Lake Mead, remnants of the structures built before A.D. 800 existed into the last quarter of the twentieth century.

Long before the Basketmaker and Pueblo peoples inhabited this section, other prehistoric tribes roamed the area. In 1933, about ten miles north of Las Vegas, an archaeologist made a discovery that indicated very old bones of man in association with extinct animals. Following long study, and after the development of carbon dating, the scientists concluded that man had inhabited this, the Tule Springs site, as long as ten to thirteen thousand years before. The Tule Springs discovery was very important, for it placed man in what became southern Nevada in Pleistocene times, thousands of years before any previous study had indicated, and furthermore, showed the aborigines to be more culturally advanced than might have been expected.

Mining Camps

The mines of southern Nevada were, like its agriculture, partly developed by Mormons. The most famous of the early mines was the Potosi, the oldest lode mine in the state. This lead-silver deposit supposedly was uncovered originally in 1847 by members of the Mormon Battalion, and named for their Indian guide. The other version of the name is that it comes from a similar district in the eastern United States. In 1856, Mormons led by another Paiute scout found metal there. The ''saints'' were unable to smelt the rather brittle ore, and the next effort came in 1861, when the Colorado Mining Company established an industrial complex that included a town and a smelter. Shortly, the place had some one hundred miners and the usual mining camp features. This operation lasted only for a couple of years, and the next reopening was accomplished by the Silver State Mining Company. The Potosi became the Comet mine.

Later developments, into the first quarter of the twentieth century, brought commercial zinc mining to the Potosi district. At one time in the 1920s, this was Nevada's largest zinc-producing operation. The production from the single mine was about $4.5 million. The most interesting part of the Potosi story, however, is in its folklore.

Because of the softness of the silver-lead ore, and the operation of the primitive smelting apparatus at the site, the Indians, the Mormons, and later travelers through the area all swore that one group or another was making *silver* bullets at the Potosi. That probably was untrue, but the tale persisted, along with legends that the mine had once been used by the Spanish—as early as the sixteenth century.

Not so romantic, but longer-lasting, were the gold and silver (later lead and zinc) operations at Goodsprings. Production followed the discoveries at Potosi, and then findings of gold ore at what became the Yellow Pine Mining District and the Keystone mine. Nearby Jean was the shipping point for the metals from Goodsprings. The industry in the area at one time made Goodsprings the largest town in southern Nevada, with more residents than Las Vegas.

A third southern mining town is Searchlight. The silver and gold mines there were discovered in the 1890s, causing a boom that lasted until about 1910. There was a narrow-gauge branch from the AT&SF railroad, marking the success of early efforts there. In 1908, with a campaign underway for a separate county in southern Nevada, it was widely believed that Searchlight, as a larger town, would win the county seat from the promoters at Las Vegas, if indeed a new county were created. But when the election was held, the vote on the matter turned up the same number of votes in both Las Vegas and Searchlight. In the 1908 election, however, Las Vegans successfully elected enough local legislators to assure both the county division and the designation of their town as the seat of government. The dealing brought a promise that Las Vegas would provide a courthouse, a feat that Searchlight was unable to perform due to a then-declining population.

The last of the early important mining districts was south of Las Vegas in El Dorado Canyon. The first

prospectors in the area were soldiers camping at a spring there in the late 1850s. They took their ore to be assayed, and caused a rush to the Honest Miner mine. The boom in the district continued for a few years, and the mines were worked for decades. By 1876, there were about three hundred miners in El Dorado Canyon, digging in the Wall Street, Morning Star, and the Techatticup mines. The latter probably was the richest of the group. The mining assisted a small transportation industry on the Colorado, Virgin, and Muddy rivers, where boats carried in freight for the population and then took the ore out for milling.

The folklore of the El Dorado district contains a tale that one day in the 1870s, a group of Spaniards and Mexicans approached John Powers, owner of the Wall Street. They showed Powers a map that they claimed to have found in a church in old Mexico, and on it was clearly marked the site of the Wall Street mine. Some people believe that the story proves an earlier penetration of the Great Basin by Spaniards than had previously been recorded. Other individuals claimed to have found Spanish coins and jewelry, including a silver crucifix and a rosary in the El Dorado Canyon. Speculation continued into the late twentieth century about where these items might have originated.

The little town of Nelson served the El Dorado Canyon with a post office, store, and saloon until the 1930s. After that, commercial facilities declined. The mines of El Dorado produced nearly $12 million; the Wall Street alone accounted for almost $3 million of that.

Las Vegas

An important city was destined to grow at the earliest-settled site, Las Vegas. Before the town was definitely established, the census of 1900 showed a population of only about 3,000 people in all of Lincoln County. The mining towns around Pioche, the county seat (see Southeastern Nevada tours), held most of the people, the Muddy or Moapa Valley settlements contained perhaps 700, and Las Vegas—mainly the area of the Stewart ranch—counted just 30. Transportation marked the greatest economic need in these isolated communities. Lincoln County's historian observed, "A generation of men had grown old in Lincoln County waiting for the arrival of the railroad." Finally, in 1900, W. A. Clark, the Montana copper king, incorporated the San Pedro, Los Angeles, and Salt Lake railroad (later the Union Pacific). Construction began, and by 1902, with its purchase by Clark's company, a townsite on the Stewart ranch was laid out. Track-layers crossed the Las Vegas Valley in 1904, and finally, the first train reached Las Vegas in January 1905.

The sale of lots for the city of Las Vegas—Clark's townsite—took place on May 15, 1905. This event was archetypal Las Vegas. To understand Las Vegas and its citizens is to know that the town is dedicated to its own promotion, nearly to the exclusion of any outside considerations. Las Vegas has always wanted to grow, to be thought well of, to offer new settlers a potential source of pride. Never mind that the summer heat is nearly unbearable, and that the winter winds transfer huge clouds of sand and dust from one end of the valley to the other on a near-weekly basis. And never mind the cost of public or private buildings; if they make Las Vegas more attractive, the money will come from somewhere. Las Vegans love Las Vegas with a passion that transcends mere patriotism and is certainly more than boosterism. Las Vegas is special, and its residents have made it so, beginning on May 15, 1905.

The railroad representatives erected a shaded platform (the temperatures in May can easily reach over 100°F), and the auction began. Excited potential buyers bid for lots on which to erect businesses or homes in the new division point for the railroad. The event went on for fully two days, and when it was over, the railroad had profited beyond anyone's dreams, for the lots were bid far over the original asking prices. This first promotion set a pattern for others. It was no accident that hotels were among the first buildings.

One railroad could easily beget another. William Clark promoted another southern Nevada route at the same time the SP, LA & SL arrived in Las Vegas. This new road's backing stemmed from important mining

"The Hotel Las Vegas was a tent building 40' by 130'. The frame was constructed, and buttons placed on the frame for anchoring the covering. The canvas was sewed in sections and the buttonholes placed at the proper intervals. There were thirty rooms, in addition to a lobby and a bar. Another tent served as a dining room and kitchen. . . .

"The life of the Hotel Las Vegas was of comparatively short duration. The intense summer heat, together with the dust and rain storms, had an adverse effect on the canvas . . . Then, also, John F. Miller started construction of the big Nevada Hotel, a two-story wooden building, so the big canvas hotel was dismantled. The pieces of canvas were much in demand and were sold to the prospectors and others."

— Florence Squires Boyer, Las Vegas pioneer (daughter of C. P. Squires)

"When I come here, the fire company had an old ranch wagon, a buckboard, and no seat or anything, just a body. And the hose was rolled up in a coil. It was parked up near the center of town, which was very small then. Fremont and First, Second, and Third Streets, where they intersected, had the buildings. And we had an old triangle, about a six-foot triangle, hung in front of Clayson and Griffith's hardware store—where the Mint is now. Everybody that had a gun . . . when there was a fire, they run out and shot in the air. Later we put that triangle up. And there was a big bolt there on a string, and you took that and pounded on the triangle. We went there with the cart . . . to find out where the fire was. You could most always see the smoke, though, because the town was small, and very few trees or shrubbery."

— Leon Rockwell, volunteer fireman, Las Vegas

discoveries to the north at Tonopah and Goldfield (see Southwestern Nevada tours). Clark helped to obtain financing for the Las Vegas and Tonopah railroad, beginning in 1905. Without the new mining developments at Tonopah, Clark probably would have found something else to engage his attention, but the enticement of still another railroad proved important to him.

The route for the LV&T was surveyed in February 1905, and early the next year, graders and track-layers were at work. The first forty-three miles of track was cause for a celebration at Indian Springs. Then "Railroad Day" festivals were held at Beatty and at Rhyolite as the tracks moved north. On October 24, 1907, the track was finished to Goldfield, joining the Tonopah and Goldfield railroad, and the rails were in place. The LV&T, however, was plagued with mishaps and strikes, and proved less than a success. Operations ceased in October 1918, and the tracks were pulled up. The right-of-way was acquired by the Nevada State Highway system, and before long, the LV&T was forgotten in the new excitement of high-

way travel. The horseless carriage quickly replaced the old iron horse.

Soon after the coming of the railroad in 1905, permanent structures arose along Fremont Street. A bank, mercantile stores, hotels, and grocery stores, along with some homes dotted the few blocks that made up the Las Vegas townsite. The railroad and its personnel somewhat dominated the economy and politics, although executives of the line did not reside in Las Vegas. Boosters complained that the corporation's policies restricted growth; by 1920, the population was only about 2,300. Still, there was a significant change. The desires of Las Vegas residents to have their own identity created Clark County, after a separation from Lincoln in 1909, so there were a courthouse, school buildings, a library, concrete sidewalks along the dusty streets, and finally, a tree-planting project sponsored by a local women's club.

The acquisition of the county seat and then the building of the courthouse formed a unique chapter in Las Vegas history. With the division of the counties

Las Vegas, ca. 1905

accomplished, the newly formed Clark County had to assume a prorated share of county debts—an amount somewhat over $400,000. This eliminated any possibility of accumulating funds for a courthouse. The solution was typical of Las Vegas then and later: the citizens took up a collection, raised $1,800 for a building, and had it put up on Courthouse Square, facing Carson Street. That building served the embryo county government until 1914, when a women's club moved in and a regular courthouse was constructed. The first courthouse of Clark County was razed in 1955, having become offensive in appearance to some progressive residents.

The prominent early citizens of the city included not just the employees of the railroad, but others who deferred to Charles P. Squires, editor of the local newspaper, the *Las Vegas Age*, and concurrently, the operators of the Las Vegas Land and Water Company. Squires, a tireless advocate for the growth of the town, used the columns of his newspaper and his own energies without stint to praise Las Vegas for its beauties and its glorious future. Squires would do almost anything for his cause. One local legend tells of his interminable puffery for the climate: Not only did he laud the weather, he created it, for, according to witnesses, on the hottest days, he would visit the weather station thermometer carrying a glass of iced tea. Then, strangely, the report went to the national weather service of a temperature several degrees cooler than anyone had thought.

Squires was also a strong believer in the possibilities of using the Colorado River not only for water but as a source of hydroelectric power. He made dozens of trips around the nation, proclaiming the need for a dam on the river, and was one of the organizers of the League of the Southwest, an interstate group that finally did convince the federal government of the desirability of building a dam in Black Canyon. Squires never let down, even after he succeeded; the name of Squires on various sites in the city of Las Vegas is testimony to his continual celebration of his adopted home town.

The Las Vegas Land and Water Company came into

being with the townsite. The place is like others in the Great Basin—low rainfall, very little water runoff in the spring, plagued by flash-floods, and, in the beginning, containing some good artesian springs. The distribution of these scarce resources necessarily made the supervisors of the company into powerful figures. The longest tenure of one of these individuals was that of Walter R. Bracken, who took over in December 1906 and reigned over the system for forty years. If Bracken proposed a fireplug in a certain location, the item appeared; if he wanted expanded service for a hotel, the hotel's request was quickly granted. Bracken oversaw the drilling of wells, the capping of springs, and laying of pipes, and the promotion of the idea that Las Vegas rested on a huge underground supply of water that was virtually inexhaustible. That was not true, and within Bracken's time it was discovered that overdrafts of the aquifers had taken place; subsidence amounting to as much as a hundred feet occurred at the site of the old Las Vegas springs.

Walls and foundations cracked with the declining hydrostatic pressure, and Las Vegans used the opportunity to begin another successful campaign to assist

---

"To supply the residents of the new town, the Union Pacific Railroad set up the Las Vegas Land and Water Company, of which Walter Bracken was made the manager. And the railroad company laid the mains and laterals in the downtown area to serve the then growing community. And the mains were all wooden mains, and this developed into quite a problem later on when the wood started to rot and leaks would appear in the wooden pipe and break down streets and flood houses . . . And incidentally, nobody kept a record of where the mains were after they were laid, because it wasn't important as there weren't very many people being served by the mains."

— John F. Cahlan, newspaperman, Las Vegas

---

their community. The result was the huge, federally assisted Southern Nevada Water Project, which took more than a decade of planning and politicking to bring into being in the 1970s. Las Vegas was then assured an adequate supply of domestic water from the Colorado River's flow by the terms of this program, and thus—with prudent management—could continue its tradition of attracting more and more visitors. The successor to the Las Vegas Land and Water Company was understandably a considerably more economical and efficient operation, but also a good deal less personal and neighborly than Walter Bracken's. And no wonder: in the late twentieth century, concerns about water treatment and sewage disposal complicated the business more than the simple laying of redwood mains and laterals.

A third highly vocal and significant promoter of southern Nevada's resources and charms was James Graves Scrugham. Scrugham served the state from the early part of the twentieth century as university professor and dean, state engineer, governor, congressman, and finally U.S. senator until his death in 1943. After his first encounter with southern Nevada, Scrugham never gave up talking about its history and archaeology, as well as about its potential for development. Scrugham counted as his proudest achievement the acquisition of the waters of the Colorado for Nevada, and the promotion of Hoover Dam. He purchased property in southern Nevada at Overton, and spent his last months of life at his retreat there. No great monuments with James Scrugham's name engraved exist in southern Nevada, a serious oversight for one of the region's ardent and effective advocates.

By many accounts, the most successful of the early promotions for Las Vegas was that for a dam on the nearby Colorado River. In 1920, Governor Emmet Boyle appointed the first Colorado River Commission. The group was composed of advocates for the area, including State Engineer Scrugham, Charles P. Squires, and others with interests in seeing the waters of the Colorado put to Nevada's beneficial use. By early in 1926, it had become evident that the dam would soon be a reality. When the bill passed the Congress on De-

cember 14, 1928, Las Vegas had a spontaneous and wild celebration, and a parade with flag-bearers and dozens of marchers up Fremont Street. Bells on churches and schools rang, railroad whistles blew, and schoolchildren, dismissed from classes, joined in. When the president signed the bill a week later, observers decided that the earlier party had been "mild by comparison." When the government engineers arrived in June, they had a hearty welcome.

With the rest of the nation in depression, Las Vegas boomed through the 1930s. With the huge dam begun, there were also roads to build, railroads to extend, and public structures needed to serve a new horde of tourists and workers. On September 17, 1930, Secretary of the Interior Ray Lyman Wilbur christened the new dam as *Hoover*, although local people referred to it as *Boulder* Dam, reflecting its first planned location in Boulder Canyon. With the dam finished on September 30, 1935, President Franklin D. Roosevelt arrived to dedicate the structure, officially calling it *Boulder* Dam, satisfying the critics of the Republican former president. In 1947, the U.S. Congress returned to the earlier name of Hoover, completing the cycle and retrieving the insult to one of the original planners of Hoover Dam.

Early in 1936, the heady days of construction at the damsite and the economic benefits of resultant crews of workers had ended. The payroll on the dam alone dropped from 5,000 to 1,500 people. The roads were built, the railroad spur finished, the public structures in place; the boom of the 1930s was over. Las Vegas turned to a new publicity campaign to rectify the losses.

Meanwhile, the state government had legalized casino gambling in 1931. At first, this seemed not so important to the southern Nevada city, although some hotels and casinos developed in the town core along Fremont Street. The city boosters turned this time to the military, promoting southern Nevada as an ideal site for training soldiers and for the manufacture of war materiel. Again, these dedicated individuals succeeded, even beyond their desires. By the end of World War II, Las Vegans were beginning to mourn

"There is quite a story regarding why Boulder City was set where it was. At the time, Ray Lyman Wilbur was . . . in charge of the Bureau of Reclamation, which was building the dam. . . . Las Vegas was being considered as the railhead for the dam supplies. Wilbur came out here, and . . . he was supposed to be quite blue-nosed. The people of Las Vegas, wanting the city to become the railhead . . . were very interested in seeing that Wilbur didn't see any of the vices that were so rampant in the city. . . .

"On the day scheduled for Wilbur's arrival, . . . the word went out . . . that all of the houses of prostitution . . . would be closed, and there would be no liquor sold in the community until Wilbur got out of the city. . . .

"Several newspapermen who were with [Wilbur] wanted to know if there wasn't a possibility that we could get some whiskey. So, being very obliging . . . we arranged to have the Arizona Club opened up. We all went down and had several libations. . . . So we all said our goodbyes and everything seemed to be all right until Wilbur announced the next day that he was putting in a model city at Boulder City . . . because Las Vegas was no place for people to live."

— John F. Cahlan, newspaperman, Las Vegas

the loss of their small-town atmosphere, but it was too late; Las Vegas had become an important city, and was destined to outstrip every dream of those early promoters.

When the war ended, Las Vegas's population had doubled since 1940, to more than 17,000 people by 1945. Any hint of decline was now past. The westward movement of the post-war years had begun; Las Vegas had been inviting people to come there for forty years, and now they accepted the invitations—in increasing numbers. A single resort-hotel, the El Rancho, built in 1941, provided a pattern for later developments.

An important event in Nevada was the revision in 1945 of the system of gambling regulation. Before that time, from 1931, enforcement of gambling behavior was the responsibility of local officials. In 1945, the legislature enacted a tax structure and licensing procedure that changed the industry dramatically, perhaps nowhere so strongly as in Las Vegas.

Because the number of casinos and resorts was growing, the Tax Commission, which had responsibility for enforcement, had some difficult times. Certain unsavory characters had moved especially to southern Nevada, none so flamboyantly as Benjamin "Bugsy" Siegel, a hoodlum with notorious connections. Siegel built the first of the flashy casinos, the Flamingo, in 1946. A national magazine named him as "the hood who invented Las Vegas," as more resorts of a similar kind followed the Flamingo. Not all of the new casino owners had antecedents like Siegel's ("Bugsy" was murdered only a year later), but many had backgrounds of illegal gambling or bootlegging elsewhere.

Las Vegas never lost its composure with any of the new citizens, but welcomed them uncritically to a new respectability. For the most part, the new resort owners responded in kind, enjoying a status previously denied them, while regulators found the owners in this atmosphere particularly easy to deal with. Moreover, customers found a special excitement in rubbing elbows with somewhat notorious characters in pleasant and safe surroundings. The area blossomed with newer, gaudier, noisier casinos, each one more elaborate than the one before. The highway west of Las Vegas was dubbed "the Strip" and became a magnet for travelers from around the world. Here was the manifestation of the "show business capital."

Concerns on the part of various critics about legalized gambling brought only more publicity, always skillfully managed by Las Vegas newspapers. Reforms in the methods of regulation, investigation, enforcement, and financing of the resorts dispelled much of the criticism, while Nevada's congressmen and senators successfully prevented federal regulation of their home industry. Eventually, a new measure of acceptance began when Howard Hughes, a famous in-

Downtown Las Vagas

dustrialist, purchased several casinos. Soon after Hughes's arrival in 1967, national hotel chains began to move in, and their corporate stocks traded well on the market. The Nevada legislature responded with statutes to make such corporate ownerships accessible. Finally, in the 1980s, when other states began to discuss legalizing casino gambling, and New Jersey did so, some Nevada establishments opened branch operations on the East Coast.

An interesting aspect of the corporate ownership authorization was a new orgy of construction. The first "biggest hotel in the world" brought on a second (and now) "biggest hotel," and an establishment down the Strip then added a few hundred rooms to maintain its status as "biggest." Hardly anyone would predict how big the hotels would be when the race ended, but it was certain that eventually, Las Vegas would indeed have *the biggest hotel in the world.*

As the resorts of Las Vegas continued to grow and expand, the population of the city doubled, and doubled again. By 1960, the census had found that more than half the residents of Nevada lived in Clark County. By 1980, the increase in population all over the state, and especially in Las Vegas, brought the granting of a second congressman for Nevada. The number of people in Clark County was so large in proportion to the rest of the state, however, that Las Vegas itself constituted one congressional district, while the suburbs of Las Vegas and all the balance of the state made up the other.

The growth was due primarily but not solely to the entertainment business. The wartime and post-war period was particularly important in other industries. Among these was air transportation. Airmail service into Las Vegas began in April 1926. The airfield was a graded strip of desert, then located about where the Desert Inn Hotel was later built. The facility was constructed by county crews who merely dragged a scraper across the ground, filled in the deepest of the gullies, and declared the place an airport.

The first airmail pilot was Maury Graham, a daredevil type who later was killed on the same run. One of the famous early-day passengers to land on this field was Will Rogers, whose plane stopped by flipping onto its top. Rogers climbed out unhurt, and told the crowd that he had been returning from a Republican National Convention, and the crash "serves me right. If I'd been going to a Democratic convention, this would never have happened." Repairs were made simply by righting the plane, and within a few hours, Rogers took off again.

"We began to find out that if legalized gaming is going to be operated in a big way, as it was apparent it was going to be in the state of Nevada, that . . . you didn't get bishops of the church and solid, upright, upstanding citizens who were in the social register . . . that wanted to go into the gaming business. They were people who were gamblers. And because Nevada was the only state where it was allowed legally, they, of course, had to get their experience in states where it was illegal. . . .

"The ones that don't know [the gambling business] can get you into far more trouble than the man who knows his business, who might have learned it in an illegal state, and who is subject to criticism, particularly from the outside press, and that has the name 'hoodlum' attached to him because he was involved in illegal gambling. These are the people who got you into the least trouble."

— Robbins E. Cahill, former head
of gambling enforcement

A few years later, the airfield moved to a better site, away from town, and was named McCarran Field. The young airlines and mail carriers used that place until shortly before the outbreak of World War II, when the leaders of the Air Corps (later Air Force) decided that they needed an area for intensive gunnery training. McCarran Field was chosen, later to be called Nellis Air Force Base. Subsequently, a new site was surveyed for commercial flight, and a new, modern, expandable air terminal arose at what became McCarran International. The McCarran International was destined to become one of the busiest such centers in the nation.

Meanwhile, Nellis Air Force Base became headquarters for a gunnery school. However, in the push of the early war period, the government failed to provide enough guns for the training of recruits. Las Vegas, true to its style, simply took up a collection among its citizens, who donated the required weapons to the Air Force; these gifts included everything from B-B guns to rifles and shotguns. Later, of course, the place became a sophisticated installation of which all citizens could be proud. Nellis had some relatively inactive periods and threatened closures following the end of World War II, but the base was never abandoned and thus provided a military presence in southern Nevada.

Faithful to their Las Vegas origins, Nellis personnel contributed entertainment of a special sort. The base became the home of the "Thunderbirds" precision flying team, providing a new dimension to the world capital of show business.

A second military installation developed under the sponsorship of the Atomic Energy Commission. Beginning in 1951, the AEC (with later changes of name) tested nuclear bombs and weapons at the Nevada Test Site north of Las Vegas. This place, like others of its sort, became controversial with the passing of time and the leaking out of information on formerly secret activities there. However, like Nellis, it was not abandoned, and seemed unlikely to be.

The University of Nevada (until then only in Reno) began in 1954 to offer classes in the south, first on an extension basis and finally as a full-fledged campus.

"It is the most awesome thing that I have ever seen. The device is exploded, and you see this terrific flash of white light, and then there is a roiling purple ball that the smoke just seems to roil around the ball, and as the ball grows bigger, it turns into all colors of the rainbow, and then all of a sudden, the sound of the shock wave'd hit you, and it's just as if somebody took a bat and hit you in the stomach."

— John F. Cahlan, newspaperman, Las Vegas

Appropriately, the University of Nevada-Las Vegas built courses in hotel management, a library collection on gambling, centers for instruction and performance in the lively arts, and some outstanding athletics programs.

True to their traditions, the people of Las Vegas continue to welcome soldiers, scientists, scholars, and professional people with cordiality matched with that for ordinary tourists. They also built one of the West's most elaborate convention facilities to underscore their hospitality.

Boulder City

At one time, the planners for Hoover Dam had thought to use the railhead at Las Vegas as a supply center for construction. Following a decision by Secretary of Interior Ray Lyman Wilbur, however, this design changed, and a town came into being at the damsite. The Six Companies, Inc., built dormitories and a mess hall for workers who came in huge numbers into the area, fleeing the depression that existed elsewhere in the nation. Not all the workers lived in Six Companies facilities, but those who did had clean beds and decent food to combat the difficulties of hard work in summer weather when temperatures often exceeded 100°. Some workers collapsed, some died, some engaged in labor union agitations, some suffered accidents, and all contributed to the making of one of the

country's engineering marvels, at that time the highest dam in the world.

Other buildings at the construction site provided office space for the Bureau of Reclamation supervisors, who would continue to oversee the place when the project ended. With the dam near completion at the end of 1935, workers began to leave. Buildings formerly owned by Six Companies were moved to other locations, some as far away as Searchlight or Overton. Blocks in the town were denuded of both structures and vegetation, lawns dried up, and the place reverted largely to desert—with paved streets and sidewalks. The Bureau of Reclamation headquarters and staff housing was about all that remained.

With the electrical work finished about 1940, the work force continued to exit. Then a Bureau of Mines installation was built to sample resources of the area. A state mining office staff studied uses of the power. Scientists of the U.S. Bureau of Mines proved their value by inventing a method for reducing titanium. During World War II, the plant evolved into processing manganese commercially. Also during World War II, a military police unit that escorted highway traffic across the dam was quartered nearby, as the dam was officially closed to visitors.

Boulder City's status as a federal reservation gave it an anomalous atmosphere for a Nevada town. No liquor was sold there, even after Repeal, and no gambling was allowed despite its legal status elsewhere. Las Vegas, 26 miles away, apparently served the needs for these outlets.

A very few early residents stayed at Boulder City, some using the materials from Six Companies buildings for construction of their homes. Not only residences, but other early structures including churches were built in the same way, using discarded materials from the construction companies. A seven-denomination community house of worship and a Catholic church had the benefits of donated labor and this scrounged lumber. In Boulder City's middle years, probably only public buildings and the Reclamation Bureau had all new materials.

"The job was as a carpenter's helper. And I had to carry water-soaked timbers away from the forms and pile them on my shoulder. One of these four-by-sixes, twenty feet long, was very heavy. Well, after two or three days there, I got working in between a couple of sets of forms, and the temperature got up to around—I think it was a hundred and thirty-seven, they said. And I passed out. Some friends got me onto a truck that was coming back to the dormitory. . . . And they advised me not to say a word about passing out, because they said, 'If you do, the doctor will simply testify that you had heart trouble, and they'll fire you. . . .' The result was that I stayed there for two days, and then I was put on bending the big steel reinforcing bars in the steel yard at night. I got by there fine."

— L. A. Ferris, Boulder Dam laborer, Reno architect

"We lived in a tent in the river bottom. We bought this tent from a widow whose husband had been disemboweled by a shovel handle when he had gone in to muck out after a blast that hadn't completely blown yet. . . . We also had to get another tent. That tent was the one I cooked and we ate in. . . . Between the tents, we spread blankets fastened to clothesline ropes with horse blanket pins so as to make a little shade for the children, because it was so hot down there. . . .

"Then, on July twenty-sixth [1931], there were three women who died in the camp right around me there. . . . [T]hey had taken two of them into Las Vegas to the mortuary, but there wasn't any transportation available to take the third woman in. Before they could get her moved, the heat had already begun to work on her body. . . ."

— Erma Godbey, Boulder City housewife

A few more Boulder City pioneers arrived or decided to stay. The first public library—with donated books—was given space in the Reclamation Bureau office. This, with other activities, set a pattern for a vigorous tradition of volunteerism in Boulder City. The list of organized and unorganized civic groups seemed outstanding in view of the supposed transient nature of the population: Boy and Girl Scouts, Parent-Teacher associations, Campfire Girls, a Cemetery Association, Junior Chamber of Commerce, Red Cross, USO, fraternal groups, veterans' clubs, and numberless ad hoc special organizations kept people busy. In wartime, many—or most—of the residents entertained soldiers and airmen from nearby bases in their homes, an extension of their customary work for the betterment of Boulder City.

After Lake Mead filled behind the dam, visitors and residents began to enjoy water sports there. Congressman Scrugham predicted a new era of prosperity for southern Nevada based on what became the Lake Mead National Recreation Area. More people began to move in. The National Park Service brought rangers to operate the facilities of the Recreation Area, which encompasses land on the Nevada side of the Colorado River.

After 1960, Boulder City became a regular, chartered city of Nevada. Although sometimes stormy, the city's government progressed so that Boulder City seems much like other Nevada places as the twentieth century nears its end. Facilities remain somewhat limited by Nevada standards, and public gambling is still outlawed by the town government. But Boulder City enjoys a stability unimagined in its first dusty days. In the 1980s, Boulder City was becoming a mecca for retired people who enjoyed the good climate and oasis-like atmosphere there.

Henderson

All of southern Nevada's important settlements came into being in the twentieth century; the most recent of these was Henderson. This city evolved from the needs of World War II. The United States required a plant for making incendiary bombs, because the only such factory available to the Allies was in England and was under threat of attack by German aircraft. Several sites were considered, and a location on a flat between Las Vegas and Boulder City was chosen. Howard Eells, head of Basic Refractories of Cleveland, Ohio, also owned some mining claims in northern Nevada, and became quite interested in the bomb problem. Eells received the contract to develop the plant at what became Henderson, with McNeil Construction Company of Los Angeles doing the actual building.

The plant began operation in 1940 and was first called Basic Magnesium. After the war, negotiations between the federal government and the state of Nevada resulted in the site's acquisition by the state. The name honors Albert Scott Henderson, a lawyer and district attorney, judge, assemblyman, and state senator. Henderson was a pioneer of Clark County, helped to prepare the first city charter of Las Vegas, served on the Clark County board of education, and was active in many of southern Nevada's civic organizations. As a judge, Henderson was instrumental in the negotiations that ended with Basic Magnesium's facilities becoming the property of the state of Nevada.

The industrial plants turned to other purposes than bomb-materials manufacture. The town of Henderson, however, retained its scientific-industrial character throughout the years, and general growth in southern Nevada spurred a certain amount of diversification there. By 1981, the Henderson chamber of commerce proudly claimed that more than half of all the non-tourist industry in the entire state was situated in their city. At the same time, there was a limited amount of commercial activity away from the plants, and only a small number of the ubiquitous Nevada-style casinos. Thus, Henderson, a relatively new city, remains a source of pride for southern Nevadans—there are some—who wished for businesses not related to tourism.

Pahrump

Of all the satellites of Las Vegas, Pahrump is probably the most unusual. This is a place devoted to com-
mercial agriculture from its beginning, and continuing as a twentieth-century scientific agricultural community. The valley has natural springs that provided succor for travelers and Indians in the days before white settlement. The first resident, Charles Bennett, lived there from the 1860s until the 1880s, when he sold the ranch to Aaron and Rosie Winters, discoverers of the borax deposits in nearby Death Valley.

Joseph Yount was also among the earliest settlers in southern Nevada. He came there from Oregon in 1876, developed a ranch around a large spring in Pahrump Valley, and called it The Manse. Yount built an adobe residence and kept a store for a while. Occasionally, for visitors, he showed what he said were samples of the ore from the ''lost Breyfogle'' mine in Death Valley. The Yount family became well known among the pioneers of southern Nevada, doing well in this isolated situation and utilizing the free-flowing water from the springs there for vineyards, until they sold out shortly before the first World War.

The folklore of the Valley surrounds its position at the doorstep of Death Valley. Charles C. Breyfogle, a resident of Austin, came through here in 1864, prospecting into Death Valley's wastes. He said that in a cliff, near a single mesquite tree, he had found a wonderful outcrop of rose quartz indicating a rich deposit of gold. The samples he took to Austin seemed to prove his claim, and he returned to try to mark the site. But when he wandered out onto the desert, a recent storm had erased his landmarks. Breyfogle continued to try to find the lost mine, attracting other prospectors to the area between Pahrump and Death Valley. On one of his treks, Breyfogle was supposedly attacked and held prisoner by Indians in Pahrump Valley. Eventually, in 1870, he disappeared, lost like his mine. ''Breyfogling'' became a weekend occupation or dedicated activity for hundreds of prospectors, but the outcrop of rose quartz never appeared again.

An important site in Pahrump Valley is the grave of the Paiute chief, Tecopa. Tecopa was credited with preaching peace to the Indian bands of the southern area, and was greatly respected for his intelligence and leadership. He told a friend before he died that he wished to be buried in a box, as white people were. The desire was fulfilled; in 1904, at a very advanced age, Tecopa was interred according to his wish, wearing a bright red band suit decorated with gold braid, his treasured high silk hat, and a red blanket. These items of clothing had marked the aged chief for many years; when they wore out, the white miners of the area, grateful for his peaceful negotiations with renegades, simply replaced them for him.

Other pioneer residents included the Buol family. The Buols had large vineyards in Pahrump Valley, where they raised grapes for wine to sell in nearby mining camps. For many years, the Buols had the only distillery license in the state of Nevada.

Later in the twentieth century, experiments and soil testing brought a new industry to Pahrump. The fields were planted with cotton and irrigated from natural springs and drilled wells. The first of these wells had a lift of only 40 feet, but with heavy irrigation the figure increased to 175 feet in the 1960s, and then increased again. By the mid-1960s, Nevada had a U.S. government cotton allotment, amounting to something

Valley of Fire

more than 4,000 acres in the Pahrump Valley; residents built a cotton gin. In addition to cotton, the valley has supported good hay growth, and harvested as many as eight cuttings of alfalfa a year. The hay is sold at markets in nearby southern California.

The agricultural activity brought many outsiders into Pahrump Valley on business. The business people believed that they could foresee a different financial environment for the site, and proceeded to create that. In the 1980s, the major business of Pahrump Valley was real estate sales and development. The most prosperous and important evidences of the modern activity were land sales offices. Agriculture began at the same time to decline somewhat. Cotton-growing was reduced in scale, and many new residents were unaware of its former importance. As the century drew near a close, in fact, the salespeople of Pahrump Valley seemed to regard the crop fields as a resource in their own future.

Recreation Areas

Southern Nevada's outdoor recreation is as interesting and colorful as the indoor variety. The first state park created in Nevada was in the Valley of Fire. In 1923, then-Governor James G. Scrugham asked and received permission from the legislature to withdraw certain scenic or recreational areas from private ownership and to create parks or game refuges. He particularly admired the Valley of Fire both for its scenic and its historic values and declared this site to be one of his first priorities. The place has startling natural beauty, being composed largely of red sandstone in strange and wonderful configurations. Prehistoric pictographs decorate the surrounding cliffs where once the Pueblo and Basketmaker people had lived. When the state park system fell into decay after Scrugham's tenure, the Valley of Fire came under the protection of the federal government, which declared it a National Monument. This dual relationship continued. When the state park system was reorganized in 1955, the Valley of Fire again received important attention. The site was more fully developed, with campgrounds and picnic tables, and the petroglyphs were protected. A visitor center was established to inform travelers, and a ranger staff installed.

Red Rock Canyon park is neither as old nor as well developed as the Valley of Fire. It is, however, a spectacular and wild display of red, white, and yellow sandstone in many of the strange shapes that wind and water can carve. Red Rock is also a National Recreation Area, and deservedly so for its splendid scenery if for no other reason. The earliest settlers in the valley called the place the Sandstone Ranch. Now, the park encompasses 77,000 acres of primitive natural beauty and contains campgrounds and picnic facilities along with a model visitor center operated by the Bureau of Land Management.

Charleston Peak stands a bit more than 11,000 feet above sea level northwest of Las Vegas. The picnic and camping grounds in its shadows in Lee and Kyle canyons have served generations of residents on pleasure trips as well as refugees from the stifling summer heat of the valley floor. More recently, some snow skiing facilities have been developed, especially in Lee Canyon. The Lee Canyon ski lifts and snow-making equipment were installed in the 1970s, making the recreation of southern Nevada truly a year-round endeavor.

The largest, and most important of the southern Nevada recreation areas is that surrounding Lake Mead. If one is interested in any sort of outdoor activity, water sports, fishing, camping, picnicking, boating, exploring hidden scenery, Lake Mead has all of that. The National Park Service has been exceedingly diligent in creating facilities of nearly all kinds around this man-made lake. The place has also become a wintertime mecca for sun-seekers, especially in the area around Overton, where travel trailers of "snowbirds" can park at low cost or free. The sections around Hoover Dam offer concessions of various sorts, giving a holiday air to an outing at Hoover Dam.

Clearly, if the traveler searches for history, archaeology, adventure, sophisticated entertainment, and spectacular scenery, the southern section of Nevada offers all of those. Although religion's proselytes began its settlement, that fact is nearly erased in a metropolitan area where the scenery changes almost weekly. Las Vegas, at the center of the southern section, is now the most energetic, lively promoter of whatever will please the hedonists, adventurers, scientists, scholars, or tourists interested in learning about the area. Las Vegas hospitality is legendary, but real in southern Nevada.

TOURING IN
SOUTHERN NEVADA

The tours in this section have been designed not to show everything about southern Nevada, but to take the traveler to some of the most attractive and accessible places within easy driving distance of Las Vegas. The traveler should be aware of temperature extremes (a fifty-degree difference between day and night is typical), the danger of flash floods in both mountain and desert areas, and the possibility of dust storms in the valley. To prepare for these events, the car should be carefully equipped with a good shovel and with extra water both for drinking and for the radiator. Dark glasses and a hat may also prove helpful.

Touring southern Nevada should not be considered a dangerous activity, but a pleasant one. Take along your camera for the wonderful photo opportunities everywhere. We have recommended picnic lunches where we thought it would make the trip more enjoyable; camping gear is appropriate for some of the tours, and we have suggested that as well.

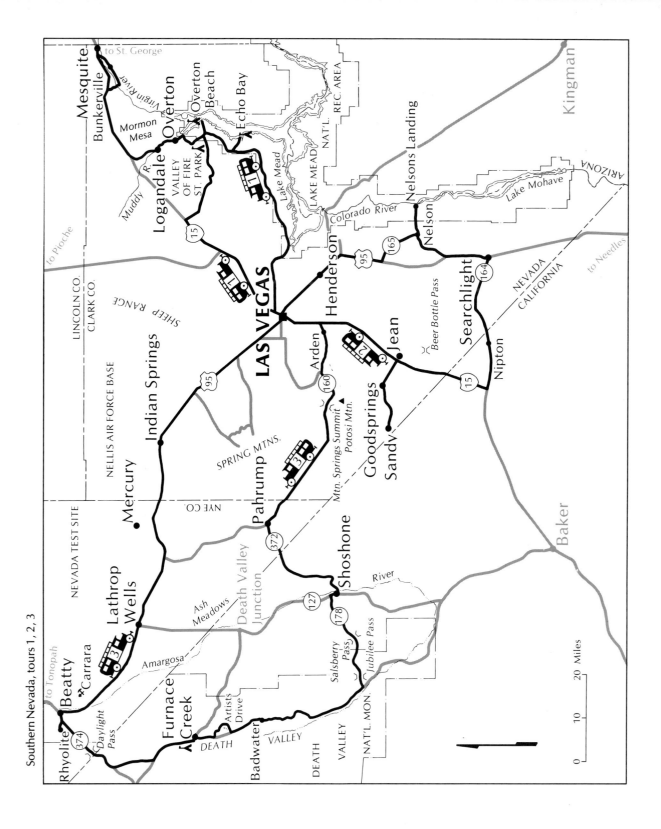

Southern Nevada, tours 1, 2, 3

What to see in Las Vegas: The Las Vegas Strip is the largest area on the planet devoted to gambling and entertainment. Here, world-famous show-business people perform year-round in the showrooms of some of the most elaborate facilities ever designed. Everything ever told or written about the Strip is either over- or understated. It is not only a place; it is an experience.

Downtown Las Vegas, "Glitter Gulch," is the original site of the development of southern Nevada's tourist attraction. There is very little that is old or historical or shabby about this section of Las Vegas; as soon as it seems about to be so, it is torn down and rebuilt. Some places have become more famous than others simply through advertising. Again, like the Strip, an experience as much as a place.

The University of Nevada Las Vegas is Nevada's late-twentieth-century university campus, on Maryland Parkway. Modern buildings, interesting architecture, and a typical Las Vegas atmosphere (minus gambling) prevail. The center of the campus is the James R. Dickinson Library.

The Old Las Vegas Fort may be the only really *old* structure in Las Vegas; it is located on North Las Vegas Boulevard at Washington Avenue. Restoration has recently been achieved, through the efforts of historically-minded people.

The Nevada State Museum and Historical Society houses artifacts, art, and relics of southern Nevada and is in Lorenzi Park, near the intersection of Rancho Road and Washington Avenue.

Southern Nevada, tours 4, 5

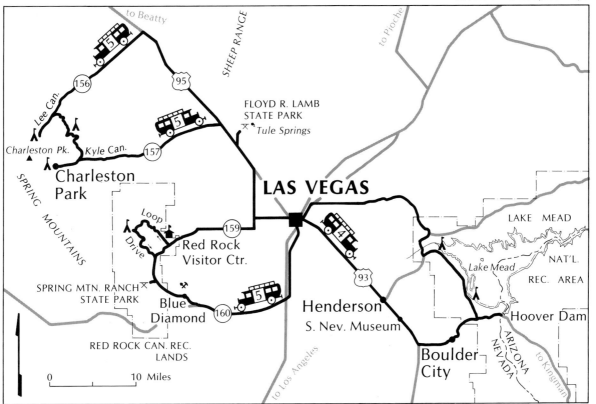

TOUR ONE, Ancient peoples and early settlers: Las Vegas — Valley of Fire — Lost City — Mormon Mesa and return. Approximately 230 miles round trip. There are commercial facilities along the way for this tour, but we suggest that you pack a picnic.

Begin the tour anywhere in downtown Las Vegas. Take an access to I-15 north, and drive approximately 20 miles to Exit #64. You may see the planes from Nellis Air Force Base practicing in the skies here. The U.S. Lime Products cement mine is on the left (west) side of the highway. At Exit #64, on the right (east) side of the highway is the historical marker for the Old Spanish Trail. Read the text on the marker to appreciate these early travelers, and return to the highway, I-15 north.

Drive 11.4 miles to Exit #75, Valley of Fire. Bear right, and follow the signs for Valley of Fire State Park, on paved SR 169. You may encounter a tortoise along this road. These interesting creatures are protected by law, they are slow and actually sort of friendly, and can grow to over 10 or 12 inches in diameter. If you see a tortoise in the road, please don't hit it; your car will crush one of the desert's rare inhabitants. The Nevada Division of Wildlife has collected tortoises from some more heavily-populated areas to release in this more favorable location. Drive 13.1 miles; here you will begin to see the red sandstone that gives the Valley of Fire its name. Continue 1.2 miles to the park boundary. Directly ahead is the first information site, and restrooms. Stop to read the maps and plaques, then continue on the paved road to the Park Visitor Center. After 2.1 miles, you will see a road to the left; return to this place after your stop at the Visitor Center, and it will be more meaningful for you. Drive 1.9 miles to the Visitor Center turn; the building is 0.2 miles on your left.

At the Valley of Fire State Park Visitor Center, you will find knowledgeable ranger-naturalists, books, maps, pamphlets, and brochures to answer your questions about this fascinating and colorful place. While you enjoy your tour of the park, you will surely want to see Atlatl Rock, a huge outcrop covered with pictographs made by ancient peoples.

Following your tour of the Valley of Fire, return to the Visitor Center and take the road east toward Lake Mead and Overton. The pavement here is purposely full of dips to accommodate the flash floods that occasionally ravage the area. In mid-October, we saw desert marigolds, sunflowers, and jimson weeds growing and blooming along the road. Drive 3.0 miles to the historical marker for the Arrowhead Trail, commemorating a historic road through here. Drive 0.4 miles to the east park boundary and Elephant Rock. Continue 2.0 miles to SR 169 and turn left toward Overton.

Drive 6.8 miles to the historical marker for Pueblo Grande de Nevada, on the right-hand side of the road. Continue then 1.1 miles to the left turn for the Lost City Museum. The museum contains relics and artifacts of southern Nevada's ancient people and early settlers. The exhibits, both indoors and outdoors are educational and excellently prepared. The museum, a state of Nevada installation, is free, although donations are welcome.

Leaving the museum, turn left into Overton. Here are necessary commercial facilities on a limited scale. Drive 0.9 miles to the junction and bear left, staying on SR 169. As you drive, look to the right to observe Mormon Mesa, a long, flat formation that gives this area its name. Mormon Peak is ahead to the north; Virgin Peak rises behind Mormon Mesa. Drive 5.3 miles through this neat, fertile farmland, and enter Logandale. Here are very limited commercial facilities, a park, and picnic tables. Continue 2.8 miles to the historical marker on the left; the marker commemorates the Moapa Valley. Drive another 3.1 miles to the junction with I-15, and turn right (northeast) onto I-15.

This route crosses a typical southern Nevada desert, with mesquite bushes and some Joshua tree forests. In the spring, the joshuas have fragrant white blossoms. Continue 18.2 miles to Exit #112 for Riverside and Bunkerville, and turn right off I-15 to SR 170.

Drive 3.0 miles, and cross the Virgin River. We have seen coyote melons growing along the roadside here. Enjoy the view of the valley of the Virgin River, with its neat fields and dairy ranches. Drive 5.9 miles and turn left on Second West in Bunkerville. At Second South, turn right to First West, and Bunkerville's landmark, the home of founder Edward D. Bunker. There are no commercial facilities in Bunkerville, but there are places of historic interest. The pioneer cemetery is at the far edge of town, just off the main highway. Here are monuments to the founders and pioneers of Bunkerville, including one for Edward Bunker, leader of the colony effort.

Leaving the cemetery, rejoin the highway and continue east on SR 170. Drive 1.6 miles and cross the Virgin River. From the bridge, drive 1.1 miles to the junction, turn right, and drive through Mesquite. Mesquite is the commercial center for this area. There is a historical marker in front of the Virgin Valley High School.

Following your visit to Mesquite, turn around, and return 2.3 miles to I-15; take the access southwest.

Drive 26.2 miles to Exit #93, take SR 169 toward Lake Mead, and now you may enjoy a second look at the Moapa/Muddy Valley.

Drive 21.2 miles, through Logandale and Overton. Notice the Mormon Mesa's dominance of the surroundings. Be aware, too, that this is flash-flood country; the soft, thin soils are nearly impermeable to water, and thus a heavy thunder shower can cause considerable havoc. Pass the Valley of Fire turnoff, and continue through the intersection for Overton Beach. Go straight through, bearing to the left. Here is a 3.0-mile scenic route to Lake Mead. Overton Beach is one of the few free trailer campsites on Lake Mead. There are a boat ramp, swimming beaches, and rest rooms. This is a very popular spot for "snowbirds"—refugees from colder climates—in the fall and winter. Except for a disposal station, there are no special facilities for trailers, but the place remains crowded. Return the 3.0 miles to SR 169, and turn left on North Shore Road.

Edward Bunker home, Bunkerville

Continue 10.5 miles to the sign for Echo Bay, and turn left toward Lake Mead. Here you may enjoy the views and facilities of the Lake Mead Recreation Area. The resort is 4.8 miles from the turn. Echo Bay is nearly the antithesis of Overton Beach in resorts and campgrounds. There are a marina, housing, developed campgrounds, and trailer parks, all oriented mainly for people who like to fish. A historical marker commemorates the contributions of John Wesley Powell to the exploration of the Colorado River. Return the 4.8 miles to the highway, and turn left.

Drive 32.1 miles. In an easy and scenic drive along a paved highway, it seems difficult to realize the adventures, hardships, and terrors endured by the early travelers and settlers here in this rough and rugged, but colorful terrain. Take time to appreciate their achievements as you drive toward Las Vegas along or near the shore of Lake Mead. Turn right on SR 147 toward Las Vegas. After 10.5 miles, the road becomes Lake Mead Boulevard; drive another 6.2 miles to Las Vegas Boulevard, and turn left for downtown Las Vegas.

TOUR TWO, Historic mining districts: Las Vegas—Jean—Goodsprings—Searchlight—Nelson and return. Approximately 195 miles round trip. There are commercial facilities along the way, but we advise that you pack a picnic.

The tour begins anywhere in downtown Las Vegas. Take an access to I-15 south and drive approximately 28 miles to Exit #12 for Jean. The highway route roughly parallels the tracks of the Union Pacific, the railroad that built Las Vegas. The scenery along the highway is typical of southern Nevada's desert. One wonders how and why prospectors, explorers, and travelers of pre-automobile days would come this way, and at the courage and determination that pushed them on.

As you approach Exit #12 to Jean, look to the left across the freeway. The concrete and steel buildings are those of a Nevada State Prison maximum security facility. The town of Jean itself is on the old highway between the freeway and the prison. After taking the exit, drive 0.4 miles and turn right (west) onto SR 161,

toward Goodsprings. You may see roadrunners and even tortoises along this way. Watch for these interesting creatures, and do not harm them. In the spring, the yucca and Joshua trees here make the desert seem like a garden.

Drive 4.3 miles. The tall peak ahead and to the right is Potosi Mountain. The visible roads lead to communications facilities and are not open for public travel.

Continue for 2.0 more miles to the junction and bear right toward Goodsprings. The cemetery is directly ahead on the right. Drive 0.4 miles and enter Goodsprings. The historical marker is directly ahead, 0.2 miles. *You will return here* after you look around the historic community of Goodsprings.

Returning, drive from the marker west (straight ahead), and turn left for Sandy Valley, following the paved road. Drive 1.2 miles to the intersection and turn right toward Sandy.

Continue 0.7 miles. This is the Argentena mine and mill. Discoveries of lead, zinc, and silver were made here in 1887. The heaviest production took place in the 1920s and 1930s, when the company shipped considerable quantities of lead ore. The place is now abandoned. Use caution in visiting old mines like this one. Timbers rot, machinery falls easily, and the place can be dangerous in ways not readily discernible.

Continue 1.5 miles to Columbia Pass summit. The road to the left leads to the Columbia copper mine. In the spring, look for ocotillo blooming here in bright crimson spikes. The mine-scarred slopes show the historic mining activity.

Drive 3.2 miles. Here is a view of Sandy Valley. The mountains across the valley are in California; the state line runs across the valley.

Continue 2.8 miles, to where the road leads around private property. Continue 0.6 miles to the intersection of Cherokee Street and Sandy Valley Road, and turn right. Drive 1.5 miles to the crossroads of Quartz Avenue and Kingston Road. Go straight ahead, but *note this place and return here*.

Drive 1.5 miles along the edge of Sandy Valley's settlement. The people who live here now are retired refugees from city life, or small farmers engaged in marginal agriculture in this fertile and well-watered environment. Earlier residents included miners and prospectors searching the nearby hills for minerals. The new Sandy Valley development came about in the general area of this intersection. The site of the Keystone Mill, one of the earliest producers in this district, is at the corner of Sandy Valley Road and Kingston. The ten-stamp mill that once occupied the site pounded out as much as $30,000 a month during its heyday in the 1890s. High metals prices caused a resurgence in World War periods, but only ruins and junk now remain. Completing your visit to Sandy, return to the intersection of Quartz Avenue and Kingston Road, and then retrace your route to the intersection of Sandy Valley Road and SR 169, 10.6 miles. Here, continue east toward Jean, 6.3 miles.

Isn't this a fine isolated place for a "max" prison? The town of Jean has enjoyed a small economic boon from the installation. At I-15, turn right (south). "Pop's Oasis" casino at Jean marks the ownership of the townsite by C. A. "Pop" Simon, an early resident of the area. Jean's name honors Jean Fayle Rasmussen, daughter of Scottish pioneer immigrants. The place has historically been only an adjunct to the town of Goodsprings, merely a railroad siding to serve the freighting needs of the larger community.

Continue 7.3 miles. Here is a rest area, with tables, toilets, trailer holding tank disposal, drinking water, and free overnight parking for trailers (if one doesn't mind the traffic or the diesel truck idling next door).

Drive 4.2 miles, and as you go under the power transmission line, look to the northeast, following the wires to a pass in the mountains. The pass is called "Beer Bottle," known thus because the thirsty construction crews who built the line in the heat of summer so littered the ground that it took the name of their trash. Drive 1.2 miles, and cross the California state line.

As you drive along the dry lake bed, you may see some interesting mirages—water on the highway, boats on the playa—all tricks of nature. Drive 9.5 miles, and turn off I-15 to SR 164, toward Nipton and Searchlight. Make a left turn at the overpass. Continue 3.9 miles; there is a turn to Cima, California, but go straight ahead to Nipton.

Drive 6.5 miles to Nipton. This is the shipping center for the mines of historic southern Nevada. There is little commercial activity here except for the railroad. There are a grocery store, bar, and post office, but you cannot depend on their being open. An outdoor mineral display is behind the store. Nipton (originally Nippeno) was founded as a mining camp in 1885; it became a siding when the SP, SL & LA railroad was built to Las Vegas.

Continue 3.1 miles, and cross the Nevada state line. The mine to the right of the highway is on Crescent Peak. The road rises into the McCulloch Range and a heavy Joshua tree forest. Remember that the desert environment is fragile, and leave the plant life undisturbed.

Drive 18.2 miles and enter Searchlight. The historical marker is 0.5 miles straight ahead at the intersection. The gold and silver mines of the Searchlight area have produced something in excess of $5 million since the 1890s, about half that of the Goodsprings district. You will find all commercial facilities in Searchlight. This typical Nevada border town tries to give tourists from California their first encounters with gambling casinos. Cottonwood Cove, in the Lake Mead Recreation Area, is a popular camping, boating, and fishing resort; Searchlight caters to these tourists as well.

Completing your visit to Searchlight, return to the historical marker and turn north on U.S. 95; go 10.2 miles to a right turn onto a good, graded gravel road toward Nelson. As you drive, notice the evidences of this historic mining district—holes, tunnels, tailings, tanks, and hoists. Many of these prospects are still active. The peaks of the McCulloch Range are on the left, the El Dorado mountains on the right. If it has been raining, do not take the dirt road without checking first; this is flash-flood country and roads usually in good condition can suddenly disappear. (If you are doubtful about the gravel road, continue 17.8 miles to the paved SR 165, and turn right, 11.1 miles to Nelson.)

If you take the gravel road through the Wall Street district to Nelson: From the turn, drive 3.3 miles to a fork in the road; stay left, on the main traveled road. Notice that the wildflowers bloom here in profusion, even into the very late summer. Continue 3.7 miles; there is a dirt road from the left, but ignore it and drive on downhill. Drive 1.3 miles; this is the Kay-E mine, active and guarded. Drive 0.2 miles and bear to the left. Do not try to visit this mine. Continue for 0.6 miles. Here is the great Wall Street mine, still active in the 1980s. There are a few ruins of the earlier workings.

Drive 1.0 mile further and arrive in Nelson. Here is an archetypal mining camp with a long history and

Headframe at Searchlight

both old and new buildings. There are no constant tourist facilities in Nelson, so one cannot depend upon their being open.

In Nelson, go straight ahead to the paved highway, and turn right on SR 165. Drive 1.7 miles; here is the great Techatticup mine on the right, and its old service center on the left side of the highway. The unfriendly warning signs should be taken seriously by any traveler. The place has a long history of conflict and bloodshed, which the current owners have apparently absorbed. The area is almost surely still haunted by the spirits of men murdered for the Techatticup's treasure. A slow drive past the works will show the area sufficiently. And you soon will be able to view it from the other direction as well.

Continue down the gorgeous El Dorado Canyon. This scenic region is colorful with peaks, pillars, and cliffs of red, purple, green, yellow, white, brown, and gray. The road is subject to flash flooding, and may have debris on it, so drive slowly and carefully and enjoy your view of Lake Mohave (this is downstream from Hoover Dam, behind Davis Dam on the Colorado River). Drive 5.6 miles, and arrive at Nelson's Landing. Go straight ahead, up to the flat parking spot. Prior to October 1974, this area was a popular campsite on the Lake Mohave shore. Then a flash flood came down the canyon, changing the landscape and killing several campers. There is a short walk and a plaque at the parking lot explaining this catastrophe.

Return 7.3 miles to Nelson, and stay on the paved SR 165, driving toward U.S. 95. Drive 11.1 miles to the junction with U.S. 95. There is a historical marker for El Dorado Canyon at your left. Turn right at the junction, and return to Las Vegas, approximately 29 miles.

TOUR THREE, Southern Nevada's outdoors and Death Valley: Las Vegas — Pahrump — Death Valley — Beatty — Rhyolite and return. Approximately 326 miles round trip. The southern Nevada area has great, varied scenic wonders, both natural and manmade. Come with us to see a few of them. Pack a picnic or camping gear (it is possible to stay overnight in camps or other accommodations in either Death Valley or Beatty), take extra water, and make sure that your vehicle is ready for a long trip.

Note: *This is not a summertime tour. Temperatures in Death Valley can soar above 130°F from June through September. The tour is recommended for the months between November and April.*

The trip can begin anywhere in downtown Las Vegas. Take an access road for I-15 south and drive approximately 10.0 miles to Exit #33 (Blue Diamond and Pahrump). At Exit #33, follow signs for Pahrump and Death Valley on SR 160.

Drive 3.1 miles and cross the main line tracks of the Union Pacific. On the left is Arden, at one time the site of the Arden Plaster Company.

Drive 7.7 miles to the road for Blue Diamond, and continue straight ahead on SR 160. The mines of this area are operated by the Flintkote Company. The company extracts and manufactures gypsum and lime products. The town of Blue Diamond houses mainly workers for the various gypsum operations. As you drive past the intersection, look to your right to see one of the Flintkote wallboard factories. Continue on SR 160, and drive 7.0 miles. As you enter the canyon, the road winds up toward Mountain Springs summit along the route of the Old Spanish Trail. Imagine caravans of pack animals sweating over this track, two days' journey from the summit to Las Vegas.

Drive 1.2 miles. To the left of the highway is a historical marker for Potosi Mine, and a few feet west of that, a concrete post to show the Old Spanish Trail. The Potosi is about 4.5 miles away on the dirt road behind the marker. The road is suitable only for high-axle vehicles, and the mine is in a hard-to-find spot at the top of a tough, steep, and rocky climb. Continue on SR 160. Drive 1.6 miles to Mountain Springs summit; there is a historical marker at the left of the highway, along with picnic tables and garbage cans. The marker commemorates the Old Spanish Trail.

Drive 12.9 miles. Look to the right at the mountain.

Here is a technical description of the formation: "a southward-plunging anticline involving Permian redbeds and the overlying Triassic Moenkopi Formation." There are numberless strange formations to enjoy along this route.

Drive 3.9 miles to the junction; go straight ahead toward Pahrump. The settlement of Tecopa bears the name of the great Paiute peacemaker. Continue 7.6 miles; here is a view of Pahrump Valley. The valley lies on an alluvial fan, and formerly had abundant free-flowing springs. Pumping has about eliminated these, and now water for irrigation comes from wells up to 900 feet deep.

Continue 1.7 miles, and cross the Nye County line. Drive another 0.3 miles. This is the site of the famous Manse ranch, which now has a considerable settlement around it. Continue 3.4 miles and enter Pahrump. The chamber of commerce and information center is 1.6 miles from this point, on the right-hand side of the road. Here is a place to obtain maps and brochures about this area. While Pahrump began as a farming and ranching center, and had a fair cotton industry in the 1960s, the main business in the 1980s is selling and promoting real estate. Almost the only agricultural activity near the end of the twentieth century involved growing and pelleting alfalfa—a good business in an area that cuts up to eight crops a year. A more controversial business is in growing turf for lawns; some people dispute the advantages in shipping the topsoil out of the valley with the grass.

To see the town of Pahrump off the highway, continue from the chamber of commerce office 1.0 mile, and turn left onto SR 372, then 0.3 miles to a right turn on East Street. Pahrump has most necessary tourist facilities, and an interesting mixture of old and new structures. Return to the intersection of SR 372 and East Street to continue the tour, and turn southwest on SR 372.

Drive 7.4 miles, and cross the California state line. The highway becomes California SR 178. The drive is across Stewart Valley into the Resting Springs Range. Drive 13.8 miles to the intersection with a sign for Chicago Valley, and go straight ahead on SR 178.

Drive 1.7 miles. This interesting road cut illustrates some of the geologic past of this region. There are several layers of volcanic material, including one layer of black obsidian. Geologists date the volcanic activity here to the Miocene era (10 to 20 million years ago). We found a geode near this place. Notice the other signs of volcanic activity as you cross the summit of the Resting Springs Range.

Drive 3.3 miles. This is a crossing of the Amargosa River. The stream, some 140 miles long, is dry on the surface for most of the year. At flash-flood time, however, the Amargosa can cause havoc and terror. The white cliffs you passed were formed during the Pleistocene era (1 to 2 million years ago) by the action of just such a flood, when the river rushed into a place where a dam grew up, and sediments collected in the resulting lake.

Drive 0.4 miles to the junction of California SR 178 and SR 127; turn right toward Shoshone on California 127, and enter Shoshone. Here are limited facilities—gasoline, groceries, a motel.

Continue 1.7 miles toward Death Valley, and turn left onto California SR 178. You will cross Greenwater Valley. As you climb out of the floor of the valley, you will see the Funeral Range on the right, Dublin Hills on the left. The road rises to 3,315 feet at Salsberry Pass. Drive 10.9 miles to the summit of Salsberry Pass.

Continue 4.0 miles to the Death Valley National Monument boundary. The road is subject to flash flooding. If you see warning signs, observe them. The highway drops down, then rises briefly to Jubilee Pass, elevation 1,317. Notice the beautiful white-leaved desert holly along the road; this is a protected plant, and you should also remember that you are now on federal lands. Continue 5.6 miles to Jubilee Pass. This is a place for wildflower enthusiasts to enjoy in the springtime.

Drive 4.7 miles to an intersection, and bear right on the paved road toward Furnace Creek. Drive 2.0 miles and look to the left; here are the ruins of the Ashford mill, a gold processing plant. Continue 0.9 miles and look to the left for a view of Shoreline Butte; the

"shoreline" refers to the fact that Pleistocene Lake Manly existed here. Watch for signs of this water body that dried up over a million years ago; at one time, it was more than a hundred miles long and 600 feet deep.

Drive 0.9 miles. The West Side Road is at the left; go straight ahead. As you drive along a scenic road in a comfortable vehicle, recall the hardships endured by the pioneer Manly party who stumbled into this area on their trek to California. The remnants of the group named it Death Valley as they left with the rescue party.

Drive 9.3 miles, past Mormon Point. Continue 16.1 miles to Badwater. You have been driving at below sea level for some time. This point is 280 feet below sea level. At Badwater there are picnic tables, garbage cans, pit toilets, and an information plaque—but don't look for a shade tree. Look up the cliff on the right; there is a sign that indicates sea level. The pool at Badwater is fed by underground springs. The water is not poisonous, but not really drinkable either. The pond supports a small amount of plant and animal life.

Drive 5.6 miles to Devil's Golf Course. You might enjoy the short drive to look at this queer deposit of halite (table salt). Below the surface here, there are about a thousand feet of alternate layers of soil and salt deposited by ancient forces.

Continue 2.4 miles, and turn right on Artists Drive. This scenic road through Death Valley geology loops 9.0 miles back to the main road. Drive slowly over this paved, one-way route, and then turn right at its end, toward Furnace Creek.

Drive 4.8 miles and turn left; here is the resort hotel at Furnace Creek. Continue 1.0 mile more, and enter the resort village of Furnace Creek. Here are food, housing, camping, and gasoline.

Drive 0.4 miles to the Death Valley National Monument Visitor Center. Stop here for maps and brochures, and look at the exhibits. Then return to the highway, and turn left.

Continue 1.3 miles, and turn left to see the Harmony Borax Works, an outdoor exhibit. This is probably the Monument's most famous man-made landmark. Return to the highway, and turn left.

Drive 9.3 miles, and turn right toward Beatty. You will leave the main part of Death Valley National Monument here. There is more to see, and we hope you will return. Now drive toward the Funeral Mountains.

Drive 10.0 miles to the intersection. The road parallels the Amargosa River's bed. In spring, the wildflowers grow here in marvelous profusion. The road will climb into the Funeral Range to Daylight Pass at 4,316 feet. At the intersection, the route joins the Titus Canyon Road; go ahead toward Beatty. The intersection is called Hell's Gate. Continue 6.3 miles to Daylight Pass. Drive 0.4 miles, cross the Nevada state line, and continue downhill across the Amargosa Desert on SR 374.

Drive 3.9 miles, leaving the Death Valley National Monument. Drive 4.9 miles, and turn left to Rhyolite on a paved road. The ruins of the ghost town are visible on the hillside ahead. Drive 1.4 miles into the town.

Rhyolite's history belongs properly in the twentieth-century mining boom (see Southwestern Nevada tours). Discoveries were made there in 1904, concurrently with those in Goldfield and Tonopah, in what was known at the Bullfrog District. By 1915, Rhyolite had passed through the familiar cycle from boom to bust. But it was great while it lasted: three railroads served the town; former U.S. Senator William Morris Stewart established a residence there and helped to promote the place; and the buildings included the depot, a bank, and one of the fanciest hotels in southern Nevada. Now, there are picturesque ruins, a few homes, the old depot that has opened or closed periodically as some sort of tourist facility, a small museum, and some souvenir shops. The paved road leads past the major ruins.

We went to Rhyolite on a weekday in the off-season for tourists, and the place was almost suffering from a traffic jam. Enjoy the sights; the old buildings are very photogenic. But do not expect to pick up relics or dig for treasure; the residents protect their town.

Concluding your look at Rhyolite, retrace the 1.4 miles to the highway (SR 374), and turn left, toward Beatty. Continue 3.5 miles and arrive in Beatty.

Beatty has all the necessary tourist facilities—gasoline, restaurants, groceries, hotel, motels, commercial campgrounds, casino.

Decision: *Las Vegas is about 125 miles away—about two and a half hours. You can stay in Beatty overnight, or continue to Las Vegas; there are no adequate facilities between Beatty and Las Vegas.*

Drive through Beatty, straight along the main street, 0.5 miles and turn right (south) on U.S. 95 toward Las Vegas. Drive 8.4 miles, and look to the left of the highway; there are the ruins of Carrara, and yes, there is a marble quarry, about a mile hike beyond the main ruins. We found a rattlesnake there one day, guarding the quarry. Continue 2.8 miles. There is a sign for U.S. Ecology to indicate the nationally-known Beatty nuclear waste dump.

The nuclear disposal site has become controversial both in Nevada and elsewhere. The items dumped there, contaminated by radiation, have included everything from small handtools to concrete mixers. Because radiation is invisible, dishonest promoters and thieves were able to sell items stolen from the dump to unsuspecting customers. Nobody knows how much material has been taken from the disposal and sold, but one investigation in 1976 resulted in the removal of more than twenty truckloads of contaminated items from homes in Beatty alone (Beatty's population is under 900). Nevada politicians have attempted from time to time to have the dump closed, but because the state is composed of 86 percent federally-owned land (and the site is on federal property), the outcome of these efforts is widely in doubt.

Drive on 5.0 miles, and look ahead to the right. There is a huge sand dune. Legend says that a wagon train camped near the dune was completely buried in a sudden windstorm, and that the train is still there—somewhere under the sand.

Continue 13.3 miles to the Lathrop Wells rest area. Here are toilets, tables, garbage cans, and free overnight trailer parking. Stay on U.S. 95 through this intersection.

Continue 22.7 miles. There is a historical marker for the Nevada Test Site. To the left, the town of Mercury is visible; this is the center for nuclear testing operations, which began here in 1951. Behind the historical marker are the remains of Camp Desert Rock, part of the Test Site. You have been driving along the border of the Test Site, and the road continues along the edge for some miles further. Drive 1.5 miles to the Mercury exit; do not take the exit, as visitors are not allowed into the area. All of the testing operations are carried out beyond the hills to the north.

Continue 15.8 miles. This is Cactus Spring, a small commercial center. Drive 2.5 miles to Indian Springs. This place has few services for the public; the U.S. Air Force has an aircraft gunnery range north of here, which is not open for visitors.

Drive 8.7 miles. The complex to your right is one of the Nevada State Prison's facilities. Continue on U.S. 95, and return to Las Vegas, approximately 33 miles.

TOUR FOUR, Science, technology, and engineering: Las Vegas — Henderson — Boulder City — Hoover Dam and return. Approximately 70 miles round trip.

The tour can begin anywhere in downtown Las Vegas. Drive south on Fremont Street (U.S. 93 & 95, the Boulder Highway), approximately 13.0 miles to Henderson. Until after the Second World War, the Boulder Highway was a two-lane road across unoccupied miles of desert. At Lake Mead Drive (the traffic light), turn right to enter Henderson. On the right-hand side of the street is the chamber of commerce. Here, you may receive maps and brochures to tell you about the area's business.

This 70-square-mile town is the fastest-growing city in southern Nevada. More than half of all the manufacturing done in the state is in Henderson; there are industrial parks, and factories producing textiles, food, and clothing. Some tours of these facilities are available; ask at the chamber of commerce office.

Back out on the main Boulder Highway, 3.0 miles beyond the Lake Mead Drive turnoff, is the Southern

Nevada Museum (on the left). This excellent Clark County-operated facility has exhibits both indoors and outdoors, including relics, minerals, photos, paintings, and diorama presentations of earlier life here. There is a nominal fee for admission, and some souvenirs including Indian handicrafts are for sale. Do also take time to visit the historic homes moved from Las Vegas and restored here. You will also find good natural history exhibits behind the main building.

Leaving the museum, turn left toward Boulder City. Drive 3.5 miles to the intersection with U.S. 95, and go ahead to the left. Continue 3.4 miles, and enter Boulder City; the Chamber of Commerce on the right-hand side of the highway is the city's main information center. You may ask for maps and brochures about the area here; Boulder City contains some surprising features. For specialists or people with specific interests, tours are available at the Desert Research Institute's Solar Research Laboratory. There is also a limited amount of "space age" manufacturing here.

Leaving the Boulder City Chamber of Commerce, continue on U.S. 93 through the business section. Drive 1.5 miles; here is a view of Lake Mead. Drive downhill toward the lake. Drive 3.5 miles to the intersection, and continue toward Hoover Dam. Continue 3.8 miles, and arrive at the dam overlook. The Visitor Center is 0.2 miles straight ahead on the left. Here, you may see a ten-minute film on the history of the dam and purchase tickets for the 35-minute tour of the dam. Do take advantage of these; it is an ideal activity, especially for a warm day.

Drive across the dam, 0.5 miles to the Arizona state line and scenic overlook, then return and drive back across the dam, 2.3 miles to the sign for the Lake View Point. The point is less than a third of a mile up the road, a good place for looking, picnicking, or resting. Return to the highway and turn right.

Drive 2.3 miles to the intersection of SR 166 and U.S. 93, and turn right onto SR 166. Now you will see the recreation facilities created by the great engineering feat. Notice the camping areas and the marinas along the lakeshore, especially at Hemenway Harbor, Boulder campground, and the Lake Mead Marina, where thousands of sailboats may be anchored. Drive 5.4 miles to the Nevada Division of Wildlife fish hatchery. Tours are available on request.

Continue past the other campgrounds, or visit a few. This area has a great deal of desert holly, a beautiful (and protected) white-leaved shrub. The flash flood activity here makes interesting landscapes. Drive 5.7 miles to the intersection with SR 167, and turn right to continue the drive through the Lake Mead Recreation Area. Continue 3.2 miles and turn left on SR 147 toward North Las Vegas. Drive 10.5 miles, and you will be on Lake Mead Boulevard; stay on this street for 6.2 miles, and you will reach Las Vegas Boulevard. Turn left for downtown Las Vegas.

TOUR FIVE, Some Southern Nevada recreation areas: Las Vegas — The Strip — Spring Mountain — Red Rock Canyon — Lamb Park — Lee Canyon — Charleston Park and return. Approximately 155 miles round trip. Southern Nevada contains some of the most varied and unusual playgrounds in the West. Pack a picnic or camping gear.

Begin your tour in downtown Las Vegas at the corner of Fremont Street and Las Vegas Boulevard. Drive 2.0 miles south on Las Vegas Boulevard to Sahara Avenue. This is the famous Las Vegas Strip, unique magnet for pleasure seekers and hedonists from everywhere. Take time to appreciate the variety of architecture and to read the marquees that advertise performances by the great stars of show business. Plan as well to return here on a night-time drive, when the lights make the place into a different kind of experience. Children are not allowed in the gambling areas of the casinos, but they can surely enjoy the strange shapes and colors of this section.

Continue driving south on Las Vegas Boulevard for 3.0 miles and cross Tropicana Boulevard. McCarran International Airport is to your left. Las Vegas promoters never lose their inventiveness and enthusiasm. For example, radio advertising told us as we drove here that McCarran International has more flights in and out of Las Vegas *per capita* than any other city airport in the United States. That is the sort of hyperbole that helped to build the Strip, and the airport.

Result of flash flood in Valley of Fire Wash

Continue 2.1 miles to the junction with I-15. Bear left, and stay on Las Vegas Boulevard south. Drive 1.5 miles and turn right toward Blue Diamond. Cross the overpass, and then continue west on SR 160 toward Blue Diamond and Pahrump.

Drive 11.2 miles, and turn right to the Red Rock Recreation Area. You will see the beginning of the formations that give the place its name. Ahead to the right is Flintkote's wallboard plant. The open-pit gypsum mine that supplies the plant is above the factory. Continue on this road. The town of Blue Diamond is on the left at 3.1 miles; this is a small residential community for the gypsum plant workers. Drive 0.8 miles to the boundary of the Red Rock Canyon Recreation Area. Stay on the paved main road; side roads lead to private property or commercial developments.

Drive 1.9 miles to the entrance of the Spring Mountain Ranch State Park, and turn left, to enter the park. There is a fee to see the park. The place was originally a ranch belonging to the Wilson family, composed of James B. Wilson and two adopted half-Paiute sons, Jim and Tweed. After the Wilsons died, the ranch passed through various hands and was finally purchased by Mrs. Vera Krupp, heiress to the great German munitions fortune. When Howard Hughes came to Las Vegas in 1967, the Hughes company bought the place, but never made extensive use of it. Finally, the ranch passed to some developers who proposed to build a condominium/townhouse on the property. Local objections to that project brought about purchase by the state of Nevada, and the current use of the ranch as a state park. The Spring Mountain Ranch park has picnic facilities, walking paths, and, on weekends, tours of the ranch house. This is an ideal stop for people who enjoy "mansion tours," for the Krupp era particularly made the house into a showplace. If your trip should be on a Saturday or a Sunday, do take time to look at the ranch house. At any time, this is a fine place for a shady picnic, and a look at a still-working ranch. Return to the highway, and turn left.

Drive 4.7 miles and turn left to the Red Rock Canyon Visitor Center. Here is almost a model for installations of this kind. There are maps, brochures, exhibits, media presentations, educational tours, self-guided hikes and drives, and ranger-led activities. The setting is one of the most beautiful of the Nevada desert area, a fact recognized by several motion picture companies who have made films here. In the vicinity are a sandstone quarry worked early in the twentieth century, a few deserted cabins (one belonged to a genuine hermit), an abandoned lead mine, and the ruins of a ranch that belonged to the "white" Wilson family (the term is used to distinguish these Wilsons from those at Spring Mountain). In the park, there are picnic facilities and primitive campsites. Make your first stop at the Visitor Center (obtain a wildlife checklist), and return to the highway, turning left onto the Loop Drive, a one-way, 13-mile trip that will display many of the features of Red Rock Canyon.

On the Loop Drive, use the wildlife brochure from the Visitor Center. This place is especially interesting for children who can use the checklist and its portrayal of desert creatures—birds, mammals, and reptiles. The Loop Drive has numerous overlooks, self-guided walks, and a seemingly endless variety of colorful desert geology, flora, and fauna. To fly over this area is to realize the fragile nature of the desert environment; wagon roads unused in over a hundred years traverse parts of the Canyon, and are visible as scars on the landscape.

Completing the Loop Drive, turn left, toward the red hills. Go 0.5 miles; here is a roadside rest, with parking, garbage cans, and an interpretive plaque. Drive 1.6 miles, this time past the Visitor Center. The road becomes an extension of Charleston Boulevard into Las Vegas. Stay on this road (and Charleston), driving 10.6 miles to the intersection with Rainbow Boulevard, and turn left.

Drive 1.2 miles to the intersection, following signs for U.S. 95 north, and turn left with the traffic light onto the U.S. 95 north freeway. The mountains to your left are those of the Charleston Range.

Drive 8.6 miles and turn right onto Durango Drive, then 1.4 miles to an intersection and bear right toward Floyd R. Lamb State Park, which is 0.6 miles ahead. This fee area state park has 700 acres of nature trails, picnic sites, lakes for fishing and boating, a state arboretum and tree nursery in a lovely, oasis-like setting. There is no campground here. The location was once a dude ranch during the heyday of Nevada's "quickie-divorce" era, and some ranch buildings remain. Thousands of years earlier, the place was occupied by the native hunters and gatherers of Tule Springs. The name of the park honors a state senator who served the area longer than any other legislator of his time. After your visit here, return 2.0 miles to U.S. 95 and turn right, continuing north on U.S. 95.

Drive 16.8 miles and turn left on SR 156 toward Lee Canyon. Just after the turn, on the right, is an information sign, placed by the Toiyabe National Forest. Take a minute to familiarize yourself with the route you will be following on paved SR 156. Straight ahead as you drive is the beautiful and rugged Mount Charleston, nearly 12,000 feet in altitude. Drive 14.4 miles to the turnoff to Kyle Canyon, but go straight ahead. *You will return here shortly.*

As you drive, notice that the vegetation changes rather suddenly from the Joshua tree forest through which you came to conifers, and then to deciduous trees and shrubs. This place is up to 30° cooler than Las Vegas in the summertime, and beautiful at almost any time of year.

Continue to drive uphill. There are several campgrounds and picnic sites in this area. After 3.6 miles, the road ends in a parking lot at Lee Canyon ski resort.

Red Rock Canyon

Skiing has not developed into a highly popular and commercial activity in southern Nevada because of the sparsity of snow; still, a few hundred people enjoy this ski lift in winter. Now, turn around, and retrace your route to the Kyle Canyon road, 3.6 miles, and turn right. If you are taking this trip in winter, you should check to make sure that the road is open. The scenic road between the two canyons affords views of the desert on the left and Mt. Charleston on the right, a study in contrasts.

As you drive this 8.9 miles, you will pass several campgrounds, picnic areas, and historic sites: Deer Creek, a walk-in picnic ground; the trailhead for a hike of the Charleston loop; Hilltop campground, a fee area for small campers and tents; and the trail to Robbers Roost cave—a hideout for badmen in the early days. Looking to the left on Angel Peak, you can see the secure military installation that houses a radar station; visitors are not allowed there. At the intersection, turn right toward Charleston. The end of the road and a place to turn around is 4.0 miles up the hill. This is the major resort area of Charleston Park, and contains summer homes, commercial facilities, fire and police stations, and a ranger station, along with good campgrounds and picnic sites. The CCC also had a camp in this vicinity, and was responsible for building many of the roads here that can now be enjoyed by everyone.

After touring the Charleston Park area, return downhill on the highway to the intersection and the National Forest boundary. Go straight ahead on SR 157. Notice again how quickly the vegetation changes back to desert Joshuas, yucca, and cactus. One can appreciate here the historic uses of Charleston Park for relief from the heat and desert environs of the valley floor. From the junction, drive 17.5 miles to the junction with U.S. 95, and turn right to return to Las Vegas, approximately 13.0 miles.

Road to Big Pine, out of Death Valley

SOUTHWESTERN NEVADA

SOUTHWESTERN NEVADA

Southwestern Nevada's history before the turn of the twentieth century is composed more of politics than of other elements. Mining became important there, as it had in other sections, yet the largest portion of the area was generally regarded as "unknown." The mining districts were famous and colorful, with names remembered in the nineteenth century, but their output pales against those of the twentieth century. Aurora, Belmont, Tybo, Hot Creek, and Jefferson City flared briefly, and died almost as quickly as their minerals played out. Tonopah, Goldfield, Rhyolite, and Rawhide all brought Nevada more celebrity and wealth than the others combined. A single agricultural complex among these, Yerington, provided contrast with the generally rougher mining camps.

Politics of the Nineteenth Century

The area that now encompasses southwestern Nevada was once western Utah. As the Mormons lost control of the section, the Nevada territorial legislature carved out nine counties on November 25, 1861. Esmeralda, with its seat at Aurora, was one of those. The new county contained roughly the area of present-day Nye, Mineral, and Esmeralda counties.

Aurora came into being as the result of ore discoveries there in 1860. This tough little gold and silver camp was accepted by Nevada government as the seat of one of the original counties. At the same time, however, the survey lines between the new territory of Nevada and the older state of California were somewhat blurred and indefinite. Mono County, California, designated Aurora its county seat. The situation could not endure, although it lasted long enough for both Mono and Esmeralda counties to send delegates from Aurora to the legislatures of their respective states, and for the citizens of Aurora to vote in the elections of both Nevada and California. In September 1863, a survey finally showed Aurora to be three miles or so inside the Nevada line.

Besides the mining moguls, probably the most famous of Aurora's early citizens was Samuel L. Clemens, later Mark Twain. The younger brother of Nevada's territorial secretary, Clemens arrived in Aurora in 1861. He tried unsuccessfully to make a living at mining there, occupying his spare time by writing pithy letters to the Virginia City *Territorial Enterprise*. With the Comstock city booming, and a labor shortage of journalists there, Twain was offered a job on the *Enterprise*. He took the post, and in Virginia City began to develop the style that later made him retrospectively the pride of Nevada's nineteenth-century press.

"We climbed far up on the mountainside and went to work on a little rubbishy claim of ours that had a shaft on it eight feet deep. Higbie descended into it and . . . loosened up a deal of rock and dirt, and then I went down . . . to throw it out. . . . I made the toss, and landed the mess just on the ledge of the shaft and it all came back on my head and down the back of my neck. I never said a word, but climbed out and walked home. . . . I sat down, in the cabin, and gave myself up to solid misery. . . . I had found a letter in the post-office as I came home from the hillside, and finally I opened it. Eureka! . . . It was a deliberate offer to me of Twenty-five Dollars a week to come up to Virginia and be city editor of the *Enterprise*. I would have challenged the publisher in the [more profitable] days—I wanted to fall down and worship him now."

— Mark Twain, *Roughing It*

Aurora's mines came to the inevitable end, with perhaps as much as $30 million worth of production. Fires took away most of the structures of Aurora, while scavengers and commercial salvage gathered the leavings. Aurora had a brief revival about the time of World War I, but finally died, and by the 1960s, there was little to mark the place except for a mill and smelter ruins and a graveyard. In the 1970s, the graveyard was disappearing to vandals and ghouls, and by the 1980s, people could only wonder what had happened to Aurora; its nearby sister city, the equally rough and tough Bodie, California, had been preserved in near-perfect state from the 1880s or so, but Aurora had evanesced.

The second important county seat of the area, Belmont, did somewhat better. With mining discoveries in a section that had previously been marked ''unknown'' on maps, the citizens of the so-called Union district petitioned Territorial Governor Nye for governmental status, complaining that the distance from Aurora or Austin was so great as to make doing business nearly impossible. Nye granted the request, seeing to the division of Esmeralda, and had the honor of seeing the county named for him. The seat was designated to be Ione City, then the only settlement in the huge area. Ione City retained the county seat for only three years; in 1867, the legislature decreed that the then fast-growing town of Belmont would be Nye County's seat.

Belmont soon had an imposing courthouse, jail, and other trappings of government. There were also homes and all sorts of commercial establishments along with many mines and mills. One of the mills, a tremendous structure with a tall chimney, had the distinction of surviving the target practice of gunners on World War II fighter planes.

Long before the turn of the twentieth century, Belmont had declined to serving only as the county seat. The mines played out, and politics was nearly the only thing keeping the place alive. Still, the courthouse supplied offices to two of Nye County's most illustrious citizens, both one-time district attorneys there: James L. Butler and Tasker L. Oddie. Both of these men ar-

rived in Nevada late in the 1890s at the behest of eastern mining speculators to investigate the possibilities of central Nevada mineral development, Butler for a company that had designs on the old camp of Tybo, Oddie with a company that had a base in Austin. Their destinies and Nevada's were intertwined from that time on.

Belmont's declines as a mining camp and then as a seat of government were permanent. Fires, weather, and collectors began to cause the site to disappear. The town was nearly gone, the courthouse endangered, and the few residents there fearful of every passing car, when finally the state of Nevada recognized its responsibility and took over a one-acre portion of Belmont including the courthouse, designating the place as a historic monument and state park. Again, politics had played its role, for only dedicated lobbying by preservation-minded people and the members of the state park commission saved the place for future generations of scholars and sightseers.

''The man who is here is named Butler and is a very pleasant young fellow and I like him. He will be connected with the company that is going to take hold of Tybo.''

— Tasker L. Oddie, letter to his mother, July 16, 1900

''[A] man named Butler who lives here [in Belmont] . . . went south prospecting. He found a group of ledges that promise to be very rich in a place no one ever was at before. . . . He has given me an interest in them. [After the assay] One piece of the ore that came from the surface assayed $206 in gold and 540 ounces of silver to the ton. This is a fine showing and an unusual one. . . . Well, I have come out for District Attorney for Nye County and people tell me there will be no opposition. . . .''

— Tasker L. Oddie, letter to his mother, September 4, 1900

Southwestern Mining Camps
of the Nineteenth Century

Although the southwestern section's history belongs mainly to the twentieth century's great mining booms, several colorful and interesting little clusters of towns and near-towns arose in the Esmeralda-Nye area. Among these were the settlements of Candelaria, Belleville, Columbus, and some of their smaller neighbors. These were about in the center of Esmeralda County, as it was constituted before 1911. The camps rose and declined from the 1860s until the 1880s, when Nevada's great depression was underway. Candelaria was named by Mexicans, who discovered silver there in 1864 on a feast day. The place was a dusty, nearly waterless camp, where people lived in dugouts in the hillsides, worked in powdery stamp mills, and finally built a town that had a reported nineteen business buildings—eleven of which were saloons.

Columbus had some fairly rich silver ore, but it was better known for some good borax deposits, discovered in 1871. By 1872, Columbus was producing the nation's first commercially refined borax. The entrepreneur of Columbus became famous as "Borax" Smith, the founder of the Pacific Coast Borax Company, owner of the "20 Mule Team" trademark. Chinese laborers at Columbus formed a typical Chinatown. The deposits lasted nearly into the twentieth century, but Columbus did not, owing partly to the fact that good transportation took care of many of the commercial needs of the people who might otherwise have lived there. By 1890, Columbus was deserted.

Belleville was mainly a mill site for the ores of Candelaria. The other little camps, Marietta, Sodaville, Rhodes, and Metallic City (Pickhandle Gulch) combined to make what writers of the mid-twentieth century called the "seven slumbering sisters." Little remained until the mining boom of the late twentieth century awoke Candelaria, under the management of the Occidental Minerals Corporation. Beginning in 1975, Occidental worked over the old deposits, established a commercial project on the sites of Metallic

City and Candelaria, and continued into the 1980s to mine profitably. By the 1980s, the Candelaria district contained the largest silver mine in Nevada, the seventh-largest in the nation. Local people in that end of the county were grateful to Occidental; the employment rolls rose to nearly 200, working at a low-grade silver leaching process that promised to keep the seven sisters awake for some time to come.

A second cluster of little camps, not so profitable for mining, but with an interesting past and future, lay around the old town of Ione City, first county seat of Nye. Ione's neighbors (the "city" was dropped when it became obviously a misnomer) included Berlin, Grantsville, and Union. Ione was established first, but the mines there lasted only a brief time; then came Berlin, with richer ore. Next was Union, near Berlin, another rich strike. Then Grantsville arose, soon larger than any other town in the county, with ore good enough to spur the building of some sophisticated mills for roasting. By the early 1880s, the entire complex was in decline, and despite occasional flurries of excitement into the World War I period, the towns decayed and became ghosts or near-ghosts.

In 1954, a peculiar event caused a partial revival in the little settlements; this was not from mining, but from science. Fossils had been known to exist in the area, which was geologically interesting enough to have paleontologists exploring there, searching out evidences of ages-old sea life. That summer, 1954, came one of the important scientific discoveries of Nevada's history; Dr. Charles Camp uncovered a giant ichthyosaur, a prehistoric sea creature. The find was so important that the state of Nevada assumed control of the site, and within a fairly short time, established a state park there. The state park arrangement proved successful, and the ichthyosaur fossils interested expanding numbers of people. Mining on a reduced scale continued around Ione and its sister towns, but science was certainly more entertaining.

Tonopah

As the nineteenth century drew to a close with Nevada's mining depression in its twentieth year, several eastern companies were investing capital on speculation in Great Basin minerals. These organizations had men in the field, exploring old districts and searching for new deposits or lodes. With this arrangement, it was no doubt inevitable that something would be found—given, of course, that the minerals existed.

The earliest of the discoveries was in northern Nevada near Golconda, but the most significant and longest-lasting came at Tonopah. James Butler, representative of one of the speculator-investor companies and an attorney who owned a ranch near Belmont, fulfilled his commission outstandingly. In mid May 1900, Butler prospected south from Belmont, crossing an area regarded as unknown and nearly inaccessible, on his way to visit and prospect a tiny settlement called Klondike. Stopping overnight at a spring called Tonopah, he found rich ledges of silver and gold ore which assayed at values of $206 in gold and 640 ounces of silver per ton.

Like all such discoveries, a body of folklore grew up around the findings. Butler himself told various stories, most consistently about having picked up a piece of rock to throw at a balky burro and finding it heavy with minerals. With this, Tonopah virtually adopted the burro as its town symbol.

"My sister was a school teacher in Tonopah. . . . Her story about the dollar-a-barrel water was that the water was used several times. She said, 'My landlady and I washed our hair, and then we washed our clothes . . .' and on and on the story went, so that it went through several uses. The story finally ended up that they scrubbed the floor with this water, and then they fed it to the burros who ranged the hills of Tonopah. . . . And the fact was that they *did* put the water out after it had been used for several purposes, put it out for the burros and they drank it. It was really getting thick by that time!"

— Amy Gulling, Reno pioneer

In any event, a townsite at what became Tonopah was established and a rush began. There were many problems in developing the settlement, for the county—largest in Nevada, and bigger than some eastern states—contained fewer than 1,200 people. Sodaville, more than sixty miles away, was the closest transportation center, and natural resources like fuel or timber or water were simply nonexistent.

Butler's eastern connections were apparently unimpressed. He took as his partner another employee of an eastern firm, Tasker L. Oddie. Together, Butler and Oddie worked the claims with pick and shovel, hauled the results by wagon to Belmont, where the ore was taken again by wagon to the railhead at Austin. After a long journey, the two tons of ore returned in the form of a check of $500. The reduction from the original assays was attributable simply to the high costs of transportation. Clearly, adequate development would depend upon on-site milling and an infusion of capital.

The money was forthcoming with the advent of a group of Philadelphia capitalists, who incorporated under the name of the Tonopah Mining Company. These men, led mainly by Arthur Brock, issued stock in the amount of $1.3 million, and ended the period of individual enterprise on the part of miners in the Tonopah ledges. Butler sold out his interests, while his partner, Oddie, remained as general manager of the corporation. A second corporation, with John Brock at its head, and also with Oddie's involvement, came into being as the Tonopah-Belmont. The latter owned claims adjoining those of the Tonopah Mining Company. For the next forty years, these two corporations accounted for some 60 percent of the production of the Tonopah mines.

The Brock family, through these two groups, gradually acquired control of the two mining companies, along with two shortline railroads, the Tonopah and Goldfield, and the Bullfrog–Goldfield. John Brock was president of the four corporations simultaneously. By 1905, their holdings increased to include stamp mill facilities and the water company.

Not so quickly in charge, but eventually with similar control, was George Wingfield. Wingfield, who

First photo of Tonopah, April 1, 1901

Tonopah

started his Nevada career as a cowboy around Winnemucca, moved into Tonopah in 1901 as a dealer in a gambling club. Within a short time, Wingfield owned the gambling concession in the Tonopah Club. Before long, he branched out to buying mining stocks, grubstaking prospectors, and generally making astute investments. He formed a partnership with financier-politician George S. Nixon, formerly of Winnemucca, and the two began to establish themselves as the barons of southwestern Nevada; Tonopah and Goldfield (to the south) fell eventually into their hands.

The original settlers continued to be prominent. Tasker Oddie, who had resigned from his earlier position with the Stokes family to associate himself with the Brocks, went into politics. He was district attorney of Nye County, state senator from that county, and in the latter post was instrumental in having the 1905 legislature designate Tonopah as the county seat. Belmont subsided another degree. Later, as his careers with the law and politics matured, Oddie became governor of Nevada and then U.S. senator. The capitalists Nixon and Wingfield sponsored his candidacies (Wingfield alone after Nixon died), and in time, Wingfield himself came to dominate not only Oddie, but also state politics as well.

Other outstanding citizens of Tonopah in the early years included attorneys Key Pittman and Patrick McCarran. Both of these men were destined to play large roles in local and national affairs, beginning with rather insignificant inaugurations of their legal careers in Tonopah. Pittman succeeded George Nixon in the U.S. Senate after the latter died in 1912, while McCarran defeated Oddie for the second senatorial seat in 1932. For decades, the men of southwestern Nevada dominated Nevada politics.

Still, all was not politics in Tonopah. In one of his political campaigns, Tasker Oddie took credit for Tonopah's stable labor force and high wages—$4 per day. This reflected the generally quiet labor history of the silver camp in its early years. In 1919, after nearly two decades of calm, the Industrial Workers of the World (IWW), one of the West's more violent labor organizations, moved in. The leaders attempted to fo-

"I thought it would be a good thing to go to Tonopah during the Boom. When I went there in 1905, it was still booming, and Tonopah, at that time, was the second or even the largest city in the state. It was the most active town in Nevada. While there I met many of the men who were interested in mining and boom excitements. . . . I met Jim Butler (discoverer of Tonopah), George Wingfield, George Bartlett, . . . Ex-Senator William M. Stewart. . . . I also met Key Pittman, Cal Brougher, Tasker L. Oddie . . . and many others. From the sporting world I met Tex Rickard and Ole Elliott. They had the Northern Saloon in Goldfield."

— Roy Hardy, mining engineer

ment a strike and succeeded for a couple of months in disrupting the relatively peaceable labor scene. But the difficulties were settled, and remained so as long as the camp was profitable, which was only to be for a short while longer.

Tonopah had numerous social affairs and organizations. Parties, celebrations, outings, charity drives, church services, and lodge meetings kept the residents involved and active. Two newspapers, the *Times* and the *Bonanza*, offered the day's information and education. In fact, the place had, quite early, all the facilities and trappings of a modern city of the 1910s. Many of these aspects of Tonopah's life continued after the decline, although on a reduced scale.

Inevitably, Tonopah's mines ran out. A bank panic in 1907, the declining mineral deposits, dropping silver prices, and another national depression all contributed to making the former silver capital of Nevada into a near ghost town. Something more than $146 million came from the mines of Tonopah during the best years. The county seat and a good situation on a major north-south highway kept a few commercial places and some politicians in business. The coming of World War II revived the place somewhat. An air base was established, along with radar installations. The military kept a few people there until the war ended, and the population again decreased. Another military push came with the Korean war, and later with the building of the SAGE system of military communication across the nation. The armed forces abandoned the SAGE system in 1971, and again, the support staff left the area. The air base site became the Tonopah airport, with some interesting ruins of the military days allowed to remain there.

As Las Vegas to the south, and Reno to the north, began to boom at mid-century, Tonopah tried in a small way to sell the advantages of holding statewide meetings there. A small convention center and a few more motels resulted from this promotion. The famous Mizpah hotel, once the setting for lavish social or political gatherings, spruced up a bit, adding some gaudier trappings. The success proved marginal; Tonopah continued to decline. In the 1950s and 1960s, Tonopah was so dim that the 1,600 or so residents there could not buy most ordinary food necessities without driving the more than 100 miles to Bishop, California, or Hawthorne, Nevada.

At the end of the 1970s, however, mineral prices rose, mining technology improved, new metals became useful, and suddenly, Tonopah revived. Larger than the previous excitement, the new boom nevertheless profited from the older setting. With over 3,000 people, the city became the largest between Reno and Las Vegas, prosperous, busy, populated, and important to the southwestern economy as it had not been for half a century. New buildings sprouted over the hillsides, traffic jams became frequent, and the Mizpah hotel became more than a tourist magnet, as it gained status with naming to the National Register of Historic Places.

Nobody could prophesy Tonopah's future. Mineral prices would no doubt go down again, but somehow the place seemed more stable in the 1980s than it had three quarters of a century earlier. Anaconda Copper Company invested hundreds of millions of dollars in a molybdenum mine and mill north of Tonopah, with a planned employee roster of up to 600 people and an expected life of more than twenty years. The reserves at the installation were said to represent 5 percent of the free world's production of the metal. Anaconda was also responsible for the building of a housing development and new roads in the area. At the same time, a ten-year project of gold mining was also underway by Cypress Mines Company, which had two open pits. In the 1980s, every sort of facility—many of them new—in Tonopah made it seem more likely that the long dream of serving as a statewide meeting center would at least partially come true. And the relative permanence of the structures of the 1970s and 1980s ap-

"At first there were many foreign groups. Right here I'd like to speak of the Austrian and Slavonian New Year's festivities. Their New Year's was, as I remember, about the seventh of January. We knew, very well, so many of these people. They held open house for their friends, and their festive tables fairly groaned with the tempting foods they had prepared for their guests. Wine was the usual liquor served. A favorite family of ours was the Chiatovich family. Mr. Chiatovich had a grocery store. This family, like so many others as Tonopah declined, moved to Reno and their names are familiar there. . . . The Beko family was another hospitable home to visit as was also the Barrovich home."

— Minnie Blair, Tonopah housewife

"Tonopah was a great place for celebrating the Fourth of July and Labor Day. They had no difficulty in collecting money for prizes for all kinds of events. . . . They had races for the children, even activities—races and nail driving contests and things—for women. They had mucking contests . . . and they had drilling contests. . . . Everybody came to the celebration. Everybody came downtown to the main street. . . . Everybody had a wonderful time; ended up with a big dance that night."

— Procter Hug, Tonopah student,
later a school administrator

peared to underscore Tonopah's modern presence as a lasting fixture of the Nevada landscape.

Goldfield

With the town of Tonopah barely out of the tent stage, in December 1902, two prospectors, Harry Stimler and William Marsh, made another strike some 30 miles south of the first, and Goldfield was born. Although it began within two years of Tonopah, Goldfield was different from its sister town, not just in the fact that its mines produced gold instead of silver, but in its leadership, its politics, its economy, and finally, in its decline.

The two towns had some similarities. Both began with tents and shanties and dugouts. Each attracted drifters and grifters among the miners and engineers, and George Wingfield and George Nixon among the financiers. The Goldfield population was noted for its law-abiding character, although there were undoubtedly a few knifing or shooting affrays. Goldfield, like Tonopah, had news service in the Goldfield *Sun, Chronicle,* and *Daily Tribune*. There were schools, churches, and the customary amenities of any town in the midst of a boom.

But Goldfield was different, too. Goldfield, unlike Tonopah, suffered from labor problems. Goldfield's labor difficulties began in 1906 and lasted for over a year. The trouble began when the Industrial Workers of the World (IWW) tried to replace the more traditional groups, including the Western Federation of Miners, as the single union representative. The IWW was a radical organization and used Goldfield as a testing ground for its revolutionary ideas. The result proved disastrous for all union groups, and brought about the founding of the Nevada State Police to prevent such outbreaks as that caused by the conflict.

At the beginning, the IWW worked to organize all crafts into "one big union." This activity caused a fair amount of difficulty with both management and labor. Still, the problems seemed to be working out until August 1907 when the Goldfield Consolidated company announced that it would institute "change rooms" to try to eliminate the losses caused by high-grading (lit-

> "Well, the Goldfield strike was—the IWW came in then. . . . [A]nd the reason they had the strike more than anything else was Goldfield was a high grade camp. And these fellows went in there, they made so much money stealing ore, high grading, that they used to even forget to go after their paycheck. And so finally, the mining company put in change rooms. And some of the guys in the miners' union thought that was wrong, that they cut off their source of supply. . . .
>
> So the strike became quite an affair. And the miners published a little newspaper there. I forgot now what they called it, a little newspaper. And it sold like hotcakes, those things did. . . . [I]t was just a rabid, red hot sheet. But it sure did sell. I used to sell those."
>
> — Joseph McDonald, Goldfield newsboy,
> later a newspaper executive

erally, the miners were stealing the best ore from the mines, secreting it in their pockets, on their persons, or in lunch pails, and carrying out pure nuggets or almost pure metal). The miners decided to strike when the mine managers announced that high-grading would no longer be tolerated.

No union leadership could successfully defend its members' right to steal, and the strike ended, but not peaceably. By December, the unions and management were again in open confrontation, this time over the issuance of scrip for pay instead of cash. George Wingfield led the management in defending the owners' privileges, and the IWW continued to agitate.

Finally, the strong and powerful owners convinced a somewhat weak (and terminally ill) governor that they needed federal troops to put down widespread violence. Governor Sparks sent a telegram to the president of the United States asserting that "domestic violence and unlawful combinations and conspiracies" were hindering work at Goldfield. Three companies of soldiers arrived the next day, rather to the surprise of

Goldfield residents who had not realized that their lives and property were in jeopardy.

President Theodore Roosevelt, unhappy that he had been misled about the alleged violence in Goldfield, demanded that Nevada put together its own force of troopers. Governor Sparks called a special session of the legislature for January 1908, at which time the Nevada State Police was created. Meanwhile, the striking miners lost every demand, and the IWW was virtually finished as a force in Nevada. Its attempt on Tonopah a decade later was in the nature of a "last gasp." Moreover, union labor was ineffective in Goldfield from that time on. No doubt, the labor troubles contributed in some measure to Goldfield's decline.

Still, it was a very interesting camp while it lasted. Goldfielders were intent on promoting their town as one of the great places of the West. In one pursuit of that aim, they attracted a world's championship light heavyweight fight. On Labor Day, 1906, in a match promoted by Tex Rickard (later of the Madison Square Garden in New York), Joe Gans won when "Battling" Nelson fouled him in the forty-second round. The fight was designed mainly to attract people who might invest in the mines, and in that, it probably succeeded. Goldfield stocks were sold and advertised on exchanges all over the nation, another scheme that brought money and people to Goldfield.

All of these activities attracted governmental status to Goldfield. In May 1907, it became the seat of Esmeralda County. Goldfield continued to be the county seat from that time forward, despite changes in its fortunes. One of those changes, as the place began to decline, was a division of the county in 1911. The people of Hawthorne (to the north) found doing business at a distance bothersome. The legislature obliged by creating Mineral County, and giving Hawthorne the status it had lost to Goldfield in 1907, albeit in a slightly reduced area.

Goldfield's mines produced about $90 million worth of precious metals in their first four decades. The society of the town was probably typical of Nevada mining camps that had a certain amount of maturity and

"When William Jennings Bryan ran for President in 1908, he said that to the precinct that gave him the greatest majority of votes, he would give a Missouri mule. Well, Goldfield did just this, in that election. Out of a clear sky one day in 1909, came by railroad car, the promised Missouri mule. He was domiciled in a livery stable on Main Street. Here he proceeded to kick down the stalls and raise havoc in general. The town looked for a likely place to put him. Burly and Woodard's corral was decided on. We lived about a half a block up the hill and many nights we were awakened by the sound of crashing boards, and the mule was on a real kicking spree. I cannot recall what they did with him."

— Minnie Blair, Goldfield housewife

"There were close to 14,000 people in Goldfield at this time [1909]. There were no paved streets . . . and the sidewalks were cement and board. There were some very substantial buildings; the tallest were the First National Bank, of quarried stone, and the Goldfield Hotel, of brick. Another word about the Goldfield Hotel—the bricks used to build this four-story structure were brought into Goldfield by parcel post. Because of an error in parcel post rates, they could be shipped cheaper this way than by freight. Each of these buildings were four stories high. There were a number of quarried stone buildings. These gave the town a very substantial appearance. Most of the school buildings, courthouse, and fire station were also built of the same material. These building stones were quarried close by and made for cheaper construction."

— Minnie Blair, Goldfield housewife

sophistication. There were motion pictures, saloons, gambling halls, and other entertainments. There were women's clubs and bridge clubs, and men's and women's fraternal organizations, in what was mainly a "white" town. Orientals were not allowed to get off the train in Goldfield, and the small black population

"[A]s I recall, the funeral services were held at an undertaking parlor there. . . . And it was the back end of a furniture store. I went to the funeral, and old man Knickerbocker, an old defrocked Methodist minister, delivered the eulogy for Riley Grannan. . . . At the time I heard it, it didn't impress me very much. . . . Some one of these newspapermen must've been in there and heard Knickerbocker deliver this eulogy. So he probably went and bought a bottle of whiskey and they went down someplace and he had him repeat it because there was nobody there to take it down. . . . Knickerbocker—he was a big, ungainly Texan. I knew him well, knew he had two kids—. He was a prospector and drunk and a Shakespearean actor, claimed to be. And he'd put on these Shakespearean acts in these saloons and pass the hat to feed his family. But he could sure make a speech."

— Joseph McDonald, Rawhide newsboy,
later a newspaper executive

was composed mainly of porters or other workers for the railroad. The people were accustomed to seeing the likes of George Wingfield or his partner Bernard Baruch and even Herbert Hoover in Goldfield. One colorful character, almost everyone's favorite fraud, was Death Valley Scotty. The place was always in the public eye during its heyday.

The customary decline set in, and fires and floods contributed to the end of Goldfield, too. After 1918, no year's production amounted to as much as a million dollars, and finally, only the trappings of the county seat remained. Esmeralda soon had only a few claims to fame or notoriety: a proud history of mining in the twentieth century, and the smallest population of any of Nevada's seventeen counties. The few brick or block buildings, along with George Wingfield's elegant Goldfield Hotel, are mostly unoccupied. The place has a pleasantly antique aura in the 1980s, and sporadic excitements about possible reopenings probably can not change that.

Twentieth-Century Mining Camps

The third of the important mining discoveries around Tonopah at or near the turn of the twentieth century was the Bullfrog district. Rhyolite grew up as the center for this activity, serving the area for mines uncovered in 1904. The Bullfrog district, although it had a heady and exciting beginning, died out rather quickly, leaving behind a deserted little city. Rhyolite became a ghost town, with little but picturesque ruins to recommend it; certainly the mines could not. Commercial establishments devoted to tourism, especially a little museum, kept the name of the town alive and some people there to guard it.

A few other notable camps of southwestern Nevada were born after the turn of the century. Some were genuinely rich, but they were mostly over-promoted. The first of these was Rawhide. Rawhide was essentially a figment of various imaginations, including that of Tex Rickard. However, in 1907, with the initial discoveries there, the place experienced a rush that brought all sorts of characters into the district. The most important production involved not minerals but legends in a section rather poor in such commodities.

The town at its peak in 1908 was typically a boom camp, tent city, full of rough miners and camp followers. Among the more colorful of these was a sometime actor named Knickerbocker. When a miner named Riley Grannan died, the town being without a clergyman, Knickerbocker undertook to see that the man had a proper burial service. He succeeded well enough to have his endeavors become a part of Nevada lore. "Riley Grannan's Funeral Oration" was adjudged by the audience to be a masterpiece of the genre and was published in little booklets that became collectors' items.

As for the town itself, Rawhide had a gaudy and rather short life of about three years. Most of it was not rebuilt after a bad fire took out a portion of the business district. And since Rawhide was situated fairly close to well-traveled roads, even the deserted ruins did not last long. The most difficult item for collectors to carry away was the strap-iron jail, and despite several attempts, the jail stood, somewhat dilapidated, but upright, into the 1980s. The balance of the town fared not so well, and the cemetery fell victim to grave robbers.

Even shorter lived and less colorful was Nevada's "last great mining boom town," Weepah. Two young men, one the son of a respected mining engineer, uncovered a very rich little pocket of gold ore, supposedly in a gopher hole west of Tonopah. Early in March 1927, the newspapers began trumpeting that Frank Horton, Jr., and Leonard Traynor had showed bar patrons at Tonopah some ore that would assay slightly more than $78,000 per ton in gold and silver (assuming that you could find a whole ton of it). The men dropped some hints about the location of the find, and soon a rush to the desert location began. Automobiles loaded with camping and mining gear crowded the site, and claims were staked in all directions from the Weepah district. Miners, movie stars, journalists, and hangers-on from everywhere owned mines or shares in Weepah.

Three months later, the rush had ended, and about 100 people were left at Weepah. By August 1927, the place was deserted, or nearly so. The last boom town had busted. Weepah was not totally false, however, for during the 1930s, Frank Horton, Sr., and his partners

Rawhide

sold out the claims they still held to a new company, the Weepah Nevada. Final statistics showed that Weepah's total production amounted to $1,622,312, of which $1,615,036 was produced in the four years between 1935 and 1939; hardly enough to justify the world-wide excitement that occurred in 1927, but apparently enough to satisfy later developers.

Manhattan

Manhattan's mines were originally discovered in 1866, but no development took place until after a rediscovery by John C. Humphrey on April 1, 1905; he named the new mine the April Fool. Humphrey and his partners found some good gold ore, one batch assaying at $10,000 a ton; that news caused a rush. By early 1906, Manhattan had two newspapers, all sorts of commercial establishments, and about 4,000 people. San Francisco financiers underwrote the first developments.

The great earthquake and fire of 1906 ruined the San Francisco investors, and the bank panic of 1907 caused difficulties with mining all over the West. Manhattan went into an early decline. Then in 1909, a mining engineer's favorable report, pointing to rich gold ore in native limestone, revived the camp. Work by the Man-

---

"In the development of Weepah—it originally was founded by a man by the name of Horton, or something like that. Anyway, they developed it into quite a little boom because they had some high grade ore. Actually, as a high-grade camp it was not too successful a producer. It was very spotty. . . . We did some development work on the possibility of open pit mining it by taking out the high grade ore as well as the low grade and averaging it out. . . . It was never a fantastic producer. From memory, I think we made about a million dollars over a four or five year period. I believe that was the first open pit gold mine in Nevada."

— Norman Biltz, speculator-broker

---

hattan Consolidated Gold Mines Company stabilized the district.

For about two decades, the company continued. A huge mill was built in 1912, and the population was static at about 2,000 people. Popularly called the ''pine tree'' camp, Manhattan continued to provide a living for varying numbers of miners, although some of the years brought in very slim profits.

In 1939, a great gold dredge was installed by the Natomas company on a flat below Manhattan, and a new era began. Dredging operations continued for about eight years, with a total production of somewhat over $4.5 million. When the dredge closed down, Manhattan's output had been in excess of $10 million.

Manhattan refused ever to become completely a ghost town. The population in the 1950s and 1960s was probably under a hundred people. Then the mining boom of the 1970s and 1980s again made the camp a lively place. As the new boom continued, Houston International Minerals Company, which had interests in several old mining towns of Nevada, including the old Comstock districts, was engaged in unwatering and redeveloping some gold mines of Manhattan's earlier

---

''The last year of high school, between the time that I was graduated from high school and was going to college, I worked for the Round Mountain Mining Company out at Round Mountain. It was a placer mining company. Louis Gordon was the superintendent of the mining company. Another fellow and I got a job there, I think, on the strength of being able to play baseball. They were quite baseball-minded out there, and they had a baseball game scheduled every Sunday. . . . We played [such] teams as Tonopah, Austin, and Fallon. And the rest of the players were Indians. But we worked there. I had a job as a carpenter helper.''

— Procter R. Hug, Tonopah student,
later a school administrator

---

days, using modern technology, and looking forward to some years of profit.

Round Mountain

Manhattan's sister city, Round Mountain, was also discovered by prospectors of the Goldfield era. The district became sporadically active after its effective discovery in 1906, operated mainly by leasers until 1915. The individuals probably took less than a half million dollars worth of gold out of Round Mountain's district in those nine years.

In 1914, the Round Mountain Mining Company started construction of a pipeline from nearby Jett Canyon, and the next phase began with hydraulicking. The same company eventually built a dam and brought in more efficient equipment to deal with the gold specks imbedded in the gravel there. Into the 1920s, production amounted to about $1.3 million, from both hydraulic and underground mining.

The Nevada Porphyry Gold Mines Company bought the claims during the 1920s. The place has not been quiet in the years since. The boom of the 1970s and 1980s, and advanced technology for dealing with difficult gold ores, have made Round Mountain into a continuously active mining town. From the beginning, the place had the usual facilities of ore camps— houses, saloons, stores, a post office—and in the 1980s, a boom camp of a different scale and type from that of earlier times.

The mines of Round Mountain underwent extensive changes with the 1970s mining boom. In the fall of 1976, the Copper Range Mining Company began a large development of gold ore deposits there. They spent about $20 million on a processing plant for a planned production of over 80,000 ounces of gold and silver per year. By 1979, there were 150 people working in the Smoky Valley development at Round Mountain. The next year, the company spent another $8 million, expecting the life of the new operation to be six or eight years longer than they had previously anticipated. Round Mountain promised to be in the ''town'' category for some time to come.

"This [1948] was a trying time for all who lived in Gabbs. . . . One day we would hear that everyone would be forced to move, and then in a few days we would get the message . . . that some large company was buying the mill and mines and houses and that would mean more people. . . . At this time upon the community descended the vultures of the business world who looked for bankrupt businesses and government boondoggles, to purchase at 10 cents on the dollar and then sell at enormous profits. . . . They came into the school without permission during the school day, measuring doors and windows and disrupting classes until I had enough and I took a ball bat and ran them off the school grounds."

— Ert Moore, Gabbs schoolteacher

Silver Peak

The geography of the Silver Peak area contains some of the most interesting landmarks in the section. Vulcanism has created a cinder cone and lava outcrops, and other natural forces have made a great dry lake stretching east from the town. Discoveries of ore were made there in the 1860s, but effective development did not take place until the twentieth century. Silver and gold mines marked the site in those first years, and prospects were owned or explored by some of the nation's most prominent mineral capitalists. In the early years after the 1860s, Aurora, more than 70 miles northwest, was the largest town nearby, and Silver Peak was only a collection of buildings.

The first developments of silver and gold were made by John I. Blair of New Jersey (Blairstown was named in his honor) and Samuel J. Tilden, once a candidate for president of the United States. Their company, the Silver Peak and Red Mountain Gold and Silver Mining Company, incorporated in 1866 and operated until about 1877 under that name and that of the Great Salt Basin Mill and Mining Company. Other miners and companies were also active, building mills and trying

to develop the ores. A few structures marked the site of what later became the town of Silver Peak; in any event, the place was largely deserted by 1878.

Silver Peak revived about 1906 and became a lively little town under the influence of the Pittsburgh Silver Peak Gold Mining Company; a company town at Blair, some three miles north, contained a population of about a thousand. This work went on until about 1915, when Silver Peak again subsided. Then in the 1930s, the Black Mammoth Consolidated Mining Company and E. L. Cord rejuvenated the camp in an operation that lasted for about eight years, 1935–1943. Silver Peak's population was probably at its highest during the 1930s. The next capitalist in the area, Avery Brundage, developed the Mohawk district and operated there for a few years, building a large mill. Brundage's era was 1955–1960. Undoubtedly, however, Silver Peak's history belongs to the late twentieth century, and to the work there by the Foote Minerals Company.

The Foote company entered Silver Peak in 1966. Not gold and silver, but lithium took their attention. The lithium deposits were first discovered in 1964, under the great dry lake or playa. The process of extracting this useful substance, a light alkali metal, is part of modern technology. The company continued into the 1980s to provide more than ordinary amounts of lithium in a fascinating procedure destined to supply American metals, ceramics, air conditioning, and drug industries for many years. Silver Peak's population did not boom under the Foote company's influence; the stable group probably amounts to under 200. Their usefulness, however, far outweighs the numbers, and Silver Peak will probably remain as an important town for the balance of the twentieth century.

Gabbs

Gabbs did not fit the mold of the mining boom camp. The place came into being at the site of an old district known earlier as Brucite. There, U.S. Brucite Company had extracted a few thousand dollars worth of the material which is used for lining refractory furnaces. With the coming of the Second World War, and the need for strategic metals, the deposit of brucite was sacrificed to the intensive mining of magnesite. The town of Gabbs was systematically developed by Basic, Inc., the same company that concurrently founded Henderson. Basic built a plant at Gabbs, along with a company town for its own employees and those of McDonald Construction Company, contractor for the building. Gabbs became somewhat of an appendage of the southern Nevada industrial complex.

The company town at first consisted of tents. Even school classes and religious services were held in tents through 1942 until the buildings were finished in May 1943. Some miners brought shacks from other towns to supplement the tent city. With the end of the war, Gabbs responded typically to the boom-bust cycle, closing down substantially in 1948, and then opening again with the coming of the Korean War. The 1950s saw considerable development of the strategic minerals at Gabbs, and then at the end of the boom of the mid-century, the place became semideserted.

In the 1970s and 1980s, with demand for strategic metals and industrial minerals again at a peak, Gabbs resumed a busy existence. Basic enlarged the big plant, and then enlarged it again. Despite the problems involved in these cycles of activity, the population retains a sort of basic core. Gabbs will probably never become a large metropolis, but the people there remain active and relatively prosperous, accepting the vagaries of the minerals business as part of their lives.

Hawthorne

Hawthorne lies on the shore of Walker Lake, remnant of prehistoric Lake Lahontan. The aboriginal inhabitants there were mainly hunters and gatherers of the Northern Paiutes. The Indians fought with early white intruders, although no major battles took place in the Walker Lake area.

Despite their relatively peaceable character, the Paiutes were placed on a reservation after the outbreak of the Pyramid Lake War of 1860. They established themselves as farmers there, on lands that encompassed over 300,000 acres and included Walker Lake. Then in the early 1900s, the possibility that minerals might exist on the reservation caused the sale of lands there to whites. Under the agreement of 1906, the reservation land was reduced, and the Paiutes lost control of their lake; Schurz, the headquarters town, went largely to white commercial interests. By the end of 1909, the reservation amounted to about 50,000 acres. Still, the Paiutes formed a tribal organization that accomplished a good deal for its members, including the building of a reservoir and recreation site upstream from Walker Lake. While they no longer controlled the lake, the Walker River Paiute Tribe did control a fair amount of land, commercial facilities at Schurz, and enjoyment of a number of privileges and typical government installations on the reservation.

Hawthorne's site was visited by some of the West's famous explorers, but its life actually began as a railroad town. Designed as a division point on the narrow-gauge Carson and Colorado, Hawthorne came into existence to serve the railroad's business. The railroad proved not economic enough to keep Hawthorne busy, and after nearly a decade of operation, fewer than 400 people lived in the little lakeside rail community.

In addition, Hawthorne seemed to exist mainly as a service center for boom towns; it was never a boom town. Its early economy and population were measured by what happened elsewhere, and hardly ever by what occurred in the town itself. When the fortunes of the railroad declined, so did Hawthorne. When mining was good at Lucky Boy or Aurora, business improved at Hawthorne. When Aurora seemed about to disappear, Hawthorne took over the county seat of Esmeralda, but when Goldfield began to rise, Hawthorne quickly lost the county seat to the boom town. When the Southern Pacific acquired the Carson and Colorado's rails and established a division point at Mina to the south, Hawthorne lost its shops and their workers. These spurts and declines made Hawthorne's population by 1920 only 244, while Mina had closer to 700. The division of Esmeralda County into Esmeralda and Mineral in 1911, and then Hawthorne's reacquisition of a county seat, apparently had no real effect on the town's development.

But 1926 was Hawthorne's turning point. In that

year, the town was nearly wiped out by a terrible fire that gutted the business district and consumed several homes. Oddly, at about the same time, another catastrophic fire was burning a continent away at Lake Denmark, New Jersey. It would take some thinking to link these two disasters, but they were inextricably tied from that time on.

Lake Denmark was the site of a large Naval ammunition depot, and the fire and explosion there killed many people and endangered a great deal of property. Demands arose all over the East Coast for an ammunition depot away from centers of population. Nevada Senator Tasker Oddie was ready with a suggestion for resettlement of strategic supplies: Hawthorne, Nevada.

Hawthorne certainly fitted the qualifications at that time. It was far from centers of population, it had plenty of space to devote to ammunition storage, and, politically for Oddie at least, there was a benefit to be gained in putting the depot in Nevada. Oddie worked hard for acquisition of the Naval installation, and earned the gratitude of the nearly destitute little town

---

"When the group building the railroad from Sodaville endeavored to obtain some trackage rights . . . the proprietor of the town of Sodaville tried to hold them up by excessive prices for the land needed for their trackage and freight yards. So the group building the railroad and financing it just moved up the valley . . . took up desert entry land at a dollar and a quarter an acre and established what is now the town of Mina. Sodaville no longer exists and Mina is an important junction point. . . . The name Mina came from the name of Wilhelmina, who was the oldest daughter of Superintendent [Alonzo] Tripp. He was the superintendent of the railroad . . . which was in the course of construction."

— Thomas W. Miller, son
of Tonopah financier

---

at the edge of Walker Lake. By 1928, contracts had been let for construction of transportation facilities, and in 1929, other contracts were awarded for buildings at the depot. The Hawthorne Naval Ammunition Depot was formally commissioned in September 1930. The increase of population brought Hawthorne's total to 680 that year.

Hawthorne could surely not have survived without a few people who believed in its future. Tasker Oddie was one of those, but the permanent residents had a stronger and more lasting effect. Probably the most celebrated of the advocates for Hawthorne was Fred B. Balzar. Balzar was a Nevada native, born in Virginia City. He moved to Hawthorne with his parents when an infant, attended schools there and in San Francisco, and then became a brakeman and conductor on the Carson and Colorado. Balzar served Esmeralda County in the legislature as a state senator, and aided importantly in the effort to create Mineral County in 1911. He then became the first state senator from the new county. In 1916, Balzar was elected sheriff of Mineral County, and served in that capacity for ten years. Then in 1926, the Wingfield machine tired of Governor James G. Scrugham, whom it had put in office, and sought out Balzar as a replacement.

Balzar conducted a winning campaign. Handsome, charming, widely known and accepted around Nevada, his victory apparently proved not excessively difficult, given the machine's support and his own considerable ability. Balzar's tenure was full of landmarks for Nevada: he signed the statute legalizing casino gambling and the law making Nevada residence for divorce only six weeks long on the same day, March 19, 1931. As the state entered the Depression, and with the failure of the Wingfield banks, the political-financial machine began to collapse. Balzar tried and failed to gain federal assistance for the faltering economy of Nevada, one of his few lost efforts. Hawthorne mourned its "most distinguished son" when the governor died in office in 1934.

A second of Hawthorne's sturdy pioneers was John H. Miller, storekeeper. Although not the discoverer of the famous Lucky Boy mine, Miller was largely responsible for its development in the Wassuk range near Hawthorne. A huge mill built on the site was Miller's contribution, along with tireless promotion for the district's possibilities. He sold his interests in the Lucky Boy in 1938. Miller served for most of twenty years in the Nevada legislature as Mineral County's senator, becoming one of the most powerful spokesmen of the conservative "bull bloc" of small-county representatives, as well as an important protector of Mineral County's citizens.

The third, longest-lasting, and probably most effective of Hawthorne's pioneer boosters is John R. McCloskey, editor and publisher of the *Mineral County Independent-News*. McCloskey arrived in Hawthorne in 1928 to work at the *Hawthorne News,* and from that time forward, never stopped extolling the town's virtues and charms. He and a partner started the *Hawthorne Independent* in 1933, and acquired the *News* two years later. McCloskey became notable for pithy commentary on the activities of the entire state of Nevada, his "Jasper" column often being quoted in other papers (sometimes without attribution, if it were considered too candid). McCloskey developed a highly respected reputation as an advisor to politicians and government officials. An authority on Nevada legal history, his memory has been called *total* for the intricacies of this topic that has fascinated him over the years. McCloskey and another newspaperman, Walter Cox of Yerington, formed an effective lobbying partnership for legislative sessions, and were conspicuous for their success, particularly in a case that resulted in an equitable distribution of gaming tax revenues among the state's smaller counties.

McCloskey, in a relatively small milieu, managed to acquire power far beyond what might have been expected from a country editor. He is regularly consulted by great or obscure public figures on all sorts of questions, and gives solid advice, humorously delivered with an Irish wit that seems never to dry up. His celebration of Hawthorne has been John R. McCloskey's main work for more than fifty years; the effects of that advocacy are illustrated all over the beautiful area that he adopted half a century before.

After 1930, ammunition bunkers began to dot the valley floor around Hawthorne. The Second World War was still some years away, and when it began to seem more imminent in 1939, the ammunition depot rapidly expanded. The outbreak of the war itself, and the resulting increases of personnel at the depot brought, in the words of Hawthorne's historian, "more of a panic than a boom." Every facility in Hawthorne and in the barracks community, Babbitt, was strained to the utmost. By the mid-1940s, the government counted more than 13,000 people—a thirteen-fold increase in only five years! The new residents included government workers, military people, temporary and permanent citizens of Mineral County.

At the war's end, of course, the population dropped again, to rise slightly with other wars and international problems. But this time the drop was not so severe, and Hawthorne's permanent residents now included those who had enjoyed their wartime living in the pleasant setting and decided to stay, or at least to retire there. Moreover, Hawthorne's businessmen, recognizing that the cyclical economic activity was unhealthy for their town, decided to work at promoting something a bit more stable. They succeeded in assisting with the building of a casino-hotel resort, and promoting tourism that centered on lakeshore recreation at nearby Walker Lake. The efforts at increasing tourism proved fruitful, and resulted not only in more traffic, but also in a more permanent and stable population to serve that trend.

The military presence continued in Hawthorne as well, with the Army taking over the Naval Ammunition Depot in 1977, and finally, at the end of 1980, a civilian contractor took over from the Army. The buildings and housing at Babbitt were gradually boarded up or sold. The bunkers dotting the desert remain to remind travelers of Hawthorne's important role in America's defense through three wars.

In the 1980s, Hawthorne celebrated its first hundred years, with old-timers feeling rather surprised that it had lasted so long, but with others looking forward to yet another hundred. In 1981, a new gold mine brought Houston International in with an industrial complex nearby at Borealis; observers believed it might, in time, match Occidental's operation at Candelaria. Travelers in the modern era could find everything they needed in Hawthorne: restaurants, casinos, grocery and drugstores, motels and hotels, gasoline, and delightful outdoor recreation.

Yerington

Yerington seems somewhat anomalous in a section of Nevada devoted so greatly to mining. Still, its social, political, and even economic ties are largely with the southwest. The town serves as the agricultural supply center for much of southwestern and western Nevada.

The aboriginal inhabitants consisted of Paiute and Washo Indians. The natives were mainly hunters and gatherers, typical of Great Basin tribes. After white settlement began, the Indians worked on ranches or in mines of the section. The most famous of the native residents was Jack Wilson, better known as Wovoka.

Wovoka was called "messiah" by Indians all over the western United States. The "ghost dance" religion, espoused by Wovoka, became the subject of controversy—and several books, including a full-length biography of the Indian Messiah. Wovoka's miraculous cures, his religious charisma, and the oddities of the ghost dance brought both white and Indian visitors to this isolated western section until Jack Wilson died in 1932.

The early white settlers included some who gave their names to places in the region. N. H. A. "Hock" Mason built the first structure in the valley later known as Mason. South of Mason Valley, Timothy Smith established a ranch and the place became Smith Valley.

Mason Valley acquired a town rather early. There was a trading post there as early as 1863, and by 1869, there were commercial establishments—saloon, post office, blacksmith shop—serving the farmers. The little community was rather isolated, off the main road through the area; it was called the "switch." Later, perhaps because of what was served at the saloon, it became immortalized as "Pizen Switch."

Although *Pizen Switch* was colorful and appropri-ate, it offended some residents who tried to call the place "Greenfield." Greenfield did not stick, but neither did Pizen Switch. In the 1890s, the town's residents thought they needed a railroad, and the most prominent railroad magnate in the area was Henry M. Yerington. Maybe, they reasoned, if the town were named in his honor, Yerington would extend the Virginia and Truckee or the Carson and Colorado—both of which he owned or managed—to assist their economy. There is no evidence that Henry Yerington even particularly noticed the proffered enticement; no railroad came to Yerington in the nineteenth century. *Pizen Switch* and *Greenfield* died out, Yerington remained, eventually to become the seat of Lyon County. Still, into the twentieth century, a few stubborn folks continued to call the place Pizen Switch, and Walter Cox, long-time editor of the *Mason Valley News,* was for many years designated as "the sage of Pizen Switch."

Yerington continued to serve the ranching interests of the Walker River area, both as commercial and governmental center. The first county seat was near the Comstock at Como, the second was nearby at Dayton. A disastrous fire at Dayton, combined with the continuing decline on the Comstock, resulted in moving the government to Yerington in 1909. The ranchers of Mason and Smith valleys, certainly more active and prosperous than the miners of the Comstock, appreciated the move and continued to support it. After the turn of the twentieth century, the brief copper mining excitements at the Bluestone mine had little effect on the rural atmosphere. Yerington's little satellites, Wellington and Smith, reflected the same agrarian economy.

In 1952, the Anaconda Copper Company made a copper strike near Yerington and opened a large pit there. Negotiations between Anaconda and the leaders of Yerington concerning the building of facilities there resulted in Anaconda's construction of a company town at Weed Heights. The mine workers and officials established homes at the town the company named for one of its vice presidents, but Yerington served many of their commercial needs. Then, inevitably, the copper deposit ran out and the pit closed in the late 1970s. Weed Heights became a virtual ghost town and began to crumble into the rim of the great pit that had spawned it. Many of Anaconda's copper workers simply moved to the new molybdenum installation at Tonopah, but Yerington suffered an economic decline following that. The huge copper pit remained as a tourist attraction, permanently closed to mining and secured by professional guards.

The Mason-Smith valley section continued into the late twentieth century to maintain its aura of pleasant rural life. The ranchers there raise cattle and hay for western markets, tourists find a quiet and restful spot, and a growing number of retired people reside in this beautiful valley's good climate.

Railroads of Southwestern Nevada

The most important of the transportation lines of southwestern Nevada, and the earliest, was the Carson and Colorado railroad. The inauguration of the road in 1880 and the subsequent lot sale on a deserted stretch of land near Walker Lake brought Hawthorne into being in 1881. Luning, some 24 miles south, came the same year, named to honor one of the railroad's bondholders. The narrow-gauge rails were planned to provide transportation from northern Nevada to southern California, and especially to take advantage of the boom at Candelaria to support freight on the road. With Candelaria's decline, the little company seemed in trouble, but in a short time, Tonopah's silver was discovered and business improved. A line joined the

Copper pit at Weed Heights, ca. 1970

tracks in 1904 as the Tonopah Railroad, to feed into the new mines.

Meanwhile, however, the Southern Pacific had purchased the C&C, with the result that, in 1905, the rails were brought to standard gauge and at the same time rerouted to bypass Hawthorne. The action was a heavy blow to Hawthorne, which remained off rail transportation lines then until the Naval Ammunition Depot needed them in 1931; at that time, the U.S. government built a spur line from Thorne to the naval facility.

The railroads of the Tonopah-Goldfield section came as the result of severe necessity there. The site of the new discoveries was so remote from other centers of population—indeed, regarded as unknown until the mining rush—that there were not even wagon roads there. Only Jedediah Smith, first white man to cross the Great Basin, had blazed any sort of trail, and that more than 70 years before the silver strike at Tonopah. John C. Frémont's explorations had passed through the present site of Hawthorne, but emigrant trains and other travelers mostly went north or south of there. It was therefore through the exercise of considerable courage that the early twentieth-century prospectors and builders came to southwestern Nevada.

The Tonopah Railroad, completed in 1904 from its junction with the Carson and Colorado, was the first such facility in the area and was greeted with considerable satisfaction. Then Goldfield's mines opened, and there was an additional need for freight and passenger haulage. The same financiers built both the Tonopah and the Goldfield railroads, and then saw to the merger of the two lines into the Tonopah and Goldfield (affectionately called locally the "*Tug and Grunt*").

The T&G had several years of typically good operation, interrupted by the usual natural and financial disasters and catastrophes. The development of local fuel at Coaldale west of Tonopah assisted in the profitability of the line. With the decline of the mines, however, the railroads also began to suffer. The last dividends on T&G stock were paid in 1926. More natural disasters followed—floods on the desert can be particularly fierce. Then there were some fairly good years,

---

"The motive power the junkie firm possessed was not capable of handling the [wartime] traffic, resulting in many derailments. . . . To relieve this situation, the Air Force supplied the T&G management with two diesel locomotives and thus the problem of servicing the air base was solved. . . . Then some fussy official decided to repossess the two diesels, and the United States attorney at Reno notified the management. The management in turn pleaded . . . that at least one diesel be continued . . . to operate what little freight and passenger traffic remained for the line. After much red tape, . . . the Air Force consented. So at the time of the [abandonment] hearing the T&G still had motive power with which to operate.

I was sitting in [the] courtroom, present at one of the hearings, when a considerable noise developed outside the courtroom doors . . . and in marched a captain of the Air Force with the requisite retinue following him, all bearing a very war-like appearance. The captain interrupted the proceedings . . . to serve notice on the general manager of the line that he was there to take, forthwith, possession of the remaining diesel."

— Gordon A. Sampson, manager of the Virginia and Truckee Railway

---

through the 1930s and up to the outbreak of World War II.

Tonopah was fortunate in receiving an air base to assist its economy at the beginning of the war. This meant, for the railroad, an increase in freight and passenger traffic. Still, plans for abandonment, reflecting the continuing decline in the mines, were already underway with the sale of the works to a Seattle firm of scrap dealers. Now the Seattle company operated the railroad for several more years, with assistance from the Army in the form of two loaned diesel locomotives. When the war ended, so did the air base, and then, so did the Tonopah and Goldfield. The T&G officially received permission to go out of operation in August 1947. The scrap dealers rather quickly completed their business, leaving only scars on the Nevada desert to mark the passing of one of Nevada's longest-lasting and most colorful shortline railroads.

The agricultural community of Yerington finally had a railroad of sorts when copper mining developed in the early 1900s on the opposite side of the Singatse Range at Ludwig. The standard-gauge Nevada Copper Belt Railroad came into being, with construction starting in 1909 to serve the mines, smelters, and resulting settlements. However, Yerington's station was placed a mile from the middle of town, considered almost a bypass at that time. The major railroad section and population center developed at Mason, a few miles south, when the trains began to run in 1910. The tracks led south from Wabuska (the division point from the Southern Pacific), past Yerington, through Mason on its main street, into Wilson Canyon, then around the end of the Singatse Range to the mine at Ludwig. But mining is a chancy and unstable business, not something upon which to build a transportation system.

After 1919, there was no passenger service to Ludwig, and other runs were continually shortened or abandoned. By the early 1920s, the Copper Belt was in receivership. Full abandonment was delayed until 1947, and the Nevada Copper Belt railroad disappeared.

There were a few other railroads or proposed railroads in southwestern Nevada, but none so interesting as the C&C and the T&G. Eventually, highways improved and truck transport became convenient. Only the main line of the Southern Pacific remained in the southwestern area, and that on a reduced scale that hardly kept its formerly important terminals at Luning and Mina alive.

Southwestern Nevada has always been somewhat set apart. The mining strikes there came later than to the rest of the state, and the cycles in the southwestern economy are more severe than those in more stable sections. The enormous expanses, the rough terrain, and the sturdy and energetic population all make for a unique mixture, special somehow, even in a state that encourages diversity and contrast.

TOURING IN SOUTHWESTERN NEVADA

PART ONE

The tours in this section have been divided for convenience into two parts: trips from Tonopah (Part One), and trips from Hawthorne (Part Two). The southwestern section is so large that it seems inappropriate to expect the traveler to cover the expanses in ordinary day-long trips. Both these centers have full facilities for tourists and are suitable as headquarters for enjoying travels in the section.

The day trips are designed, not to show every feature of this interesting area, but rather to lead tourists to some of the most attractive and accessible sites. There are many such places, both on our suggested tours and off. While traveling in this section should not be considered dangerous, the prudent traveler will make sure that the vehicle is in good condition, and that the fuel tank is full before beginning any trip. We have recommended picnic lunches where we thought it appropriate, and included a few special instructions with some of the tours. You will surely want a camera, for this section has lovely scenery and interesting man-made structures.

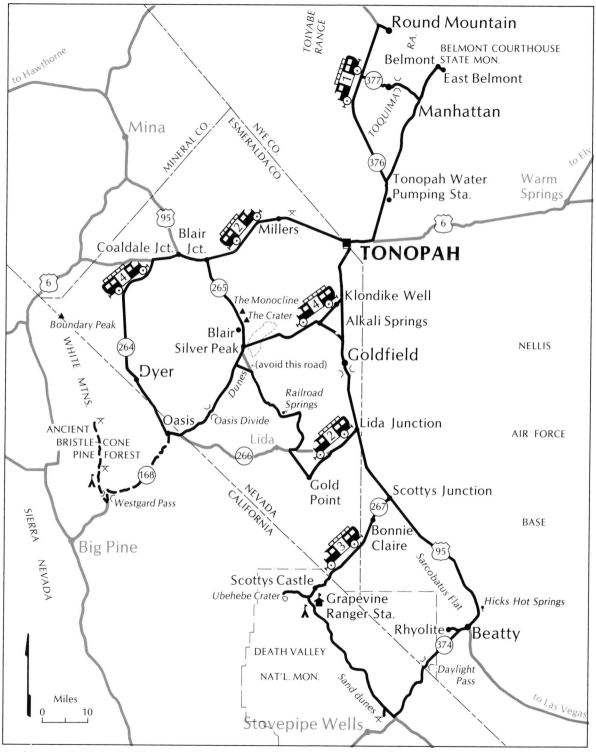

Southwestern Nevada, Part One, tours 1, 2, 3, 4

What to see in Tonopah: Stop at the Convention Center, two blocks above Main Street on Brougher Avenue to obtain a city map and brochures on Tonopah business. The map brochure contains directions for a short driving tour of the town. Driving around the city is highly recommended; many of the homes and business buildings date from Tonopah's earliest days.

The Central Nevada Museum, opened in 1981, is at the south city limits on U.S. 95. The museum contains professionally-prepared indoor and outdoor exhibits of artifacts, relics, documents, and photos of the area. Copies of the journal of the Central Nevada Historical Society are on sale. The museum's hours are limited, but it is a ''must see'' while you are here. All the tours in this section begin in front of the museum.

The city park, a source of considerable civic pride, is near the northeast city limits off Mizpah Circle (turn off Main onto Florence, go east on Florence to Mizpah Circle, turn left on Mizpah Circle to the park). Here are a children's playground, picnic tables, barbecues, and one of the very few lawns in Tonopah.

The Tonopah public library is on Central, two doors west of Bryan (behind the Telephone Company building). The building is one of the early-day block structures, and looks like a home. There is a local history collection and a knowledgeable staff at the library.

TOUR ONE, The evolution of mining in southwestern Nevada: Tonopah — Belmont — Manhattan — Round Mountain and return. Approximately 142 miles round trip. Pack a picnic.

Leaving the museum, drive 0.2 miles north (downhill) to the intersection of U.S. 95 with U.S. 6, and turn right (east) on U.S. 6.

Drive 5.5 miles. Note the Tonopah air base skeletons (now on the grounds of the Tonopah airport) on your right as you turn left on SR 376.

Drive 8.9 miles on SR 376. The dirt road on your right leads to the pumping station and well in the grove of trees. This is the basic source of Tonopah's domestic water supplies. You may have noticed that there are very few trees in Tonopah, and fewer lawns. The sparseness of this water supply here explains the lack.

The trees west of Tonopah were started and raised on sewer effluent. Please notice these facts, and do not waste water in Tonopah!

Continue on the paved road for 3.8 miles. The ruins are of the Midway mine. Drive 0.8 miles, and turn right on SR 82, toward Monitor Valley and Belmont. As you drive 18.8 miles along a modern paved road, it is interesting to think about the courage of prospectors like Jim Butler, traveling across these desolate miles of uninterruptedly barren land with only a horse or mule for companionship. Mining as a profession seems to attract or create uncommonly tough people. The plant life along this stretch consists largely of sagebrush, rabbit brush, russian thistle (tumbleweed), and patches of white sage—not much for livestock feed, and certainly not for human consumption.

When you come to the junction, the road to the left goes to Manhattan. Go straight ahead, across the cattle guard on the paved road, but note this intersection, as *you will return here.* Drive 0.9 miles, and the pavement ends. Continue on this wide, good, graded gravel road into the Toquima Range toward Belmont. Drive 4.3 miles, and note that as the road begins to rise toward the old town, the landscape changes to piñon-juniper forest and a somewhat more friendly environment.

Continue another 2.6 miles. The Monitor-Belmont mill ruins are at the left. The famous Belmont courthouse is straight ahead. Drive 0.6 miles and enter Belmont.

We hope you will enjoy exploring Belmont. There are no dependable commercial facilities here (including no electricity and no developed domestic water supply), although this is not a ghost town, and never has been completely deserted. There is a historical marker in the courthouse yard. Just beyond the turn into the courthouse yard on the main road is the information center for the courthouse. *This is a private residence; the attendant is paid mainly to guard the premises.* The attendant here will conduct tours of the courthouse for groups, or by private arrangement for individuals through the Nevada State Park System. The courthouse was scheduled for restoration in the 1980s, but that project depends upon public and legislative support. Enjoy Belmont from your car and from the road; all buildings are on private property and guarded.

At the information center, the road veers to the right. East Belmont's ruins and the old Combination Mill (the World War II fighter pilots' target) are 1.1 miles ahead on a scenic drive past a number of interesting rock ruins.

Completing your tour of the area of Belmont and East Belmont, return to the courthouse, and then return downhill toward the intersection. There is a cattle guard in 6.4 miles, the pavement begins 1.2 miles after you cross the cattle guard, and in another 0.9 miles you will arrive back at the junction. Now turn right toward Manhattan, and drive along a graded dirt road into the Toquima Range.

This road has fairly heavy use by ranchers and miners, so drive slowly and stay alert for trucks. Drive 2.2 miles; there is a road on the right, but keep going straight ahead. Continue 1.0 mile; there is a miner's cabin on the left. You can notice signs of mining on the hills all around here in this beautiful juniper-piñon forest. Continue 3.7 miles to the summit; stay on the main road as you drive downhill. After 1.3 miles, there is a mining road at the right; do not try to approach working mines. Continue 0.3 miles, and here is the Manhattan water supply. Drive another 0.1 miles and the pavement begins as you enter Manhattan.

Manhattan has very limited commercial facilities, mainly bars. There are a telephone booth, picnic tables, and barbecues at the fire station. From the place where you entered Manhattan, in 1.2 miles there is a road to the left leading uphill to a combination museum/rock shop, housed in a building that was once a power substation. Watch for heavy trucks on this road; Houston International has a busy operation that may yet revive anything that is still sleeping in Manhattan. The rock shop/museum has free admission, and some interesting exhibits, along with jewelry and relics for sale. Return to the highway, and continue downhill on SR 377.

Drive 6.3 miles past the gravel piles and mill ruins from hydraulicking days, toward the elegant, rugged

Toiyabe Range. Turn right on SR 376 (north). Drive 0.1 miles; there is a historical marker for Manhattan on the left side of the highway.

Drive 6.1 miles across the Big Smoky Valley; the Toiyabe Range is on the left, Toquima Range on the right. The Round Mountain mining operation is visible ahead to the right. The huge tailings piles give an indication of the work that has gone into the development here since the early 1900s.

Drive 4.4 miles. There is a dirt road on the right that leads to the modern-day mining operation. Do not take this road. The company does not entertain tourists, for your protection and theirs. Continue 1.2 miles to the junction with SR 378. There is a historical marker for Round Mountain on the left. Turn right to go to Round Mountain, drive 2.7 miles on the paved route, and enter the town.

It used to be, if you had a job as a miner in a booming camp, you put up a tent, then in your spare time, threw together a shack for shelter. Now, the process involves merely having a mobile home, complete with whatever amenities you need, moved onto a ready piece of ground. In Round Mountain, this has resulted in an instant population of several hundred people—families, children, and some service delivery—and the necessity for a new school and fire house.

Round Mountain's facilities are still fairly limited. There are picnic tables at the fire house. The most interesting and picturesque features are the seemingly endless piles of scrap and junk that used to be mining machinery. Enjoy your look around Round Mountain, then return the approximately 2.7 miles to SR 378, turn left, and return via SR 378 and U.S. 6 to Tonopah, approximately 51.5 miles.

TOUR TWO, Ghost towns: Tonopah — Klondike Well — Alkali Springs — Goldfield — Gold Point — Silver Peak — Blair Junction — Miller's and return. Approximately 160 miles round trip. There are literally hundreds of ''ghost towns'' or nearly-deserted mining camps in Nye and Esmeralda counties. Pack a picnic, take some extra water, and make sure your vehicle is full of fuel. (Some of the roads are dirt, but

Belmont

suitable for any vehicle in good condition and with a careful driver.)

Leaving the museum, drive south (uphill) on U.S. 95, 1.0 mile to the Esmeralda County line. Continue 7.5 miles to the crossroad, a gravel road, with large mining operations visible on either side of the highway; do not approach working mines, but continue south on the paved U.S. 95. Drive 3.5 miles, and turn right on a well-maintained, gravel road; watch for big trucks here, as there is active mining in the area. Drive 1.6 miles. At this point, the Tonopah and Goldfield railroad bed crosses at right angles to the road. The ruins to the left are what remains of Klondike Well, a watering stop on the railroad; you can see the railroad's curve just beyond (south) the ruins of the settlement.

Continue 6.4 miles down the gravel road to the intersection with a paved road. The ruins to the right of the intersection mark the site of Alkali Springs. During Goldfield's heyday, this was a favorite spa for residents there. Then, during Prohibition, Alkali Springs became a combination resort and speakeasy. At one time, there were extensive swimming and bathhouse facilities here, and now the little cabins are kept by an ''oner'' [sic] who wants you to stay out; please observe his signs. Turn left (heading southeast) at the intersection, and go down the paved road 6.8 miles, and turn right onto U.S. 95. Drive 4.3 miles into Goldfield.

Drive 0.7 miles to the historical marker in front of the Esmeralda County courthouse. Then enjoy your tour of this interesting, turn-of-the-century mining camp. The Goldfield Hotel, opposite the courthouse, has had several owners since George Wingfield's day. Many of these have promised to restore the building to its former status. In the early 1980s, still another new purchaser acquired the hotel and announced designs for extensive rehabilitation. Goldfielders greeted the proposal with hope—and some skepticism, stemming from similar encounters over the years since 1938, when the hotel closed the first time. The Goldfield Hotel was open during World War II, mainly as housing for soldiers stationed nearby. There are many homes and other buildings dating from Goldfield's boom time. The cemeteries are near the northern edge of town, visible from the highway. Goldfield has rather limited tourist facilities, and some very friendly residents who operate the stores and antique shops. Completing your tour of Goldfield, return to the historical marker and continue driving south on U.S. 95 for 15.1 miles to Lida Junction, and turn right onto SR 266 (heading southwest).

You are driving across the northern end of Sarcobatus Flat, one of Nevada's most desolate and seemingly endless deserts. It is hard to imagine why a prospector would push out here, but the lure of precious metals is so strong that men have endured much on the basis of their gold-and-silver dreams alone. Drive 7.3 miles to the historical marker for Gold Point, on the left side of the highway. (A mindless "sportsman" with a shotgun seems to have feared the vicious nature of the marker, and thus blown a hole in it.) Proceed to the intersection just ahead, and bear left on SR 774. The dirt road is graded, graveled, and adequate for any vehicle.

Drive 7.5 miles, and arrive in Gold Point. This interesting old village has been open and closed numerous times over more than a hundred years. The activity depends on metal prices and capital for development or reworking. In the 1980s, the settlement is partially occupied, mainly by leasers. Picturesque wooden structures, one of the state's best collections of headframes, some trailers, and a wearily reminiscent aura of "Well, just maybe—" mark this community. Although the town has been dim over the years, it has never been totally vacant, and thus vandalism has not destroyed Gold Point as it has many other places. A sign at the entrance to the town prohibits picking up relics. Observe this stricture; local residents, including the Esmeralda County deputy sheriff stationed here, stand ready to enforce it.

Leaving Gold Point, return to the intersection where you entered the town. Go straight ahead on the road that leads north*west* directly across the valley (don't take SR 774, the road you came on). Pass the old busi-

ness buildings, and stay on this straight road. Drive 0.2 miles to a fork in the road, and keep right. Drive 3.2 miles; here is a corral and water tank that serves a local livestock rancher. Continue 3.9 miles to a crossroad and turn right. Drive 0.3 miles to SR 266, and turn right (east).

Drive 1.0 mile to an unmarked graded gravel road, and turn left. Mount Jackson is the flat-topped rise ahead. The road heads northerly, and passes near the west flank of Mount Jackson. Stay on the main graded road, ignoring side roads, and drive 2.9 miles. At the fork in the road here, go to the left (the right hand road leads back to Goldfield). Again, stay on the main traveled road; side roads lead to deadends or private holdings. The road leads across the valley toward the Montezuma Range, with Montezuma Peak just ahead. The area is a rather sparse Joshua forest that becomes somewhat thicker as the road rises. Drive 6.4 miles; there is a road from the right that leads back to Goldfield. Keep straight ahead.

You may see some wild horses in this section. Despite what you may have heard about wild horses here, they are not mustangs. Mustangs as a breed died out many years ago. The horses you will see roaming wild in this area are either horses turned out by local ranchers or descendants of such animals. They are beautiful and photogenic nonetheless, and sometimes quite bold. The livestockmen of the region consider them pests, competing for scarce forage with range cattle.

Drive west for 4.3 miles. This is Railroad Springs. The springs here are part of an underground thermal system that you earlier observed at Alkali Springs. We noticed obsidian chips around the spring here, perhaps indicating some aboriginal use of the site. Continue on the main road to the right, driving 1.1 miles to the summit. Now continue downhill into Clayton Valley, staying on the main road. Drive 3.4 miles; here is a view of Clayton Valley, its great playa (dry lake), and a line of lovely gray sand dunes. You can also see in the distance the evaporation ponds of Foote Minerals' lithium operation off to the right. There will be an opportunity for a closeup view of all of these features shortly.

Drive 1.4 miles to the intersection. There is a road

from the left, but continue downhill to the right, driving 0.8 miles. Look to the left; the natural dry stream bed is Lida Wash. Clayton Ridge is ahead on the right, Montezuma Peak is the tall mountain directly to the right and in the distance, and the Silver Peak Range is ahead and to the left. Continue on the main traveled road, driving 2.2 miles to the cattle guard. The town of Silver Peak is visible ahead in the foothills to the left of the formations called Alcatraz and Goat islands. The cinder cone is visible behind the "islands."

Drive 3.3 miles; there is a road coming from the right, but go straight downhill toward Silver Peak. Drive 0.5 miles to a fork in the road, and take the left hand one (the road to the right looks as if it heads straight for Silver Peak, but that is true only in ideal weather; otherwise, it can disappear or become impassable). Drive 0.9 miles; there is a road at the left, but go straight ahead toward the Silver Peak Range. Drive 3.0 miles to the intersection with the main, graded road, and bear right. Drive another 3.5 miles to the next intersection (a road from the right), and keep going straight ahead. Drive 0.3 miles and turn right onto the pavement, the beginning of SR 265. The Foote Minerals plant is straight ahead. Enter Silver Peak, and stay on the pavement through town. Services are very limited here.

The lithium operation that dominates Silver Peak in the 1980s serves an almost endless variety of industrial, environmental, and medical uses. Lithium is used in bakeware and ceramics, in air conditioners both for buildings and for space ships, in the manufacture of aluminum, in lubricants, and in drugs for treating mental disorders. Drive 0.9 miles to leave Silver Peak, and look to the right of the highway. The evaporation ponds for extracting lithium are south of Goat Island on the playa. The water is pumped through deep wells from under the Clayton playa. The water is piped into a series of ponds; then as solar power evaporates the fluid, the concentration of lithium salts becomes higher. Quicklime is added, which precipitates out magnesium. A fairly concentrated solution of almost pure lithium chloride is then pumped to the plant and treated, and powdered lithium carbonate is the result.

The powder is trucked to the railhead at Mina, where it is shipped by rail to be manufactured into its many possible products.

Continue north on SR 265, along the edge of the playa for 2.0 miles to the historical marker for Blair, on the left side of the highway. Remnants of Blair are visible behind the sign in the foothills. Blair was the terminus for the Silver Peak railroad, a spur from the T&G that led from Blair Junction to this place, from 1906 to 1918.

Drive 2.2 miles. This splendid little cinder cone is a valley landmark and also illustrates the relatively recent volcanic activity in this area. Continue on SR 265.

Drive 1.5 miles, and look to the right. Here is another valley geologic landmark, a monocline. As the earth's crust shrinks, it can create a fold, then part of the fold falls away and leaves the slanted mesa that geologists call a monocline.

Continue driving 13.7 miles on SR 265. The white structure is a VORTAC radio transmitter, an FAA installation used for aircraft navigation. Drive on 0.4 miles. Here is the T&G railroad bed, crossing the highway at right angles. Here also you can see the ruins of Blair Junction. Drive 0.7 miles to the junction with U.S. 6 & 95 and turn right; the historical marker for Silver Peak is at the right.

Drive toward Tonopah on U.S. 6 & 95, 20.9 miles to Millers. This site at the right side of the highway was once an important milling site, owned by the Tonopah Mining Company. The place name honors Charles R. Miller, one of the members of the company. There is a historical marker inside the roadside rest on the left side of the highway. At the roadside rest are tables, toilets, water, and free overnight parking for trailers and campers.

Return to Tonopah, straight ahead, approximately 14 miles.

TOUR THREE, Southwestern Nevada's early days: Tonopah — Goldfield — Scotty's Castle — Death Valley — Rhyolite — Beatty and return. Approximately 257 miles round trip. Bring a picnic or camping gear.

Note: *This trip is not for summer months. Plan to go between November and April.*

Starting at the Central Nevada Museum at the southern city limits, drive south (uphill) on U.S. 95 toward Goldfield. Drive 1.0 mile to the Esmeralda County line. Continue 7.5 miles; here is a gravel crossroad, where you should be alert for big trucks involved in a mining operation. Continue on U.S 95, and drive 3.5 miles to the road to Silver Peak, on the right (see Tours Two and Four in this section). Continue on U.S. 95.

In the early automobile days, the route of this pleasant, easy-to-drive highway was covered by multiple ruts across the desert. The cars would come out across the flats, and if one bogged down, then the others would press out new tracks. Citizens of Goldfield and Tonopah held annual ''good roads days'' when men with picks, shovels, and rakes labored to widen and smooth the primitive routes to make travel easier and safer. A 55-mile-per-hour drive under those conditions, however, was unthinkable.

Drive 14.0 miles and enter Goldfield, and then go 0.7 miles further to the historical marker in front of the courthouse. We hope you will enjoy exploring this old town. There was some active gold mining in the 1980s just north of town, by the Pacific Gold and Uranium Company. Facilities in Goldfield include most necessities in limited quantities, along with antique stores, rock shops, and ''museums.'' These establishments are not always open but are more likely to operate on weekends than on weekdays. The pioneer cemeteries are at the north edge of town.

Leaving the historical marker in front of the Esmeralda County courthouse, continue south on U.S. 95 toward Beatty. The mesa at the town's edge is named Malpais (pronounced locally as *mal*-a-pie). Drive 2.1 miles to Goldfield summit, and continue on U.S. 95. The Joshua forest here extends for many miles. The Joshuas (a type of lily) demonstrate the ability of plant life to evolve and to adapt to arid conditions.

Drive 13.0 miles to Lida Junction. Stay on U.S. 95. Drive 4.2 miles, and reenter Nye County, leaving Es-

Esmeralda County courthouse, Goldfield

meralda. As you drive along this long, straight stretch of highway, you may note a tendency to lean a little harder on the accelerator. You should be aware, however, that even sharp eyes may fail to reveal a Highway Patrol car.

Continue 12.2 miles to the junction with SR 267, Scotty's Junction, and turn right. For many years, there were commercial facilities at the junction to serve the leisurely traveler. Autos with greater mileage capacity reduced the need for such services, and then a fire caused the end of Scotty's Junction as a tourist rest.

Drive 6.6 miles. Here are the ruins of the town of Bonnie Claire on the left, the Lippincott mine on the right. Drive ahead 5.7 miles into the Grapevine Mountains, reentering Esmeralda County. Continue to drive on SR 267 for 9.5 miles to the California state line and the boundary of the Death Valley National Monument.

Death Valley was named by survivors of an 1849 emigrant party who met disaster here. They called it Death Valley as they left with their rescuers. The valley floor is the bed of Pleistocene Lake Manly, named for the leader of the emigrant train. The road leads down Grapevine Canyon. Flash floods can surprise you on this route. If it has been raining, be alert for washouts. The flora of this area is exceedingly interesting and colorful, and includes many thrifty desert plants—and wild grapevines as you approach Scotty's Castle. We also enjoyed seeing some ripe coyote melons on the roadside.

Drive 4.7 miles and arrive at Scotty's Castle. Here you may picnic, and you will find gasoline and a snack bar in addition to the Castle tour. There is an admission fee for the tour; it may be a lengthy wait, but we think it is worth some extra time. There is a pamphlet available with directions for a walking tour of the grounds while you wait your turn to see the Castle.

Leaving Scotty's Castle, continue downhill toward Stovepipe Wells. Drive 2.9 miles, and make a right turn for the Ubehebe Crater. Note this junction; *you will return here*. Continue on the paved road, ignoring side roads, 5.8 miles into the Last Chance Range. At the junction, follow the signs and drive 0.3 miles to the crater. Notice, too, the beautiful desert holly in the area—all white, holly-like leaves. The plant is protected, so do not pick it. The Ubehebe Crater is one of the scenic and geologic wonders of Death Valley. At the parking lot, there are an information board and pit toilets.

Return to the junction, 5.7 miles, and turn right toward Stovepipe Wells. Drive 0.2 miles. Here are the Grapevine Ranger Station and an information booth. Continue 0.5 miles to the turn for Mesquite Springs. There are developed campsites, a trailer disposal station, a fee for camping. Continue on the main road toward the valley floor. The geologic formations on this old lakebed are endlessly fascinating and varied in color. Watch, too, for the blooms of desert flowers on shrubs, cactus, or standing alone.

Drive 18.2 miles. The Titus Canyon road comes in here; it is a one-way road into the Valley. Continue 3.0 miles; here is an information board that explains about weather and valley geologic phenomena. Drive 9.1 miles to the sign for the sand dunes.

It is so quiet at the picnic grounds at the sand dunes that you can almost hear yourself think. Turn right, and drive 0.3 miles. Here is a grave marker for a man who died from Death Valley's heat in August 1931. Continue 0.5 miles; there is a monument and historical marker for old Stovepipe Wells at the right side of the

road. Continue 0.9 miles, and arrive at the Sand Dunes picnic site. Here are tables and pit toilets. The dunes cover about 14 square miles. Return to the highway, 1.7 miles, and turn right at the intersection.

Drive 0.4 miles. A historical marker here points out the fragility of the desert environment, where wagon tracks endure for over a hundred years.

Continue 1.9 miles. Here are a roadside rest, picnic tables, pit toilets, information board. Drive 0.2 miles to the junction.

Decision: *If you are planning to camp in Death Valley, take a map from the container at the roadside rest, and enjoy your stay. Then, to continue this tour, turn left at the junction toward Beatty and Rhyolite.*

Drive 6.9 miles. The drive will take you into and over the colorful Funeral Range via Daylight Pass. Particularly notice the desert holly, beavertail cactus, cholla, old man cactus, mesquite, and other interesting desert plants. Arriving at Hell's Gate, continue straight ahead, uphill. If it has been raining, be alert for washouts or other evidence of flash flooding on the highway. Drive 6.3 miles to Daylight Pass, and then drive downhill toward the Amargosa Desert. Continue 0.4 miles, and arrive at the Nevada state line; the highway becomes Nevada SR 374 here.

Drive 1.8 miles. Rhyolite, the queen city of the Bullfrog district, is visible in the distance ahead and to the left of the highway. The scar on the desert leading to Rhyolite was a road, abandoned following a washout. Stay on the highway, and drive 2.2 miles to the Death Valley National Monument boundary, then 4.9 miles, and turn left for Rhyolite. Drive up into the town, which is directly ahead, and enjoy your tour of this interesting and historic spot. The important buildings include the old railroad depot, which is now a private residence, ruins of the John S. Cook bank, the Porter store, and the school building. A small museum is maintained in the famous "bottle house." At the museum, there are books and pamphlets along with some souvenirs for sale. Admission is free, but donations are welcome.

Rhyolite has never been deserted, and is not now. The residents here are very protective of their property, so take the "no trespassing" signs seriously. The cemetery is about a mile southwest of the town, near the highway. This town was the last Nevada home of Nevada's first U.S. senator, William Morris Stewart. Death Valley Scotty was a frequent visitor, too. One of the legends about Scotty says that a Chinese friend, denied service in the cafes of Rhyolite, shared a picnic with Scotty on the curbstone in front of the Cook bank. Completing your tour of Rhyolite, return to the highway (SR 374), and turn left, toward Beatty. Drive 3.7 miles, and enter Beatty.

Beatty was the site of a ranch owned by Montillus Murray Beatty, a pioneer in the area from the 1860s. Beatty was an Iowa native and veteran of the Civil War. His wife was a Paiute woman, born near Death Valley. Beatty bragged to local residents that he had crossed Death Valley in every month of the year with-

out trouble. If that is so, he probably was unique. Beatty served as his town's first postmaster, for just over a year (1905-1906), until he became bored with the job. Beatty died in December 1908, victim of a fall from a wagon.

The town of Beatty celebrated two "railroad days," honoring the coming of the Las Vegas and Tonopah in October 1906, and then the Bullfrog Railroad in April the next year. Although the railroads are long gone, the little town enjoys a favorable place on highways and contains all necessities for tourists.

Drive through the town of Beatty along the main street, staying on U.S. 95 toward Tonopah. Drive north on U.S. 95 for 0.5 miles, and cross the Amargosa River. No water in the bed of the Amargosa today? That is the usual situation, for this river is mainly underground except at certain times of the year when it is likely to flood. The Amargosa in flood can be a fearsome sight, so do not be disappointed at the

Railroad depot at Rhyolite

dry riverbed. Continue driving 6.9 miles. The ride is along the valley of the Amargosa. At Boiling Pot Road, notice the little settlement against the hills on the right; this is Hicks Hot Springs, one of several such thermal springs of the area. The hottest water here is about 109°.

Continue 0.6 miles. The historical marker at the left side of the highway commemorates the old Nevada-California boundary. Drive on 26.3 miles; the ride will take you across the desolate Sarcobatus Flat, in the earlier days one of Nevada's most dreaded desert trips and now accomplished in less than an hour of easy travel. At the rest area, there are picnic tables and pit toilets.

Drive 1.0 mile; the "new" Scotty's Junction, unlike the old one that you saw earlier on this trip, has a store, gasoline, and an air strip. Continue 1.2 miles to "old" Scotty's Junction, on the left.

Return now to Tonopah, approximately 58 miles.

TOUR FOUR, Southwestern Nevada history and scenery: Tonopah — Klondike Well — Silver Peak — Fish Lake Valley, with a side trip to the Ancient Bristlecone Forest, and return. Approximately 226 miles round trip. Make sure your vehicle is filled with fuel, pack a picnic or camping gear.

Note: *The road over Oasis Divide is maintained except in winter, and can be negotiated in good weather by most vehicles except big campers or motor homes. The trip is for careful and adventurous drivers. Be advised, however, that the road is narrow, winding, and fairly steep. Some parts of the road thread along the wash created by streams, which make narrow passages and sharp turns, with no room to maneuver. If the weather has been unsettled or if it is stormy on the day of your drive, postpone the trip. If you are driving an unsuitable vehicle, take another tour. And if you are inexperienced at dirt road driving, we suggest that you obtain your first experience elsewhere (see, for example, Tour Two in this section).*

Leaving the museum at the south limits of Tonopah, drive south (uphill) on U.S. 95 for 0.7 miles to To-

nopah summit. Continue 0.3 miles to the Esmeralda County line. Drive another 11.0 miles, and turn right on a good, well-maintained dirt road. Watch for big trucks; there is active mining in the area.

Drive 1.6 miles. Here is a view of the grade of the Tonopah and Goldfield railroad. The ruins of Klondike Well are at the left side of the road. There is not much besides trash, a ruined well, a tree stump. This is near the place that Jim Butler was headed when he found the ledges at Tonopah. The assayer there told him his rocks were worthless.

Continue 6.4 miles to the intersection, and turn right on the paved road. This is the settlement of Alkali Springs. Here next to the power substation are the ruins of one of the Goldfield-Tonopah boom era's hot spots. This was a favorite recreation site for tired miners in the early days of the twentieth century. There was an indoor wooden swimming pool and bath houses, along with other facilities, operated by the Guisti family. During Prohibition, old-timers declare, Alkali Springs was a popular party resort, with bootleg liquor flowing as freely as the hot springs. Alkali Springs was also part of the mining business. A drilling and pumping operation here supplied the Combination Mill at Goldfield, with water at this source measured as hot as 140°. Tourists should take seriously the "no trespassing" warning here.

From Alkali Springs continue driving 6.5 miles west on the paved road to an intersection. The dirt road to the left leads to the ghost town of Montezuma, which has been thoroughly, totally vandalized. Continue on the paved road. The view ahead is of the Clayton Valley playa. The cinder cone across the playa shows the relatively recent vulcanism of this region.

Drive west 3.0 miles. The pavement ends. Continue downhill toward Clayton Valley on the main traveled road. Be alert for big trucks, as this is an active mining area. Ignore the side roads; they lead to deadends or to private holdings.

Drive 4.2 miles. Look ahead and to the right and you will see evaporative ponds used by the Foote Mineral Company for extracting lithium. You will see others, close up. A number of deep wells in the Clayton playa produce water containing lithium salts in the form of lithium chloride. This water or brine is pumped into large ponds, and in several stages the water is evaporated, the magnesium is precipitated, and then the brine containing almost pure lithium chloride is pumped to the plant at Silver Peak. At the plant, the material is further processed, and the result is powdered lithium carbonate. The powder is trucked to the railhead at Mina for distribution to manufacturers of aluminum, air conditioners, space ships, ceramics, bakeware, lubricants, batteries, and drugs. The company began this work in 1966, expecting to continue for some decades to process lithium salts here.

Stay on the main traveled road, and out of the dike areas. Drive 3.4 miles; Silver Peak is visible ahead to the right. Drive 1.2 miles to the junction, and bear right toward the town of Silver Peak. Watch out for trucks. Continue 0.2 miles, pass a transformer bank, and turn left on the pavement into town. Here are limited facilities—homes, mobile homes, old buildings from earlier mining booms, ruins from still earlier days, and a modern swimming pool, tennis courts, and 0.4 miles from where you entered the town, the Foote Minerals plant.

At the plant, drive on the paved road to the intersection and the sign for the end of SR 265. Turn left (south) on the graded dirt road toward Oasis. *If you did not read the warning at the beginning of this tour, read it now.*

Drive 0.5 miles to a fork in the road, and bear right (the left hand road leads to the town dump). Drive 3.4 miles; there is a road at the left leading to the sand dunes and over the hill to Lida, but stay to the right, on the main road. Continue 0.9 miles, another road to the left leads to the sand dunes; stay on the main road. Drive 1.2 miles to a fork in the road, and take the road to the left. (The right-hand road leads some 20 miles to the Mohawk mine. The Mohawk was discovered in the 1920s, later purchased by a firm owned by Avery Brundage, former chairman of the U.S. Olympic Committee. Brundage's company spent some hundreds of thousands of dollars on development and a

mill between the 1950s and 1975. The Foote company owns the property now.)

Continue 3.0 miles to a fork in the road. Keep to the right on the main traveled route. The road climbs from here to Oasis Divide in the Silver Peak Range. We saw a pair of golden eagles playing "Lazy Eight" above this Joshua and cactus covered incline. Drive 4.3 miles and cross the cattle guard. From this point, you can look back at Clayton Valley and appreciate the rugged character of the mining business. This wide expanse contains two little settlements that you can see with field glasses: Silver Peak on the road on which you came, and a more recently-built mill west-southwest of Silver Peak on a little flat between two hills. The high peak west of the new mill is (appropriately) Red Mountain. The sand dunes that looked so huge a few minutes ago are now a dim gray line on the desert floor.

Continue uphill through the piñon-juniper-Joshua forest, 3.3 miles to the summit of Oasis Divide. Here is a breathtaking view of the West's most beautiful mountain range, the Sierra Nevada. The Sierra's rugged peaks are on the left; the White Mountains are on the right in your view ahead.

Drive downhill 1.9 miles to the ruins of a little settlement. Here is the end of some miner's dream—a cabin, mine, small mill, and corral all lie in pieces here.

Drive 1.6 miles to the second summit, and continue downhill into Fish Lake Valley. Cross a cattle guard after 0.9 miles. Drive 3.9 miles to a fork in the road and go to the left on the main road. Drive 0.2 miles and turn right on the paved road. You are in Inyo County, California on SR 168. Continue 1.8 miles on the paved road to the junction with SR 266.

Scenic side trip to see the ancient bristlecone forest. Allow a minimum of three hours for the side trip. If you have camping gear, there will be an opportunity to use it at the Bristlecone area. The way is all on paved road, and a walk to see the bristlecone pine trees is less than a quarter mile. Mileage for the side trip including the drive to the bristlecone site is approximately 70 miles round trip from here.

Turn to the left at the intersection, toward Westgard Pass. Drive 5.3 miles to Gilbert summit, and continue on the paved road. The rugged peaks of the Sierra Nevada are visible in the distance.

Drive 4.9 miles; the Deep Springs Highway Maintenance Station is on the right; stay on the main highway. Drive 1.1 miles; the Deep Springs ranch road is at the left; stay on the paved highway. Drive across the desert valley, and uphill 8.9 miles to the Inyo National Forest boundary. Continue through this fascinating canyon with its volcanic formations and deposits, 4.3 miles to Westgard Pass. Drive downhill 0.8 miles, and turn right to the Bristlecone Forest. This is a paved road, but there are no services and no supplies. Drive 0.5 miles to the entrance station, pick up a brochure, and then explore the area. You can enjoy camping, picnicking, hiking, and spectacular scenery in this beautiful park. The drive to the first of the ancient bristlecone trees, nature's oldest living things, is seven miles up the highway. There is a self-guiding, one-mile walk among the trees. Remember that the altitude is above 9,000 feet, and take it slowly. Completing your visit here, return to the highway, and turn left to retrace your route over Westgard Pass and Gilbert Pass to the junction of California SR 168 and 266, 25.8 miles.

At the junction of California SR 168 and 266, go straight through the intersection on SR 266. You will be driving across Fish Lake Valley, with the White Mountains on the left, toward the valley commercial center at Dyer, Nevada. Millionaire auto manufacturer Errett L. Cord made his home at a ranch near Dyer and became prominent in Nevada politics and business after World War II. Cord was state senator for Esmeralda County in the Nevada state legislature in 1957.

Drive 7.5 miles to the Nevada state line. The highway becomes SR 264 in Nevada. Stay alert for cattle grazing in this ranching district. The chief crop here is alfalfa for livestock feed.

Drive 6.9 miles. Here at the Bar Double 9 ranch, we saw some elegant-looking Black Angus bulls taking their ease in the yard. Continue 1.1 miles, and arrive in Dyer. In this small village there are very limited facilities, including a gas station, store, telephone, emergency medical clinic, and air strip.

Continue 2.6 miles; there is a historical marker at the left side of the road with a brief history of Fish Lake Valley. Continue 15.3 miles to the junction of SR 264 and SR 773; turn right on SR 773 (east) toward Tonopah. The drive is into the Volcanic Hills, where you can see strange shapes and lovely colors.

Drive 10.7 miles to the junction with U.S. 6, and turn right (east) toward Coaldale and Tonopah on U.S. 6. Drive 6.3 miles to Coaldale Junction, and bear right toward Tonopah.

Coaldale was formerly called Coal Wells. Nevada Fuel and Manufacturing Company built a settlement here, becoming the first suppliers of fuel for the T&G. The company mined coal from deposits south of the junction site. There is nothing to indicate that history here except the name. Yet, Coal Wells began as a stage stop, so there is a certain appropriateness to its present condition.

Return to Tonopah via U.S. 6 & 95, 40.1 miles.

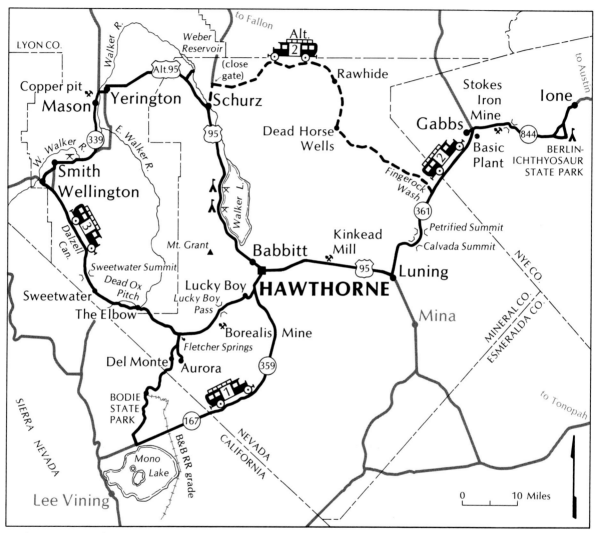

Southwestern Nevada, Part Two, tours 1, 2, 3

TOURING IN SOUTHWESTERN NEVADA

PART TWO

The trips contained in this section are designed for people touring out of Hawthorne. The tours are composed to show some of the most accessible and interesting natural and manmade scenery. Still, tourists should note the warnings at the beginning of some of the trips, for travel in ordinary passenger cars may require some extra caution.

Travel in the area, while pleasant at all seasons, may be somewhat limited in winter. We advise leaving dirt-road trips to the dry seasons—late Spring, Summer, early Fall. If it has been storming, check locally to learn about road conditions before undertaking any trip; the Mineral County sheriff's office is the best source for this kind of information.

The prudent traveler will make sure that the fuel tank is full and the vehicle in good condition before starting any trip. We have recommended picnic lunches where we thought it appropriate, and camping gear when useful. You will surely want your camera, for the scenery in this section has some outstanding features.

What to see in Hawthorne: The Mineral County Museum is at the corner of D and Tenth streets. The museum contains interesting relics of Hawthorne's early history and some well-prepared displays and exhibits. The museum's hours are limited, but this is a "must see" in Hawthorne. Admission to the museum is free, but donations are welcome, as this is an all-volunteer effort. All the tours in this section begin in front of the museum.

The outdoor recreation areas along Walker Lake merit more than a passing-by in the car. There is good fishing, picnicking, and camping in these well-maintained areas.

The chamber of commerce is housed in an insurance office on the main street. Stop there for a brochure and business directory of the area.

Hawthorne has all necessities for tourists—hotels, motels, casinos, grocery stores, drug stores, gasoline stations, and so forth. Take time to drive around this little city and to appreciate the contrasts between its historic and modern aspects.

TOUR ONE, Scenes of the early days: Hawthorne — Aurora — Bodie — Mono Lake and return. Approximately 108 miles round trip. Pack a picnic, make sure of your vehicle's good condition, and take extra water. There are no commercial facilities of any kind on this tour.

Note: *The roads over Lucky Boy Pass and in the Aurora-Bodie area are unpaved, but graded and fairly-well maintained. The novice dirt-road driver should be aware that this tour requires some skill and considerable patience in negotiating the rough spots. The reward comes in seeing some very interesting historic and scenic places. No driver should attempt the tour if it has been snowing, as there is no road maintenance or snow removal during the winter.*

Leaving the museum at the corner of D and Tenth streets, drive east one block, turn right (south) on E Street (the main street), and drive through town on E Street toward SR 359 and Mono Lake. Drive 1.0 mile;

E Street becomes SR 359. Continue on this paved highway. Drive 3.5 miles, and turn right onto the Lucky Boy road.

Drive 1.4 miles. The tailings pile is about all that marks the historic part of Lucky Boy. The people who live here now are reworking the mine. Here, the pavement ends. *If you did not read the note at the beginning of this tour, read it now.*

As you drive over this good, graded road, you can see remnants of the original wagon road. Think of the strength and endurance of men and animals who used this track.

Drive 2.4 miles. There is a rock ruin on the left, and a good spot to pull off the road to see the valley floor. From this place, Hawthorne and nearly all of the hundreds of ammunition bunkers are visible along with other structures of the military installation. A careful look will show almost the entire valley floor covered with the bunkers.

Continue on the uphill road 3.2 miles to a crossroads, and go straight ahead. The road at the left leads to the mine you can see on the hillside above it; the road is blocked just beyond the intersection, and the mine is deserted. The road at the right leads to the Corey Peak communications installations.

Drive 2.2 miles. Here is Lucky Boy Pass summit, and a view of the splendorous peaks of the Sierra Nevada. Drive downhill, and as you make the first turn, look straight ahead to see the Aurora Crater, a volcanic cone with a mound in the depression. There are several other evidences of vulcanism in this area.

Drive 2.4 miles, and see the road at the left leading to Mineral County's new Borealis mine, opened by Houston Minerals in 1981. Do not try to visit the mine, but continue downhill for 0.7 miles to the National Forest boundary, then 5.9 miles, where you will see a road to the left leading into the trees at Fletcher Springs. This road is not always passable, owing to spring activity, so go straight ahead 0.7 miles to the junction.

Turn left (south), and as you make the turn, bear right at the fork in the road. Drive 1.1 miles; the road at the left leads back to Fletcher Springs. Keep going straight ahead on the main road, 1.0 mile. The road may be rough and have some water running across it, but drive carefully, and it can be passable. The next fork is the intersection with the Bodie Road.

Note the intersection with the Bodie Road; *you will be returning here*. Now, go to the left toward Aurora. The road is rough, but passable. Drive 2.2 miles. There is the ruin of a smelter on the left. Continue 1.1 miles to a junction, and take the right-hand road. There is a large tailings dike to the left.

Drive 0.2 miles to the big mill ruin. Keep heading straight uphill, 0.7 miles to the summit. From here, the road winds down to the Aurora townsite. Explore the area, and then return to this point. As late as the 1940s, Aurora's brick buildings stood intact on this site. Then a contractor from southern California discovered the place and salvaged the buildings for use in his business of constructing stylish "used brick" edifices. Vandalism, collecting, and scrap salvage have about finished what he started. There was also some active mining by leasers in the early 1980s that further contributed to Aurora's demise even as a "ghost town" tourist attraction.

One of the old legends about Aurora and its notoriously wicked sister city Bodie has a little girl, about to move from Aurora to Bodie, praying, "Goodbye, God, we're going to Bodie." The people who thought Bodie's badness had been exaggerated declared that it wasn't a prayer at all, but, "Good! By God, we're going to Bodie!" Maybe you will be able to decide which it was by the time this day is over.

Return now to the summit, and retrace your route downhill for 4.2 miles back to the intersection with the Bodie Road, and make a hard left turn to drive up the canyon. Drive 0.2 miles, cross Bodie Creek on a narrow bridge, and continue up the canyon. Drive 1.1 miles and cross a cattle guard; notice the nice talc formations in this area. Continue 2.3 miles to a deserted cabin. This is the site of Del Monte.

At Del Monte, there was a junction of the 2-mile road from Aurora and the main road into the old California roaring camp of Bodie. The route from this place into Bodie follows the historic wagon road track between the two cities. In the boom days, the way had heavy traffic of freight teams and stage coaches. The Aurora road is visible by walking up the canyon to the left of this main road. Continue up the canyon on the main road, 0.7 miles to a rock ruin on the left across the creek from the road. The drive will take you through pleasant aspen groves, wild roses, willows along the creek, wildflowers in season, a piñon-juniper forest, and rock palisades lining the road. The rock ruin is part of the remnants of Del Monte, and there are several similar structures nearby.

Continue up the canyon, over several crossings of Bodie Creek. Drive 1.5 miles to one of these bridges, and a fork in the road; keep to the left here, and drive another 0.3 miles to another bridge over the creek. Continue 0.3 miles to the California state line.

Drive 3.6 miles to the next stream crossing. This is summer grazing land for livestock from Bridgeport, and Smith and Mason valleys; watch for animals on the roadway. From this point, you will notice rock ruins, mills, and evidences of mining. These are all part of the Bodie activity. Drive 3.2 miles and enter Bodie State Park. The parking lot is 0.5 miles beyond the park boundary.

Tours of Bodie State Park are self-guiding. A brochure is available at the visitor center, a short walk into the town from the parking lot. This photogenic place is just begging for you to explore it, so we hope you'll do that. Completing your visit to Bodie, return to the parking lot, then drive 0.5 miles to the fork in the road, and go to the left.

Stay on the main road as you drive uphill here, 1.2 miles south to the summit, for a stunning view of the mighty Sierra Nevada. Watch for glimpses of the little Bodie and Benton railroad bed along the mountainside. The Bodie and Benton never went as far as Benton, and it lasted only a few years from its construction in 1881. Continue downhill from the summit through the lovely desert scenery, 5.6 miles. Here is a good place to stop along the road and admire the area ahead.

This view of Mono Lake and the Sierra Nevada is beautiful at all seasons of the year, and worth driving many miles to see. Mono is a remnant of an ancient inland sea. The wild peach, bitter brush, rabbit brush, and tall sage provide fragrant flowers nearly year-round. We picked up some nice water-rounded pebbles from this prehistoric beach. Continue on the main road.

Drive 2.3 miles to a crossroads (a ranch on the right), and go straight ahead. Drive 0.3 miles to the next intersection; go left, staying on the main road. Continue 1.7 miles to California SR 167, and turn left (east). The rest of the tour will be on paved highway.

Drive 6.2 miles. Here is a historical exhibit, an ore car on rails, and with a plaque, on the right-hand side of the highway. The exhibit commemorates the Bodie and Benton railway. The roadbed of the railroad is visible on both sides of the highway at right angles to the pavement.

Continue 8.3 miles to the Nevada state line. The highway becomes Nevada SR 359. Return to Hawthorne via SR 359, 34.2 miles.

TOUR TWO, Old and new: Hawthorne — Gabbs — Ichthyosaur State Park — Ione and return. Approximately 165 miles round trip; with alternate scenic return through Rawhide, approximately 215 miles round trip. Pack a picnic or camping gear.

Leaving the museum, drive east one block to E Street (Hawthorne's main street), and turn right. Follow this, U.S. 95, through town, turning left at the intersection of Fifth and E streets, and head east (toward Tonopah). As you leave Hawthorne's city limits, you will be able to see a large part of the Ammunition Depot's installations, ''mothballed'' in peacetime, but ready in case of military action. The hundreds of divided mounds that dot the desert floor are munitions storage bunkers. This underground system provides constant temperature for storage. Separation of the structures protects them against chain-reaction explosions. Drive 2.1 miles and cross the railroad track, part of the spur brought in by the government to service its installation here. Continue 4.3 miles, and cross the second set of rails.

Drive 7.1 miles to Kinkead. The mine and mill operation at this old railroad siding on the left is sporadi-

cally active, depending upon metals prices. Ruins at the right of the highway are remnants of the town of Kinkead. The name honors a Nevada governor who took an early interest in promotion of the area.

Drive 11.7 miles to the junction, and turn left on SR 361. Luning is visible ahead on U.S. 95. This survivor from the Carson and Colorado days still serves the Southern Pacific as a siding. The town has very limited commercial facilities. Head north on SR 361 into the Gabbs Valley Range. These mountains are typical Nevada landscape, rugged and colorful peaks and rounded hills covered with desert vegetation.

Drive 9.4 miles to Calvada summit, then continue on SR 361 for 2.1 miles to Petrified summit. Continue 7.9 miles; the dirt road on the left leads to Rawhide. Note this intersection, as *you will return here.* Continue driving now on SR 361 for 3.0 miles to the Nye County line. At this point, look at the hilltop to the left. The concrete shells are remnants of the post-World War II SAGE radar system—a ghost now of the Cold War. The structures are deserted. Drive 1.4 miles, and here is a view of Gabbs and the huge Basic plant, the town to the left of the highway, the plant to the right. Continue driving toward Gabbs.

Drive 7.8 miles to enter Gabbs. The plant is up the road to the right, the town of Gabbs down to the left. Gabbs has very limited commercial and other facilities—gasoline, bar, cafe, motel, post office. After touring Gabbs, return to the intersection, and continue north on SR 361.

Drive 1.9 miles to the junction with SR 844, and turn right, driving into the Paradise Range. Continue 4.9 miles, and look to the right; there is the famous Stokes iron mine, no longer active. Stay on SR 844, and continue driving 3.5 miles to Green Springs summit. The Shoshone Mountains are in the distance, the drive is down into Ione Valley.

Drive 4.1 miles, and the pavement ends. Continue on this good, well-maintained road. Drive 3.5 miles to a fork in the road, and go left to the Ichthyosaur park. Continue 0.6 miles to the next fork in the road, and go straight ahead to the right; the park is visible on the hillside. Drive 1.9 miles, and enter the ghost town of

Berlin and the Ichthyosaur State Park. The ranger station is on the left, well-marked.

This fascinating historical/paleontological site offers many hours of entertainment, education, and recreation. See the ranger for a brochure, and tour in your car. There is a small museum, open on request, in the ranger residence area. The road is well-marked with numerous plaques and information sites. The "Fossil House," with an open-pit display of the prehistoric sea lizard skeletons is 2.4 miles beyond the park entrance. On the way to the Fossil House, you will be able to see the historic little town of Berlin, some excellent campgrounds, and picnic areas. Rangers conduct tours and lectures at the Fossil House at 10 A.M., 2 P.M., and 4 P.M. daily during the summer, and on weekends (Thursday through Monday) in the off-season. There is a self-guided walk at the Fossil House as well, to acquaint you with the area. The park is open all year, but snow is not removed. You are cautioned to control pets or children; there are still some open mine shafts in this old mining camp. Facilities include water at campsites, flush and pit toilets, picnic tables, and numerous self-guided hikes. Enjoy your stay here, and when you are ready to leave, return to the fork in the road just below the ranger station where you entered, and turn right (north) toward Ione.

Drive 0.9 miles; ignore the road from the left, and go straight ahead toward Ione. Drive 1.0 mile; there is a road at the left, but bear right on the main route, a good, graded, gravel road. Stay on this main-traveled route, staying away from side roads.

Drive 3.1 miles to a fork in the road, and keep to the right. Drive another 0.4 miles and enter Ione. The historical marker is 0.3 miles ahead on the right, at the city park. This now tiny little town, once briefly the county seat of Nye County, has very limited facilities, but an interesting lot of historical buildings and plenty of atmosphere. Look around, then return to the historical marker, and start back toward Berlin.

Drive 0.6 miles to the fork in the road, and go to the left (south), staying on the main road. Drive 3.1 miles to the next fork, and stay to the right on the main road. Continue 2.8 miles to the intersection, and turn west,

to the right (the park is to the left).

Drive 0.6 miles; ignore the road at the left, and go straight ahead. Drive 3.5 miles, and the pavement begins on SR 844. Now retrace your route, 12.5 miles via SR 844 to SR 361. At the junction with SR 361, turn left (south).

Drive 1.9 miles to return to the Gabbs intersection, and now continue on SR 361. Drive 9.2 miles to the Mineral County line, then 3.0 miles to the graded dirt road with the sign that directs to Rawhide.

Decision: *This dirt road will offer a scenic return route to Hawthorne via Rawhide. The road is good most of the way, although it may be rough near the end. There will be approximately 60 miles of dirt-road driving, and another 35 miles of pavement to return to Hawthorne, about 95 miles total. If it is late in the day, save it for another time, but if you are ready for an adventure, follow the directions below. If you are returning to Hawthorne via the paved highway, retrace your route back to U.S. 95, then turn right, and return to Hawthorne, 44.6 miles, all paved.*

Alternate return: Turn right onto the graded dirt road. The drive is along Fingerock Wash in Gabbs Valley, with the Gabbs Valley Range on the left. We saw many golden eagles playing soaring games above the flat along here and spotted a herd of wild horses grazing. Drive 7.3 miles. The road at the right goes to the windmill; go straight ahead on the main road. Continue 5.7 miles; the Bender ranch road is to the right. Stay on the main road. Drive 0.4 miles; this is the Gabbs Valley ranch. Stay on the main road. Drive another 1.4 miles to the second Gabbs Valley ranch road, and stay on the main road. Continue 1.2 miles to a junction, and bear right on a wide gravel road.

Drive 6.5 miles to the junction with a road from the left; go straight ahead on the main road. The settlement to the right is Dead Horse Wells, a stage stop in the early 1860s and 1870s, and where there was a stamp mill during the Rawhide boom. Drive 0.6 miles to the intersection and go straight ahead on the wide main road. Drive 0.2 miles to a second intersection, and continue straight ahead (north). Drive 0.6 miles to the junction with a road from the right; continue straight ahead, 3.2 miles to the next intersection. A note of caution: sometimes poison for coyotes is put out in this area, something you should know if your pets or children will be out of the car.

At the intersection, keep to the left. (The ruined mill and the Nevada Scheelite mine are on the right-hand road. The road coming from the right behind leads to Murphy's Well.) Drive 3.7 miles, staying always to the left. Here are tailings piles as you approach the old camp of Rawhide. Continue 0.6 miles; the mill ruin on the left is the National Mill, once the pride of the camp. Drive 0.4 miles, and there is an adobe ruin that once was a home. There are other ruins along this road; stay on the main road, drive 0.5 miles, and you will be in the center of what is left of Rawhide. The jailhouse is on the right, with its cage still intact. A vandal tried with a torch to remove the cell, and when the sheriff found him, was forced to replace the metal and repair the damage. Continue 1.2 miles on the main road, enjoying the ruins and mine dumps of one of the last real ghosts of this section of Nevada. At the fork in the road, keep to the right, drive 1.0 mile to the next fork, and go to the left.

Drive 3.2 miles to the boundary of the Walker River Paiute Indian Reservation, cross the cattle guard, and stay on the main road. Drive carefully over the rough road, 2.7 miles to a crossroad, and go straight ahead. There is a rather lush stand of Great Basin rice grass along here, which was part of the aboriginal food supply. Continue 4.0 miles to the next cattle guard, and go straight ahead. Drive 0.5 miles to a fork in the road and go to the left. Continue 1.6 miles to a cattle guard, and enjoy a spectacular view of the Wassuk Range; Mount Grant is the high peak to the left.

Staying to the right, drive 7.7 miles to a fork in the road, and go to the right. Drive 2.7 miles west to the crossroads and go straight ahead. Drive 1.0 mile to the gate; make sure that you leave it closed after passing through. Highway U.S. 95 is just ahead; turn left there.

Drive 3.0 miles south on U.S. 95 and enter Schurz. This is the headquarters town of the Walker River tribe. The historical marker is 0.4 miles ahead on the right, in the park.

Drive straight through Schurz on the main highway, 0.7 miles. At the junction with Alternate U.S. 95, go straight ahead toward Hawthorne. The drive will take you along the shore of Walker Lake, where you may enjoy watching the shining waters. Drive 18.4 miles; the historical marker for Mineral County is on the left-hand side of the highway. Continue driving to return to Hawthorne, 14.4 miles.

TOUR THREE, Recreation and agriculture: Hawthorne — Walker Lake — Yerington — Smith — Lucky Boy and return. Approximately 152 miles round trip. Bring along your picnic.

Leaving the museum, drive one block north on D Street to U.S. 95, and turn left (northwest). Drive 0.9 miles, and notice the base housing at Babbitt on the left. The major part of this facility is now abandoned or ''mothballed.'' The name honors one of the base commanders.

Continue 0.9 miles. The plant entrance is on the left. There are no tours of the base without prior arrangement. Continue on U.S. 95, northwest. The drive will be along the west shore of Walker Lake.

This highway was built beginning in 1920, then just a few feet above the water's edge. Because of the cliffs and the water line, there was no road along the west side of the lake prior to that time. The railroad was on the east side. Then a mining boom struck Dutch Creek (about 11 miles north of Hawthorne on the west side of the lake), and the only way to haul supplies was by rail to Walker siding directly across the lake, and then by boat to Dutch Creek. The steamers of the Walker Lake Navigation Company have provided an interesting bit of lore for the area, with some people asserting that the water was once high enough for boats to sail between Schurz and Hawthorne, a pleasant, but doubtful claim.

Drive 13.1 miles to the Sportsmen's Beach recreation site. There is a historical marker for Mineral

County at the entrance. At Sportsmen's Beach, there are shaded picnic tables, paved trailer pads, pit toilets, and a boat ramp for people wishing to take advantage of the regular plantings of cutthroat trout in the lake. Shore fishing is also enjoyable here.

Continue 3.2 miles to Tamarack Point recreation site. Here are shaded tables, paved campsites, pit toilets. Beach fishing is pleasant here. There is no tamarack in this area; the name is a corruption for the tamarisk shrubs that grow in lovely pink springtime profusion.

Continue 2.2 miles to the boundary of the Walker River Indian Reservation. The Walker River tribe has its headquarters at Schurz, and owns some of the recreation facilities in the vicinity.

Continue on U.S. 95 for 12.9 miles to the junction with Alternate U.S. 95, and turn left on Alt. U.S. 95 (the community of Schurz is ahead on U.S. 95). You will drive briefly along the border of the Walker River reservation.

Drive 6.9 miles to the sign for Weber Reservoir, and turn right to see this interesting recreation site. The road is graded dirt, and passable for all vehicles. The reservoir is 2.4 miles from the turn. The water of the Walker River here is impounded behind a small dam for irrigation and flood control, mainly for the use of the Paiute tribe. There is primitive camping and fishing by permit from the tribe. On a sunny morning in autumn, we enjoyed seeing some Great Blue herons on the pond below the dam, and listened to a coyote concert from the hills across the reservoir. In the spring and summer, the tamarisk shrubs blooming here create pink blossom clouds. Return to the highway (2.4 miles) and turn right.

Drive 7.9 miles. The view is of Mason Valley. The town of Yerington and its suburbs and adjacent ranches are spread across this fertile valley. Drive straight across the lush and beautiful agricultural section, 7.4 miles past the fairgrounds (on the right) and another 0.7 miles to the Yerington city limits. Cross Goldfield Avenue here, and one-half block on the left, the information center is in the appliance store. You may request a city map and brochure here. Continue south on

Main Street through the business district. Yerington has all necessary services, and some very friendly and helpful people.

Drive 0.7 miles through town to the Lyon County Museum, on the right (215 South Main). The museum has excellent indoor and outdoor exhibits of regional artifacts and relics. There are some nicely-restored historic buildings in the museum complex. The museum also features a gallery of works by local artists. This museum has weekend hours only; admission is free, and donations are welcome and needed by a totally-volunteer staff.

From the museum, continue one block on Main and turn right onto Bridge Street. Drive 1.1 miles to SR 339 and turn left, toward Wellington. Drive 0.4 miles. Here is an opportunity to view the copper pit abandoned by Anaconda Copper Company. The view point is a short, safe walk from the parking place. The deposit is completely mined out; the company has no plans for reopening it. Many people formerly employed in this operation for Anaconda moved into molybdenum processing for the same company in Tonopah, giving the two cities a new link.

Continue south on SR 339, 1.7 miles and enter Mason. Mason's boom days as a mining town are over, and it is now mainly residential. There are some old buildings below the highway; the old Mason Hotel is picturesque.

Continue driving on SR 339 along the mining area, 8.7 miles to the intersection with SR 208, and go straight ahead on SR 208 toward Smith. Leaving Mason Valley now, the road leads into the beautiful Wilson Canyon and along the Walker River. If it is a summer day, and if the river is high enough, you may see some local residents pursuing the popular activity of floating on inner tubes or rafts down the river.

Drive 2.6 miles to a crossing of the Walker River, then 0.4 miles to the rest area. Here are picnic tables, barbecues, pit toilets, shade trees, and an opportunity for river fishing or wading.

Return to the highway and turn right, continuing on SR 208. Drive 3.6 miles to a crossroads, and go straight ahead on SR 208. The road now leads down into Smith Valley. Drive 2.0 miles and enter Smith. There are few commercial services in this little center of an exceedingly prosperous agricultural community. Drive 0.1 miles and bear left at the intersection. Drive 0.3 miles; the ranch of the Fulstone family is at the right. The Fulstones are among the area's most celebrated and respected pioneer families. Dr. Mary Fulstone, Nevada's longest-practicing physician, delivered babies for several generations of valley residents, working out of her office here. The Fulstone ranching operation spreads from this ranch over counties in both Nevada and California.

Continue 0.5 miles to the junction and bear right, staying on SR 208. Drive 2.1 miles to the intersection, and stay on the main road as it curves around to the left. Drive 1.5 miles and enter Wellington.

The historical marker for Wellington is straight ahead in the vacant land created by the highway intersection Y. Take a few minutes to look around this quaint old town, then come back here and head south-

---

"I was married my last year [of medical school], and then I came up here and moved to this house and have been here ever since, fifty-three years. When I came up here it was kind of nice because they'd never had a doctor here before. . . . I think they were so happy to have a doctor right in the community; they'd had to send to Yerington for their doctors before. And you know that was a horse and buggy drive up here, which was kind of long, and they had all gone through that influenza epidemic without having a doctor here. I think they were very happy, because there were a good many deaths and very serious illnesses, and they were very happy to have one. But of course, there were probably some who think, 'Oh, a woman doctor, how terrible!'"

— Dr. Mary Fulstone, Smith Valley physician

---

east on SR 338. (If you don't want to look the town over, just go straight ahead, and turn left onto SR 338.)

Drive 3.2 miles to the junction and stop sign. Bear right on SR 338 (toward Bridgeport). Drive 17.0 miles. The road rises through Dalzell Canyon into the Sweetwater Range, an area of piñon-juniper forest, typical desert hills, and mountain meadows fed by springs and streams. The grasslands are important adjuncts to livestock ranches in western Nevada and eastern California, as well as for local cattle raisers.

At Sweetwater summit, continue downhill on SR 338, 3.4 miles to the Sweetwater ranch. This was a stage stop in the 1860s, serving the traffic to Aurora. Continue 3.7 miles to the junction with a dirt road, and turn left onto the unpaved road (east, toward Hawthorne). This was the historic stage road to the Aurora mines. The road from this point is occasionally rough, but drive carefully, and it can be pleasant.

Drive 1.0 mile. The road at the right leads to the Conway livestock ranch, which you have been able to view for fully a mile, and will see for about two more miles. Continue on the main traveled road for 0.5 miles to a picturesque bridge over the East Walker River. Continue 0.4 miles to a fork in the road, and keep to the left (the road to the ghost town of Masonic is undependable). Drive 1.0 mile; there is a road at the left, but go straight ahead.

Drive 2.0 miles, and now start down the steep grade that has the colorful name of Dead Ox Pitch. Send your imagination back to the 1860s and you will see how this stretch of wagon road acquired its name. In 0.7 miles, go straight through the intersection, crossing a road even rougher than the one you're driving on. The river's bend here is called "the elbow." The place is a popular fishing spot for local sportsmen.

Continue 0.6 miles, and look to the right. There is a rock pile that once was a stage station. In the 1860s, the station and a small ranch here were known as "Elbow Jake's." Dairy products from the farm supplied Aurora. There was a post office here in 1881, but the place has been unoccupied except by transients and cattle for nearly a hundred years.

Drive 0.2 miles to the Toiyabe National Forest

boundary. Stay on the main road through this area, and ignore the side roads that lead to dead ends or private holdings. Drive 4.0 miles. The view is of the Wassuk Range, and Corey Peak is the large mountain just ahead and to the left.

Drive 1.2 miles. The road to Rough Creek is on the right. Stay on the main road across the valley. Drive 1.4 miles. This is Ninemile ranch (it's surely nine miles from somewhere!). Cross Rough Creek through the ranch; it may be flowing across the road, but slow and easy will get you through. We saw some very fancy Hereford bulls lazing around here.

Drive 2.3 miles to a junction, and go straight ahead (east) toward Hawthorne. The road at the right leads to Aurora (see Tour One in this series). The road improves from this point. The patch of trees to the right of the intersection is Fletcher Springs, a stage stop on the Aurora road.

Drive 0.8 miles. The road on the right is another to Fletcher Springs. Stay on the main road, driving straight ahead.

Drive 6.6 miles. The road at the right leads to Min-

eral County's newest, richest gold mine, the Borealis. Do not try to visit working mines, for your safety and for the protection of the mining company. Go straight ahead, and watch out for big trucks.

Drive 2.7 miles to Lucky Boy Pass. The road leads downhill from this point into the Hawthorne area. Drive 2.1 miles. The road at the right leads to a deserted mine, and is blocked just a short way down. The road at the left leads to communications facilities on Corey Peak.

Drive 3.1 miles. On the right is a place to park your car and view the valley below. This is probably the best vantage point to understand the magnitude of the Ammunition Depot installation, as a careful scrutiny will reveal literally hundreds of bunkers almost covering the valley floor.

Drive 2.3 miles. This is the site of the Lucky Boy excitement and John Miller's mill. The pavement begins just ahead. Drive 1.4 miles to the intersection with SR 359 and turn left toward Hawthorne. Return to Hawthorne, approximately 3.7 miles.

A LIGHT-HEARTED GUIDE TO PRONOUNCING PLACE NAMES

YOU'LL HAVE more fun here if you don't reveal yourself as a stranger to Nevada. One way to avoid that appearance is to say our place names correctly. Most of the geographical locations are pronounced as you recognize them, but it's the exceptions that will mark you if you say them wrong to a local resident. Of course, we realize that some of our ways are strange, but we still say the names as they sound best to us.

Amargosa. We don't know why some people put an *r* in the first syllable, but you will hear arm-uh-*go*-suh; we like am-ar-*go*-suh.

Beatty. This southwestern town is not a remnant of the "beats"; say *bait*-ee.

Beowawe. Here's one of our northeastern favorites: bee-oh-*wow*-ee.

Caliente. A lovely Spanish name for a southeastern town, but don't try the Spanish form. They say cal-ee-*ant*-ee (a very few old-timers still say cal-ee-*ant*). Use a flat *a*.

Cortez. A little mining district named to honor the conqueror of Mexico, but you would never guess the correct pronunciation. It's *cort*-us.

Denio. The northeastern town on the "Highway to the Sea" is den-*eye*-oh.

Ely. This east-central town can fool you. Say *ee*-lee.

Fallon. This western Nevada farming community was named for a man who said it with a flat *a*, *fal*-un.

Genoa. Nevada's birthplace in western Nevada was named to honor Columbus's native city, but local residents pronounce it their own way, jin-*oh*-uh.

Goshute. An Indian tribe left its name on several sites; we say *go*-shoot.

What follows is not a place name directory, but merely some suggestions for finding your way around linguistically.

First, say the name of the state with a flat *a*. Only outlanders say ne-*vah*-duh. Residents call it ne-*va*-duh, with the *a* as in *a*spirin or *a*pple. Now with that out of the way, here are a few more local pronunciations.

Hiko. The residents of this southeastern settlement call it *hy*-koh.

Jarbidge. The name preserves the legend of the evil giant Ja-ha-bich; *jar*-bidge—and don't make the mistake of saying *jar*-bridge.

Lahontan. This prehistoric lake once covered a large part of the state, and there are several sites with its name. Call it luh-*hont*'n.

Lamoille. A fancy French name for a northeastern community, pronounced locally, luh-*moyl*.

Las Vegas. Local residents like to hear the whole name, lahs-*vay*-gus. Only outlanders and admen are nervy enough to say *vay*-gus.

Lehman. The cave in east-central Nevada is *lay*-man.

Moapa. The name attached to southern Nevada has more syllables than you might think; say mo-*ap*-uh.

Osceola. The mining camp on Mount Wheeler is called oh-see-*oh*-luh.

Pahranagat. The southeastern valley and wildlife refuge looks hard to say, but it isn't: puh-*ran*-uh-gut.

Paiute. The Indian tribes left their names in several places (sometimes as Piute); say *py*-yute.

Panaca. This Mormon village in southeastern Nevada is pronounced with all flat *a*'s, pan-*ack*-uh.

Pioche. The Lincoln County seat's residents call it pee-*oach*.

Potosi. This looks like a hard Spanish name for mines in two sections of Nevada, but it isn't difficult to say *poh*-tuh-see.

Riepetown. The whoopee town in east-central Nevada was named to honor a rancher whose name was pronounced ''reep,'' so call it *reep*-town.

Shoshone. This central Nevada Indian tribe's name is sometimes spelled Shoshoni, which makes it easier to say sho-*sho*-nee.

Sierra. This is a common place name in Nevada; a few old-timers said sy-*ar*-uh, but see-*air*-uh is correct here.

Tahoe. Here is the lovely western lake's name: *tah*-hoe. Some old-timers said *tay*-hoe.

Techatticup. The mine in Clark County is pronounced tuh-*chat*-i-cup.

Toiyabe. The mountain and forest name is toy-*yahb*-ee.

Tonopah. A Shoshone word, said to mean no-wood-no-water. There is your clue: *toh*-noh-pah.

Truckee. The name of the western Nevada river looks unlike its real pronunciation, *truck*-ee.

Verdi. The western Nevada lumber camp was named for an Italian composer. We don't care; we call it *vurd*-eye.

Washoe. Indian tribe or county name, it's *wash*-oh.

FLEISCHMANN: A NAME ON OUR LAND

IN ANY NEVADA community, if you see an ambulance, a bookmobile, a swimming pool, a library, a youth facility, a museum, a university building, or a hospital, the chances are that if you look at the dedicatory plaque or ask an attendant, you will learn that the Fleischmann Foundation of Nevada was somehow involved in construction of the building, purchase of the vehicle, or training of the technicians. The rural and urban centers of Nevada contain these special facilities, all donated through the generosity and foresight of some extraordinary people.

Max C. Fleischmann was an Ohio native, born in 1877. His father founded the company that produced yeast and gin and that later was renamed Standard Brands. As a young man, Max Fleischmann worked in the family business and then attended military schools. He fought in the Spanish-American war, serving with Theodore Roosevelt, who became a close friend. During World War I, Fleischmann served in the pioneer U.S. Air Force, then called the Balloon Service of the American Expeditionary Force. He advanced during the war to the rank of major, and ever after retained the title (or nickname) of "Major."

Fleischmann had intense interests in the out-of-doors and in sports. An avid fisherman, sailor, baseball player and manager, he also wrote a book on big game hunting. All of these avocations were probably typical of the extremely wealthy soldier-playboy that he might have become. Fortunately for us, Fleischmann was made of better stuff.

Max Fleischmann became a resident of Nevada in 1935. At that time, many millionaires had found in the Silver State a "cyclone cellar for the tax weary," a place with no sales, income, or inheritance taxes.

Fleischmann was not much different from the others at that time; wealthy industrialists and heirs to great fortunes had discovered some of the same things about Nevada, including the fact that people mostly left you alone, no matter who you were. Fleischmann soon had a comfortable place at Glenbrook, on the shore of Lake Tahoe, and some ranch properties in nearby western Nevada.

Then he became really interested in the Silver State. Nevada was relatively poor at that time, with few tax sources and almost no industry. Fleischmann became a philanthropist on a rather grand scale. He supplied the money so that the Nevada State Museum could open and begin to become a distinguished institution. He liked the Nevada Boy Scouts and gave the organization money for what later was called Camp Fleischmann. He became interested in medical research, and realized that there was a need for money in that field. Just after his seventy-fourth birthday, Fleischmann established a charitable trust to help provide funding for worthy organizations, with his wife and some of his fishing pals as trustees. Just a few months later, in October 1951, the Major died, leaving the Max C. Fleischmann Foundation of Nevada an estate amounting to about $63.8 million. The trustees were directed to use the money to benefit mankind, with a time limit that, after Mrs. Fleischmann's death, became 1980.

The fishing pals and Mrs. Fleischmann began then in 1952 to carry out the Major's wishes. Eventually, they surely did so, distributing about $192 million, nearly half of it in Nevada and with the bulk of the rest going to medical research. The list of grants made through the Foundation is truly staggering; probably the benefit to mankind could never be measured.

Youth activities like Boy and Girl Scouts and the Ys received more than $11 million for facilities like swimming pools and clubhouses; the University of Nevada, the Foundation's largest single grantee, had more than $30 million for buildings and environmental studies; some 3,400 Emergency Medical Technicians (EMTs) had training with Foundation grants; libraries in Carson City and Clark, Churchill, Douglas, Elko, Humboldt, Pershing, Washoe, and White Pine counties came from the Foundation; and so did medical installations in Carson City and Clark, Elko, Humboldt, Lander, Lincoln, Mineral, Nye, Washoe, and White Pine counties. The EMTs represented one group of scholarship recipients, while students across the state had $1,000 annual Max C. Fleischmann Foundation scholarships for college training for nearly the entire life of the Foundation. There were swimming pools, state and local parks, money for local charities, ambulances, pollution control systems. The Nevada State Museum and Elko's Northeastern Nevada Museum, the University of Nevada Press, and the National Judicial College all were grateful beneficiaries of the Major's generosity.

When the Foundation made its final payments and filed its last report in 1980, some people were surprised that it had ended so quickly, and most Nevadans were saddened to know that their best benefactor had at last come to an end. Owing partly to the employment of the fishing pals, the Max C. Fleischmann Foundation of Nevada has been called an "amateur" endeavor, but no professional organization of its type could have done more, or better, for the benefit of mankind.

INDEX